North-East Scotland

To Alison

North-East Scotland

Sir Edward Peck G.C.M.G.

John Bartholomew & Son Limited
Edinburgh

Other titles in this series:

Cumbria JOHN PARKER

Devon & Cornwall DENYS KAY-ROBINSON

The Scottish Highlands JOHN A. LISTER

Somerset & Avon ROBERT DUNNING

South-East England OLIVER MASON

South Wales RUTH THOMAS

First published in Great Britain 1981 by
JOHN BARTHOLOMEW & SON LIMITED
12 Duncan Street, Edinburgh EH9 1TA

ISBN 0 7028 8021 3

British Library Cataloguing in Publication Data

Peck, Edward H.
    North East Scotland.
    1. Scotland — Description travel
    I. Title
      914.12   DA867

Printed in Great Britain by John Bartholomew & Son Limited, Edinburgh

Contents

Acknowledgements

I am greatly indebted to the many authors who have written about the North-East of Scotland. A number are listed in the notes for Further Reading. I have not attempted to use the standard guide-books but, for historical and architectural background, I have drawn on such sources as Hubert Fenwick's *Scotland's Castles* and his *Abbeys and Cathedrals* and, in particular, Nigel Tranter's three invaluable volumes of *The Queen's Scotland*. These, together with Tranter's series on *The Fortified House in Scotland*, have been my constant companions. The excellent Forestry Commission handbooks, Whittow's *Geology and Scenery in Scotland* and Millman's *Making of the Scottish Landscape* have been particularly valuable for background on the section on landscape and nature. The excellent publications of the National Trust for Scotland, the equally good ones issued by the Ancient Monuments Division of the Department of the Environment, as well as innumerable local guide-books and newspaper articles, have also been of great assistance.

I am especially grateful to the Ministers of the West Kirk of St Nicholas, Aberdeen, of Brechin Cathedral and of Fyvie Church, for showing me the churches in their care. I am also most grateful to the owners of Balbithan, Craigston, Delgatie, Fyvie, Muchalls and Towie-Barclay Castles for opening their doors to me. I wish to thank the staff of the Scottish Tourist Board for the trouble they have taken to meet my requirements and also the many friends and advisers who have helped with the text and in other ways.

A special word of thanks goes to Mrs Fenella Corr, who has spent many hours deciphering my handwriting to produce a faultless text.

Above all, I should like to express my gratitude to my wife, who has not only endured the frustration of living with an author but has also shared long journeys to out-of-the-way places at unseasonable times of year, and has volunteered much valuable criticism of the text.

Grateful acknowledgement is made to the Executors of Charles Murray and Aberdeen University Press for permission to quote from *Hamewith — The Complete Poems of Charles Murray*.

Edward H. Peck,
Tomintoul, 1981

Preface

North-East Scotland has its own special characteristics, moulded by geography and deeply rooted in history. The fortress of Stirling, dominating the principal crossing of the River Forth, is the key to the historic route to the North-East through Strathearn to Perth, along Strathmore to Aberdeen, and so by way of Buchan to the fair and fertile land of Moray. This guide-book covers the administrative regions recently named Grampian and Tayside, and also the eastern half of the Central Region. The western half of the Central Region, extending as far west as the Trossachs and Loch Lomond, is another story; so is the historic Kingdom of Fife to the east. To the south is the industrial belt; to the north is the Highland Region, which is the subject of a companion volume in this series, *The Scottish Highlands.*

North-East Scotland is a wonderful blend of highland and lowland, of farmland, moor and mountain, of scattered villages and a few not-too-big urban centres, of salmon rivers and coastal fishing communities, and enough industry to bring prosperity without pollution. Before the Industrial Revolution, this was the most populous and settled part of the Scottish Kingdom. Nowadays its population of rather over one million, of which some 400,000 reside in the two cities of Aberdeen and Dundee, is a well-balanced proportion of Scotland's total of 5.2 million inhabitants spread over nearly one fifth of the country's area.

These lands owe their distinctive character in part to their historical development. The Romans came north this way but did not cross the Spey. The enigmatic Picts left characteristic traces in their unique symbol-stones from Forres to Angus. The Normans pushed up into Moray, bringing the power of the Catholic church, the principle of feudal rule responsible to a central authority and, in their train, the English language. By contrast, the Highlands to the north and west retained the Gaelic language and the tradition of loyalty to the clan and the chieftain.

To the south, the River Forth is a clear dividing line between southern Scotland and the northern part of the country, of which the area covered by this book is essentially the non-Celtic half. The Romans, those empire-building strategists, saw fit to site their Antonine Wall across the 'waist' of Scotland, just south of the Forth. None can doubt the vital importance of Stirling Castle perched on its strong isolated rock beside the only river-crossing, nor wonder that many battles would be fought for the possession of the Stirling gap. Long before it was fixed at Edinburgh, the royal capital of Scotland was at Perth and then at Stirling, and it is from these two cities that the high hills first loom on the northern horizon.

The new names recently given to these three regions — Grampian, Tayside and Central (of which only the eastern half is covered) — are not particularly imaginative. They were created in May 1975 on the reorganisation of local government in Scotland, at the same time as the Highland Region was formed out of the seven former crofting counties. The administrator's labels represent a regrouping of earlier counties with more familiar names, for Central Region comprises the large district of Stirling stretching far to the west and tiny Clackmannanshire, while Tayside groups Perth and Kinross alongside Angus:

Grampian has swept up the former counties of Moray, Banffshire, Aberdeenshire and Kincardine (better known as the Mearns) and re-shuffled them into slightly different districts. These county names cover in turn much older earldoms, with resounding historic names like Breadalbane, Atholl, Gowrie, Strathbogie, Formartine, Buchan and Mar, which are evocative of many stirring events in Scotland's history.

Too many visitors see too little of this magnificent part of Scotland as they hurry up the A9 trunk road, sparing a glance for Stirling and Perth and perhaps Blair Atholl, on their way to the better known beauties of the Highlands beyond Inverness. Both west and east of the highway there is a wealth of lovely scenery and historic associations to be sought out: deep-set glens, rushing rivers, forests of silver birch and ancient pine, high, snow-capped mountains, long sandy beaches and rugged cliffs, as well as hill-forts, ruined castles, fantastic tower-houses and cities in superb sites.

From Forres to Dunsinane, this is the land of the Macbeth of history, certainly an ambitious king, but by no means the villain of Shakespeare. This is Norman Scotland, with its great cathedrals at Elgin, Dunblane and Dunkeld, its motte-and-bailey castles and its French-style fortifications. This is the land where Wallace and Robert the Bruce fought for the independence of Scotland; and the land where the Stuart kings loved to sojourn. Here, the laird's private fortress grew into that unique and delightful style of dwelling, the tower-house, of which Craigievar is the foremost example of many. This is where the Great Montrose was born and where he won his greatest victories; and he passed through Donside on his last humiliating pilgrimage. This is the land of Royalist and Covenanter, of the great families of Gordon, Fraser, Graham, Erskine, Hay and Keith; the land where the Jacobite Rising of 1715 counted for more than that of 1745; the land of planned villages rather than of clearances, of secret Catholics and disruptive Presbyterians and of the historic cities of Stirling, Perth, Dundee and Aberdeen. Nowadays, to all this has been added the wealth of beef cattle, malt whisky and North Sea oil.

Practical Notes

In introducing the reader to the places outlined in this book, it is assumed that travel will be generally by car but that certain spots will be visited on foot. Specialist knowledge of geology, botany, zoology or architectural detail will neither be offered nor required. The intention is simply, by sketching enough of the background in geography, history or literature, to enable the discerning traveller to judge why the mountain, valley, village or castle he sees before him has come to be where and what it is, and to whet his appetite for seeing more.

The section on Climate emphasises the unpredictability of Scottish weather, but it is worth bearing in mind that the eastern half of Scotland usually enjoys a drier, if sometimes colder, climate than the west. The period from May to October is generally pleasant, though August is apt to be a rainier month than the others. One good feature of the drier climate is that midges and clegs (horseflies) are not the pests they are in the west, though the common fly can be tiresome in windless forests in hot weather.

The red deer-stalking and grouse-shooting seasons begin in July and August respectively. It is then advisable to seek local advice before venturing off the road into a private deer-forest or grouse-moor, but, with goodwill, a friendly arrangement can be reached between sporting and other interests.

It would be misleading in a guide-book of this nature to give detailed information which may vary from year to year, such as opening times of castles and other places of interest, accommodation, or facilities for specialised recreations. This deliberate gap is more than adequately filled by the excellent publications of the Scottish Tourist Board (23 Ravelston Terrace, Edinburgh, EH4 3EU, with an office in London at 5-6 Pall Mall East, SW1). In addition to the Board's three booklets on *Where to Stay — Hotels; Bed and Breakfast;* and *Self-Catering Accommodation,* an indispensable 'must' is the Scottish Tourist Board's new Touring Map (the Bartholomew 5 miles to the inch map, overprinted with symbols of places of interest). The annual companion booklet, *Scotland: 1,001 Things to See,* gives current opening times of castles, museums, etc. More specialised Scottish Tourist Board booklets cover angling, golf, pony trekking centres, winter sports, historic hotels and inns, motoring, walks and trails, shooting and stalking, camping and caravan sites and, for those who like to see others working while they themselves are on holiday, *See Scotland at Work.*

As regards maps, those who wish to supplement the sheets of the Bartholomew 5 miles to the inch series included in this volume can make use of the revised Bartholomew 1:100,000 series, with the original coloured layering. The Ordnance Survey series on a scale of 1:50,000 also covers the area, with special sheets (on the old scale of one inch to the mile) for the Cairngorms and the Trossachs, and at 1:25,000 for the High Tops of the Cairngorms. In addition, there are specialised maps showing Whisky Distilleries, Clans and an Historical Map, all issued by Bartholomew.

A number of castles and houses in private ownership are open on request, or at limited times. Other castles, country houses and monuments are in the care of either the National Trust for Scotland (NTS) or the Ancient Monuments Division of the Department of the Environment (AM).

Regional Map

Showing the Area Covered by this Guide

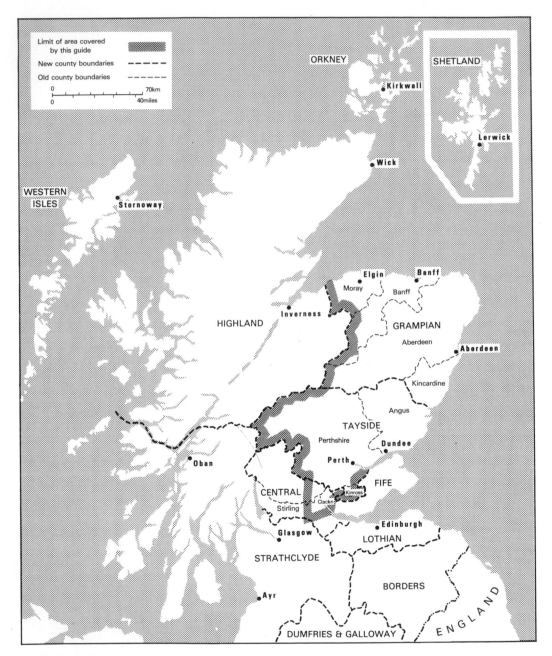

Publisher's Note

The publishers of this guide are always pleased to acknowledge any corrections brought to their notice by readers. Correspondence should be addressed to the Guide-book Editor, John Bartholomew & Son Limited, 12 Duncan Street, Edinburgh EH9 1TA.

Introduction

Landscape and Nature

Landforms

The beautiful and varied region between Stirling and Elgin, part Highland, part Lowland, is a tapestry of moorland and mountain, forest and farmland. The evolution of this landscape over millions of years has governed Man's brief occupation of less than 8,000 years in many ways: the routes he has followed, the animals he has bred, the types of tree he has planted, and even the colour of his house.

A glance at the map shows a great wedge of land, like a blunt triangle, jutting out into the North Sea in the direction of Norway. Its seaward limits are the straight east-west coast of the Moray Firth, from the mouth of the River Findhorn to Kinnaird Head, and the fretted, cliff-bound coast, alternating with sandy beaches, of the North Sea from Peterhead to the Tay Estuary. A conspicuous line of hills runs in a straight line diagonally across Scotland for nearly 100 miles (160 km.), from the south end of Loch Lomond northeastwards, to dip into the North Sea by Stonehaven. This is the Highland Boundary Fault, a geological feature where the sandstone of the Lowlands comes up against the hard, igneous rock of the hills, which has resisted erosion more successfully than the softer, sedimentary rocks of the valley. There is still instability along this fault, as the early recorders of earthquakes at Comrie discovered.

From anywhere beyond Stirling or Perth, this continuous line of hills dominates the northern horizon. The scarp is at its steepest 20 miles (32 km.) west of Stirling; further east, the rivers from the Angus glens twist their way through the hills of the Fault in spectacular falls and canyons. In the past, this line divided the lawless Highlands from the settled, orderly Lowlands; nowadays the southern boundary of the Highland Region runs along the watershed well to the north of the Fault. Nevertheless, to pass through these hills at one of the natural gaps, the Sma' Glen or the Tay gap at Dunkeld, is still, for the modern traveller, a most dramatic entry into the Highlands.

South of the dividing line of the Fault is a broad belt of undulating country, the so-called Midland Valley of Scotland, its central section better known as Strathmore (the great vale), which narrows at its eastern end into the Howe of the Mearns. This wide valley is intersected by winding rivers, the largest being the Tay and the Forth, with their respective tributaries, the Isla and the Teith. South of this broad vale runs a series of hills, breached at two points, Stirling and Perth, where the Forth and the Tay start to broaden out to become arms of the sea, or firths. West of the Stirling Gap are the lava terraces of the Gargunnock Hills; east of it come the Ochil Hills, steeply scarped above the Firth of Forth. Northeastwards from Perth is the line of the volcanic Sidlaw Hills, which run behind Dundee and peter out just south of Montrose; the little Garvock Hills close off the tip of the Howe of the Mearns from the North Sea, leaving the harbour of Stonehaven squeezed between them and the seaward end of the Grampians. Further north, two more large rivers, the Dee and the Don, run eastwards into the sea on either side of the great city of Aberdeen.

North of the Boundary Fault, the landscape presents a very different picture: a jumble of high mountains, with rounded or flat-topped summits. These are the Grampians, mostly over 3,000 ft (900 m.), the largest area of high country in Britain. On the west the land is cut by deeply incised troughs, some containing long, narrow stretches of water, like Loch Tay or Loch Rannoch. In the centre is the high, dissected plateau of the Cairngorms, with four summits over 4,000 ft (1,200 m.). To the east, the hills fall away to form enclosed inland basins, or 'howes', and eventually to the undulating land of Buchan, the 'cold shoulder' of Scotland. West of Buchan and along the south shore of the Moray Firth stretches another broad band of low country, the Laich (lowland) of Moray.

The line of the Highland Boundary Fault determined Man's communications, north-eastwards along Strathmore to the sea, over the gentle end of the Grampians into Buchan and then north-westwards to Moray. Strathmore, Buchan and Moray formed a crescent of habitable land where prehistoric Man could scratch a living. Since the beginning of the historical era, Man has penetrated further into the Highland mass between the horns of the crescent, using the transverse valleys that cut across the general grain of the country.

But how was this landscape formed in the millions of years before Man put his mark on it? For the non-geologist, the scenery gains greatly in interest if four simple, if gigantic, geological processes are borne in mind. First, the basic rocks are laid down in layers, either as sedimentary rocks or as igneous rocks, the latter being solidified molten rock. Next, metamorphosis can occur, when heat and pressure from within the earth alter their chemical structure. Third, folding and faulting distort the layers of rocks, wrinkling them into undulations; sometimes the older, lower layers are thrust on top of the upper, more recent strata, and inversion occurs. Finally, the forces of erosion — wind, water and ice — 'sand-paper' the surface, leaving the hollows and summits that we see today.

Unlike England, where much of the land is composed of sedimentary rocks, Scotland's scenery has been subject to volcanic action and glacial erosion. The yellow sandstone of the Moray coast is one of the few undisturbed areas and interesting fossils have been found there; some are to be seen in the Elgin Museum. The red sandstone of Strathmore has been mixed with pebbles or covered with enormous quantities of eroded material washed down from the hills. The coal-bearing limestone south of the Forth is penetrated by the hard, igneous basalt (dolerite) plugs of the Castle Rock of Stirling and other neighbouring crags. Volcanic lavas have poured out and hardened in terrace-like escarpments, as in the Sidlaw Hills east of Perth. Limestone has been converted by heat into marble and sandstone into quartzite. A narrow band of Tay limestone runs from Blair Atholl, with its prominent quarry, up Glen Tilt, past the suitably named Marble Lodge, to emerge again near Tomintoul and continue through Dufftown to the Moray Firth near Portsoy. Its presence shows not only in the valuable quarries, providing lime to correct the acidity in peaty soils elsewhere, but also in the greener, more prosperous-looking grazing. At Portsoy, there is an attractive vein of red and green 'marble' (actually serpentine).

The inversion — or over-folding — of the strata produces some odd effects. Sedimentary rocks from near the bottom of the original layers have been metamorphosed and inverted to appear on the summit of Ben Lawers (3,983 ft/1,214 m.), a 'mountain turned upside down', as the schoolboy perceptively observed. Here, the friable, mineral-rich soils provide a foothold for an unusual arctic-alpine flora. The shapely summit pyramid of Schiehallion (3,547 ft/1,080 m.) is of the same quartzite that forms the spectacular Bow Fiddle Rock on the coast of Portknockie near Cullen.

Less dramatic at first sight are the great igneous masses of granite — the whale-back humps of the Grampians, the high, flat plateaux of the Cairngorms, and lesser hills like Bennachie and the Hill of Fare in Aberdeenshire. These hills have resisted the forces that wore down the softer surrounding rocks; it is on their flanks, sculptured by erosion, that fine scenery is to be found in corrie and gorge, rather than on the summits.

The inexorable forces of erosion — wind, water and ice — were the principal agents in creating both the rich soil of Strathmore and the mountain scenery we enjoy today. In the first glacial period, two million years ago, Scotland was under a huge ice-cap, probably centred on the Moor of Rannoch, covering all mountains up to a height of 3,000 ft (900 m.), with huge glaciers flowing from it. Erosive action by these glaciers planed down the Cairngorm summits to a level plateau, and at a later stage the spiky tors of Ben Avon and others, now fretted by wind and snow, probably stood out above the ice, as nunataks now do above the Greenland ice-cap. Glacial ice gouged out the Dee Valley, Loch Tay and Loch Avon. Ice, too, ground out the hanging corries on the slopes of Braeriach and above Glen Clova. Ice swept over or round isolated volcanic plugs like Stirling Rock or Dundee Law, revealing the direction of its flow by the 'crag-and-tail' effect, the steep crag on the west where the ice first hit the harder rock, trailing away to the east as it flowed round the obstruction.

The glaciers pulverised the softer rocks into fertile soils: the vivid red earth of Strathmore, the yellowish tilth of Moray and the mineral-rich gabbro soil of the Garioch basin. The granite was harder to grind down, and the thick layer of grey, glacial 'till', sometimes called boulder clay, that the glaciers spread over Aberdeenshire was mixed with boulders great and small. These were later painstakingly collected by Man to form rubble buildings or field-walls, of which the most spectacular is the great 'Consumption Dyke' at Kingswells, just west of Aberdeen. The terminal moraines of the glaciers left piles of gravel to form the up-and-down miniature landscape which geologists call 'kame and kettle-hole', kames being the ridges of gravel deposited by the melting water of glacial streams, and kettle-holes the depressions formed by the melting of a mass of dead ice, once buried under rubble. The hillocks on which Aberdeen is built show that the Deeside moraine once reached that far. The nature reserve of the Muir of Dinnet on Deeside, with its two kettle-hole lochs (Kinord and Davan), and the hummocky Gleneagles golf-course also represent moraine landscapes. Curiously enough, none of the glaciers reached the inner part of Buchan, which has no moraine drift over it, and no boulders to build dykes with; consequently, wire fences rather than stone walls nowadays divide the fields of this rolling, fertile, and rather treeless country.

Wind and water have played their part in the erosion process, the wind blowing the dust of the frost-shattered granite gravel from the tops, the streams carrying the residue away. Some streams have eaten back into the hills at their source, producing the phenomenon of the 'captured river'; this explains the curiously erratic course of some rivers which strike the eye of the map-reader. Thus, the Don must once have had its source in Loch Avon, before the Avon, cutting its way back into the limestone gorge of Inchrory, captured the Don headwaters, diverting the stream northwards instead of east and leaving the sources of the Don in the boggy hills behind Corgarff. The twisting course of the Deveron evidently links sections of other rivers and it may once have joined the Ythan to flow into the North Sea instead of the Moray Firth.

On both Moray Firth and North Sea coasts, spectacular cliff scenery alternates with immensely long, sandy beaches, among the longest in Britain. To the west of the River Findhorn are the Culbin Sands where an estate was once covered by wind-driven sand dunes; the sands of Forvie engulfed much of a parish at the mouth of the Ythan; and the sand dunes by Carnoustie form one of the famous golf-courses of Scotland. Between Burghead and Lossiemouth, the wind and sea have eroded the yellow Moray sandstone cliffs into weird shapes, and the same phenomenon, but in the vivid red sandstone, is to be seen on the cliffs north of Arbroath. From Buckie eastwards the Moray Firth coastline is a succession of cliffs culminating in the dramatic, 400 ft (120 m.) vertical red sandstone cliffs of Troup Head. On the North Sea coast between Stonehaven and Aberdeen there is a fascinating succession of stacks, coves, rock arches, and narrow inlets known as 'yawns'. Further north, towards Peterhead, pink granite cliffs plunge into the sea, with ledges providing exiguous nesting-places for sea-birds, or sensational features like the open-roofed sea-cave of the Bullers of Buchan, in stormy weather a giant blow-hole.

Granite, gneiss, basalt, quartzite, limestone and sandstone, red in Angus, yellow in Moray — these are the basic rocks, not difficult to identify by the non-geologist, either in surface outcrops, in the soil or in the buildings of Man. The sandstone of the Moray is easily cut into ashlar blocks and this freestone, in shades varying from light brown to pinkish yellow, is characteristic of buildings in Moray: Elgin Cathedral is a fine example. The Moray stone was used as far afield as Aberdeen, at least before it became the Granite City of the early 19th century. The millstone grit of the Stirling region can be similarly handled as a freestone, but its dull and often grimy look is generally disappointing, though there are great exceptions, like Stirling Palace itself.

The sandstone conglomerate, a strange, dull red stone larded with big pebbles, is to be seen where the North Esk breaks through near Edzell and in the cliffs near Stonehaven. Indeed, Dunottar Castle is built of this strong, 'pudding-stone' material. Much more striking is the vivid red of the Old Red Sandstone, characteristic of so many of the buildings of Strathmore, from Inverquharity Castle to Arbroath Abbey. It is found again in the broad band which emerges near Turriff in Buchan and comes down to the Moray Firth at Pennan; here are the fine, red sandstone castles of Delgatie, Craigston and Towie-Barclay, and the rich, red earth reminiscent of Devon.

Though popular because so easily cut into blocks, even the best of sandstones weathers too easily. Granite is the king of building materials: solid, lasting, colourful and often sparkling with mica crystals. In earlier times granite was used in the shape of so-called field gatherings, that is, those boulders of varying sizes that protrude from the soil or lurk close under it, wherever the glaciers deposited their sprawling moraines. At best, these stones were rough-hewn, but they were often so hard that they were left in the odd shapes of rubble that can be seen in many farm buildings today. Granite only became manageable in quantity when specialised cutting machinery came in with the Industrial Revolution. Then, Aberdeen grey granite from the Rubislaw quarry became known all over the world; white granite was quarried on Deeside for Balmoral; and the Peterhead cliffs provide a deep pink variety.

In striking contrast though they are to the sharp ridges of the West Highlands, these high granite hills, flat-topped or great whale-backs of moorland, also provide vast areas of solitude for grouse, red deer and even modern man, and wild places remain in the remote corries. Moreover, not only have the peat-bogs supplied the tangy fuel for the whisky-distilling process over the centuries, but these hills also hold the secret of the crystal-clear water that flows over the granite gravel, pink or grey, to provide an even more essential ingredient of that delectable nectar of Scotland — the *uisge beatha*, or water of life.

Climate

Generally speaking, the climate gradually becomes drier the further one goes from Rannoch in the west towards Peterhead in the east, while the chances of rain and snow are greater the higher one climbs. Strathmore, Buchan and especially Moray are protected from much wet weather by the Highlands to north and west. As elsewhere in Scotland, no reliance can be placed on the weather remaining stable at any time of year, though when an anti-cyclone comes to rest over Scandinavia, the Eastern Highlands can usually count on settled, dry weather. Moreover, when the prevalent westerly winds bring a succession of 'lows' in from the Atlantic, they drop most of their precipitation in the west and centre, while only the occasional shower penetrates east of the Cairngorms. Thus, more sunshine and less rain are likely to be found east of the north-south line from Elgin through Braemar to Blairgowrie than west of it.

If rain is about, it is likely to fall most heavily in the west, the annual average rainfall at the west end of Loch Tay being 60 in. (1,524 mm.). On the other hand, recorded precipitation is surprisingly low in the Laich of Moray and the tip of Buchan, where the annual average is only 25 in. (635 mm.); while even in Glenlivet it is only 37 in. (940 mm.), little more than in London, increasing to 60 in. (1,524 mm.) on the high Cairngorms. Winter temperatures can be severe, with January averages no more than 34°F (1°C) at Braemar, 38.7°F (3.75°C) at Aberdeen, and minimum temperatures down to zero Fahrenheit (-18°C). The July average at Braemar is 55.6°F (13°C) and at Aberdeen 57.6°F (14.1°C). Arbroath, with 1,500 hours of sunshine *per annum*, is reckoned one of the many 'sunniest places in Scotland'.

The generally dry conditions have two unusual effects. In spring and early summer, an easterly wind can bring a sea mist — known as the 'haar' — over the North Sea coastal strip from Montrose to Fraserburgh, while two or three miles inland the sun is shining from a clear, bright blue sky. The 'haar' is, however, almost unknown in the Laich of Moray, which is thus an ideal area for the R.A.F. airfields at Kinloss and Lossiemouth. Secondly, in Moray and Strathmore, the light soil can be whipped up by the wind to cover the roads to a depth of several inches, and in a dry summer irrigation may be necessary.

For summer visitors, once the May snow-showers, known in the North-East as the 'Gab o' May', are over, the summer months can often provide good weather up to October, though August has a reputation for being a rainier month than the others. The length of the summer's day surprises visitors from the south: in mid-June one can read out of doors at 11 p.m. and first light is flushing the sky by 3 a.m.

In the winter months, from mid-December to mid-April, the eastern half of Scotland is also drier, if colder, than the west. When cold winds blow from north or east, falls of rain and often snow (rarely lasting for more than twelve hours) are to be expected. If heavy falls of snow are accompanied by driving winds, high passes like the Lecht or the Cairn o' Mount, and even the main A9 road at Drumochter Pass, may be blocked for a time. These storms are, however, often followed by periods of severe frost with days of brilliant sunshine, giving near-Alpine conditions and tempting skiers to the tows and slopes of Glenshee or the Lecht. The roads, even the notorious Lecht Pass, are rarely closed for long. Avalanche conditions can occur when a warm spell immediately follows a snowfall, and climbers and cross-country skiers should then be especially cautious. Wind-speed, too, increases with height and dangerous near-Antarctic white-out conditions can occur when snow is falling on the high plateaux. These hazards emphasise the need for being well-equipped before venturing high in doubtful weather.

On hot, still days in summer, visibility is liable to be limited by heat haze, but amazing clarity can occur at any time of year, and then nothing can be more exhilarating than to walk the ridges, with visibility of more than a hundred miles, and to see fold after fold of mountains stretching out to the western and northern horizons.

Flora and Fauna

Most visitors to Scotland have three great expectations: to see the heather in full bloom with a red grouse rising from it; to sight a herd of red deer; and, if very lucky, to catch a glimpse of a golden eagle. Between mid-August and early September, the Eastern Highlands can offer a fair certainty of seeing the first of these, whether it is the brighter, dramatic bell-heather or the more common ling that suffuses these hills with purple. Earlier, in June or July, the pale flush of the cross-leaved heath, or later, in October, the maroon of the spent flowers spread their own subtle colours on the hillside, interspersed with bright green patches of blaeberry or sphagnum moss. On these drier eastern hills, the heather is both more widespread and has a greater intensity of colour than in the damper west. The practice of 'muir-burning', which produces characteristic grey stripes across the hillside, encourages fresh heather shoots which are the main food of the red grouse, while leaving high heather as cover for the nesting birds. Most hill-roads will, at some point or another, cross a moor where the red grouse, with its prominent red hackle, will start from cover uttering its warning cry 'go-back, go-back'. They will be seen in plenty up to the opening of the shooting season on 12 August, but after that date those that do not fall victim to the guns will be more wary.

The burning of the heather may extend the territory of the grouse but it has prevented the natural re-growth of trees and has driven the red deer, formerly inhabitants of the once widespread native forests, to spend their summers on the high tops and their winters in glens where shelter and grass are to be found. Over most of the year, the red deer, the largest of British wild mammals, divide into separate groups of stags (hence the term stag-party) and of hinds with their calves, only coming together in the autumn for the rutting, or mating, season. A mature stag with a full set of antlers is a magnificent sight at the beginning of the rut in October, but his energies are often so exhausted by the task of defending his numerous harem of hinds against rival stags that he starts the winter in poor condition. Severe winters may mean deaths from starvation, and in some deer-forests fodder is provided to keep the hills well-stocked while the carefully-controlled deer-stalking culls the weaker beasts. (A 'forest' is uncultivated ground, not necessarily wooded; and a deer-forest is notable for its lack of trees.) Quite apart from the income derived from sportsmen, the venison is a valuable export, and both help to maintain the estate. For the casual summer visitor, the best chance of seeing red deer is either to keep watch on a high skyline for an unmistakable silhouette or, better still, to drive through one of the mountain glens at dawn, when herds of deer come down from the tops to graze.

It is more difficult to see a golden eagle, gliding in effortless flight or dropping like a stone on its prey, and this needs time, special knowledge and luck. The osprey, which lives primarily on fish, can provide almost as impressive a sight, and has the advantage of being more certainly observed. A victim of vandals and egg-hunters, the osprey was long absent from Scotland, but since the late 1950s it has returned to breed in the Highlands. A number of pairs regularly mate, nest and produce chicks in the wild. Two sites can be visited under protected conditions, between early April and mid-summer, one at Loch Garten (in the Highland Region), the other at the Loch of the Lowes (q.v.) near Dunkeld. Their numbers are on the increase, but the whereabouts of other ospreys is a closely-guarded secret.

If these major attractions are elusive, there is a wealth of flowers, animals and birds to be seen, far more than can be dealt with in this brief chapter: those interested should consult the specialist handbooks (*see* Further Reading). Basically, flora and fauna vary with the climate, location and height above sea-level. Above 3,000 ft (900 m.) on the high plateaux, it is not difficult to see the ptarmigan, which changes its plumage from pure white matching the winter snows to a speckled brown later in the year. Flocks of snow-buntings breed near the melting snow-fields, the dazzling white wings of the males giving them the nickname of 'snow-flakes'. The snowy owl, a huge white bird, is a rare summer visitor. The scanty grass of the whale-back ridges is the nesting-place of the dotterel, the smallest of the plovers, of which the female, with chestnut breast and yellow legs, is more colourful than the male. Where the melting snow-water wells up through the frost-shattered pink granite rock are startling yellow and bright green patches of moss, while in June the creeping azalea *Loiseleuria procumbens* with its tiny flowers makes a pink carpet. At this level, too, are to be seen the pink stars of the moss-campion and some of the rare saxifrages, including the purple *Saxifraga oppositifolia*. Arctic-alpine flora that survived the last glacial period, like the snow-gentian, the alpine lady's mantle, the alpine fleabane and others, are to be found on the calcareous schists of the higher parts of Ben Lawers (q.v.) and of the Caenlochan reserve at the head of Glen Isla, on ledges immune from the attentions of sheep or deer.

Below these high-living species, and down to 1,500 ft (450 m.), there is more wild-life to be seen: the peat-bogs accumulate water; sphagnum moss and heather begin to flourish, with green patches among it denoting the common blaeberry, the less frequent red cranberry and the delightful cloudberry, a kind of single-stemmed orange-coloured bramble. Voles, shrews, and the young rabbit provide food for the golden eagle and the peregrine falcon, while the common buzzard glides serenely over the moors on the look-out for similar prey. The heather is the home not only of the red grouse but also of its less voluble companion, the glossy blackcock (its undistinguished female a mere 'greyhen'), with its fine, lyre-like tail. Here too is the blue mountain hare, whose coat changes to pure white in winter. The shy ring-ouzel, resembling a blackbird with a white bib on its breast, is an attractive, if elusive, bird of the moorland.

Few trees now survive wind and snow above 1,800 ft (550 m.), and re-afforestation does not succeed much above 1,500 ft (450 m.). The forest, whether of old established Scots pines, of rough birch or the recent Forestry Commission plantations, provides cover for a variety of animals and birds. These range from the dainty roe-deer, displaying its white scut as it bounds through the trees, to the strange, parrot-like cross-bill, the cock rusty-red and the hen olive-brown, whose curious bills are admirably suited to extracting the seeds from pine-cones; the rare crested tit and the diminutive goldcrest are also to be seen. Open clearings in the forest, if well-provided with its favourite blaeberries, are the home of the extraordinary capercailzie, the large cock to be mistaken only for a turkey clattering about in the trees. In spring, the cocks assemble to leap up and down, fanning out their tails and uttering their strange song, a sequence of rattles, corks popping, siphon-squirting and muffled knife-grinding. The 'caper' became extinct in Scotland in the 18th century, but was re-introduced by the Earl of Breadalbane in 1837, and is now fairly wide-spread. The woods are also the haunt of predators such as the tawny owl, hooting by night and occasionally by day, and the wild-cat, nocturnal in habit and distinguishable from the domestic tabby by its larger size and the set of dark rings on its thick, stubby tail; a terror of young rabbits is the agile brown stoat (the ermine), whose coat turns white in winter, except for the black tip of the tail.

Rather lower, in the pastures and farmland, the shrill cry of the smart black and white oyster-catcher, with its long orange bill and red legs, mingles throughout the summer with the evocative, liquid, bubbling song uttered by the curlew, or whaup, of the long, curving bill; flocks of golden plovers make their mournful cry, and the elegant lapwing, with its 'peewit' call, performs its complicated aerial evolutions over the fields. A flutter of white seagulls, behind a tractor-drawn plough turning up red soil, is a brave sight and a reminder that the gulls, like the grey-backed hoodie-crows, are the noisy scavengers of the farmland.

In May and June, the side-glens foam white with the blossom of the gean, or wild cherry, of the rowan, or mountain ash, and with the fragrant flower-spikes of the bird-cherry *Prunus padus*. The banks and hillsides flare with the brilliant yellow of the broom bushes and, in places, the prickly gorse or whin; a little later, the shingly beds of the streams are covered with tawny-yellow mimulus. The purple spotted orchis is plentiful in boggy patches and the yellow globe-flower *Trollius europaeus* is to be found. The solitary grey heron can be seen flapping up and down in search of fish; the blackish-brown white-throated dipper enlivens the fast-flowing streams by alighting on stones to mark the end of its beat, or diving under water to walk about on the stream bed; and the pied wagtail, and the less frequent grey wagtail with the yellow underparts, bob up and down, or chase each other in jerky flight.

The middle reaches of the main rivers, Dee, Tay, Spey, Avon, North Esk, are the favourite haunt of the salmon, where these great fish, instinctively homing from their feeding grounds in the Arctic Ocean, congregate before moving upstream to the headwaters where they spawn. On their way they leap formidable waterfalls, sometimes with the assistance of fish ladders, a sophisticated, enclosed fish-pass at Pitlochry on the Tummel, rough ones elsewhere as on the North Esk near Edzell. Best of all is to see the fish leaping free, as at the Feugh Bridge near Banchory or the Linn of Dee above Braemar. After spawning the spent fish return downstream, the majority to die. After a period of up to three years in the river, the smolts make their way out to sea, some returning after a single year — grilse — but most after two or more years of rich feeding. Unerring instinct brings them back to the river where they were bred, to continue the extraordinary life cycle.

The coast, alternately rugged and sandy, offers many delights to the naturalist. In winter and spring, the shallow estuaries, like the mouth of the Ythan or the Montrose Basin, carry vast populations of wading-birds and water-fowl. On the long, sandy beaches are myriads of sandpipers and other waders. On the mud-flats and banks of the Ythan estuary, geese — greylag and pink-footed, swans and duck congregate, and there is the largest breeding colony in Britain of the eider duck; she lines her nest with the softest of down but is a drab bird compared with the showy drake, resplendent in his black and white plumage. In early summer the grassy cliff-tops by the Moray Firth are a riot of red campion, blazing yellow gorse, thrift, bladder-campion, scurvy-grass and the rare vernal squill. The finest sight of all is where the cliffs fall sheer into the sea, as at Troup Head or at the Bullers of Buchan: here, a wild tumult of sea-birds — kittiwakes, guillemots, razorbills and fulmars — whirl to and fro between the sea below and cliff-ledges above; scores of cormorant and shag fish from the rocks awash in the tide. The comic parrot-like puffins shuttle like small torpedoes between their feeding-grounds in the sea and their burrows in the cliffs, while the rare sea-otter or, more frequently, the common seal bobs on the surface.

At whatever time of year one comes, there is always something of interest in the world of nature. Even in the depths of winter, when the rivers and waterfalls are frost-bound and the snow drags down the branches of the stoutest pines, the tracks of deer, ermine and blue hare are to be read in the snow, and the geese and eider congregate on the estuaries. In high summer, the hills are purple with heather and the mountain tops a joy to walk, while the farmlands are yellow with ripening barley. In autumn, the rowans are afire with red berries, the birch foliage turns to a pale gold, and the plough and stubble make a patchwork pattern over the low ground. Best of all seasons is spring and early summer, when the trees put out their first flush of delicate, varied green, the first lambs appear, the salmon make their way up-river, and curlew, oyster-catcher and peewit utter their evocative calls, against a background of snow-flecked hills.

The Historical Landscape

The forces of nature have moulded the general outline of this landscape over millions of years. Man's imprint on it is a mere 8,000 years old, and much of what is seen today took shape within the last 800 years. Man has turned the rocky waste of the glacial moraines into a green and fertile land, setting up the boulders in his megalithic monuments or piling them in long stone dykes. Man almost annihilated the ancient Caledonian forest; in the past 250 years the hillsides have been replanted with species of trees the early Caledonians never knew. By introducing sheep, Man has not only kept the old forests from regenerating but has also encouraged heather to spread its purple mantle over the hillsides. Man settled in strategic points, at river junctions, on isolated crags or hill-tops, or where a gap in the rock-bound coast gave him the chance to harvest the sea. He used the stone that lay to hand - grey or pink granite, yellow or red sandstone — to build castles, churches and towns agreeable to the eye and blending with the landscape. Nowadays, there are dissonant patches of modern housing or installations related to North Sea oil and gas and to whisky, but they do not, yet, significantly interrupt the basic pattern of the bright green or gold of the fields, the darker green of the forests, the purple of the moorlands, the blue of the hills and the snow of the high tops — a pattern laced with the shimmering waters of loch and burn. Man's bridges may span rivers and estuaries and his roads cover the countryside with a thin network, but a sudden flood or snowstorm can halt all movement. Such events bring a sharp reminder that, up on the mountain plateaux, the primitive forces of snow and ice, wind and water, are still at work, eroding or shattering the rock and forcing vegetation to cower close to the ground. Signs of Man's cultural and artistic aspirations range from the stone-circles of Donside and the Pictish symbol-stones of Angus to the Renaissance front of Stirling Palace and the great garden of Pitmedden. Battles have been fought and much blood shed over the ownership of this land, but the most lasting works of Man have been those of peace.

Stone Age to Romans

As the ice receded and the climate improved, the first men penetrated to Scotland, probably about 6000 B. C. They landed first on the shores of the Forth and later in the Tay Estuary, but they left few traces of their occupation beyond heaps of shells. Some 2,000 years later others came from the continent of Europe who brought grain, sheep and cattle. They left no evidence of houses or farms, but the long cairns or barrows, elongated piles of boulders, are their graves. They used flints and stone axes and made some kind of primitive stone or earth circle for ritual purposes.

More striking are the standing-stone monuments left by the Beaker Folk (named from the shape of the drinking-vessels or beakers found in their graves). They came in considerable numbers about 2300 B. C. and are probably the basic stock of the stubbornly individual Aberdeenshire folk of today — the 'Buchan loon' who, with a later admixture of Viking, Flemish and other blood, is the antithesis of the Highland Gael. These Beaker Folk left a large number of standing-stone circles, particularly in the area north of the River Dee. Stone-circles are, of course, known elsewhere, as at Stonehenge, but in North-East

Scotland the material, brought down by glaciers, is ready to hand. Here, too, the stone-circle has its special variant, the Recumbent Stone-Circle, of which there are about eighty in Aberdeenshire. This consists of a circle of stones, graded in height, the two tallest set invariably on the south-west and always flanking a huge block laid on its side. A magnificent example is at Loanhead of Daviot, an Ancient Monument (AM), five miles (8 km.) north of Inverurie; here, ten stones, up to six feet high, are set in a circle approximately sixty feet in diameter. There is evidence of cremation burials within the circle and a separate, and later, cremation area alongside. Other recument stone-circles are those on Tyrebagger Hill (with a recumbent weighing twenty-four tons) overlooking Aberdeen's Dyce Airport, and at Tomnaverie (AM) on the south edge of the Howe of Cromar. There are two splendid and easily visited circles just north of the A974 near Midmar Castle; one is in the churchyard of Midmar Kirk, the other, with a huge recumbent sixteen feet long, near the farm charmingly named Sunhoney. The effort, organization and manpower needed to construct these monuments must have been tremendous, while quarrying and dressing the stones would have been a major task with stone tools. The dead seem to have been disposed of in two ways. One was by collective cremation, the ashes being gathered in cinerary urns or buried under little cairns as in the stone-circle at Cullerlie (AM). Alternatively, the body was buried in a small stone-lined grave, not more than three feet long, the body laid on its side with knees drawn up to the chin, and accompanied by a pot — the position in which the body was laid could indicate sex or rank. These 'short cists' were usually placed under round piles of stones like the huge, well-preserved Cairn of Memsie, (AM), about fourteen feet high (three miles south of Fraserburgh). A good re-arrangement of a short cist, complete with skeleton, is displayed in the Marischal College Museum in Aberdeen.

Standing-stones, stone-circles, round cairns and short cists: these give little idea of how these people lived, though on remote hillsides, it is sometimes possible to pick out the stone foundations of huts. From about 1000 B. C. onwards there is a big change: instead of burial grounds and ritual monuments, a wealth of settlement sites have been found. The settlements of these Later Bronze Age people were defended by wooden stockades, by banks and ditches, by walls of stone or, most interesting of all, by structures built up of interlaced timber and stone. These fortified settlements are usually located in superb strategic sites, either on a promontory overlooking the sea, or on a hill-top with uninterrupted views far and wide. Such is the Barmekin of Echt, on a 900 ft (270 m.) hill between the A944 and the A974, some 12 miles (19 km.) west of Aberdeen — an area about 450 ft in diameter enclosed within three distinct circular ramparts. The largest of these hill-forts is in Angus, the White Caterthun (AM), on a hill-top north of Brechin, with double walls that may have been 40 ft thick. The 'vitrified' hill-forts are the most puzzling of all: in these, the timber beams running through the stone walls have been burnt, either in an enemy attack or because wooden buildings inside the protecting wall caught fire, and the intense heat has fused the stones into a vitrified mass resembling glass. The most complete vitrified fort, the highest in Scotland, crowns the summit of Tap o' Noth, a sharp hill 1,850 ft (560 m.) high, west of Strathbogie, and from it the whole of Aberdeenshire north of the Don and much of Moray is at one's feet. Another superbly situated hill-fort or dun is on the Mither Tap (1,650 ft/500 m.), the easternmost of the three summits of Bennachie, the hill that dominates Gordon District.

By the beginning of the Christian era (though Christianity did not come to Scotland until about A.D. 400) the inhabitants of the North-East were tillers of the soil with their smiths skilled in handling bronze and iron, and, militarily, sufficiently well organised to present serious opposition to the Roman invaders who, by A.D. 80, had penetrated to Scotland.

The first and effectively the sole Roman occupation of Scotland north of the Forth lasted a bare ten years (A. D. 81-90). Nonetheless, the Romans, under Agricola, left a remarkable legacy: on the ground, with their forts and camps; in literature, with Tacitus's account of his father-in-law Agricola's campaign; and on the map, with the name Grampian (q.v.) - a distortion of Mons Graupius. Two great forts, one at Ardoch, alongside the Stirling to Crieff road north of Braco, and the other at Inchtuthil, in a bend of the River Tay 11 miles (18 km.) north of Perth, are clearly visible to this day, Ardoch being the more impressive. A Roman road connected them, making a dog-leg at the River Earn crossing at Strageath. East of this, a line of nine signal stations runs along the low ridge north of the Earn, parallel with the A9 between Auchterarder and Perth. An outlying screen of lesser forts, at Dalginross by Comrie and at Fendoch, where Glenalmond narrows to the Sma' Glen, defended the passes to the north. The port for landing the large amounts of grain required to feed the legions was at Carpow on the south bank of the Tay Estuary.

From Inchtuthil, a string of marching camps stretched north-east at regular intervals across Strathmore to Raedykes near Stonehaven, then turned north to cross the Dee at Normandykes to the last fully identified camp, down in the vale of the Banffshire Isla at Auchenhove near Keith. The legions may have penetrated as far as the place called Roman Camp at the Spey crossing near Fochabers but, though tradition has it that they reached Burghead, there is no evidence that they ever went west of the Spey.

Agricola moved across the Tay in A. D. 83 to bring under Roman jurisdiction the Venicones of Strathmore, the Taixali of Buchan, and their more distant allies, the Vacomagi of Strathspey and the Caledonii of the Great Glen and Atholl. It was a well organised operation with the Roman fleet sailing up the north-east coast to keep the legions supplied. In A. D. 84 he ordered the fleet to sail round Britain, thus providing the material for Ptolemy's map (see Mapmakers) and identifying the rivers Deva (Dee), Dabrona (Deveron), Tuessis (Spey) and Loxa (Lossie).

On land, Agricola was manoeuvring to bring the Caledonians to a pitched battle and he did just that, according to Tacitus, in A. D. 84 at Mons Graupius, defeating and killing Calgacus, the first Scot to be named in history. The precise site of the battle of Mons Graupius has been the subject of dispute by scholars and archaeologists for the past couple of centuries. Tacitus failed to identify the site at all clearly: he was not there himself and had to rely on his father-in-law's description years after the event. Until recently, the site generally favoured was the hill-top of Raedykes near Stonehaven, but it is not far enough north and there is no distinctive mountain in sight. In 1978 aerial survey, followed by excavations near Durno, just north of Bennachie, revealed a huge camp, as big as or bigger than Ardoch, which is thought to have been the assembly point for the whole Agricolan army for a special action. The little river Urie lies between the site and the modest but prominent mountain range of Bennachie (q.v.) where, according to Tacitus, 'the British army was posted on higher ground in a manner calculated to impress and intimidate the enemy; their front line was on the plain, but the other ranks seemed to mount up the sloping hillside in close-packed tiers'. The unmistakable Mither Tap, the easternmost of Bennachie's three summits, with a hill-fort on the summit, is a landmark seen over most of Aberdeenshire and even out to sea. Bennachie is more likely to have been of significance to the Romans than the rolling skyline of the distant range which (thanks to a medieval clerical error) we now call the Grampians (q.v.).

.Tacitus, in a remarkable effort of imaginative oratory, puts into Calgacus's mouth a fierce and bitter speech in defence of Caledonian independence — 'We, the most distant dwellers on earth, have been shielded till today by our very remoteness ... Now, the farthest bounds of Britain lie open to our enemies; and what men know nothing about they always assume to be a valuable prize. But there are no more nations beyond us; nothing is there but waves and rocks, and the Romans more deadly still than these'. The speech included the memorable words: 'They create a desert and call it peace' (*Solitudinem faciunt, pacem appellant*). Tacitus gives Agricola a brave counter-speech, extolling the virtues of Roman rule to the 'bewildered band' of Caledonians, and though the 10,000 legionaries did defeat 30,000 Caledonians, the Roman effort petered out somewhere short of the Moray Firth. As O.G.S. Crawford (*Topography of Roman Scotland*) so correctly observes, Calgacus was, in the end, right, for on these remote and breezy uplands 'one can understand the uneasy feelings of the Romans as they advanced ever further into the endless, hostile land and surveyed ... first the illimitable prospect of tree-fringed moorland, and then, beyond the sea, yet another line of mountains fading away over the distant skyline'. The view over the Moray Firth into Sutherland and Caithness, a fair prospect today, must have been daunting indeed to legionaries so far from home.

Agricola might have consolidated Roman rule north of the Tay had he not been recalled to Rome by the Emperor Domitian in A. D. 85. Inchtuthil was evacuated in A. D. 90. Some 50 years later, under the Emperor Antoninus Pius, Governor Lollius Urbicus built the Antonine Wall across the waist of Scotland, as a barrier against the tribes who became collectively known as the Picti, or painted men. This name was at first possibly a piece of propaganda to impress the folks back in Rome, but the later image of a ferociously painted or tattooed warrior dreamt up in the 16th century has stuck. In 208-216 there were a couple of campaigns by Emperor Severus and his son Caracalla against the Maetae, subject tribes around Stirling and in Perthshire beyond the Antonine Wall. Their name survives in Dumyat (*pron.* Dum-my-at), a peak in the Ochil Hills. The Romans may then even have penetrated as far as Normandykes on Deeside but after that there were no further incursions north of the Forth.

Picts to Macbeth

The Picts, known to their Celtic neighbours as Cruithni, have virtually no recorded history. Their language, a form of Celtic more akin to Welsh than to Gaelic, gave way to the Irish Gaelic of the Scots who invaded them from the west. A list of thirty Pictish kings from 586 to 843, with splendid names like Gartnart, Onvist and Talorcan, indicates a fair degree of social organization. The intricate tracery of their enigmatic carved stones shows a high sense of artistry. Their place-names are identifiable by the prefix Pit (a 'piece' or 'share' of land), e.g. Pitfour, the same as Balfour — 'pasture settlement'. Of the 280 'Pit' names, all but a very few lie east of a line from Inverness to Stirling. Even the few Pictish inscriptions turn out, when transliterated, to be totally unintelligible. Apart from the hill-forts, which may date back to the Bronze Age, Pictish 'architecture' is confined to those strange underground passages known as souterrains or earth-houses (*see* Architecture) and the Anglian importation of the tower of Restenneth (q.v.). These earth-houses gave rise to the legend that the Picts must have been short, dark, painted men who emerged from holes in the ground. On the contrary, the skeletons of men buried in the long stone cists of the period indicate a people of average height, about 5 ft 9 in., and they were probably red-haired like many of their descendants today.

Scraps of historical evidence suggest that the Pictish Kingdom emerged about A. D. 300, that its greatest extent ranged from Orkney to Fife, and that it lasted until its absorption by the Scots in 843. The heart of Pictland was certainly the crescent of fertile land from Moray round to the Tay Estuary, north and south of the 'Mounth' or Grampians. Although it was at Inverness that St Columba preached to a King Brude, who reigned from about 555 to 585, the seat of subsequent Pictish kings was in Strathmore, a region rich in Pictish stones.

We hear of external pressures on the Picts from the Venerable Bede, the chronicler of the Angles of Northumbria. He records that, in the 7th century, the Anglian kingdom stretched at least as far as Edinburgh, and that in 685 the invasion of Angus by the Anglian King Egfrith was soundly defeated by the Pictish king, another Brude, the son of Bile, at Nechtansmere, south of Restenneth. Only 25 years later, in 710, King Nechtan sought advice from the Northumbrians on various matters, including the construction of a stone church 'after the manner of the Romans'. This survives in the lower section of the tower of Restenneth (q.v.), a rounded arch built by masons from the monastery of Wearmouth in Northumbria. From about this time, the beginning of the 8th century, a change in style is noticeable in the Pictish symbol-stones. The earlier stones (Class I) are rough, undressed boulders, the symbols simply incised. The later stones (Class II) are hewn, shaped stones, carved in rich intricate relief with more elaborate scenes and symbols and bear the Christian cross on one side, which is absent from Class I stones. (More on Pictish symbol-stones can be found under Aberlemno).

Towards the end of the 8th century, Viking raids on the west coast put pressure on the Scots who had earlier crossed from Ireland into Argyll. These Gaelic-speaking Scots began to move steadily eastwards into the fertile Pictish lands of Strathmore. The Picts united with the Scots against the Vikings but, about 843, Kenneth MacAlpin acquired the throne of the Picts, established his seat at Dunkeld and was crowned at Scone as the first King of Scots and Picts. The Picts lost their cultural identity and their language, and were absorbed into the Kingdom of the Scots, which can be said to have begun at this period. But the Picts, who were not lacking in intellectual, artistic or technical capacity, live on as the inhabitants of the Grampian and Tayside Regions.

Whereas the 'white-haired' invaders from Norway found the islands and sea lochs of the west coast of Scotland not so different from their own fjords, the Danes, or 'black' invaders, preferred the sandy beaches of the Moray Firth or such sheltered bays as there are on the iron-bound North Sea coast. There were Danish landings along the Banff-Buchan coast, one at Gamrie Bay where St John's Chapel, on the grassy cliff near Gardenstown, still commemorates a victory by the Earl of Buchan over the Danes in 1004. The half-dozen castles inland from Kinnaird Head, from Inverallochy to Pitsligo and Dundearg, are on the sites of forts intended for defence against Viking raids. In 1010 Malcolm II 'ramscuttered' the Danes near the modern Dufftown and his victory is marked by the Battle Stone in Mortlach churchyard. In 1153 Eysteinsson, though he was probably an Icelander, carried out the raid on Apardion (Aberdeen) noted in the Icelandic *Heimskringla* saga. On the whole, the Danish Vikings must have found the rugged east coast of Pictland a tough proposition, and concentrated their efforts further south in Northumbria.

INTRODUCTION

This complicated struggle between Celt, Angle and Scandinavian is well illustrated by the career of Macbeth, the Celtic mormaer or earl of Moray, who ruled Scotland from 1040 to 1057 — a rather different story from that told by Holinshed, on which Shakespeare based his drama. Claims to the throne operated under a kinship system which effectively meant that it went to the strongest. Macbeth probably had as good a claim as any to be High King of Scotland through his wife Gruoch, who descended from Kenneth II, as Duncan did through his mother, the daughter of Malcolm II. If Macbeth did consult witches about his claim to the throne, he may have done so at Macbeth Hillock west of Forres, or in a wood near Dunsinane. Duncan was not the venerable old king of the play, murdered at Inverness, but a rather arrogant young man who had already tried to eliminate Macbeth. With the help of his cousin Thorfinn, the Norse Earl of Orkney, who had a base at Burghead (also known as Torfness), Macbeth ran Duncan to earth near Elgin and killed him in battle at Pitgaveny on 14 August 1040. For 17 years Macbeth ruled over a relatively stable and prosperous Scotland, moving his headquarters from Moray down to Gowrie, in the fertile land east of Tay and south of Isla, between Blairgowrie and Scone. From here he was able to hold back for a time the advance of Siward the Northumbrian, fighting a defensive battle where the Earn joins the Tay. His enemies, the implacable Macduff of Fife and Duncan's son, Malcolm Canmore ('Big Head'), were in league with the southerners. Only a year or so later, in 1057, the leafy branches of the famous wood of Birnam near Dunkeld began to move — and here Shakespeare is historically correct — across the Tay, covering the advance of the English forces towards the hill-fort of Dunsinane (q.v.) where Macbeth had moved for safety. But, as dramatically related by Nigel Tranter in *Macbeth the King*, Macbeth's end did not come on that hill-top in Angus. He slipped through the circle of his foes, making his way northwards by Glenesk over the Mounth to Deeside, aiming for his own country of Moray, but before he could reach safety he was caught and slain by Macduff and Malcolm near Lumphanan (q.v.). With Macbeth ended the rule of the Celtic mormaers who contended for the office of High King of Scotland.

Norman Scotland

Two factors helped to transform Scotland from the loose federation of Celtic mormaers under a High King to a largely feudal Norman kingdom. First, Malcolm III (Canmore) returned to Scotland with English support and with an English wife, Queen Margaret. Second, in 1072, only six years after his landing at Hastings, William the Conqueror invaded Scotland and, by the treaty of Abernethy, exacted homage from Malcolm, some say merely for the lands he held in England, though others maintain it implied the feudal subjection of the whole of his Kingdom of Scotland. This ambiguous arrangement bedevilled Scottish history for at least the next 240 years, until Robert the Bruce confirmed the independence of Scotland at Bannockburn in 1314. Whether or not Malcolm became 'William's man' at Abernethy, there is no doubt that the strong Normanising influence both of his Queen, and of her son, David I, who reigned from 1124 to 1153, brought about the unity of Scotland outside the Highlands. This was achieved by the Norman feudal instruments of castle, burgh and church. The development of the Norman castle from the wooden palisade on a motte, or earth-mound, of the 11th century to the great stone castles of the 13th century is outlined in the section on Architecture. The feudal lords, usually Norman knights from England, with French names like Brus or Commines or

Somerville, or Flemings like Freskyn (who founded the de Moravia or Moray line), were licensed by the King to build castles and rule as sheriffs on his behalf. To keep the Celtic Highlanders away, and their own Gaelic-speaking peasantry in subjection, these knights used cavalry, which could be best deployed in the open, undulating country of Moray and Strathmore, areas which were themselves attractive for their fertility and generally fair climate.

Craftsmen and tradesmen were encouraged to establish themselves under the protection of these castles, and in due course received recognition as royal burghs, with special trading privileges, sometimes local, sometimes overseas. The herring-bone layout of the medieval burgh, with its wide, wedge-shaped market street and 'mercat cross', and a pattern of lesser 'gaits' and connecting 'wynds' (once enclosed by a city wall), has left its mark on the Scottish townscape. Towns on this plan are immediately recognizable as much older than those built to the grid-iron pattern of the 18th-century planned villages. At Stirling, the medieval plan is conditioned by the steep sides of Castle Rock but on flat land it is unmistakable, as in the centre of towns like Montrose, Elgin or Inverurie.

The Church was firmly reorganized on continental lines, with a structure of dioceses and parishes, in addition to monastic foundations, in place of the looser Celtic system of religious communities to which bishops and priests were attached — the Culdees or *celi dei*, servants of God. A first step in the process was the establishment of outposts of the recently revitalised religious orders in France. Encouraged by David I and his grandson William the Lion (1165-1214) with rich endowments of land, the Augustinians, the Tironensians and other monastic orders established new abbeys or priories at Kinloss (now in ruins) or Pluscarden (now restored to a living monastic house) in Moray, or absorbed old Celtic establishments like the Abbey of Deer, and they also founded magnificent new establishments like Arbroath Abbey. These monks were the improving landlords of their time, worshipping God in church and cloister and, in the fields and woods, developing new methods of farming or forestry. The burghers and country folk did not normally worship in the abbey church but in their own local parish church, like the ancient kirks of Birnie near Elgin, or St Vigeans by Arbroath, which came under the jurisdiction of bishops, who ruled from their cathedral churches. In calling David I 'a sair sanct for the Crown', James I may have meant that, by endowing monasteries with so much land, David had deprived the Crown of wealth and power. Be that as it may, there is no doubt that the monks, lords and burghers brought to the North-East a degree of civilisation which was not seen in the Highlands until centuries later.

The rule of the House of Canmore brought stability and some prosperity to the verge of the Highlands. Its end came with the accidental death in 1286 of Alexander III and the sad fate of his grand-daughter and heir, the Maid of Norway, who, if she had not died on her way to Scotland, was to have become the bride of the son of Edward I of England. The resulting dispute between the numerous claimants to the throne of Scotland, in particular the Balliol and Bruce families, gave opportunities to Edward I of England and his successors to intervene in Scottish affairs on the assumption that Scotland was a subject kingdom.

Struggle for Independence

The long-drawn-out struggle for independence between Scots and English, which began in 1296, continued after the Battle of Bannockburn in 1314 until after the Battle of Culblean in 1335, the turning point of the Second War of Independence. Edward I, called upon to arbitrate between the dozen rival claimants to the Scottish throne, decided in favour of John Balliol — a weak man whom he proceeded to treat as a vassal until Balliol, when called upon to furnish troops and money for the English war against France, renounced his homage. Edward I stormed northward in the summer of 1296: thanks to a contemporary chronicler, we can trace his march through the north-east of Scotland stage by stage. From Stirling (when 'they that were in the castell ran away') he went on to St John's (*i.e.* Perth), a 'metely goode toune'. Crossing the Tay at Kinclaven Castle, at its junction with the Isla, Edward proceeded through Angus to Stracathro near Montrose, where there came to him 'Kynge John of Scotland to his mercy, and did render quietly the Realme of Scotland'. Balliol, then and there stripped of his kingship, exiled with his son Edward to England, and later allowed to return to his estates at Bailleul in northern France, goes down in Scottish history as the Toom Tabard — the empty coat.

After receiving homage from the Earls of Mar, Buchan and many others, Edward of England crossed the Mounth from Glenbervie to Durris and spent five days in 'Dabberden' (Aberdeen), continuing by Fyvie Castle and Banff to Elgin. On his southward progress, Edward went through the desolate Cabrach ('where there was no more than iij houses in a rowe between two mountaignes') to the great castle of Kildrummy in Mar on Donside. Recrossing the Dee at Kincardine O' Neil, where the 'hospitall' for travellers using the ferry still stands, though now a ruin, Edward went over the Cairn o' Mount to Brechin, and back to 'St John of Perte'. There he ordered the Stone of Scone, on which the Kings of Scotland had traditionally been crowned, to be removed to Westminster Abbey (from which it made a brief and clandestine return to Arbroath in 1951).

This peregrination ended in Edward's setting up a government for Scotland under English lords, similar to that given to conquered Wales. Scots blood was up. Andrew de Moray moved against the English garrisons in the north-east. William Wallace started a movement of revolt in the south and joined de Moray to oppose the northward move of the English forces in September 1297, taking up position at the wooden bridge crossing the Forth by Stirling. At the Battle of Stirling Bridge the English troops were forced back in disorder; de Moray was killed, or died of wounds soon after; Wallace, after various exploits including the destruction of the English fleet in Aberdeen harbour, was defeated at Falkirk in 1298. After a period in exile, Wallace was captured in 1305 and hurried through a form of trial to the horrible execution reserved for traitors. But Wallace was no traitor, for he had never sworn loyalty to the English King. He has become Scotland's national hero and some of his courageous sayings can be read on the pink granite plinth of the huge monument on Union Terrace in Aberdeen, or in the memorial hall of the Wallace Tower on Abbey Craig near Stirling.

In 1303, Edward I made a second triumphal progress through the north-east, following very much the same route to Elgin and back as in 1296, and in 1304 Stirling Castle, the last outpost of Scottish resistance, fell to the English. The two contestants for the leadership of Scotland were Robert Bruce and the 'Red' John Comyn. After murdering his rival in February 1306 in Dumfries, Robert Bruce had himself hastily crowned at Scone in March. Routed by the English at Methven near Perth in June, he fled with a few followers to spend two years wandering in the Highlands, Ireland and the Western Isles before returning to the North-East in the winter of 1307-8. Though sick in camp on the hill above Inverurie, Bruce was determined to crush the other John Comyn, who held the north-east earldom of Buchan, and did so, with devastating effect, on the hill of Barra near Oldmeldrum. There followed the 'herschip' or harrying of Buchan, which brought a redistribution of the Comyn lands to his supporters, the Frasers, the Stewarts, the Hays of Erroll, the Keiths, the Barclays of Towie, Irvine of Drum and Burnet of the Leys (and later of Crathes, q.v.), not to mention the 'braif toun' of Aberdeen itself, which gained the countryside adjoining the town known as the 'Stocket Good'. The tide began to turn in Bruce's favour when Edward I died in 1307, to be succeeded by his son Edward II. The English strongholds of Brechin, Dundee and Perth fell in turn. Only Stirling held out.

The story of Bruce's triumph is well-known: the English, aiming to relieve Stirling before the bargain struck by Edward Bruce with the Governor expired on Midsummer's Day 1314, were manoeuvred to disaster in the marshy hollows of the Bannock Burn, and Edward II was driven, a fugitive, from the field. The great statue of Bruce in armour on horseback, brandishing his sword, stands on the Borestane Hill, now part of an area owned by the National Trust for Scotland, (NTS). Bruce continued to consolidate the Kingdom of the Scots, asserting its independence in the sonorous words of the Declaration of Arbroath (q.v.) delivered to the Pope at Avignon in 1320, holding the first genuine parliament at Cambuskenneth (q.v.) and finally obtaining reconciliation with Edward III and recognition from the Pope just before he died in 1329.

Robert the Bruce left a son and heir, David. Unfortunately, as so many other sovereigns of Scotland were to do for the next 250 years, David II succeeded as a minor. Edward III, who had succeeded Edward II in 1327, set up Edward Balliol, son of John Balliol, as a puppet king in opposition to David II, who was sent by the Scottish nobles to France for safety. David's guardian, the Earl of Mar, was defeated by the Balliol forces at Dupplin near Perth in 1332, and for a time Scotland endured Balliol rule again. David de Strathbogie, no longer Earl of Atholl since he fought on the English side at Bannockburn, was despatched in 1335 to root out Scottish resistance to Balliol north of the Forth. He concentrated his attention on Kildrummy, where Lady Christian Bruce, aunt of David II and wife of Andrew Moray, son of the hero of Stirling Bridge, was determined to hold out. Strathbogie, learning that Moray, was moving north to relieve Kildrummy, aimed to intercept him in the Howe of Cromar and there, on 30 November 1335, the two forces clashed below the hill of Culblean. Strathbogie was killed and his forces fled. Though the Second War of Independence grumbled on, this was the turning-point and six years later in 1341 young David Bruce, seeking refuge from storms at sea and pursued by English ships, leapt dangerously ashore on his kingdom at Craig David, on the coast of the Mearns. He reigned for another 30 years (of which six were spent as a prisoner of the English) but died childless in 1371, and the crown passed to the 55-year-old Robert, son of Walter the Steward, the husband of Marjorie, daughter of Robert Bruce. This Robert was the first of the Stewart line (or Stuarts, as they later became known).

The Stuart Kings

The feebleness of Robert II, the incompetence of Robert III and the minority and exile of James I meant that, for over 50 years, until 1424, effective power rested in the hands of the Dukes of Albany, father Robert and son Murdoch, who operated from their impressive and strongly fortified Castle of Doune (q.v.). When James I returned from exile — an exile prolonged by the Albanys' reluctance to raise the ransom money — he promptly executed Murdoch. However, James's efforts to reduce the power of the nobles only brought them to conspire against him and in 1437 the King was himself assassinated in the Blackfriars monastery in Perth.

This was the tragic sequence: first, an infant king, with rival leagues of nobles contending for his person and, through him, for the power to govern; next, an adult king endeavouring to centralise power in his own hands, disposing of regents and over-powerful lords; and eventually the early death of the king, to be followed by yet another minority. This pattern was to haunt the Scottish monarchy until the Union of the Crowns in 1603, but the fundamental loyalty to the royal dynasty did mean that the interest of nobles and king alike centred on the palace and castle of Stirling. Stirling Castle, which James II strengthened by building the great curtain wall across the entrance, became the favourite residence of the Stuarts. Admittedly, in 1452, James II personally stabbed to death the over-powerful Earl of Douglas and disposed of the body by throwing it out of the window of the highest building on Castle Rock, but on the whole the Stuart kings enjoyed themselves in Stirling. They were born and christened there, they feasted and jousted, encouraged science and the arts and built the fine Renaissance palace we see today.

Outside the capital, the conflict between Gaelic Highlander and Anglo-Norman Scot affected the lands north of the Forth and east of the Spey throughout the Stuart period. Already in 1411 the burghers of Aberdeen together with the Gordons, Frasers and other noblemen of the North-East had gone out to repel the Highlanders under Donald of the Isles at Harlaw (q.v.) near Inverurie. Forty years later, an alliance of Douglas and the 'Tiger' Earl of Crawford, (a vigorous man who 'held all Angus in his bandoun and was richt inobedient to the King'), with the Lord of the Isles might have overthrown the Stuarts had not James II, with the help of the Gordons of Huntly, defeated the Crawfords at Brechin. James IV reckoned to have solved the problem by appointing two great nobles — the Campbell Earl of Argyll and the Gordon Earl of Huntly — as royal lieutenants with vice-regal powers, to control the west and the north-east respectively. Much of the subsequent history of the area is the history of the constant rivalry between these two great families. The Campbells, both the senior branch of Argyll and the Campbells of Glenorchy, who became Earls of Breadalbane (q.v.), pressed eastward to drive the Macgregors to seek refuge as landless men in Rannoch and elsewhere. The Campbells of Glenorchy took over Glenlyon and the lands along Loch Tay, and dominated the Menzies of Weem by Aberfeldy. The Earls of Argyll exercised their influence over the King from their eyrie of Castle Campbell (q.v.) near Dollar, conveniently close to the royal palace at Stirling. The rivalry between Argyll and Huntly was accentuated when the fourth Earl of Argyll was persuaded to turn Protestant by John Knox, who preached to him at Castle Campbell in 1556, while the Gordons remained determinedly Catholic.

The second half of the 16th century was dominated by the conflict between the Protestant and Catholic factions, their attempts to hold the person of the sovereign, whether Mary, Queen of Scots, or her son the young James VI, and their respective links with Protestant England or the Catholic powers of France and Spain. This belongs to the history of Scotland as a whole, but had its impact on the lands between Forth and Spey. Mary, Queen of Scots, makes two important appearances on our scene during her short and tragic reign. One was the royal progress through the North-East in 1562, which ended after the battle of Corrichie (q.v.) on Deeside in the execution in Aberdeen of the amorous John Gordon. The other was her imprisonment in Loch Leven Castle (q.v.) in 1567 and her dramatic escape, recounted by Sir Walter Scott in *The Abbot*.

The young James VI, proclaimed King in 1567 at the age of 13 months, suffered, too, from predatory designs on his person by his nobles. The Earl of Gowrie captured the 16-year-old King from the power of his Regents Lennox and Arran, and detained him for six months in 1582 at his castle, the House of Ruthven near Perth, now known as Huntingtower (q.v.). James never forgave the Ruthvens; as soon as he had power in his own hands, he had the Earl executed in 1585; and in 1600 he used the extraordinary episode of the Gowrie conspiracy in Perth (q.v.) as a pretext to extirpate the family name in addition to executing the supposed conspirators.

James VI became personally involved in the conflict between Argyll and Huntly as a result of the battle of Glenlivet (q.v.). A brief account of the Affair of the Spanish Blanks is essential to an understanding of this important episode in the history of the North-East, in which the Catholic Earls of Huntly, Erroll and Angus were alleged to be plotting with Spain. Letters intercepted in 1589 by Elizabeth of England's efficient secret service indicated that Huntly and others were proposing that a Spanish force should be landed in Scotland to stir up trouble in England. When this evidence was forwarded to James VI, who may have himself toyed with such a scheme, he twice went through the motions of arresting the 'Papist Earls', releasing them after a short period. In 1592, 'blank' letters, signed by Huntly, Erroll and Angus, and supposedly addressed to Philip II of Spain, were revealed and again no action was taken against the earls. In July 1594, a known papal agent and three strangers, 'suspect like papists', were arrested by the city authorities on arrival by ship in Aberdeen, but handed over to Huntly in response to his threatening demands. James again urged delay but, in October 1594 the impetuous 7th Earl of Argyll (then aged 18), impatient to get to grips with the Catholics, led his Highlanders right across Scotland to meet Huntly and his allies in battle on the steep bank of the Allt-na-Choileachan (burn of the hillocks) in Glenlivet. Huntly's new-fangled field artillery threw the Highlanders into confusion. Erroll was surrounded, only to be rescued by Huntly. After a prolonged battle, the earls carried the day and Argyll fled sobbing, westwards, to the secret delight of James. But, as so often happened with the Campbells, they lost the battle but won the war, for James VI was reluctantly persuaded, with the strict Presbyterian divine, Andrew Melville, at his side, to take the field in person to bring the 'Papist Earls' to heel, and to 'ding doon' their castles at Huntly (q.v.) in Strathbogie and Slains (q.v.) on the Buchan coast. Huntly and Erroll went into exile but two years later they were back in favour, Erroll building his 'new' castle of Slains, Huntly promoted Marquis and constructing his palace at Huntly on the model of Blois. All of which goes to prove that the Gordon family was a necessity to the Crown to keep order (of a kind) in the North-East.

Union of the Crowns to the Forty-Five

When, in 1603, James VI left his unruly northern kingdom to become James I of England, his last act was to sign the decree ordering the extirpation of the Macgregors. The following 36 years, not solely on account of the outlawing of the Macgregors, were an interlude of peace and prosperity, especially in the North-East. It was a period when the lairds who had benefited from the division of church lands after the Reformation were able to expand or build their tower-houses (see Architecture). This peaceful period came abruptly to an end in February 1639 when the first shots of the Civil War were fired at Turiff against Covenanters (adherents of the National League and Covenant to uphold Presbyterianism) by Royalists under the Earl of Huntly, who then retreated; this was known as the Raid of Turriff. Three months later there was a reversal of fortunes at the Trot of Turriff, when the Gordons gained the day.

The Covenanters gave the saturnine 8th Earl of Argyll (1607-61), whose father had been defeated at Glenlivet, a blank cheque to rout out the Catholic lords. He made a dramatic start by ravaging the lands of Atholl and burning the 'bonnie House of Airlie' (q.v.) in Angus. Argyll was, for a time, in alliance with James Graham, the 'Great Marquis' of Montrose, but when Montrose refused to subscribe to the more far-reaching Solemn League and Covenant, and was appointed by Charles I his Royal Lieutenant in Scotland, Argyll and Montrose were in deadly conflict with each other. In Montrose's whirlwind campaign of 1644-5, his brilliant leadership out-manoeuvred the cautious Argyll and the Covenanting commanders. In 1644, Montrose and his 'Irishes' (mainly Highlanders) sacked Aberdeen in a manner remembered for a long time. In February 1645 he marched his men through the mountains to surprise Argyll at Inverlochy (now Fort William). Dodging back and forth between Blair Atholl, Corgarff, Speyside, Don and Dee, Montrose lured General Baillie to defeat across the boggy meadows of the Don by Alford in July 1645. Montrose then swept south across the Mounth to Brechin and Perth, and on through Kinross, past Argyll's Castle Campbell (q.v.), to his last victory at Kilsyth (between Stirling and Glasgow). After this Montrose's luck and his Highlanders deserted him and the imprisonment of his king drove him abroad. After five years in exile, Montrose returned to Scotland, only to be betrayed in Sutherland and to make a final, pitiful journey through the North-East, pausing at Pitcaple (q.v.) on the Don on his way to execution in Edinburgh in May 1650.

On the execution of Charles I in 1649, Argyll, with an eye to the main chance, encouraged Charles II, then in Holland, to support the Covenanters. The young King landed at Garmouth at the mouth of the Spey in July 1650, where he reluctantly signed the Solemn League and Covenant. He was crowned by Argyll at Scone, was bored by Presbyterian sermons in Perth, escaped to Cortachy and the Angus glens, and finally met disaster at Worcester a year later. Argyll, too self-seeking to support a loser, threw in his lot with the Cromwellian forces which occupied Scotland, but met his fate on the execution block after the Restoration of Charles II in 1660.

Another Graham and another Argyll flit across the scene before the troubled 17th century ends with the Union of Parliaments in 1707. John Graham of Claverhouse, Viscount Dundee (1648-89), encouraged by James II of England (James VII of Scotland) to suppress disobedient Covenanters in the Lowlands, roused the Highlanders, after James's deposition, to rout the troops of 'the Dutchman', King William III, at Killiecrankie (q.v.). Killed in this battle, he goes down to history as 'Bonnie Dundee'. Four years before, the 9th Earl of Argyll (1629-85) had attempted a Scottish rebellion against the Catholic James II of England, timed to coincide with Monmouth's rising in south-west England, but its failure led him, like his father, to the execution block and caused some 165 unfortunate Covenanters to be confined in the 'Whigs' Vault' at Dunnottar Castle.

Dunnottar (q.v.), the grim fortress on a promontory by Stonehaven, impregnable until the days of artillery, became for a time the magnificent residence of the Keith family, who had been hereditary Earls Marischal of Scotland since the days of Robert the Bruce. The 5th Earl Marischal, George Keith (1552-1623), who became an ultra-Protestant, founded in 1593 the Protestant University of Marischal College in Aberdeen as a rival to King's College, established by papal decree a century before. The Protestant affiliations of the

Keith family did not inhibit them from supporting the Jacobite cause in the Rising of 1715. This uprising, less romantic but probably better organised than the Forty-Five of 'Bonnie Prince Charlie', was enacted largely between Peterhead and Stirling. 'Bobbing John' Erskine, the hesitant Earl of Mar, raised the standard of revolt under cover of a hunting-party at Braemar in September 1715. When the ill-fated Old Pretender, James Edward, son of James II of England, landed at Peterhead on 22 December, he learnt that Mar had, a month earlier, effectively lost the battle of Sheriffmuir (q.v.) (near Dunblane) against another Argyll, the 2nd Duke. James, suffering from an 'anguish distemper' — or a plain cold — was entertained by the Earl Marischal in his landward castle of Fetteresso (now a ruin) from 24 December until 2 January 1716. Though proclaimed King, he had no time to be crowned at Scone before he hurried back to Montrose to embark for France on 4 February 1716, leaving his disconsolate followers to retreat through Aberdeen to Strathbogie.

The Jacobite Rising of 1745 brought Prince Charles Edward and his Highland followers down through Atholl to Perth, and the Murrays of Atholl were involved on both sides (*see* Blair Atholl). The festivities in Edinburgh and the retreat from Derby are beyond our province, but the Prince comes again into our sight in January 1746 when his forces spent a month besieging Stirling Castle. The Jacobite forces abandoned the siege to take the Highland road northwards through Atholl, while 'Butcher' Cumberland followed by the lowland route through Strathmore to the ultimate decision at Culloden.

The romantic wanderings of the 'Prince in the Heather' do not concern us here, but many Jacobites fled to take ship for exile from some small port in the North-East. The fate of 'Old Glenbucket' (*see* Glenbuchat), a loyal Jacobite in both Fifteen and Forty-Five, is typical, but there are many others — the Airlies went to France, the Keiths to Prussia or Russia, and some of the lesser Gordons found their way abroad to make a name for themselves. Smuggling on the east coast, into the little coves along the rugged coasts north and south of Montrose, was a profitable enterprise, defrauding the English of their customs duties on tobacco and spirits and giving a chance for Jacobites to slip away into exile. The Earls of Huntly, now Dukes of Gordon, who supported the Old Pretender in 1715 but were equivocal in 1745, continued to be the indispensable Cocks o' the North and, under their protection, the Catholics were saved from the worst persecution, and able to continue their activities in secret in the Braes of Glenlivet (q.v.) or in the remote Cabrach.

The failure of the two Risings meant the end of the quasi-independence of the Highlands: General Wade built his military roads, and his work was continued by Caulfeild (*see* Communications). The Black Watch Regiment, so named because its dark tartan distinguished the Highland soldiers from the English redcoats, was raised at Aberfeldy to patrol the Highlands. The Earls of Atholl put their soldiers at the disposal of the Hanoverian Government, retaining a small bodyguard. The need for manpower in the Indian, American and Napoleonic Wars led to the formation of other famous Highland regiments; not the least of these were the Gordon Highlanders, raised by the 4th Duke of Gordon with the help of his flamboyant Duchess, Jane Maxwell, who enlisted the men with the bait of a shilling between her lips.

Agriculture and Industry

Apart from the Jacobite Risings, the 18th century was a time of steady economic progress. This was particularly so in agriculture, where the rotation of crops, the cultivation of the turnip as winter feed for sheep, the abandonment of the wasteful 'run-rig' system of farming in strips in favour of enclosures and, above all, the prospect of long tenure for tenant-farmers, brought about a revolution in farming methods. These changes presaged the dramatic transformation of the landscape from ill-drained, raggedly cultivated land, and poor, untidy, thatched cottages, into the prosperous, well-tended farmlands of waving barley or fine grazing cattle, and the solid, stone-built slate-roofed farmhouses that greet the eye in the smiling landscape of today.

The name of Sir Archibald Grant of Monymusk, who introduced clover and turnips and tried out new crop rotations on his Donside estate, is well-known from the *Monymusk Papers*, but there were scores of other improving landlords and innovators, like the Barclays of Ury by Stonehaven (q.v.), who turned a stony waste into fertile land, Lord Kames of Blair Drummond, who drained the Forth Mosses and resettled Highlanders on them, or Patrick Bell, the Angus minister who invented a reaping-machine. Others, like the planting Dukes of Atholl, covered thousands of acres with plantations of larch and pine and, later, of Norway spruce and Douglas fir. Their work is continued today by the Forestry Commission.

The improving landlords of the 18th century and early 19th century left another permanent mark on the land: the planned villages, laid out on a grid-iron pattern, like Tomintoul (1776), Burghead and New Deer (both 1805), Ballater (1808), Dufftown (1817) and many others. Some were founded, like Fochabers or Cullen, to rehouse the populace away from a grandee's doorstep. A few were genuine settlements for the unfortunate victims of the Highland clearances. Others again, in the unctuous jargon of the day, were intended 'to Reclaim the inhabitants from their long habits of Sloth and inactivity and reconcile them to the love of Labour, Industry and Good order'. Though these good intentions have not always borne fruit, the planned villages, some of them now substantial towns like Keith (1750) or Laurencekirk (1770) or successful fishing ports like Macduff, are characteristic features of what were once the less fertile parts of Buchan, Moray and the Mearns.

The activities of the Duff family and of the York Buildings Company made their own contribution to this transformation. Starting as merchant bankers in the 17th century, the Duffs acquired property throughout the North-East, including some of the estates forfeited after the two Jacobite Risings, and brought in capital from outside for their improvement. The York Buildings Company (originally founded to supply water to the Adelphi Terrace in London) also aimed to acquire, finance and develop the forfeited estates. When their activities became frustrated by the loyalty of Jacobite families who clubbed together to buy back the estates for their exiled members, the Company expanded its schemes to develop an iron-mine at the foot of the Lecht Pass by Tomintoul, and in felling timber in the Cairngorm forests to be floated down the Spey for ship-building at Garmouth (*see* Spey). In the end, the Company, unlike the Duffs who went on to become Earls and Dukes of Fife, over-reached itself and went into liquidation.

The general effect of this increasing prosperity was to help reconcile Highlands and Lowlands. The rehabilitation of the Highland image, which was begun by Sir Walter Scott with *Waverley* and other works, was continued by General Sir David Stewart's *Sketches of the Characters, Manners and present State of the Highlanders* (*see* Fortingall). Royal approval was achieved in 1822 when, at Sir Walter Scott's suggestion, George IV visited Edinburgh: tartan was draped round the royal person (and round the even stouter waist of Sir William

Curtis, Lord Mayor of London) and the King drank a glass of Highland malt whisky, probably Glenlivet. Queen Victoria set the seal on this revival of interest in the Highlands when Prince Albert acquired Balmoral on Deeside as their 'holiday home'. Meanwhile, the first parties of tourists, of whom the English naturalist, Pennant, in 1769, Dr Samuel Johnson with the ineffable Boswell in 1773, and the Wordsworths in 1803, were the distinguished precursors, began first to venture, and then to pour, across the Highland Line, to risk the rapidly diminishing hazards in order to view the beauties and wonders beyond.

Agriculture, no longer confined to the fertile Laich of Moray and the wide valley of Strathmore, spread into the bleaker parts of Buchan and into the rolling Aberdeenshire uplands. Once the boulders, the legacy of the glacial moraines, had been painstakingly dug out and piled in great 'consumption dykes' along the edges of the fields (one ton of stone representing a yard of dyke 4½ feet high), this land provided fine pastoral farms, with sufficient arable to keep the stock, cattle and sheep, over the winter. Interbreeding between the Buchan Humlies and the Angus Doddies produced the world-famous strain of Aberdeen-Angus cattle. William McCombie of Tillyfour developed the prize herd which was visited by Queen Victoria, and Aberdeen-Angus beef cattle have been exported all over the world, as far as Argentina and Australia. The peaceful-looking Aberdeen-Angus bulls, now sometimes crossed with a Charolais strain, are to be seen in many farms from Buchan to Strathmore.

The labour-intensive agriculture of the mid-19th century meant the growth of the 'farmtouns'. These were not towns, but groups of houses associated with a big farm: there was the bothy for the single men, tied cottages for the married cottars, stables for the much-prized horses, with a 'chaumer' for the men above, and byres for the cattle. These communities developed traditions and a ballad literature of their own, which has now largely disappeared under the impact of mechanisation. A nostalgic reminder of those times is to be found in the agricultural museums; there is an excellent one at Adamstown near Huntly, another (with a startlingly realistic horse, cart and driver) on the road from Elgin to Rothes, and a collection of implements is being made at Pitmedden.

Though agriculture is the mainstay of Moray, Buchan, the Mearns and Strathmore, the sturdy prosperity of the area does not rest on that alone: there is, or has been, fishing, shipbuilding, whaling, as well as a variety of light industries, especially the whisky industry (see Whisky). The trawlermen of the Moray Firth coast, based on Buckie, Macduff and Fraserburgh, together with the east coast ships operating from Aberdeen, Montrose and Arbroath, have built up a fine seafaring tradition which has largely adapted itself to the fluctuations of the herring, white fish or mackerel trade.

Ocean-going wooden sailing ships were built at Kingston at the mouth of the Spey (q.v.) until superseded by iron and steam in the late 19th century. Aberdeen's clipper-ships on the Cape Horn run were long famous for speed and seaworthiness. Whaling vessels were built and operated from Peterhead, which was the leading British whaling port until it lost its supremacy to Dundee in the early 20th century. Perth can thank the River Tay for its bleaching and dyeing of fine wools, and Inverurie's railway workshops are now used for light industry.

Heavy industry first appeared north of the Antonine Wall in 1760 with the Carron Iron and Steel works, its furnaces the wonder of 18th-century travellers. When Burns was refused admittance, he wrote:

We came no' here to view your works in hopes to be mair wise,
But only, lest we gang to hell, it may be nae surprise.

The Carron works produced not only James Small's newly invented iron plough in 1765 but also the 'carronade' of which Wellington ordered a battery, considering them the best of field-guns. Together with the Grangemouth oil refinery, the Carron works still dominate the Falkirk region, but their production is now more peaceful, including stoves, kettles and the like.

Even Dundee, which once made a grimy, 19th-century fortune out of gunny-bags and linoleum, has now had a face-lift and is turning out cash-registers (or their modern equivalent — computers), textiles, carpets, cameras and cake, as well as continuing the traditional jam industry, based on the rich raspberry fields of Angus and the Carse of Gowrie.

Since 1970, the oil and oil-related industries have brought a new prosperity to the North-East, with a bustle round the depots at Montrose and Peterhead servicing the North Sea oil industry, a plethora of strange vessels in Aberdeen and other harbours, a vast increase in helicopter activity at Dyce airport, and mobile homes for oil-men up and down the south Buchan coast. The oil pipe-line terminal at Cruden Bay scarcely obtrudes on the landscape, but the gas complex of St Fergus is a large and unsightly industrial installation on the coast between Peterhead and Rattray Head. The folk of the North-East have adapted themselves to this new-found oil wealth as readily as they did to the new methods of agriculture two centuries ago. Should this new wealth prove short-lived, as some fear, the well farmed land, the beautiful mountains and the sea are still assets which their inborn thrift and industry will unfailingly develop.

Man in the Landscape

Architecture, from Souterrain to Tower-House

The stone circles of the Beaker folk may have had some astronomical or religious significance. The Iron Age hill-forts are built to a defensive plan, but are now mostly mere heaps of stone. Any domestic buildings were temporary huts of wood and thatch on circular stone foundations. The Pictish symbol-stones are a form of art or communication. Consistent building style can be said to begin with the curving, vaulted, flagged underground passages known as souterrains, weems or Pictish earth-houses. Examples unroofed can be seen at Ardestie and Carlungie north of Dundee, and one in Arbroath East Cemetery, where it was unearthed by a surprised grave-digger; but the best-preserved, to be inspected with a torch, is at Culsh on the A949 as this road drops into the Howe of Cromar from the east. Opinions differ as to whether they were storage places, cattle-sheds or refuges for the above ground inhabitants in times of trouble. 'Enigmatic' is the general verdict.

It is more rewarding to follow the development of architecture in castle, church and cottage, particularly in the castle. The earliest castles were not the stone-built affairs of the picture-books — those came later. Essentially, an 11th century castle was a motte — a large circular mound of earth thrown up, sometimes leaving a ditch round it; the mound was defended by the lord and his warriors from behind a wooden palisade (or peel) round the top. Beside it there was a lower mound, the less well-defended bailey for the domestic staff and animals. A good example of a motte and bailey can be seen where the rivers Don and Urie join at the Bass of Inverurie (q.v.). An impressive high, round peel can be seen at Lumphanan (*see* Cromar).

The next step was to strengthen the earth walls with stone, as in the oval mound of the Doune of Invernochty in Strathdon. Lords who wanted to go one better and build a stone castle might well do so on their motte, but not always with satisfactory results, for the great castle of Duffus (q.v.) has suffered the fate of the Biblical house built on sand and has slipped part-way down its mound. In the 14th century the more powerful lords surrounded the bailey with a strong wall, and so developed the castle of *enceinte*, with thick, high curtain walls enclosing a courtyard, round which were disposed the lord's hall, retainers' establishment, the kitchens and temporary huts. Balvenie Castle at Dufftown (q.v.), the old Comyn castle, is an impressive example, and so is the great ruined shell of Kildrummy (q.v.) on Donside. Modelled on Coucy in France, Kildrummy's *enceinte*, shaped like a shield with five towers, with the chapel projecting rather incongruously through the curtain wall, recalls Edward I's great castles of Wales; indeed his master-mason, James of St George, may well have suggested improvements in the defensive plan. Two rival theories of defence can be seen here: the French concept of a fortified *donjon* or keep, and the Edwardian idea of forward defence with a strong gatehouse. In Albany's castle at Doune (q.v.), keep and gatehouse coalesce into one great building which is itself divided into two sections: one hall for the great lord and his immediate retainers, placed on top of the gateway passage, controlling portcullis and well, the other accessible only after entering the courtyard, and designed for the hired mercenaries, whose loyalty was not to be trusted.

As space and comfort became more important than defence, the great hall, instead of being on an upper floor in the tower, became a horizontal extension of the tower. This was a 'palatium' or palace, like the great Gordon palace of Huntly (q.v.) with its row of oriel windows inspired by Blois, or the hall of Druminnor in Strathbogie (q.v.), or the royal palace within the castle of Stirling.

Lesser lairds could not afford to be so expansive. Their grim fortress-homes were originally tall keeps, accessible only at first-floor level by a wooden stair that could be drawn up, and they had little in the way of surrounding wall, perhaps no more than a barmkin, an enclosure providing refuge for peasants and cattle. The 13th-century laird's sturdy keep, tower or fortalice had a slightly sloping (battered) base, probably rounded corners as in the tower of Drum (q.v.), and a wooden gallery projecting from the top level with holes (machicolations) through which boiling oil could be dropped to splash off the sloping base among the attackers below. The chief weapon was the long-bow. By the 15th century, the wooden gallery had been replaced by stone parapets built out from the walls on stone supports (corbels), with machicolations between them and, at the corners, turrets for cross-fire by the defending bowmen. A late and well-preserved tower of the bow and arrow era is Affleck (q.v.). The invention of the firearm in the 16th century changed the style: defence works had to be in a horizontal plane with gunports, as at Claypotts (q.v.).

In parallel with the evolution of weapons, the tower-house itself developed. A single rectangular keep (as at Drum) meant that all four of the corner turrets had to be manned to watch against attackers. Why not, instead of building a second tower, extend one wing to provide flanking defence to cover the main entrance, which could then be in the re-entrant angle at ground level instead of inconveniently on the first floor? And so the L-plan castle, as at Auchindoun, Towie-Barclay and later Craigievar, came into being. The next step was to cover all four walls by building out towers at two diagonally-opposite corners, making two turrets do the work of four. Thus the Z-plan castle, so characteristic of the North-East, evolved. Of the supporting towers, one could be round and one rectangular, as at Midmar or Castle Fraser (q.v.), or they could both be round, as at Claypotts, or both square as at Castle Menzies.

After the Reformation of 1560, church lands were distributed to the lesser nobility, but the lairds so favoured were required to build themselves a 'house of fence', that is to say, a fortified country-house intended as a base from which to keep the peace in a countryside plagued by marauding bands. What was not foreseen was that these tower-houses would encourage rival clans, like Gordons and Forbes, to pursue vendettas against one another. Nonetheless, the growing prosperity of this new plutocracy, and the lessening of general turbulence towards the end of the 16th century, brought about a period known in Scotland as 'King James's Peace' which lasted until the beginning of the Civil Wars in 1639. Lairds of elegance and taste like Lindsay of Edzell (q.v.), or the Gordons of Huntly, who had travelled in France and Germany, made good use of the skills of master-masons, released from 300 years of building purely for military purposes, to give expression to their desire for ornament in the exuberance of the tower-house.

Wealthier lairds, like Willie Forbes of Craigievar, or the Bowes-Lyon Earls of Strathmore at Glamis, wished to bring some comfort as well as splendour to the rough and draughty keeps of their ancestors, but true Scottish caution made them wary of abandoning all considerations of defence. So the base of the tower remained sturdy and the single entrance in the re-entrant angle was heavily guarded by a 'smiddy-made' yett or wrought-iron grille, the bars dextrously interwoven by the smith to give extra strength.

New architectural forms could produce a bizarre but thoroughly pleasing skyline. Corbelling went mad and became an art-form, converting rounded corners into square ones; supporting over-sailing turrets on a whole range of corbel courses, up to eleven varied concentric ones at Fordyce; under-pinning dormer windows and crowning the conventional tower with a romantic silhouette. This could include exotic elements like crowstep gables from the Low Countries, ogee-shaped, helmeted turrets from Germany, balustraded balconies and ornamented windows from Renaissance France. These dream castles, floating in the sky yet blending with the rich countryside, are to be found in Angus and the Mearns, but it is in Aberdeenshire that they are most numerous and at their finest. Claypotts by Dundee has a crudely rustic air with its little square 'cottages' perched on round towers, and it was conceived more for defence than for ornament. Elegance begins to show at Midmar, to be developed into magnificence at Castle Fraser, planned splendour at Crathes, and to reach, at Craigievar, the perfection of a unique architectural form.

Inside the castle too there was scope for ornament and improvement: the entrance usually gave onto a wheel-stair (sometimes of grandiose proportions, as at Glamis and Fyvie) leading to the main hall on the first floor. Large timbers for ceilings and floors were hard to come by, so that it was often cheaper and stronger to build stone-vaulted rooms one above the other than to expand horizontally. In this vertical living, bedrooms and other apartments higher up the tower were reached by narrow stairs in the thickness of the walls, equivalent to the corridors of horizontal dwellings. Turrets no longer needed by sentries could be roofed over to serve as convenient studies, or as garderobes (privies). Where timber was available, it could be used for the glorious painted ceilings of Crathes and Delgatie, or for the carved oak panels of Craigston and Stirling Palace. An even higher degree of refinement came with the splendid plaster-moulded ceilings of Glamis, Craigievar or Brodie, intertwined as at Muchalls with brightly-painted blazons. This was Scots-baronial at its best, though by the Restoration in 1660, the tower-house as an architectural form was in decline. In 1677 the Earl of Strathmore reckoned that 'Tower-houses are quite out of fashion, as feuds are, . . . the country being generally more civilised than in ancient times'. It was Sir William Bruce (the architect who rebuilt Holyrood for Charles II) who first brought Scottish country-house architecture back from the vertical to the horizontal with his own French-style house at Kinross.

The Union of Parliaments in 1707 meant that English and Scottish architecture developed on common lines, with a substantial Scottish contribution from the Adam family — William the father (who completed Bruce's work at Hopetoun), and his three famous sons, Robert, James and John. Instead of tower-houses, mansions were built in the Palladian classical style, as at Haddo and The Burn (near Edzell), or in the baroque manner that William Adam used so expensively for the Earl of Fife's Duff House at Banff (q.v.). In the 18th century the Duke of Atholl converted his old castle of Blair Atholl to something resembling a Georgian mansion, but a later duke caused the Victorian architect, David Bryce, to reconstitute the castle with turrets and square English-style battlements. These square battlements are not a characteristic of Scottish military architecture; ornamental versions are to be seen at Fasque (q.v.) and in William Atkinson's 'Gothick' facade of Scone Palace, while John Adam used them in the military mode in his conversion of Braemar Castle (q.v.). The star-shaped curtain walls surrounding Braemar and Corgarff are also English military importations.

More cheerfully, follies and gardens made their appearance. Existing follies include 'Ossian's Hall' at the Hermitage (NTS) near Dunkeld (q.v.) and the incredible Pineapple (NTS) at Airth (q.v.). The formal garden, like the knot-garden below the Castle Rock at Stirling, was already in fashion in the 17th century, and Sir David Lindsay's lovely walled heraldic pleasance at Edzell (AM) is an early example. Under the influence of the French landscape designer, Le Nôtre, formal gardens were elaborated and expanded. They developed into Sir William Bruce's carefully aligned garden at Kinross, into the magnificent Great Garden of Pitmedden (q.v.) to which Sir Alexander Seton devoted 30 years, now restored to full glory by the NTS, and, in a modern idiom, into the delightful planned confusion of the seven gardens of Crathes.

The late 18th and early 19th centuries saw the Georgian tradition of Edinburgh New Town extended to the genteel streets of Perth, to Gillespie Graham's fine steeple at Montrose and the town-planning of Archibald Simpson's granite city of Aberdeen. Archibald Simpson (1790-1847), taking advantage of the new mechanical techniques that made it possible to work the white, grey or pink granite of Aberdeenshire, used this unforgiving material to transform his native city, largely in the classical style. Simpson's rival, John Smith ('Tudor Johnny'), and his son William, were employed by Prince Albert to create, in the finest white granite, and with immense attention to detail, the Royal Palace of Balmoral. Incorporating, as it does, many — some would say too many — features of the traditional tower-house, Balmoral has been maligned and abused. This is unfair, for Balmoral has its own charm. Its fate has been to give birth to 'Balmoralism' and the revival of the 'Scots-baronial' tradition that had reached its fine climax with the tower-house of more than two centuries before. Happily, modern restoration is being carried out nowadays on the basis of sound historical research, the Victorian clutter swept away at Udny, ruined castles like Towie-Barclay, Harthill and Inchdrewer carefully restored by private owners, while great castles like Brodie, Craigievar and Castle Fraser are not merely preserved and restored by the NTS but made into living properties.

Church architecture, on which the Reformation of 1560 had several dramatic effects, developed on different lines. Not only did the mobs inflamed by the preaching of John Knox destroy the houses of the great religious orders in the cities of Perth and Aberdeen, but neglect, following the misappropriation of funds by the pre-Reformation lay commendators, brought Arbroath Abbey to its state of magnificent ruin, reduced Kinloss to a few ivy-clad walls, stripped the lead from Elgin Cathedral and so on. It was not always so. When the saintly Queen Margaret (1046-93), wife of Malcolm Canmore, and her son David I (1084-1153) introduced the Roman Church into Strathmore and Moray, they had the political aim of pushing back, or absorbing, the Celtic Church of the Culdees by the establishment of religious foundations. There was plenty of scope for fine building, for the early Kingdom of the Scots and Picts could not boast much more than the Pictish tower at Restenneth and the two Irish-style tall round towers at Brechin and Abernethy. David, or his successors, founded the Anglo-Norman cathedrals of Dunkeld, now partially restored, of Brechin, now much re-built, of Dunblane, with its free-standing Norman tower, and, more glorious than all these, though now a sad if magnificent ruin, the great cathedral of Elgin, reminiscent of the cathedrals of northern France. Among these cathedrals must be numbered St Machar's of Old Aberdeen, though scarcely a stone remains of the Norman building. The 15th-century military-style west front with heavily-buttressed towers, its corbelled and machicolated parapet, built of granite long before this became the predominant material in Aberdeen, and the gloriously political heraldic ceiling within, make this the most unusual ecclesiastical building in Scotland.

Well-preserved pre-Reformation churches include the chapels of Tullibardine (*see* Auchterarder) and Innerpeffray (q.v.) in Strathearn, the church of St Mary's, Grandtully (q.v.), with its painted wooden ceiling, and the great nave of the Holy Rude at Stirling. The best is King's College Chapel (1505) in Old Aberdeen, with its Renaissance Gothic windows and its closed-crown tower. Early pre-Reformation parish kirks still in use are at Birnie near Elgin (continuously since 1140), at Fowlis Wester and at Cullen. The great city kirks of St Nicholas in Aberdeen and St John's in Perth have been so divided, disused, restored and reunited as to retain little of their original character, while at Dundee the three kirks under the shadow of the Old Steeple are of the 19th century. The strictly Presbyterian post-Reformation churches have an austerity that provoked the quip that, in some, our Lord still seems to be worshipped in a stable. In others, the social distinction of the Laird's Loft and the pumphels, or box-pews, for other worthies, seems nowadays strange, as does the canopied box for the Provost and Town Council in James Gibb's attractive conversion of the West Kirk of St Nicholas in Aberdeen. In the later 18th century, light and airy churches were built, like the graceful, spire-crowned Bellie Kirk at Fochabers, built by John Baxter for the Duke of Gordon's new village. The 19th-century ecclesiastical restorers, like Sir Giles Gilbert Scott at Dundee, Sir Rowand Anderson at Dunblane, or Dr Honeyman at Brechin, have been kinder to the restored churches than their counterparts were to the castles.

Turning to domestic buildings, while lairds and ecclesiastics built themselves houses of stone, the common people had for centuries to be content with cottages of rough stone walls, roofed with wooden branches and heather. Yet the relative prosperity of the fertile lands between Moray and Strathmore and the availability of building stone meant that proper stone houses were built earlier here than in the Highlands. This is reflected in the solid, red-sandstone farmhouses of Angus, the farmtouns of Aberdeenshire, built from granite 'field-gatherings', and the yellow freestone houses of Moray. Some, indeed, are not without architectural merit and though this vernacular architecture may lack in elegance, it gains in its close connexion with the rock and soil to which it belongs. A glance at farm buildings is a useful reminder of the age of horse-power, whether in well built barn and stable or in the circular or hexagonal wheel houses or horse mills with a conical roof, where the unfortunate beasts plodded round and round to drive the farm equipment — 'a most pernicious work'. Examples are to be seen just off the A9 near Pitlochry, in Glenshee and on the Airlie estates.

An interesting minor form of architecture is the doocot — *anglice* pigeon-house. In the main, they date from the 16th and 17th centuries and are confined in this area to the rich farmlands and estates of the Laich of Moray and of Strathmore in Angus. There is good reason for this. Since the only means of preserving meat during the long winter was by salting, some fresh alternative was a welcome change of diet — at least, for those who could afford it. Pigeons provided just this; attracted to roost in a well-equipped and sheltered doocot, they grew fat by feeding on the grain of the fields of landlord and tenant alike over a wide area. This unneighbourly procedure led to disputes and litigation until a regulation of 1617 forbade a landlord to put up a doocot unless there were two miles round of his own land for the greedy birds to plunder. The doocot thus became a prerogative of the wealthy, and in due course — inevitably — a status symbol.

Doocots usually provided roosting-boxes for about 500 pigeons and come in two different basic shapes. In the 16th century, the fashion was for circular ones with tapering walls and a domed roof, rather like an enlarged beehive, equipped with a revolving ladder inside (known as a 'potence') and string-courses outside to keep out the rats. In the 17th century, the tendency was to build doocots to a rectangular plan with a lean-to roof, known as the lectern type, with crowsteps for the pigeons to perch on. Within these two major types, there is an interesting variety of architectural detail. One of the biggest doocots is a double one for 2, 000 birds at Finavon (q.v.) in Angus. By the early 18th century, however, the efforts of the improving landlords rendered fresh pigeon-meat an obsolete luxury and, as a status symbol, the doocot ceased to attract the laird with pretentions to one-upmanship. Indeed, the heritage of the lesser lairds was by this time 'a pickle land, a muckle debt, a doocot and a law-suit'.

Communications, from Agricola to A9

The Highland Boundary Fault determined that the main line of communication should be, from earliest times until the 18th century, from south-west to north-east. The two brief Roman occupations of Scotland north of the Antonine Wall left no heritage of roads; it was to be another 1, 500 years before any seriously-planned road system emerged under General Wade. Meanwhile the horse, mainly the sturdy Highland garron, and the boat, by sea and to some extent by river, were the only supplement to 'Shanks's mare'. The wheel was almost unknown in the Highland districts until the early 18th century and, even in the lowland areas, such carriages as there were easily bogged down on the appalling tracks.

Transport by water was thus a useful adjunct to travel by land — at least for organised bodies such as invading armies. Agricola made good use of his fleet, as we have seen. Fourteen centuries later John Hardyng, an English spy sent to Scotland in the reign of James I, was reporting 'how to conveigh an armie as well by lande as water, into the chiefest partes' of Scotland. His quaint account in verse describes the Forth as 'that river principall, of right faire waye' and the Tay as 'so navygable, From the East Sea to Saynt Jhon's towne (Perth), For all suche shippes as bee able, Fortie tunne of wyne to carry up and doune'. He, too, notes the convenience of ports all the way up the east coast for the navy to come 'with vitailes to refresh your whole armye'.

One invader who did not seem to need naval support was Edward I, with his force of 30, 000 foot and 4, 000 horse. On both his Scottish campaigns, in 1296 and 1303, he took the easy lowland route from Stirling through Perth and along Strathmore on his northward journey to Elgin. On his return journeys, he ventured into the Highlands as far as Mortlach (Dufftown) and through the Cabrach to Kildrummy and, after crossing the Dee at Kincardine O' Neil, he went over the exposed Cairn o' Mount to Brechin. Admittedly, as the month was August, he probably suffered no great hardship,. On his first journey, he sent the unfortunate Bishop of Durham from Badenoch over the mountains by another way. This might have been through the Drumochter Pass, the route now used by the A9 highway and the Highland Railway, or this *pessimum passagium sine cibo* (worst of passages without fodder) could have been the more direct Comyn's Road, from Kingussie to Blair Atholl.

This Comyn's Road, now a track, was used as long ago as the 13th century by the powerful Comyn lords of Badenoch and Atholl, before their destruction by Robert the Bruce. It represents a substantial saving — 15 miles (24 km.) — off the Drumochter route between the strongholds of Blair Atholl and Ruthven (near Kingussie) on Speyside. Although the summit of the pass at the head of Glen Tromie is, at 2,500 ft (760 m.), 1,000 ft higher than Drumochter, a man on foot could cross from shelter to shelter within the hours of daylight. A shorter variant of Comyn's Road, the Minigaig (which is signposted at Calvine on the A9 as a walking route to lead over into Glen Feshie), figured as the only route through the Western Cairngorms on maps up to Moll's map of 1718, which was all General Wade had to use when building his military road over Drumochter between 1728 and 1730.

Directness and the need to move quickly over the exposed summit, from the last house in one glen to the first house in the next, were much more important to a man on horse or on foot than the gentler gradients required by wheeled vehicles. In medieval times, there was continual traffic between the fertile lands of Strathmore and the fair land of Moray. This meant either taking the long way round by Aberdeen and the undulating country of Buchan and Banff, or tackling direct the principal obstacle in the way, that is the Grampian range, or as it was then called the White Mounth. So the long, north-pointing Glens of Angus became important routes. Here, a man could travel up Glen Isla or Glen Clova or the winding glen of the North Esk, spend a night in some kind of shelter, and see how the weather might turn out before making a quick dash over the high plateau down to Deeside by the Monega, the Tolmount, the Capel Mounth or the Fungle. Nowadays, these Mounth roads are for the hill-walker, since there is no motor road crossing the Mounth between the Cairnwell Pass (on the A93 at the head of Glenshee) and the Cairn o' Mount (on the B974 north of Brechin).

The Mounth roads have a creditable history, being used by royalty, armies, monks, pedlars, whisky-smugglers and cattle-drovers. The cattle certainly trod out ways across these moorland hills for many centuries. It is a little difficult to determine just when the traffic ceased to be north-bound with cattle stolen from Strathmore to be driven to the raiders' homes in Badenoch, but by the end of the 17th century there was certainly a legitimate traffic southward in cattle being sold to the English market through the great trysts at Crieff and later Falkirk. These drove-roads, while making use of much the same glens and mountain passes as the raiders, had other requirements: the route must be broad enough for great masses of cattle, there must be sufficient pasture at convenient intervals and river-crossings should be broad and neither too rocky nor too swift. The drove-roads south through the Cairngorms, the long, impressive, rocky defile of the Lairig Ghru, or the somewhat easier way, softer underfoot for the calves, the Larig an Laoigh (Pass of the Calves), are still popular walking routes from Braemar to Speyside. In the days of the Crieff tryst, drovers from the West Highlands would come over the hills from Loch Tay to Comrie. As cattle production in Aberdeenshire developed in the 19th century, the Mounth routes came into their own again. These drove-roads persisted after the construction of the military roads of the 18th century, for the good reason that the gravelly surface of the latter hurt the feet of the cattle, which would have to be shod for travelling long distances by road. For the same good reason the drove-roads make good walking routes today.

It was the Jacobite Rising of 1715 that brought the military roads to the Highlands. In 1724, Simon Fraser, Lord Lovat, reported to George I's Government that the Jacobites were ready to rise again. As a result an Irishman, General George Wade, was promptly sent to investigate. He returned with the recommendation that keeping control of the

Highlands was not merely a matter of troops and barracks, but that roads and bridges were essential to maintain communications for His Majesty's troops between garrison towns and outlying barracks. Between 1726 and 1739, Wade built some 250 miles (400 km.) of new roads, of which two main ones concern us here. One is the route from Dunkeld to Inverness over the Pass of Drumochter, the route followed by the A9. The other Wade road of importance provided a direct route from Stirling to Inverness, by way of Crieff and Aberfeldy, where the Tay was spanned by the ornamental bridge designed by William Adam, to join the road from Dunkeld at Dalnacardoch. Here, at the junction, Wade set up the 'hut' from which he directed operations on both roads and, in September 1729, celebrated their conclusion with a feast that included four roast oxen and four kegs of brandy. The Crieff-Aberfeldy-Dalnacardoch route is still an attractive scenic alternative for those who prefer to eschew the traffic of the A9 and do not mind steep hills and a tight Wade zigzag or two.

After Wade's transfer and promotion in 1739, his work as road builder was continued and expanded by his Inspector of Roads, Major William ('Toby') Caulfeild, another Irishman who, over the following twenty-seven years until 1767, built some 850 miles (1, 350 km.) of road. It was his Irish wit that inspired the couplet:

> If you'd seen these roads before they were made,
> You'd lift up your hands and bless General Wade.

The popularity of this quip probably deprived Caulfeild of credit for his own roads, for most military roads are currently spoken of as 'Wade roads', with never a mention of a 'Caulfeild' road. Caulfeild's road-building took on a new impetus after the Rising of 1745, and of his major roads the one that concerns us here runs from Blairgowrie in Perthshire, up Glenshee, over what was once known as the Devil's Elbow and is now the Cairnwell Pass, to Braemar on Deeside. From there it followed — and its modern successor, the A93/A939, still does — a winding course over the hills to Corgarff (q.v.) on the Don with its small military outpost, before rising sharply to the 2,000 ft (600 m.) Lecht Pass — this last an extraordinary piece of road-engineering, first along a broad-backed ridge, and then slung along the hillside between the two summits of the pass. At the northern foot of the Lecht, a rough-cut slab notes 'A.D. 1754, Five Companies The 33rd Regiment Right Honbl Lord Chas. Hay Colonel made the road from here to the Spey'. Tomintoul was not yet founded and the road crossed the clear River Avon by the two-arched bridge which still exists, though damaged by frost in the severe winter of 1978-9. The road went on to Grantown-on-Spey heading for Fort George, the great military base then being built on the promontory between the inner Moray Firth and the Firth of Inverness.

There are two particularly fine bridges on this splendid route. Between Braemar and Balmoral, the modern A93 by-passes Caulfeild's five-arched Invercauld Bridge, with its sturdy cut-water buttresses; this presents an unforgettable foreground, among the dark Scots pines, to the peak of Lochnagar. Between Balmoral and Donside, the A939 still makes good use of the impressive, steeply hump-backed bridge of Gairnshiel, arching high over the little River Gairn. These magnificent bridges, admired today, and the hundreds of culverts and lesser bridges, made Highland travel a possibility for the early tourists, for until Wade and Caulfeild, there were almost no bridges north of the historic Stirling Bridge over the Forth, except for the ancient 14th-century Brig o' Balgownie across the Don at Old Aberdeen (q.v.) and its 16th-century companion over the Dee.

After Caulfeild's retirement in 1767, a few more military roads were built — from Aberdeen to Keith, the link from Coupar Angus to Dunkeld, and the Deeside road west from Aberdeen to Braemar which might have continued, as has often been since proposed but never carried out, down Glen Feshie to Speyside. As a result of General Wade's dispute with the Duke of Atholl, there was still no bridge at Dunkeld until Thomas Telford, that great civil engineer who earned the title of Pontifex Maximus from Southey in 1803, built the present fine bridge over the Tay there. Then, turnpikes and bridges were built quickly for the brief era of the fast stage-coach, before steam took over. To show the speeds stage-coaches could reach, Captain Robert Barclay-Allardice of Ury by Stonehaven, the famous 'Pedestrian', started the 'Defiance' stage-coach which did the 129-mile (200 km.) run from Aberdeen to Edinburgh in 12 hours. Smeaton's bridge at Perth, built in 1766, was the first for centuries to stand against floods; another Telford bridge spanned the Don at Aberdeen; and the graceful Telford/Simpson iron bridge of 1815, with its castellations, crosses the Spey (q.v.) at Craigellachie. The Morayshire floods of 1829 swept away many bridges in that district and gave scope for new bridge-builders, as can be seen at Fochabers and Glenlivet. Modern bridges include the Tay Railway Bridge, opened to passenger traffic in May 1878, struck by disaster eighteen months later, and rebuilt with superb Victorian confidence in 1883-8; also the parallel two-mile-long Tay Road Bridge of 1966, linking Fife to Dundee; and the Friarton motorway bridge of 1978, springing high over the Tay outside Perth.

Inland waterways enjoyed a brief era of activity between the age of the turnpike and the age of railway, and steam-boats were seen on Loch Tay. Timber was floated down the Spey during the late 18th and early 19th centuries. Interesting too was the Aberdeen-Inverurie canal, built by John Rennie in 1795, with its terminal at Port Elphinstone; an old information board in the Inverurie Museum states that 'The passenger boat sails from Inverurie to Aberdeen every afternoon at half-past 2 o'clock, Sunday excepted'. The canal was bought out in 1852 by the Great North of Scotland Railway — 'the wee railway with a big name' — to form part of their main line out of Aberdeen.

The G.N.S.R., its passenger service now sadly reduced to part of the British Rail single main line from Elgin to Aberdeen, was a pugnacious but efficient little railway system that spread its tentacles all over the north-east corner of Scotland, branches penetrating to Fraserburgh, to Alford on the Don, to Turriff and Macduff, with forgotten junctions at Maud and Tillynaught — and, of course, the Royal Deeside Line to Ballater of 1853, closed in 1963. The twisting bridge over a grassy ditch is the only reminder of most of these branch lines, except for the one from Dufftown down to Keith, still essential for the carriage of whisky from that town of distilleries. In the age of cut-throat railway competition, the G.N.S.R. did battle with its neighbour the Highland Railway which, starting from modest beginnings as the Morayshire Railway of 1852 from Elgin to Lossiemouth, set out to capture the traffic from the Highlands to the south. The Highland main line, the Inverness & Perth Junction Railway, originally ran south from Forres (open to traffic in 1863), over the exposed expanse of Dava Moor, where the track, its stations converted to trim dwelling-houses, is still to be seen along the A939 north of Grantown-on-Spey. The present Inverness main line, built by the engineer Joseph Mitchell, by way of Tomatin to Carrbridge, was not opened until 1898. In the interim, the G.N.S.R. hoped to catch some of the passenger traffic between the Highlands and the south by offering a fast connexion at Aberdeen with the great expresses of the North British and Caledonian Railways, speeding south by the Tay Bridge and by Perth respectively. The aggressive tactics of the G.N.S.R. proved counter-productive, leading to some hilarious episodes at Keith, where the G.N.S.R. passengers from Aberdeen had less than a minute to make the connexion with the Highland train to Elgin. A network of competing lines ran between Keith and Elgin, one along the coast through Buckie and across the Spey by what is now a useful footbridge at Garmouth; it has left us a magnificent relic in the great viaduct that bestrides the seaside town of Cullen (q.v.). The G.N.S.R. pushed its way, too, up the south-east bank of the Spey, offering day excursions at the cost of 2s. 6d. (12½ pence) from Aberdeen to Boat of Garten in 2½ hours.

Rail traffic concentrated on two main arteries. One was the Highland Line pushed by Mitchell over the Drumochter Pass and down to Dunkeld and Perth in 1863. This main line carried immense burdens during the Victorian shooting-seasons and two World Wars, battled through snow-storms, and is now restored once more to double-track in parts. The other main line was the joint North British/Caledonian Line out of Aberdeen, which carried the urgent fish-traffic southward to London. Their lines parted company at Kinnaber junction just north of Montrose, and crack north-bound expresses from King's Cross and Euston competed to be the first at Kinnaber and thus command the line on to Aberdeen. Carrying Royalty to their summer residence at Balmoral certainly put the train crews and the station staff on the Deeside line on their mettle. The amalgamations after World War I into the four great companies, and later the reduction to the uniformity of British Rail, has taken the colour out of North-East train travel. It is worth recording that until well into the 20th century, the passenger car on the two-mile line connecting Inchture station in the Carse of Gowrie with Inchture village was drawn by a horse!

Nowadays, rail takes second place to road. Virtually all public roads have tarmacadam surfaces, though some are narrow and winding and a few, like the Lecht Pass with a gradient of 1 in 4, or the Kenmore to Amulree by-road, steep and zigzagging as well. It is worth pursuing the by-ways, despite some loss of time, if only to enjoy the marvellous and unexpected views to be obtained. For the traveller who must be in a hurry, improvements are already in hand: the M90 motorway into Perth from the south by-passes the winding bottle-neck of Glen Farg; the fast road from Perth to Aberdeen now skirts the towns of Forfar and Brechin; and the improved A9 trunk-road which follows the line of General Wade's road from Dunkeld, will soon be complete.

Mapmakers from Ptolemy to Bartholomew

On my wall there hangs a well-reproduced facsimile of the map of the 'Duo Vicecomitatus Aberdonia & Banfia, auctore Roberto Gordonio à Straloch' included in Blaeu's *Atlas Scotia* of 1654. This attractive map, a milestone in the history of map-making of Scotland, is by no means the first in the field: there were mapmakers before Blaeu's sources assembled their material and the first of them was a Roman. When Agricola sent his fleet to circumnavigate Britain in A. D. 84, it returned with information for a map of Scotland which is a good deal more accurate on the relatively straight eastern coastline than on the heavily-indented west coast. Tacitus writing in A.D. 98 added the laconic statement that 'Caledonia stretches a vast length of way to the north ... sharpens to a point and terminates in the shape of a wedge'. With this material, Claudios Ptolemaios of Alexandria (A. D. 87-150) did his best and produced a crude but recognizable map of Britain. Unfortunately it twisted the whole of Scotland through a right angle so that the west coast faces north and the Moray Firth opens to the south-east. Nonetheless, the east coast shows with reasonable accuracy details such as Taezalorum Promontorium (Kinnaird Head), the rivers Tuessis (Spey), Dabrona (Deveron), Loxa (Lossie) and Deva (Dee). Even more unfortunately Ptolemy's map lay undiscovered until about 1475, and although medieval maps of the intervening period are relatively good for England, they are quite hopeless for Scotland. Matthew Paris (d. 1259) had a deplorable tendency to write essays in the blank spaces of his map, and Scotland showed plenty of those. The so-called 'Gough' map of 1360, now in the Bodleian Library in Oxford, was better, in that the anonymous author was aware of the place-names recorded in the royal progresses of Edward I of 1296 and 1303, when he travelled through north-east Scotland from Stirling to Elgin and back (*see* Communications). Only in the 16th century was there some advance in cartography and a map of 1546, while not much more detailed than Ptolemy's, at least shows Scotland the right way up, and, for the first time, 'Grampius Mons' appears for the Grampians.

The first effective map of Scotland was 'Scotiae Tabula', engraved by Mercator in 1564, published by Ortelius in 1573 and incorporated in Mercator's Atlas of 1595. The east coast is accurate enough, but the western half is still distorted. Mercator's map, hailed as 'one of the most perfect cartographic works of the 16th century', was widely copied and served as a basis for most maps of Scotland for the next 60 years. In 1654, the Amsterdam family firm of Blaeu published their completely new Atlas of Scotland. Behind that achievement lies the strange tale of Timothy Pont, the minister of the Caithness parish of Dunnet, who, after the 'hardships of a dangerous journey round Scotland', produced a painstaking survey in 36 sheets but failed to find a publisher. On his death, early in the 17th century, Pont's maps came into the possession of the 'doyen of geographers', Robert Gordon of Straloch (1580–1661), who revised them and, with Sir John Scott of Scotstarvit as intermediary, arranged publication by Blaeu. Charles I saw some of the sheets in 1641 and commended them: the Civil Wars delayed and complicated the transfer of the maps to Holland, and after 25 years of preparation Volume V of Blaeu's *Atlas Novus*, entirely devoted to Scotland, was published in 1654. In a letter to Scott, published with the Atlas, Robert Gordon pays a warm tribute to Timothy Pont: 'I wish he had been fated to outlive his own works . . . and not that I, as a substitute for him, should have laboured in this duty with abilities less than his'.

Even so, the shape of Scotland was not quite right, and it was still some time before it was generally realised that the Gordon-Blaeu map did not square with subsequent observations of latitude and longitude. John Adair, who set about revising the Blaeu map in the 1680s, made a coastal survey which served as a more correct outline for the 1718 map of the Dutch cartographer Hermann Moll.

In 1661 James Gordon, the minister of Rothiemay on Deveronside, son of Gordon of Straloch, produced his beautiful plan of Old and New Aberdeen, with its delightful marginal engravings depicting King's College and a 'prospect of New Aberdeen'. This plan (also available in facsimile) shows that New Aberdeen stopped at the 'Great Church' of St Nicholas beside the Denburn and was separated from Old Aberdeen by the moraine hummocks of Spital Hill and the Gallow Hill. The undredged estuary of the Dee and, in an inset, the 'ager Abredonensis', or adjacent countryside, stand out clearly. So does Gallowgate, which was then the axis of the town, for Union Street was still 150 years in the future.

Gordon's maps, half picture, half plan, came towards the end of the period of the old style map, which gave few details beyond localities, rivers and some hills. More accuracy and greater detail would be required by the new generation of military men and road-makers. When first commissioned in 1725 to build his roads, General Wade demanded maps of the area, but he probably had to put up with Moll's map of 1718. His successor, Caulfeild, built up a set of his own manuscript maps of his roads, and these came in useful when, in 1746, the Duke of Cumberland complained of the lack of maps of the Highlands. Caulfeild put young William Roy (then just 21 years of age) on the job, and in the years 1747 to 1755 Roy produced the 'Military Survey of the Highlands' on a scale of one inch to 1, 000 yards, the forerunner of modern surveys. Roy became fascinated with Roman and other antiquities of Scotland and later devoted himself to archaeology. For instance, it is to Roy that we owe the detailed plan of Burghead showing the fort on the promontory before the town-planners of the early 19th century did their destructive work.

Meanwhile, the improving landlords of the second half of the 18th century required not only maps of their estates in their unimproved state, but also plans as to how they might be best developed. The Commissioners who, in 1755, were put in charge of the 'Forfeited Estates' also needed to have the lands surveyed. The earliest estate surveyors were the local gardeners, mathematicians or schoolmasters, who had no qualifications beyond a knowledge of measurement and drawing. Sir Archibald Grant of Monymusk, the pioneer of the improvement of agriculture in the North-East, found that his English farming adviser needed plans drawn up. The Earl of Breadalbane had a 'Survey of Loch Tayside' made in 1769 which took 286 days to survey on the ground and another 198 days to draw the plans. Sir John Sinclair's compilation of the *Statistical Account* of 1791-5 recorded details of practically every parish in Scotland: this marked the culmination of the process whereby descriptive information ceased to be included on the margins of maps, but required recording on its own. A few of the estate surveyors enlarged their scope to cover whole counties, like the map of Kincardineshire of 1776 engraved from a survey by William Garden of Laurencekirk, showing roads with complete accuracy and with a 'meticulous delineation of enclosures and plantations'. These county surveyors combined accuracy with elegance: it was said of one of them that 'The Nobleman and Gentleman's domains, the towns and villages, with the roads, the sea-coast, the woods and rivers, are presented on paper as if reflected in a glass'. Their work was to lead to surveys of the whole country, until John Ainslie (1745-1828), who started as an estate surveyor, produced his 'Scotland drawn and engraved from a series of angles and astronomical observations in 1789', which rendered all previous maps out of date.

As early as 1763, William Roy had advocated an official national survey. The Ordnance Survey was stared in 1791, the year after his death. The original seven-mile-long base-line for the Ordnance Survey's triangulation of Scotland in 1817 was laid out on the sandy coastline north of Aberdeen, between the mouths of Don and Ythan, where neither tree nor hill interrupted the visibility. Map-making and map-production were becoming big business, beyond the capacity of the successors of skilled amateurs like Timothy Pont or Gordon of Rothiemay. By the beginning of the 19th century, with the spread of education and the interest in geography roused by the growth of the British Empire, cartography passed into the hands of the engravers and the publishers. They first combined existing county maps into Atlases, and later commissioned their own surveys. The Edinburgh engraving firm of Lizars employed one George Bartholomew as an apprentice. It was his son John (1805-61) who, starting as a freelance engraver, founded the great family firm of

John Bartholomew and Son in 1826. It was, in turn, his son, John the Second (1831–93), who made the vivid innovation of 'contour layer colouring' that startled cartographers at the Paris Exhibition of 1878. In the early 19th century the old system of depicting hills, and even ranges of mountains, as a series of conventional 'mole-hills' had been superseded by the caterpillar-like hachure and this, in turn, was giving way to black and white contouring. John Bartholomew's inspiration was to contrast the greens of the lowlands with the browns of the uplands, shading these into mauve and grey tints for the snowy highlands, in the way that became familiar with the Bartholomew half-inch to the mile series, and still makes the hills surge up out of the map so as to rejoice the heart of every mountain lover.

Whisky, from Illicit Still to World Drink

The Whisky Map of Scotland shows a surprising concentration of distilleries, 55 out of a total of 105 making Highland malts, in the Speyside triangle, its base between Forres and Macduff and its apex at Glenlivet. Travelling down the A95 from Ballindalloch, below the slopes of Ben Rinnes to Rothes and on to Elgin, one is rarely out of sight of the puff of blue smoke, the pagoda-like stack and a fragrant aroma in the air, that denote this pleasant and profitable industry. The happy combination of plentiful grain from Moray, an abundant supply of water of exceptional purity from the granite hills, and peat for the cutting, gives Speyside the ideal conditions for the production of Highland malt whiskies. The idiosyncrasies of these components make it impossible for even the keenest American or Japanese competitor to imitate them, and have given 'Scotch' a world market.

How is this magic liquor produced? In principle, quite simply, and you can even do it yourself. Take a sack of barley, steep it in pure mountain water, spread it out to germinate for ten days or so, dry it over a peat fire, crush it and put it in a container with a hole in the bottom, pour hot water through and collect the liquor in a cask, ferment it with yeast for 40 hours; pour it back into your container (having first filled up the hole), and heat the concoction, making sure that the vapour is expelled through a spiral copper 'worm', which is led through cold water to distil the spirit. If you drink or sell what comes out, take care: not only will you be acting doubly against the law, by failing either to pay excise duty or to mature your whisky for at least three years, but you will also be taking serious physical risks. Edward Burt, one of General Wade's assistants, tells of three English officers drinking raw spirits: one was afflicted with gout, another fell ill of a fever, and the third lost all his hair. He did not mention the risk of blindness.

The process of producing whisky in modern distilleries is not essentially different, though the technology, with its impressive copper retorts, huge vats, automatic machinery and oak sherry casks (and even oil in place of peat), is highly sophisticated. The secret of making the spirit drinkable lies in the process of maturing, in the course of which the noxious impurities are lost. The law requires that no whisky shall be sold less than three years old, and effectively none goes on the market under six years old. This maturing involves an enormous loss of whisky through evaporation, so that, in Lower Speyside, one can become mildly intoxicated on the 'angel's breath'. It also ties up big stocks in bonded warehouses. Despite all this mechanisation, each malt whisky retains its individual character, deriving from the peculiarities of its place of origin.

Single malt whiskies made by this 'pot-still' process take time, since the barley must germinate into malt before being distilled, and two separate processes are involved. Unmalted barley, maize or other grains can be distilled direct as a colourless alcoholic spirit that does not deserve the name of whisky (certainly not 'Scotch') and can equally well be made into gin or vodka. Distilling of this kind was greatly accelerated by the 'patent-still' invented in the 1830s by an exciseman called Coffey. This method could produce forty times as much spirit, and by a continuous process, in the same time as the malting method, and production of alcohol in this way was carried out on an industrial scale in the Lowlands.

The individual character of Scotch whisky is obtained by blending a selection of malt whiskies — maybe as many as forty malts — with the colourless spirit. Large quantities of malt whisky go to the blending industry, in the Lowlands and in Perth. With the development of many more Highland malt distilleries, particularly on Speyside, and the education of taste towards the single malt whiskies, a whole new market has grown up for a discriminating drinking public which can appreciate the individual bouquet of a malt.

Certain of the larger distilleries welcome the public to Visitor Centres, provide an exhibition or film of the history and craft of whisky-making, and a visit to the works, concluding with a sample dram. The Whisky Trail is well-marked on Speyside, leading from Craigellachie to Glenfarclas and Glenlivet, and on to Dufftown which, with more than seven distilleries, is the 'capital' of Eastern Highland malts.

Whisky is, however, more than just an industry: it is part of Scottish social history, with its own mythology of the smuggler and the illicit still. From medieval times whisky-making was as much part of the Highland way of life as cider-making still is in Devon. Whisky not only kept out the cold but also enabled the farmer to dispose of surplus barley in a form which provided a cash return and helped to pay the rent. It was only after the Union of Parliaments in 1707 that the Government in London attempted to tax spirits, but no enforcement of the excise laws was possible until after General Wade's roads gave access to the Highlands, in the 1740s. From then until the Excise Act of 1823 the 'smuggler' — which meant both the distiller and the transporter of illicit liquor — was the hero of the times.

Smuggling was a way of swindling the English and, because the whisky was made in remote Highland glens, the trade carried undertones of Jacobitism and repressed Catholicism. Moreover, the grain spirit of the Lowlands, where they could not evade the tax, was of poor quality and gave the good burghers of Perth and Dundee headaches. They would much rather pay more for a Highland malt which, as well as being more palatable, carried the cachet of having been smuggled. So the illicit trade flourished and the spirit distilled in the hills was carried in kegs on the backs of sturdy garrons from the Braes of Glenlivet (where there were over 200 illicit stills) over the Ladder Hills and by the 'Whisky Road' through the Angus glens to Brechin, where it was sold openly from house to house, or to the outskirts of Perth, where it was carried in cans secretly into the city after dark.

The excisemen or gaugers did their best to check the trade and there were violent clashes — one Malcolm Gillespie receiving forty-two wounds in the course of duty — but the gaugers were few and public opinion, Highland and Lowland, was against them. The poet Burns, though himself an exciseman for a time, railed against the 'curs'd horse-leeches of the excise, wha make the whisky stills their prize'. The authorities from London not only stationed military outposts at Corgarff and Braemar in support, but also varied the excise duty in the hope of inducing the black market to turn legal. Illicit stills flourished in, or even under, the heather, the smoke-outlet from the underground chamber cunningly led up a neighbouring chimney, and a convenient fast-flowing burn providing both the water intake and the drainage. The essential piece of equipment was the spiral coil of copper, the worm, and it was not unknown for the owner of an illicit still to 'find' for an exciseman his own worn-out worm, claim the £5 reward, and once more start up his still. A dramatic impression of an illicit still is to be seen in Landseer's picture of that title, which is reproduced with life-size figures at the Glenlivet Visitor Centre.

The Napoleonic Wars put French brandy out of favour as the drink of the wealthier gentry and whisky, particularly Highland malt whisky, rapidly grew in popularity. On his visit to Edinburgh in 1822, George IV took a great liking to the Highland malt whisky recommended to him by Sir Walter Scott. At about the same time the 4th Duke of Gordon explained to Parliament that whisky-distilling was part of the Highland way of life, and proposed that, if a reasonable tax could be devised, he would lend his power and influence in making the whisky trade legal. The Excise Act of 1823 imposed a flat licence rate of £10 on a 40-gallon still, those below that limit being illegal. This was a great inducement to legal distillers, with the dramatic result that the amount of duty-paid whisky doubled in one year. In 1824 George Smith, whose illicit whisky had been drunk by the King, decided to take out a licence for his distillery at Glenlivet. Though threatened by the owners of illicit stills, to the extent that he carried pistols, George Smith persisted. So good were both the quality of his whisky and his salesmanship that other Speyside distillers not only took out licences but also made use of the name 'Glenlivet', though little of the precious water of the Livet can have gone into their products. In 1880 George Smith's son, John Gordon Smith, decided to go to law to protect his product and obtained a High Court ruling that his was the only whisky entitled to the name 'The Glenlivet'. All other distilleries wishing to use the name must hyphenate it with the name of their own distillery, and some twenty-seven do just that, all the way from 'Glenburgie-Glenlivet' by distant Forres, up the Spey past 'Glenrothes-Glenlivet', past the junction of Livet and Avon to 'Tomintoul- Glenlivet'. No wonder that the brief 12 miles (19 km.) of the River Livet proper have been nicknamed the 'longest glen in Scotland'.

Well-matured malt whisky — the older the better — is a drink for the gods if taken in moderation after a long day in the open air, whether fishing, stalking deer or simply walking the hills. Neither soda-water nor ice should be added, but a little water, preferably straight from the burn, enables the drink to be savoured. Taken in excess, whisky may lead not to the gods, but to the devil. Like liberty, whisky must be enjoyed with discretion. Truly, as Burns said, 'Freedom and whisky gang thegither'.

The North-East in Language and Literature

World-wide literary figures have their special associations with the North-East of Scotland. Sir Walter Scott describes the Arbroath area in *The Antiquary*, wrote of Aberdeen in *A Legend of Montrose*, and was inspired by the Covenanters' Stone at Dunnottar church to write *Old Mortality*, while various castles, in particular Grandtully, claim to be the original of Tullyveolan in *Waverley*. The Wordsworths walked down the Tay in 1803, William musing on Ossian and Killiecrankie. Dr Samuel Johnson rode with Boswell through the North-East from Montrose to Elgin, pausing to converse with Monboddo, or to dine at Slains. George Gordon Byron, 'the brat from Aberdeen', expressed his nostalgia for Lochnagar and Deeside in verse. Rabbie Burns dashed round the North-East in 1787, visiting his relatives in the Mearns, praising the Birks of Aberfeldy and exhorting the Duke of Atholl to plant more trees. R. L. Stevenson wrote some of his stories during a wet summer spent in Pitlochry and Braemar, and J. M. Barrie's birthplace in Kirriemuir is now a literary museum.

Less well-known is how the Scots of the North-East developed their own speech, more than a dialect of English but not quite a separate language, and the intensely local literature of the North-East that sprang from it — manifesting itself in the early historical ballads, the Jacobite verse of the 18th century, the down-to-earth bothy ballads of the 19th-century farmtouns, and, in our own day, the nostalgic poems of the Buchan exiles and the 'couthy' writing of Lewis Grassic Gibbon in his *Scots Quair* trilogy.

The Picts left no literature because they had no written language, and even their spoken word was replaced by the Gaelic of the Scots from Ireland. These Scots left a considerable heritage of Gaelic place-names across the landscape, from Abernethy to Auchindoun. Outside the Highlands, Gaelic lingered on in the remote Banffshire glens until late in the 19th century, and the last sermon in Gaelic was preached in Tomintoul in 1895, though few can have understood it. From the 11th century onwards, the language and literature of North-East Scotland developed on quite different lines under the Normanising influence of Malcolm Canmore and his descendants. In those days official documents were in Latin, the high and mighty conversed in French, but the language of the stewards, bailiffs, and hangers-on was the tongue spoken in the north of England, where most of the nobility also had lands. This was a basic Anglo-Saxon, which had acquired a number of Scandinavian words from the Danish occupation and was now picking up some Norman-French as well. The Viking raids on Buchan and Moray had also left some Norse words, and the numerous Flemings who came up with the Normans brought their own guttural cadences. The resulting language became known in Scotland as 'Inglis' and, with its peculiarities of spelling, pronunciation and vocabulary, persisted as the official written language of Scotland (by then called 'Scottis') until after the Union of the Crowns in 1603. When the Court moved to London, standard English developed a prestige value and, by the Union of Parliaments in 1707, had established itself as the official written language of the whole of Britain. The spoken language in Scotland remained Scots-English, with the marked distinctions of pronunciation and special vocabulary that we know today, local variants depending on district and social standing. Gaelic was, at least until after the 'pacification' of the Highlands after 1746, still the language of the clans living in the hills north and west of the Highland Boundary Fault. This served as a linguistic as well as a geological boundary, but Gaelic had long before ceased to be the speech of the inhabitants of the farmlands of Buchan, Banff and Moray. These folk developed a strongly percussive speech of their own, classified by linguists as 'Mid Northern Scots', by the literary-minded as 'the Doric', and by ordinary people as 'good old Buchan'.

The historical ballads, many of them anonymous, record, with varying degrees of accuracy, the bloodthirsty events of the 15th, 16th and 17th centuries: for instance, the defence of the North-East against the Highlanders at Harlaw (q.v.) in 1411 (with its bagpipe refrain 'in a dree, dree, drady, drumtie'); the frequent feuding between Gordon and Forbes, as in Edom o' Gordon's burning of Corgarff (q.v.) and the Battle of Corrichie of 1562 (q.v.), where the ballad writer laments:

> I wis our quine had better friends,
> I wis our country better peice,
> I wis our lords wid nae discord,
> I wis our weirs at hame may ceise.

The Jacobite theme runs through the 17th and 18th centuries. The most picturesque Jacobite poet was William Meston (1688-1745) — that 'gay, thoughtless, clever, extravagant, restless, indolent, careless, unsteady, witty, dissipated dog', as a contemporary described him. The two Risings inspired a great deal of verse, much of it over-sentimental; the best probably came from the pen of Lady Caroline Nairne (1766-1845) of the Jacobite family of Oliphant. Writing under the pseudonym of Mrs Bogan of Bogan, she contributed to the Highland revival of the 1820s with her lilting songs like *Charlie is my Darling, Will ye no' come hame again?* and *Hundred Pipers*. Some of her literary relics can be seen at Ardblair Castle near Blairgowrie (q.v.).

The rollicking *Reel of Tullochgorum*, which Burns reckoned the best song to be danced to a Scottish reel, came, surprisingly enough, from John Skinner (1721-1807), who was for over 64 years the Episcopalian priest of Longside in Buchan:

> Let Whig and Tory all agree,
> To spend the night wi' mirth and glee,
> And cheerful sing along wi' me,
> The Reel of Tullochgorum . . .

As a piece set to music, it was used by two great fiddlers; Skinner's contemporary, Neil Gow of Inver by Dunkeld (q.v.), and Scott Skinner (1893-1923) of Banchory (q.v.). Robert Burns's cousin, John Burness (1771-1824) of Bogjordan in the Mearns, put into verse, in something resembling Rabbie's style, the story of *Thrummy Cap*. So named from his weaver's cap of odds and ends, this fictional character, well-known in the North-East, gets lost in a snowstorm, spends a night in a haunted room, drinks with a ghost in the cellar and undergoes other adventures.

The 19th-century prose work that best catches the spirit of the North-East is William Alexander's *Johnny Gibb of Gushetneuk*, a novel of 1870 based on life in an Aberdeenshire village called 'Pyketillim' (in fact Chapel of Garioch), with characters enjoying such splendid Dickensian names as the Reverend Sleekabout the minister, Sir Simon Frissal the impecunious laird, and Dr Drogemweal. The novel turns on two themes: the Disruption of 1843, when the Free Kirk broke away from the established Church of Scotland, and the relationship between farmers, farm-labourers and laird. It makes fine reading, providing one can manage the language: the opening words are 'Heely, heely, Tam, ye glaiket stirk', but enthusiasts will be relieved to know that a recent edition is equipped with an extensive glossary.

A very different writer from the same area — now the Gordon district of Grampian Region — was George Macdonald (1825-1905), preacher, poet and novelist, of Huntly. He wrote prolifically, mostly novels with odd titles like *Marquis of Lossie, Guttapercha Willie, David Elginbrod, Alec Forbes of Howglen*, some set against a background of Huntly Castle and the Banffshire coast. These are coming back into vogue, but Macdonald is better known for his mystical fairy-tales, like *At the Back of the North Wind, The Princess and the Goblin* and *The Princess and Curdie*.

During the 19th century, a much more down-to-earth form of verse was circulating with the Bothy Ballads — the songs of the young, unmarried farmhands who lived above the stables or in quarters known as bothies. Collected by Gavin Greig, a schoolmaster from New Deer, and John Ord, a Glasgow policeman, these ballads reflected the rough agricultural life of the North-East and circulated widely as the men changed their employment from farm to farm. Woe betide the farmer who was mean with his men, or the farmer's wife who skimped the rations. They were punished with ruthless ballads, known as cornkisters, the rhythm hammered out on the corn-chests, with no concealing the true name of the farm. The farmer of Drumdelgie, a farm near Huntly, 'he is baith hard and sair' — and his workers 'a maist unceevil crew'. And as for the food:

> The breid was thick, the brose was thin, And the broth they were like bree,
> I chased the barley roon the plate, And a' I got was three.

One of the best-known is *The Barnyards of Delgaty,* where the farmer

> Promised me the ae best pair (of horses) I ever set my eyes upon;
> But when I gaed home to the Barnyards There was nae thing but skin and bone

and a lot more in this vein before the end comes:

> Sae fare ye weel ye Barnyards,
> Ye'll never catch me here again.

These humble ballads caught the dour spirit of the land. It was expressed with greater sophistication and more intense feeling by Lewis Grassic Gibbon, pseudonym of Leslie Mitchell (1901–34), the outstanding writer of the North-East who now lies in Arbuthnott kirkyard. The first two volumes, *Sunset Song* and *Cloud Howe*, of his trilogy *A Scots Quair* are written in a prose which catches the cadences of the local speech without inordinate use of dialect. Brought up in the Mearns (q.v.), Mitchell makes his hard-working farmers and obstinate townsfolk come vividly to life, whether in the Guthrie farm of Blawearie or in 'Seggat', the little weaving town of Drumlithie. His third volume, *Granite City*, is set in a city that might be Dundee or Aberdeen, though he claims it to be imaginary.

This deep-rooted nostalgia for the North-East goes back to the old song about the lovely Garioch (q.v.) with the refrain 'Gin I were whaur Gadie rins, at the back o' Bennachie'. In modern times this theme recurs again and again, perhaps best in the poems of Charles Murray (1864–1941), a native of Alford in Aberdeenshire but for many years an exile in South Africa. His poem *The Whistle* ('He cut a sappy sucker from the muckle rodden tree . . .') is a popular tongue-twister for Scottish school-children. Murray's roll-call of the hills of his native Donside in *Hamewith* is the essence of non-Celtic Scotland:

> There's Tap o' Noth, the Buck, Ben Newe,
> Lonach, Benrinnes, Lochnagar,
> Mount Keen, an' mony a Carn I trow
> That's smored in mist ayont Braemar.
> Bauld Ben Muich Dui towers, until
> Ben Nevis looms the laird o' a';
> But Bennachie! Faith, yon's the hill
> Rugs at the hairt when ye're awa'! . . .
> There's braver mountains ower the sea,
> An' fairer haughs I've kent, but still
> The Vale o' Alford! Bennachie!
> Yon is the Howe, an' this the Hill!

There can be no finer introduction to this splendid country, part tamed by Man, part still mountain wilderness. Once this land has taken hold of you, it is hard to shake off its fascination.

Short-Stay Guide

The following selection — inevitably a subjective choice — is intended for the visitor whose time is limited to a few days in the area. The lists are alphabetical. Those places that are not covered by an independent Gazetteer item may be traced through the Index.

Archaeological Remains
Aberlemno Pictish stones
Bennachie hill-fort
White Caterthun hill-fort
Loanhead of Daviot stone circle
Midmar Kirk stone circle
St Vigean's Pictish stones museum
Sueno's Stone, Forres
Tap o' Noth hill-fort

Bridges
Aberfeldy, 18th century, over Tay
Balgownie, 14th century, over Don
Craigellachie, 19th century, over Spey
Dunkeld, 19th century, over Tay
Friarton, 20th century, over Tay
Gairnshiel, 18th century, over Gairn
Invercauld, 18th century, over Dee

Castles, Country Houses and Gardens
Blair Castle, Blair Atholl
Branklyn Gardens (NTS), Perth
Brodie Castle (NTS)
Castle Campbell (AM)
Castle Fraser (NTS)
Craigievar (tower-house) (NTS)
Crathes, Castle and Gardens
Dunnottar Castle
Edzell, Castle and Garden (AM)
Haddo House (NTS)
Pitmedden Great Garden (NTS)
Scone Palace
Stirling Castle (AM)

Cathedrals, Churches and Abbeys
Arbroath Abbey (AM)
Dunblane Cathedral
Elgin Cathedral (AM)

Fowlis Wester Church
Grandtully Church (AM)
King's College Chapel, Old Aberdeen
St Machar's, Old Aberdeen

Scenery, including Nature Reserves
Arbroath cliffs
Banff Coast: Troup Head
Ben Avon, from Tomintoul
Ben Lawers (NTS)
Bennachie
Bullers of Buchan
Cairngorms, from south side
Cairn o' Mount Pass
River Dee near Braemar
River Findhorn: Randolph's Leap
Glen Clova
Glen Isla: Reekie Linn
Glen Lyon
Glen Muick and Falls
Lecht Pass
Loch of the Lowes (SWT)
Lochnagar (mountain)
Loch Tummel: Queen's View
Kinnoull Hill, Perth
Moray Firth, looking to Sutherland
Speyside
Ythan Estuary

Towns and Villages
Old Aberdeen
Banff
Crovie (Banff coast)
Fochabers
Fordyce
Perth
Portsoy
Stirling

Gazetteer

Abbreviations

AM   for Ancient Monument (i.e. in the care of the Ancient Monuments Division of the Department of the Environment)

NTS   for National Trust for Scotland

RSPB for Royal Society for the Protection of Birds

SWT   for Scottish Wildlife Trust

Entries in the Gazeteer

The first figure of the map reference supplied to each entry refers to a page number in the map section at the back of the book. The subsequent letter and figure give the grid reference.

Aberdeen (*see* also **Old Aberdeen**)

Grampian 5 H1 (*pop.* 210,362)

Aberdeen, the most northerly city of its size in Britain, has been called many names, of which 'Silver City by the Golden Sands' is the most complimentary, 'Granite City by the Sea' the most accurate, and the 'Oil City of the North' the most up-to-date. There are really two towns, the University and Cathedral 'village' of Old Aberdeen (q.v.) or 'Aulton', a mile or so to the N, quite distinct in character from the busy port and commercial capital of the North-East, though the two now form a single city. Etymologists speculate whether they derive their joint name from the Gaelic *aber dubh abhainn,* 'mouth of the dark waters', or whether, more ingeniously, Old Aberdeen is really 'Aberdon', giving rise through the Latin to 'Aberdonian', while Aberdeen is really 'Aberdene', at the mouth, not of the Dee, but of the Den, or Dene, Burn, that narrow chasm to the w of the city centre where the railway now runs.

Unlike Stirling or Dundee, the physical site of Aberdeen is not dramatic. The low sandy hills on which the city is built are the last humps of the terminal moraine left behind by the glacial ice-cap that once covered the Cairngorms and flowed down Deeside. The two rivers, Dee and Don, hem in the city with a broad sweep of two miles of sandy beach along the North Sea between them. This only comes into view after leaving the city behind. Yet Aberdeen is, with its harbour, its seagulls and the 'haar' or sea mist that rolls in on warm days, very much a city of the sea. Aberdeen has overcome its grey, gloomy reputation of the 1930s and with the coming of North Sea oil it has an air of prosperity and brightness, especially when the mica spicules of the grey granite sparkle in the sun.

It is also a city of fish and of flowers: fish because of the fishing port, the exciting fish auctions at the covered market that are vociferously conducted on most mornings (though now sadly diminished); flowers because of the city's foresight in planting flowers and shrubs in many open spaces. This means a multitude of daffodils on the banks of the River Dee, the imaginative development of roundabouts with heathers and shrubs and, above all, the abundance of roses that bloom for eight months of the year along the central reservation of the Ring Road.

Aberdonians are well known to be a race apart; some say this goes back to Flemings who came here in the early Middle Ages, and did not inter-marry with the surrounding Celtic people. However that may be, Aberdeen has shared most of the troubles of the Scottish nation from Independence onwards. The Aberdonian reputation for parsimony, which has formed the subject of innumerable jokes, often by Aberdonians against themselves, is no more than a matter of hard-headed husbandry of their own, and of the City's, resources. A sturdy independence, well rooted in a sound economy based on farming and fishing, now supplemented by North Sea oil, give the folk of the broad Doric speech of the North East the capacity to absorb outsiders, from Normans to Texans, without losing their own individuality — an untranslatable 'couthiness'.

The earliest known Aberdonians based their little township at the mouth of the Denburn on The Green, now overshadowed by the Union Street Viaduct. As the city's importance grew as market and port for the North-East, and when the Scottish kings after Malcolm Canmore extended their rule to the fertile lands of Moray, they found it essential to control Aberdeen. The first extant charter of the town dates back to William the Lion, 1179, and trading privileges were probably granted under David I. Since then, Aberdeen has seen plenty of violence: in 1336 it was totally devastated by Edward III; in

1411 the burgesses sallied out to the Battle of Harlaw (q.v.); in 1525 Leslies from the Garioch attacked the city and injured the Provost; shots were fired in the streets of James V in 1537; Gordons and Forbeses fought family squabbles in 16th-century affrays, of which the worst was the Battle of the Craibstone in 1571; Reformers brought 'fire and spulzie' (spoliation) in 1560 to the churches and the three great monastic foundations of Aberdeen — Greyfriars, Dominicans and the Trinitarians; while the plague killed off a quarter of the population in 1647.

The worst devastation was in the 17th century when Montrose, who had, in 1639, chased out the Gordon defenders of Aberdeen, reappeared 5 years later. In 1644, infuriated at the shooting of a drummer-boy on The Green after the Battle of Justice Mills, Montrose gave his 'Irishes' full rein to pillage, rape and murder. In the Jacobite Risings of 1715 and 1745, the City Council backed the losing side, but Cumberland's occupation was relatively peaceful, though his cavalry's fodder was stored in St Nicholas Church.

Nonetheless, Aberdeen grew steadily and, on the whole, prospered. Robert the Bruce had reason to be thankful to the Provost and men of Aberdeen who, in 1308, ejected the English garrison from the castle using, tradition has it, the password of 'Bon Accord'. This is now the city's cheerful motto, coupled with the toast: 'Happy to meet; sorry to part; happy to meet again'. Bruce rewarded the Aberdonians with the gift of the Forest of Stocket, which provides the Common Good Fund, used for the entertainment of visitors. It is a pity that, although Aberdeen owes much to Bruce, there is no statue to him in the city, whereas Wallace, whose legendary exploit of destroying part of the large English fleet in the harbour in 1297 is his only connexion with Aberdeen, is commemorated by the huge bronze statue on a pink granite plinth which towers over the N end of Union Terrace.

After the destruction of 1336, the centre moved up from The Green to the present Castlegate. Though there was once a castle here, no traces remain on the site now occupied by the neo-baronial Salvation Army citadel. Since the 14th century, authority was exercised from the old Tolbooth, now incorporated in the heavy arcaded facade of the pretentious Town House of 1868, surmounted by a top-heavy pepper-potted spire in Flemish medieval style. Within, there is a fine statue of Queen Victoria, historical documents including the original charters, a finely emblazoned Council Chamber and the flags of the Gordon Highlanders (the famous regiment's museum is on the outskirts of the town). The old Tolbooth (admission by arrangement with Town Clerk) is marked by the more slender spire at the other end of the frontage. In 1627 it replaced an earlier jail and ceased to be used as a prison in 1820. One of the condemned cells, with shackles, chain and bar, has been preserved. The gentry were given the privilege of speedy execution by the headman's axe or the Maiden, an early

form of guillotine: its blade can be seen in Provost Skene's House. Mary, Queen of Scots, was obliged by her half-brother James to watch the execution here of John Gordon after the Battle of Corrichie (q.v.) in 1562. In Castlegate too is the elaborate Mercat Cross in red sandstone, built in 1686 as a circular arcade containing a unique portrait gallery of Scottish sovereigns from James I to James VII, said to be very good likenesses.

Round the corner in Broad Street, two controversial examples of 19th and 20th century architecture strike the eye. To the left is the towering glass and concrete block of St Nicholas House, the new headquarters of the City Council. To the right is the granite western exterior of Marischal College, completed by Marshall Mackenzie in 1905. Some talk of the 'exuberant fretted detail' of the Gothic facade; a poet writes of 'pinnacles and minarets most excellently fair'; while others condemn the 'wedding cake in indigestible grey icing'. Whatever view one takes, Marischal College occupies a major site in central Aberdeen — the second largest granite building in Europe, after the Escorial. The College was founded in 1593 by George Keith, 5th Earl Marischal, on land expropriated from Greyfriars monastery after the Reformation; Greyfriars Church is incorporated in the south-west corner. The College was intended as the Protestant counterpart to the 'Papist' University of King's College, founded a century earlier in Old Aberdeen (q.v.). Until 1860, when the two colleges were amalgamated, Aberdeen enjoyed the distinction of being the only city in Britain with two universities. Of the original building there remains only the inscription bearing the Earl Marischal's defiant retort to his critics, 'Thay haif said, quat thay say: lat yame say', when they claimed he had misused the funds of the monastic foundations. The three sides of the quadrangle, including the Mitchell Tower at the east end, were designed in a less exuberant Gothic style between 1837 and 1844 by Archibald Simpson, Aberdeen's leading architect in granite. The Mitchell Tower houses the grandiose hall for examinations and graduation ceremonies, as well as the interesting Anthropological Museum containing a valuable, if mixed, collection of Greek vases, Egyptian mummies, stone axes from New Guinea, Chinese bronzes of 1500 B.C., Australian boomerangs, and drums from Fiji. There is also a fine short stone cist of the Beaker Folk, skeletons of Stone Age inhabitants, medieval weapons and a testimony to John Forsyth of Belhelvie, inventor of the percussion lock introduced by the British Army in 1839.

Thanks to the inspiration of Queen Elizabeth the Queen Mother, and the support of the City Council, Aberdeen enjoys two fine examples of well-to-do houses of the 16th and 17th centuries. Provost Ross's House (NTS) on the Shiprow is partly the local headquarters of the British Council, and part is being made into a maritime museum (to be completed by late 1981). Originally built in 1594 for the father of George Jamesone, the portrait painter, the house was acquired a century later by Provost

Mercat Cross, Aberdeen

Ross, who was able to keep an eye on his own trading ships in the harbour. 'The house he bought and plenished so fine lived on when he was dead . . . But a graceless age took little care of the house on the Shiprow Brae'. In the 19th century it came near to demolition, but was restored in 1954. Provost Skene's house, similar in period, and open to visitors, is off Broad Street in the shadow of the 15-storey modern office block of St Nicholas House. First mentioned in 1545, the house was in 1622 owned by Matthew Lumsden, who commissioned the fine painted ceiling in the chapel, well restored. In 1669, when Provost Sir George Skene of Rubislaw acquired the house, he made substantial exterior alterations, which give the pleasing aspect of today. The main rooms are carefully furnished with Georgian, Regency and Victorian period pieces, and the long gallery on the top floor houses a small museum showing the development of Aberdeen.

From the N end of Broad Street, turn left down Upper Kirkgate and up Schoolhill where the Grammar School, attended by Byron, once stood. (The Grammar School is now housed in a fine granite building in Skene Street, with the poet's statue in front of it.) Across St Nicholas Street is St Nicholas Church, the 'Mither Kirk' of Aberdeen. The general outline of this great parish church as we see it today was completed in 1520, built by funds

collected by the citizens of Aberdeen who, 'canny by nature and suspicious of innovation', had already disposed of the rood screen and high altar by the time the band of Reformers arrived at Christmas 1559 to 'ding doon' the religious houses and the Mither Kirk. The citizens refused to allow the roof to be stripped and see good money go to waste. After the Reformation, St Nicholas was divided into three, the w end becoming the Auld Kirk, and the E end, or former choir, becoming the New Kirk, with a common central area at the crossing. After 1689, the church was neglected and in 1708 the roof fell in. However, after 1751 the Auld (West) Kirk was rebuilt by James Gibb, the Aberdeen architect who also designed the Senate House at Cambridge, the Radcliffe Camera at Oxford and St Martin's-in-the-Fields in Trafalgar Square. The result is an unusual church, with box pews in dark oak and extensive galleries, one with a majestic *baldacchino* or canopy for the Lord Provost. In the entrance are four large tapestries worked by Mary, daughter of George Jamesone the artist: the left-hand one depicts the finding of Moses beside a river, clearly spanned by Aberdeen's Bridge of Dee. To the right is a large monumental brass commemorating the great scholar and mathematician Dr Duncan Liddel (1561-1613). The Middle Kirk is largely bare, with

Collison's Aisle (a former Provost) to the north and the Drum Aisle to the south, containing the recumbent stone effigies of Alexander Irvine of Drum (q.v.) and his wife Elizabeth. Passing into the East Kirk is to move from the intimacy of the 18th century to the chilly splendours of High Victorianism. In the 19th century the medieval choir was pulled down and replaced by a pretentious work in granite by Archibald Simpson, which fails to harmonise with the West Kirk, either inside or out. A long flight of steps descends to St Mary's Chapel, known as 'the Lady of Pittye, her vault', the only medieval part of the church, with its ribbed groin-vaulting. After the Reformation, it was used successively as a prison for witches, a plumber's shop, a Gaelic chapel and a soup kitchen, before being well restored at the end of the 19th century: two small windows of modern stained glass glow in the dim light. The spire of St Nicholas was rebuilt in Gothic style in 1874, after the old wooden steeple had burnt down. The old bells of 1351 were recast in Louvain to make part of the carillon of 48 bells which now bring the pleasant notes of a Belgian Grand' Place to the grey streets of Aberdeen. The graveyard round St Nicholas is crowded with tombstones, some with beautiful 17th-century lettering. It is separated from Union Street by the heavy classical columns of 'Tudor Johnny' Smith's great granite screen.

To the w of St Nicholas, on Schoolhill, the pleasant Georgian James Dun's house of hand-dressed granite has changing exhibitions for children of all ages. James Dun was Rector of the Grammar School in Byron's day. In the small square opposite, the statue of Gordon of Khartoum stands at the entrance to the Robert Gordon's College. Now the Institute of Technology, it was founded by a wealthy Danzig merchant, grandson of Gordon of Straloch, the mapmaker. The older buildings with slender spire, visible in the distance through the modern arch, were designed in 1731 by William Adam, but occupied by Cumberland in 1746 as his headquarters. The entrance arch in pink granite is of a piece with the Art Gallery facade and the War Memorial nearby. The Art Gallery contains a certain number of French Impressionist paintings, as well as paintings by Aberdeen's own artists George Jamesone (1588-1644), (the 'Scottish van Dyck'), William Dyce (1806-44) and John ('Spanish') Phillip (1817-67). There are also changing exhibitions of modern art. Opposite the Art Gallery are the Belmont Triple Kirks, built by Archibald Simpson in incongruous red brick in East Prussian-style for parsimonious parishioners who wanted three kirks in one in a cheap material. After being declared unsafe, the building is now restored and converted to secular use.

Across the Rosemount Viaduct, spanning the steep-sided little Denburn where the railway now runs, are, side by side, the Public Library, St Mark's Church and His Majesty's Theatre, jocularly known as 'Education, Salvation and Damnation'. Beyond Rosemount Viaduct and the pleasant Union Terrace Gardens Aberdeen really begins to deserve its epithet of 'Granite City'. This was

Provost Skene's House, Aberdeen

made possible by two developments. The first was the discovery of building stone in the 'quarry in the den of Rubislaw', mined by John Gibb at the end of the 18th century. This huge hole off the Queen's Road, 450 ft (137 m.) deep, was closed to working in 1970 after providing granite for houses in Aberdeen, pavements in London and even temples in Japan. The second development was the Act of Parliament of 1800 authorising two new streets in Aberdeen: King Street to the N and Union Street to the w. The latter, named to commemorate the Union of Great Britain and Ireland in 1801, is one of the great streets of Europe. It gives a fine vista of uniform granite buildings as it dips from Castlegate to span the Denburn on the bridge designed by Telford to rise again to the junction at Holburn Place. The bridge, though hardly noticed by the passer-by on Union Street, is a fly-over half a mile long, as can be seen by taking one of the twisting wynds below it. At the w end, the vista is closed by the attractive 19th-century Tudor-style Christ College; at the east end, in Castlegate, the pepper-pots of the Salvation Army Citadel give a rather grimmer look. The street was not completed until 1805, and the cost virtually bankrupted the city – a fact which may account for subsequent Aberdonian financial caution.

The two Aberdeen architects responsible for many of the granite public buildings and the planning of the Granite City were John Smith (1781-1852) (known as 'Tudor Johnny', because of his predilection for the ogee-fronted coping of the Tudor tradition), and Archibald

Simpson (1790–1847). 'Tudor Johnny's' work, in addition to the St Nicholas granite screen on Union Street, includes the North Parish Church in King Street (now the Civic Arts Centre) and the schools in Little Belmont Street. Archibald Simpson, a prolific architect whose work is to be seen throughout the North-East, not only designed a number of public buildings, mostly in granite and in classical style (such as the Music Hall — former Assembly rooms in Union Street), but also had a vision of a planned 'silver city by the sea'. His design for a new Aberdeen envisaged wide streets, dignified squares, crescents and terraces; some of this may be seen off the middle section of Union Street, particularly in Bon-Accord Square, where a rough-hewn block of granite commemorates the architect himself — 'A Pioneer of Civic Design in this, his Native City'. Incidentally, Archibald Simpson's first major work, St Andrew's Episcopal church (now cathedral) in King Street, completed in Gothic style in 1817, has close links with the United States, for the first American bishop, Samuel Seabury, was consecrated in Aberdeen in 1784 by three Scottish bishops in an upper room in the Guestrow, since the Government in London had refused to permit his consecration as a bishop unless allegiance were sworn to King George III (which Seabury could obviously not do).

Two important aspects of Aberdeen remain to be mentioned: its harbour and its parks. The harbour developed from the estuary of the Denburn, without making much use of the River Dee. This sweeps majestically under the seven arches of the old Bridge of Dee, built in 1527, and past most of the docks, except Torry. It runs out to the North Sea between the N pier by Footdee (an 18th-century fishing community which has preserved its character) and the bold promontory of Girdle Ness, providing a stance for one of Robert Stevenson's many lighthouses. The harbour entrance was once impeded by sandbanks and a great rock, the Craig Metallan, which an ingenious Aberdonian, David Anderson (known as 'Davy do a' thing'), removed in 1610 by floating it away at high tide with a string of empty casks. The sandbanks were dredged and the harbour isolated from the spates of the River Dee as part of Smeaton's and Telford's schemes for constructing the dock basins in the late 18th and early 19th centuries. Since then, Aberdeen harbour has remained prosperous and busy, dependent not only on the fish trade, but also active in ship-building. In the mid 19th century, clippers for the Australian wool and the China tea trade were built here, *Thermopylae*, the *Black Prince*, the *Cairngorm* and others, averaging 67 days from London to Melbourne. Later there were hundreds of fishing vessels and, most recently, the multitude of activities connected with the oil industry

Aberdeen harbour

The Wallace statue and His Majesty's Theatre, Aberdeen

The former Town House, Old Aberdeen

development out in the North Sea.

Aberdeen has a fine variety of parks, large and small. Of the larger, special mention must be made of Hazlehead, with its maze, rose garden, sports grounds, small zoo and free-flight aviary; of Duthie Park with its Winter Gardens, where tropical flowers and birds can be found in the depths of the Aberdeen winter; and the vast open expanse of the King's and Queen's Links, between Dee and Don, backing onto the two-mile raised beach promenade and its golden sands.

From the summit of Brimond Hill (846 ft / 265 m.), a good overall view can be had of the city, from the cluster of spires and pinnacles that mark St Nicholas, Marischal College and the Town House to the high-rise blocks of Bridge of Don. The modern outskirts include many new housing developments and caravan parks inevitably needed by the developing oil industry and its ancillaries, as well as the rapidly growing international airport at Dyce.

Just as, in earlier days, Aberdeen looked to the Baltic trade, to Prussia, to Holland and to Scandinavia and had links with Danzig, Veere and Bergen, so now she looks to Norway and has developed a close connexion with Stavanger, that other oil port across the North Sea, while Grampian Region is suitably twinned with Houston, Texas. Aberdeen can absorb it all, for it is an historic city, an exciting city, a prosperous city, closely linked to the sea on the one hand, and on the other to the well farmed Aberdeenshire countryside, with its many castles, its rich herds of Aberdeen-Angus cattle and its high moors fading into the hills of the 'White Mounth'.

Old Aberdeen   Grampian 5 H1

The 'Aulton of Aberdon', with St Machar's Cathedral, King's College, and its delightful, ancient High Street, is an oasis of quiet between the swirling traffic of King Street and the heavy lorries hurtling by on the A94 from Dyce and Inverness. Whether 'Old Aberdeen' is older than 'New Aberdeen' is a matter for debate, but the old town on the Don has had a longer continuous existence than the city on the Dee, destroyed by the English in 1336. The 'Aulton' had an independent municipal life from 1498 to 1891, when it was absorbed into the City of Aberdeen. Old Aberdeen has many buildings of historical and architectural interest, which the University authorities have been at pains to preserve, and to keep apart from the newer, functional buildings of the University. Skilful use of the old wynds and closes has been made to connect old and new.

The University, the fourth oldest in Britain, was founded by Bp Elphinstone (1431-1514) under a bull issued by the Borgia Pope, Alexander VI, dated 10 February 1494, in response to King James IV's petition that in the northern parts of his kingdom there were 'men who were rude, ignorant of letters and almost barbarous', and so incapable of the ministry of the church. The papal bull encouraged mortal man to win by earnest study the pearl of knowledge, showing the way to live happily and raising to eminence those born in the lowest estate. The University opened in 1505 with Bp Elphinstone as first Chancellor and, as the first Principal, Hector Boece, native of Dundee, friend of Erasmus, Professor of Philosophy from Montpellier in France, and a most

King's College Chapel, Old Aberdeen

credulous and imaginative historian.

Oddly enough, after descending Spital Brae when coming from Aberdeen, the first building to strike the eye is not Christian at all, but Moslem. This is the incongruous Powis Gateway, now leading to two Halls of Residence. The gateway consists of a pair of 100 ft minarets, each complete with muezzins' gallery and oriental crescent on top, and joined by a central arch. These were built in 1834 for John Leslie, a laird of Powis, who, as a young man, became a devotee of Byron's Turkish romances and wished to leave this memorial to the Byronic cult. After this initial surprise, it is reassuring to find, on the opposite side of College Bounds, the crowned tower of King's College Chapel, and the complex of older University buildings in Scottish Gothic style built, not in granite, but in the yellow Moray freestone.

The picturesque crown tower of King's Chapel is similar to that surmounting St Giles Kirk in Edinburgh. Modelled on the Imperial Crown of the Emperor Charlemagne and his successors, it denotes the universality of education, and, as a closed crown, was an assertion of the independence of the Scottish nation. The crown was blown down in 1633 and rebuilt in the crocketted style we see today. The tower stands beside the crowstep gable and fine traceried window of the w front of the chapel. Outside the w end of the chapel is an elaborate bronze cenotaph, commemorating the founder bishop, supported by figures of the Seven Virtues, which

have acquired a deep green patina, because, after being cast in Venice in 1914, they spent the years of World War I under the Grand Canal. The interior of the chapel is very fine, particularly the carved oak rood-screen and stalls of Flemish work, the shallow arched wooden ceiling with decorated ribs and bosses, and the carved pulpit transferred in the 19th century from St Machar's.

The rest of the older University buildings, decorated with brightly tinctured coats of arms, centre round the small quadrangle to the s of the chapel. The squat, rectangular tower, looking like a Norman keep, built about 1658, was known as 'Cromwell's Tower', because some Roundhead officers contributed to the cost. In the quadrangle too is the magnificent library, restored in the 19th century after a fire. It is a long, lofty hall with a low-arched decorated ceiling, which is only visible on climbing to the upper galleries.

North of the chapel, College Bounds becomes the cobbled High Street, lined with grey stone houses of rough hewn granite, and closed at the N end by the granite Tolbooth (1788) crowned with a lead belfry, now the Police Station. Here the old roads N from Aberdeen diverged: to Inverurie to the left, and across the Don to the right. Before reaching this division, however, take a glance down some of the wynds that link the 18th-century High Street with the modern buildings of the University in Elphinstone Road to the w (largely scientific) and in Dunbar Street to the E (largely political and social). In particular Wright's and Cooper's Close is a delightful row of dons' houses, ending in a waterlily pool and metal astrolabe in front of the memorial to the three MacRobert brothers killed while serving with the R.A.F. between 1938 and 1941. In the modern idiom, the Edward Wright building in Dunbar Street sinuously adapts itself to the curves of this old street, while the Faculty of Natural Philosophy sports a mushroom dome.

Across the busy St Machar's Drive is the quiet Chanonry. The dignified granite houses, formerly the manses of the cathedral canons, are now occupied by University professors. This street leads past the Botanical Gardens to the gateway of the former cathedral (since 1690 a parish kirk) of St Machar, unique both for its long history and for its unusual architectural features. According to legend, St Mochrieha, a Celtic missionary from the west, was in the 6th century inspired to found a place of worship on a water-meadow, or machair, in a crook of the River Don 'like a bishop's staff'. St Machar's, as his church became known, was at first probably no more than a heather-covered hut. David I created a Bishopric of Aberdeen and in 1165 there was a Norman cathedral on the site, of which only one single piece of stone remains. A second cathedral in red sandstone was built by Bp Kininmund in the late 14th century. All that remains are the two big piers at the E end of the present main aisle, best seen from outside.

In 1424, Bp Leighton came to St Machar's from Elgin, where he had rebuilt the cathedral after its destruction by the Wolf of Badenoch. The usual building material of the time was the easily-worked yellow freestone from the Moray coast, but the extraordinary thing about St Machar's is that it is in granite. From 1420 to 1440 is the so-called 'granite interregnum', for granite was not used again until the Granite City of Aberdeen developed in the early 19th century. It is uncertain whether this was due to difficulties in shipping the Moray freestone, or because Bp Leighton, unable to find (or afford) a skilled foreign mason, was thrown back on a local master-mason, accustomed not only to shaping the granite boulders that emerge from the soil in many parts in Aberdeenshire, but also to using his material more in a military than in an ecclesiastical mode. In either event, this apparent setback turned into the success of St Machar's unique w front, with its strong towers, machicolated in the military tradition, and surmounted by battlemented parapets. (The octagonal spires of sandstone are a later addition by Bp Gavin Dunbar (1455-1532) who also commissioned Alexander Galloway to build the Bridge of Dee.) In between these towers, the mason set a great window divided by six enormously tall mullions into seven round-headed lights of unusual height. Bp Elphinstone completed the central tower of the cathedral. In the neglect of churches following the Reformation, St Machar's fared better than many, but the central tower fell in a storm in 1688, damaging the transepts, so that the present church is little more than Leighton's nave

St. Machar's Cathedral, Old Aberdeen

screened off at the crossing.

Entering the cathedral by the s porch, one is impressed both by the strength of the pillars and by the airiness of this remarkable building. The flat wooden ceiling with its 48 heraldic shields was inspired by Bp Gavin Dunbar and executed by Alexander Galloway about 1520. The layout of the shields is interesting: on the N side they record the sovereigns of Europe, in the centre the pope and the bishops of Scotland, and on the s King James V and the earls of Scotland, the last three shields on the w side being those of Old Aberdeen, the University and New Aberdeen respectively. This remarkable ceiling gives a lecture on European contemporary politics, just as the Lutheran revolt was about to disrupt the concept of feudal Europe. It shows the widely-travelled outlook of the Aberdonian clergy, and was intended as a reassertion of Scottish national identity after the defeat at Flodden (1513). The Reformers of only 40 years later failed to notice, despite their desire to destroy all signs of the papacy, the arms of Pope Leo X (Giovanni de Medici) under which present-day Presbyterians unconcernedly worship. The stained glass is all of the 19th century. The story of St Machar and the founding of the cathedral, together with the works of Bps Kininmund, Leighton and Elphinstone are depicted in two of the windows on the s side porch, executed by Douglas Strachan. There is also the Artists' Window, commemorating Jamesone, Dyce and Phillip.

Beyond St Machar's, in the bend of the River Don, is Seaton Park. On a mound, a former motte, to the left is the mis-named Wallace's (for Wellhouse) Tower, an attractive 17th-century miniature tower-house. It was rebuilt here after being moved in 1963 from the present site of Marks and Spencer's store in central Aberdeen. It must be the only town-house built to the defensive Z-plan, but no doubt the troublesome Robert Keith of Benholm, brother of the fifth Earl Marischal, needed to defend himself against enemies when he built it in 1616, just outside the city walls.

Across the park to the N runs the Don, through its last little rocky gorge, spanned by the splendid Brig' o' Balgownie, a triumph of 14th-century engineering. The idea of a bridge at this strategic point seems to have originated with Richard Cementarius (d. 1294), the mason-provost of Aberdeen, and his successor Malcolm de Pelgouenie (d. 1317), who owned the lands of Balgownie on the N bank. Suspended during the War of Independence, the work was encouraged by Robert the Bruce and completed in 1320. Picturesque, strongly built and with a defensive kink at the south end, the Bridge of

Balgownie has a single span of 67 feet from where the arches spring out of the living rock on either side. A modest fund started by Sir Alexander Hay in 1605 and carefully husbanded has ensured its upkeep. On the bend above the s approach to the bridge a delightful group of houses known as Cruickshank's Lodging, built in 1655, was recently given the Saltire Award for careful restoration. On the other side of the bridge are the red-tiled little houses of Cot-town, carefully restored. It is pleasant to return to Aberdeen by the fine Bridge of Don, half a mile downstream, built in 1830 to Telford's design, the cost being wholly met out of the Alexander Hay fund.

Aberfeldy   Perthshire   Tayside 3 H6

Aberfeldy is pleasantly situated in the Tay valley between the mouth of Loch Tay and the junction of Tay and Tummel. The up-and-down route to Speyside, favoured by General Wade for his military road from Crieff to Dalwhinnie, makes a splendid introduction to the Highlands for the modern traveller determined to shun the A9 trunk road. General Wade, as the result of some dissension with the Duke of Atholl, refused to build his bridge across the Tay at Dunkeld, chose Aberfeldy for his

Wade's bridge across the Tay, Aberfeldy

main crossing and, with advice from William Adam, built a bridge which, with its obelisks, is of some architectural distinction, even if Dorothy Wordsworth had the nerve to call it 'ambitious and ugly'. Begun on 23 April, 1733, as the long Latin inscription records, the Aberfeldy bridge was finished the same year — in fact, within 8 months. It has lasted well and carries the modern road which, following Wade's line, continues over the shoulder of Schiehallion and down to Tummel Bridge.

On the s side of the bridge is the fine monument (erected in 1887) to General Wade's other achievement — the Black Watch. The tall cairn with a Highland gentleman volunteer wearing a single eagle's feather in his cap and flourishing his sword commemorates the first parade here in May 1740, of this famous regiment based on the six original companies raised in 1725. The men, who wore the now familiar dark tartan to distinguish them from the redcoats, became known as the Black Watch.

Across the Wade bridge is the little hamlet of Weem, its inn with a portrait of the General who made it his headquarters while building the bridge and this section of his road. Here too is Castle Menzies, a fine example of a 16th-century Z-plan fortified tower-house of 1570 or so, but now rather overwhelmed with Victorian additions. It has been acquired as the headquarters of the Menzies clan. The old church of Weem, since 1839 the Menzies mausoleum, houses two sanctuary crosses removed from nearby Dull, and some interesting Menzies memorials.

Aberfeldy also inspired Robert Burns's poem on the *Birks of Aberfeldy*, associated with the Falls of Moness, up a steep path on the s side of the town. There were no birches (only laburnum) when the Wordsworths looked for them a few years after Burns was there, and such as are now there seem of more recent date. Unkind critics of the Bard suggest he intended to recall the birch-clad slopes near Abergeldie on Deeside, where he had previously been entertained by the laird.

Aberlemno Angus Tayside 5 E5 (AM)

Three splendid collections of Pictish symbol stones can conveniently be considered under one heading. The four stones at Aberlemno are in their original setting, three on the roadside and the best near the parish kirk. At Meigle, just over the Perthshire border, 6 miles (10 km.), w of Glamis, and at St Vigeans (q.v.) just outside Arbroath, there are two collections assembled from stones found in each area. Little is known of the Picts because of the virtual absence of written material, but these stones, with their intricately-carved tracery, their puzzling symbols and their dramatic scenes, afford a vivid, if tantalising, glimpse of a high degree of artistic culture in what is often thought of as the Dark Ages.

The symbol stones divide into two broad categories. The first comprises those from about A.D. 500 (possibly earlier) to about 700, with symbols incised on boulders or on roughly-dressed stones, and without any Christian cross. The second category, following the conversion of

Pictish symbol-stone, Aberlemno

the northern Picts to Christianity in the 8th century, are heavy up-standing slabs with the symbols carved in relief and usually confined to one side, the other bearing some form of Christian cross with intricate ornamental tracery. The Christian elements increasingly dominated the carved surface and the symbols became fewer and less significant so that, by about 1000, only the traditional Christian Celtic cross remains.

The symbols comprise on the one hand apparently abstract designs which have become known by simple and obvious names, such as Crescent and V-rod, Rectangle and Z-rod, pair of discs, triple disc, mirror-and-comb, etc., and probably had some hieroglyphic significance for the 'reader'. On the other hand, there are recognizable pictures, skilfully carved, of animals such as bull, boar, wolf, horse or fishes and birds, and a very peculiar beast with a long snout dubbed an 'elephant'. In addition, more important stones may carry a vivid representation of some outstanding event, a hunting or battle scene.

At Aberlemno, the two Christian-cross stones are magnificent examples of their type, one with a superb stag-hunting scene on the back, the other with a splendid combat scene with charging horsemen, brandished spears and even a fallen soldier attacked by a bird of prey.

The little museum at Meigle contains some 30 symbol

stones and slabs belonging to the period between the 7th and 10th centuries A.D. There are several examples of the mysterious 'elephant' and a number of grotesque beasts with long snouts or claws, biting or interlaced with each other. The most readily identifiable scene is a graphic representation of Daniel in the Lions' Den, with Daniel raising his arms as he appeals to the fierce lions.

At St Vigeans 32 Pictish stones have been assembled in a cottage-museum. The best-known is the Drostan stone, which has actually a written inscription, in the Irish Ogam alphabet, though in an unknown language. The other stones include scenes such as an archer shooting at a tusked boar, an osprey eating a fish, two clerics reading a book, and St John being martyred head down in a pot of oil.

These collections are a 'must' for anyone interested in the Picts and amusement may be had in trying to decipher the cryptograms, which surely convey some message, possibly the names of the chiefs taking part in the scenes depicted. There are well over two hundred stones scattered over the former Pictish kingdom, covering Angus and Grampian, but virtually none elsewhere (the Dunfallandy stone near Pitlochry is the furthest west). Particularly fine examples are the 9 ft high, intricately decorated cross-stone outside the manse at Glamis, the interesting Picardy and Maiden stones in the Garioch (q.v.), the Rodney Stone with huge symbols in high relief near Brodie Castle (q.v.) and the finest of all is the 23 ft high so-called Sueno's Stone outside Forres (q.v.). On the near side, this shows rows of horsemen, spearmen, captives and headless victims, probably commemorating some Pictish victory of the 9th century, and certainly nothing to do with Sweyn the Dane, as Boece suggested, though the name has stuck.

Three miles (5 km.) E of Meigle, towards Forfar on the A94, is the Eassie Stone, well-preserved as an AM, in the ruined, roofless church of Eassie. This fine cross-stone, with intricate interlacing, has a hunting scene well portrayed on the back and various 'enigmatic' Pictish symbols.

Abernethy   Perthsire   Tayside 2 E3

Not to be confused with the Abernethy on Speyside, now generally known as Nethy Bridge, the Perthshire Abernethy, hard up against the Fife border, is a place with roots far back in Scottish history, having been one of the capitals of Pictland. It was probably in the ninth or tenth century that the free-standing 70 ft high Round Tower was built. This closely resembles the tower at Brechin (q.v.), though it has no octagonal cap, and is clear evidence of Irish influence: there are over 70 of these towers in Ireland though only these two in Scotland. They served as watchtowers or places of refuge from Viking invaders.

It was at Abernethy in 1072 that Malcolm Canmore is said to have met William the Conqueror of England, who had penetrated this far north. By paying him homage, Malcolm persuaded the Normans to retire southwards,

Round Tower and Mercat Cross, Abernethy

but he has been criticised for becoming William's man. In the subsequent Normanising of Scotland by the foundation of abbeys, the Culdee community at Abernethy was transformed into a monastery of Augustinians.

High on an outlier of the Ochils, behind the village, is an Iron Age hill-fort, Castle Law, well sited with timber-laced dry stone walls still standing to a height of 7 ft.

Affleck Castle   Angus   Tayside 2G1   (AM)

Just W of the village of Monikie, 4 miles (6 km.) N of the Dundee seaside suburb of Monifieth, is the well preserved 15th-century keep of Affleck. Built as a rectangle with a slight projecting jamb (or wing), the tower stands 60 ft high, its walls sheer to the projecting corbels of the battlements, surmounted by two unusual square cap-houses. Affleck's clean lines belong to the age of bow-and-arrow, unlike the ungainly additions of nearby Claypotts (q.v.), intended for defence against firearms. The rubble exterior is unharled; the window-finishes and corner-stones are of trimmed stone. The hall stands on a vaulted stone floor, one and a half storeys up; and the lord's solar (or drawing-room), with its massive columned fireplace, is on the next floor up. The spiral entrance stair, as far as the hall in the small projecting jamb, continues up to the battlements in the opposite corner, so that anyone mounting to the roof, for good or evil purposes, had to cross the hall. On the solar level, the space thus freed in the wing is used for a small chapel, unique in being perfectly preserved with its holy water stoup, an aumbry to hold the sacred vessels of the Mass, and corbels to support candles. A feature of Affleck is the little closet and garderobe fitted in beneath the chapel, but above the head of the main staircase, with a secret spy-hole covering both the hall and the stair — an early version of the 'laird's lug', but intended more for seeing than for hearing.

Affleck was the home of the Auchinlecks, hereditary armour-bearers to the Earls of Crawford, but the laird who was the father of Boswell, the biographer of Dr Johnson, moved to Ayrshire in the early 18th century. The castle passed to the Reid family who lived in it until they built the Georgian farmhouse nearby and thus ensured its present excellent state of preservation. Affleck is now an AM (temporarily closed).

The area between Affleck and the sea has a number of features of interest. There is Monifieth Laws, the 400 ft (120 m.) hill with the great vitrified fort of the Pictish King Hungus, whose name survives in the district of Angus; many relics, including swords and burial cists, have been unearthed here. There are the two Pictish earth-houses or souterrains, (both now AM), of Ardestie and Carlungie, respectively about a mile SE and due E of the Laws. The roofing slabs have been removed, so that the course of these curious underground passages, which were probably used by the Picts of the 2nd century A.D. as refuges or storehouses rather than as dwellings, can be inspected without the inconvenience of stooping and taking a torch, as is needed for a visit to the covered souterrain at Tealing, 5 miles (8 km.) to the W.

To return to more modern times, the tall tower on the wooded hill NE of Carlungie is the Panmure Testimonial known as the 'Live and Let Live Monument'. It was erected in 1839 by the grateful tenants of William Ramsay Maule, who was reinstated in the title of Panmure, which his ancestor had forfeited after taking part in the 1715 Rising.

Airlie and Glen Isla   Angus   Tayside 5 D5

Airlie Castle, celebrated in the ballad of the burning of *The Bonnie Hoose of Airlie*, has been since the 15th century (except when in ruins from 1640 to 1794) the home of the staunchly Royalist family of Ogilvy, Earls of Airlie. It is superbly situated on a wooded promontory where the Melgam Water joins the River Isla. The long, E-facing curtain wall, 30 ft high, and the fortified gateway, built in the 15th-16th centuries by earlier Ogilvys, are all that is left from the burning of the castle. Within is a late-18th-century Georgian house, built over the old north wall, and a charming garden, occasionally open to the public.

GLEN ISLA is Ogilvy country. It differs from the more easterly Angus glens (q.v.) in that the River Isla emerges from the hills into Strathmore to become a lowland stream and joins the Tay by Meikleour. The remote uppermost part of the glen has to be reached on foot from the road-end at Tulchan. At its head, the Monega track crosses the watershed to Deeside, only a couple of miles E of the A939 at the Cairnwell Pass but, at 3,300 ft (1005 m.), over 1,000 ft (300 m.) higher. Here is the Caenlochan Nature Reserve, where the geological formation is such as to encourage the growth, on the crags and steep slopes, of the rare alpine-type flora found on Ben Lawers.

The middle glen has a settled look, with a church and hotel at Kirkton of Glenisla, and two roads lead over the ridge westwards to the main A939 up Glenshee. The more northerly takes off at Forter Castle, a tall, grim-looking fortalice of rough rubble. An outlier of the Airlie-Ogilvy domains — their principal castles being Inverquharity, Cortachy and Airlie itself — Forter served either to catch marauders coming over the high passes from Deeside or as a refuge from their enemies encroaching from the south.

An exciting section of the Isla is that below the Bridge of Craigisla, where the river gouges a deep canyon through the Highland Boundary Fault. A short distance below the bridge, and easily accessible from it, the river leaps over the spectacular 80 ft high waterfall known as the Reekie Linn, the spray rising like smoke. Lower down, it runs through a 10 ft wide chasm, the Slug of Auchrannie, continuing in its deep canyon past Airlie Castle.

The Ogilvys led adventurous lives. As Bailies of Arbroath Abbey (q.v.) they fought the Lindsays in 1445 and feuding between the two families continued for centuries. As supporters of Mary, Queen of Scots, one of them helped her escape from Loch Leven (q.v.). As Catholics, they were involved in the intrigues with Spain in the early years of James VI. In 1639 the 7th Lord Ogilvy, with a troop of his men, joined Charles I's army at York and was created Earl of Airlie on the spot. His son, who took the title of Lord Ogilvy, remained at Airlie but refused to show allegiance to the Protestant cause by signing the National Covenant. This refusal brought down on Airlie the wrath of Argyll who, in 1640, obtained authority to root out by fire and sword the enemies of the Covenanters. When Argyll reached Airlie, the Earl was still in England, his wife had gone for safety to Forter, and only the young Lady Ogilvy was in Airlie Castle with her children. After she had fled, Argyll spent nearly a fortnight destroying the castle, himself, according to the historian Spalding, 'tacking a hammer in his hande and knocking down the hewed worke of the doors and windows, till he did sweate for heate at his work'. Meanwhile, Argyll's lieutenant Dougal Campbell was similarly busy at Forter, acting under sly instructions from Argyll — 'ye sall fyre it well, so that it may be destroyed. But ye need not to lat know that ye have directiounes from me to fyre it'. The famous ballad has the facts slightly wrong, for it was not Lady Airlie who was at Airlie but her daughter-in-law. Nonetheless, the spirit of the lady is caught in the verse:

> Had my ain Lord been at his hame, As he's awa' with Charlie,
> There's no a Campbell in a' Argyle Daur hae trod in the bonnie green o' Airly.

When the Earl did return, he made Cortachy, at the mouth of Glen Clova, his home. The Ogilvy adventures were, however, far from over: they fought with Montrose at Inverlochy and at Kilsyth too. They shared Montrose's defeat at Philiphaugh and Lord Ogilvy made a dramatic escape from Edinburgh Castle, his sister substituting herself for him. Charles II spent the night at Cortachy in 1650, between his flight from Covenanting sermons in Perth (q.v.) and his ignominious recapture in Glen Clova. In retaliation, Cromwell's troops sacked Cortachy. In the quieter years at the turn of the 17th and 18th centuries, Cortachy was enlarged, and in the 19th century it was heavily 'baronialised' by David Bryce. It now gives an impression of being all white harling, red quoins and wimple-like pepper-pots masking the old tower.

In 1715 the young Lord Ogilvy of the day joined the Jacobites at Sheriffmuir (q.v.) and went into exile in France. In 1745 his brother, who became Earl of Airlie, cannily remained at home, while his son David joined

The Pineapple, Airth

Prince Charles Edward's army. This David Ogilvy fought with the Prince from Edinburgh to Derby and back to defeat at Culloden. His adventures in disguise and his escape by ship from Dundee were sensational enough, but his courageous wife, who had held his spare horse at Falkirk and at Culloden, had even more exciting tales to tell. She was imprisoned in Edinburgh Castle, from which she made a dramatic escape disguised as a lame laundress, and was mistaken for the Prince himself when she boarded a ship at Hull; she later returned secretly to Scotland so that her son should be born in Angus. Meanwhile her husband, 'le bel Ecossais', had become a French general. Pardoned in 1767, he made Cortachy into a little corner of France. He also rebuilt Airlie Castle, living there from 1794 till his death in 1803. The prominent monument on the wooded hill of Tulloch (1,246 ft / 380 m.) between Prosen and Clova, visible far out into Strathmore, is the Airlie Tower, in memory of the earl who fell on 9 June 1900 leading a cavalry charge at the battle of Diamond Hill, near Pretoria, in the South African War.

Though the misfortunes that have befallen some of the Ogilvy ladies in the past may have inhibited marriage between Royalty and this most Royalist of families, there was no such hesitation over the marriage in 1963 of H.R.H. Princess Alexandra with the Hon. Angus Ogilvy.

Airth   Stirling   Central 1 C5
Once a medieval port and a royal dockyard, Airth is now on the reclaimed Forth marshlands above the Kincardine Road Bridge. The A905 from Grangemouth to Stirling passes through the modern part of Airth, but it is worth turning off to look at the High Street, leading up to the Mercat Cross with some fine traditional houses, in particular the Herring House. Airth Castle, restored and now an hotel, has a tower attributed to Wallace, because he sacked it.

In the grounds of the Dunmore estate, is the remarkable folly called the Pineapple. Given by the Countess of Perth to the NTS in 1974, it is available for letting, through the Landmark Trust, to holiday-makers with an eye for the eccentric. The Pineapple is a bizarre summer-house, two storeys high, built in 1761 for the 29-year-old Earl of Dunmore, later Governor of New York and Virginia. In the words of the Landmark brochure 'classical and orthodox at ground level, it grows into something entirely vegetable: conventional architraves put out shoots and end up as prickly leaves of stone'. This 'eccentric work of genius' is built of the finest masonry and every leaf of the colossal pineapple is drained to prevent frost damage. It presides over a large walled garden replanted by the NTS, with crab-apple trees giving a fine show of blossom.

Glens of Angus   Angus   Tayside 4 C4
The broad farmlands of Strathmore are dominated by a rampart of hills known as the Braes of Angus. The five

Glen Doll, at the head of Glen Clova

main valleys that pierce this rampart are the Glens of
Angus; their head streams share with Lochnagar the
peaty plateau of the Mounth, stretching away to the
Cairnwell Pass at the head of Glenshee. From E to W the
principal Glens of Angus are Glen Esk and Glen Lethnot,
which join to form the River North Esk (*see* Glen Esk),
Glen Clova (q.v.) and Glen Prosen which form the River
South Esk, and Glen Isla which joins the River Tay and is
dealt with under Airlie.

These lovely glens are favourite excursions for townspeople from Dundee or Aberdeen, but lie off the direct
track for visitors from further afield aiming north or
west. They are well worth visiting for their own beauty,
provided it is borne in mind that, with the exception of
Glen Isla which has an escape route westwards to
Glenshee about half way up, each of these glens is a cul-
de-sac for the motorist and, after 15 miles or so (24 km.),
the route must be retraced. For those prepared to
adventure on foot beyond the road-heads, in particular
from Lochlee in Glen Esk and from Braedownie in Glen
Clova, there is a great deal of wild beauty to be discovered.

Arbroath Angus Tayside 2 H1 (*pop.* 22,586)
This busy town at the mouth of the little Brothock Water
(hence its name in medieval times, Aberbrothock) is well-
known for three things: as a seaside resort; for its

'smokies', the haddocks cured in the smoke of wood-chip
fires in the fisher-town; and for its magnificent abbey
(AM).

The roofless ruins of the abbey, in the deep red sandstone of Angus, still dominate the town. Though the
central tower has gone, enough survives to indicate the
one-time grandeur of this great abbey church of the late
12th and early 13th century. The S transept, of which the
arcades and triforium are intact, has a huge circular
window; it carried no tracery, but was used for a light to
guide ships at sea – the 'Round O of Arbroath'. The
deeply-recessed W doorway most closely resembles contemporary cathedrals in England and France; sadly, only
the lower arc of the great rose window remains. An
unusual feature is the elevated gallery above the door,
reached by a wheel stair in the S tower, and with access to
the gallery inside the arcades of the church.

The domestic buildings of the abbey – the cloister, the
warming-house, the kitchen – are only traceable in
ground plan. Three surviving buildings have kept their
roofs. The first is Abbot Paniter's fine lofty double-
vaulted sacristy of the mid 15th century, inserted in the
corner between the S transept and the S wall of the choir
– the little corner room was probably a strong-room,
but was used for confining lunatics in the 18th century,
acquiring the name of Jenny Batter's Hole. Next, the massive Abbot's House (now the Abbey Museum) of the late

15th or early 16th century, built over the rib-vaulted undercroft of the 12th-century cloister. Finally the gate-house set of buildings extend westwards from the w porch of the Abbey. The vaulted entrance, or Abbey Pend, through which traffic still passes once controlled the entrance to the monastery and was defended by a portcullis (which now figures in the town's arms). The N entrance of the gateway presents an imposing facade crowned with a Dutch-style crowstep gable. This range of buildings to the w ends in a stout, three-storeyed tower, the Regality Tower, with the abbot's court of justice in the Regality Chamber between it and the gateway.

But why is this fine abbey now in such a state of ruin? In the days of which Sir Walter Scott wrote in *The Antiquary*, the locals showed no more interest than to say of the ruins 'They were made by the monks lang syne'. On the other hand, Dr Johnson on his tour in 1773 was most impressed — 'Its ruins afford ample testimony of its ancient magnificence . . . I should scarcely have regretted my journey had it afforded nothing more than a sight of Aberbrothick'. Though the abbey was raided by English sea-raiders in 1350 and seriously damaged by fire 30 years later, Arbroath was restored soon after. Nor did the Reformation mobs here do much more than strip the images and cast down altars, allowing the monks to end their days in the precincts. The cause of the destruction was rather the neglect of the centuries that followed,

when there were no funds for the upkeep of the ruins, and the thrifty burghers of Arbroath built much of their town, including a new Presbyterian kirk, from this convenient quarry of fine stones. In the 19th century, measures were taken to preserve what was left, but it was not until 1924 that the AM took the ruins into its care.

This neglect is all the more shameful because of the abbey's close connexion with the history of Scotland. During his young days at the court of Henry II of England, William the Lion (1143-1214) became a close friend of Thomas à Becket. His murder in 1170 by Henry II's knights, when he was Archbishop of Canterbury, must have shocked William, as it did most of Christendom. Henry did humble penance at Canterbury in 1174. A few days later William, by then King of Scotland, was captured at Alnwick in Northumberland. Held prisoner by the English for 3 years, William vowed on his return to Scotland to found a monastery in honour of God and St Thomas. Not only was this monastery richly endowed but William took a close interest in its construction, which bears resemblances to Canterbury. Grey-robed Tironensian monks, who later assumed the black habit of the Benedictines, were brought from Kelso. William himself was buried behind the high altar in 1214, and his coffin discovered 600 years later.

The early abbots tended to side with the English invaders. Very different was Abbot Bernard de Linton,

Arbroath Abbey

who had carried the Brecbennoch, a relic of St Columba housed in the Monymusk (q.v.) Reliquary, at Bannockburn. A good Latin scholar, it was he who drafted, under Bruce's guidance, the famous letter now called the Scottish Declaration of Independence, signed by the nobles of Scotland and dated 6 April 1320; it was despatched from Arbroath to Avignon to be read to Pope John XXII by two of their number. This splendid document traces the Scots back to Scythia, comparing Robert the Bruce to Joshua and Maccabeus (which accounts for the popularity of these figures in Craigston (q.v.), Crathes (q.v.) and elsewhere). It also affirms the signatories' determination to uphold Scottish independence and support Robert I unless he 'leave these principles he hath so nobly pursued', and contains the ringing words:

> For so long as there shall be but one hundred of us remain alive we will never give consent to subject ourselves to the dominion of the English. For it is not glory, it is not riches, neither is it honours, but it is liberty alone that we fight and contend for, which no honest man will lose but with his life.

The letter asks the pope to 'admonish and exhort the King of England (Edward II) to suffer us to live in that narrow spot of Scotland beyond which we have no habitation'. As a first step, the pope did urge Edward II to make peace with the 'aforesaid Robert', but it took another 9 years before the pope actually recognized Bruce (then on his deathbed) as King of Scotland.

In the 15th century, the abbot established a proper harbour, put his beacon light in the 'Round O', and his bell on the Bell (or Inchcape) Rock. Southey's ballad of Ralph the Rover recalls how that evil man, to spite the abbot, cut off the bell and was himself later wrecked on the rock. Already the monastic ideal was fading and the abbey's revenues attracted the greedy nobles. The abbot deputed his judicial powers, with its profitable pickings, to a bailie — a post which the Ogilvy family came to consider theirs as of right. In 1445 the impecunious Alexander Lindsay, son of the Earl of Crawford, challenged the appointment of an Ogilvy and there followed the disgraceful Battle of Arbroath, in which 500 Ogilvys and 100 Lindsays perished, including the white-bearded Earl of Crawford himself. The next hundred years up to the Reformation saw the decline of the abbey under abbots whose interests were more material than spiritual; one of them, the covetous Patrick Graham, secured the grant to himself of the Abbey *in commendam*, that is to say, the dignities and the emoluments of the abbot without any of his duties. So there were pluralist abbots, absentee abbots, even youthful abbots like the illegitimate son of James IV. Cardinal Beaton, when Archbishop of St Andrews as well as Abbot, made grants of its lands to his mistress Marion Ogilvy, the mother of seven of his children (*see* Melgund), bestowed churches on two of his illegitimate sons, and bequeathed Arbroath to his nephew. By the end of the 16th century the pious

foundation of William the Lion had become simply a source of wealth for anyone strong enough to seize it. The Hamiltons did so and in 1608 were granted a charter transforming its still considerable possessions into a temporal lordship. And so, by neglect, to the 'fragments of magnificence' as Dr Johnson termed them, that we see today.

Life in the Royal Burgh of Arbroath went on alongside the life of the monastery where the monks, so long as they remained truly religious, devoted themselves to the worship of God. The burghers worshipped elsewhere, either at St Vigeans (q.v.) or later at the 18th-century 'old' parish kirk in the town.

Between the abbey and the harbour, the town of Arbroath has not much of interest to offer, beyond a pleasant classical-style Town House of 1803. Down by the harbour are the old-style houses where fisher-girls gut the fish which make the delicious home-cured smokies. Here also is the Signal Tower Museum, looking like a fort with whitewashed gateway, quadrangle and crenellated Signal Tower. It was designed by Robert Stevenson, the lighthouse builder, grandfather of Robert Louis Stevenson the author, as the shore establishment for the famous Bell Rock Lighthouse built by him between 1807 and 1811 on the dangerous Inchcape reef at the entrance to the Tay Estuary, for neglect of the abbot's bell had, with increasing sea traffic into Dundee, led to numerous wrecks. The Signal Tower is now a well laid out and welcoming museum (awarded the Museum of the Year Award in 1975). Here, one can gain some idea of the difficulties and hazards overcome by Stevenson in his skilful construction of the lighthouse, as well as see displays of early life in the area, the growth of the town, first as a commercial harbour and in the 19th century, as a fishing port.

Arbroath appeals as a seaside resort both to those who prefer long, sandy beaches, like the one stretching sw towards Carnoustie (celebrated for its golf-course), and those who prefer rocky coastlines. A cliff-top walk starts NE of Arbroath, continuing for 3 miles (5 km.) to the fishing village of Auchmithie. The deep red sandstone is fretted by the sea into a medley of headlands, arches, caves and stacks, with names such as the Needle's E', the Deil's Head (a pillar bulging at the top), Forbidden Cave and a blow-hole, where on rough days the sea spouts up inland. Auchmithie itself is the 'Musselcrag' of Scott's *The Antiquary*, just as 'Fairport' and 'St Ruth' are Arbroath and its abbey in the same novel. Northward, the rugged coast continues, culminating in the dramatic 250 ft cliff of Red Head, just short of the southern tip of the great sandy crescent of Lunan Bay (q.v.).

Arbuthnott Kincardine Grampian 5 G3
In the narrow glen by which the Bervie Water drains the northern part of the Howe of the Mearns (q.v.) is the lovely little sandstone church of Arbuthnott, glowing a deep red in its green 'den'. This is the 'Kirk of Kinraddie'

The Falls of Bruar

described in Lewis Grassic Gibbon's *Sunset Song*; his tomb-stone is to be seen in the graveyard. The church, dedicated to St Ternan, is of considerable antiquity; the chancel dating back to 1242 is a burial place for the Norman family of Allardyce. The Arbuthnotts, who were also lairds hereabouts — and still are — built the w bell-tower and the Arbuthnott Aisle about 1500, a beautiful example of late Scottish Gothic style. The church has happily survived the Reformation and two 19th-century restorations.

The Arbuthnotts have held these lands since the 12th century, and were relied upon by the Stuart kings to keep the peace in the Mearns. Dr John Arbuthnot was Physician Extraordinary to Queen Anne and wrote political satires as witty as Swift's. One of these, *Law is a Bottomless Pit* (1712), was re-published as *The History of John Bull*, establishing the Englishman's nickname once and for all.

Allardyce Castle, a mile or more down Bervie Water, recently restored, is an interesting fortalice with unusual corbelling supporting the twin turrets of the staircase tower.

Ardvorlich   *see* **Loch Earn**

Atholl   Perthshire   Tayside 3 H4
Atholl is not just Blair Castle, at Blair Atholl (q.v.) but also a wild and beautiful land with an ancient history, extending far on either side of the Highland railway line and the modern A9. Between the great humps of Grampians known as the Boar of Badenoch and the Sow of Atholl, road and rail come together at the summit of the Drumochter Pass (1,516 ft/472 m. above sea-level), still a remote and desolate place, especially in a winter snow-storm, before entering the Highland Region. This route gives a rapid cross-section of Atholl, but provides no more than a glimpse of the entrancing side-valleys — Tummel leading to Rannoch, Glen Errochty of the Robertsons, or the deep trench of Glen Tilt leading from Blair Atholl to Deeside over an imperceptible watershed. Here, men of Atholl once clashed with men of Braemar, who were trying to divert the water of Loch Tilt into the Dee. A better way to catch the spirit of Atholl is to take, instead of the A9, General Wade's other military road, now the A826, that rises out of Crieff through the Sma' Glen and drops to Aberfeldy, continuing over the corner of Schiehallion to Tummel Bridge as the B846. Carry on northwards by Trinafour and up the tight zigzags of the Wade road, past the Loch Errochty dam, but do not fail to pause before dipping down to rejoin the busy A9 at Dalnacardoch, where Wade had his headquarters. From this vantage point, the eye travels over the immense tree-less desolation of the so-called Forest of Atholl, rising to the great whale-back hills of the western Cairngorms where the snow lingers until early summer, so very different from the thickly forested valleys by Pitlochry.

As the Pictish province of Athfodla, Atholl was a bul-wark against the Scots moving east in the 8th and 9th centuries from Ireland and Argyll; after the unification of Picts and Scots under Kenneth MacAlpin in 843, Dunkeld became for a time the capital of the joint kingdom, and Atholl an outpost against the Norsemen. Its subsequent history is closely connected with the Earls (subsequently Dukes) of Atholl who, whether Comyn, Stewart or Murray, ruled this mountain province from their stronghold of Blair Castle (q.v.), with their own law court on the hill at Logierait where Tummel joins Tay, now marked by a 19th-century Celtic-style cross.

Like many mountain-folk, the people of Atholl were individualists: even Ptolemy noted that the Caledonii, who spread from Badenoch into Atholl, were different from the tribes in the lower lands with whom the Romans came into contact. Most of the Atholl men who fought for the earl were not of his clan but belonged to a more ancient race, the Clan Donnachaidh (Duncan). Their clan museum can be visited beside the A9 at the Falls of Bruar. Members of Clan Duncan were originally followers of the Celtic King Duncan, who was killed by Macbeth. Another Duncan (the 'Stout') led a local force at Bannockburn. On the hill to the south, towards Tummel, his grandson Robert captured Sir Robert Graham, one of the murderers of James I, and was rewarded with the barony of Struan. His descendants and tenants peopled the glens of Atholl; the majority took his name, calling themselves Robertson, which became the predominant name of Clan Duncan. They were more loyal to the Stuart kings than the earls themselves, whose devotion some-times wavered. The most persistent Jacobite of them all was the poet-laird Alexander Robertson (1670-1749), who fought in all three Jacobite Risings: with Dundee at Killie-crankie in 1689, at Sheriffmuir (q.v.) in 1715 and with Prince Charles Edward in 1745. The relics in the Clan Museum include the Clach-na-Brataich, a crystal-stone with magical powers carried at Sheriffmuir and at Culloden.

The Falls of Bruar, a succession of cascades in a narrow cleft with deep gouged-out pools, lie just off the A9 near the museum and must be visited on foot. Once bare of trees, they are now thickly wooded, thanks to Burns's successful appeal to the 'planting' Duke of Atholl:

Would then my noble master please
To grant my highest wishes,
He'll shade my banks wi' tow'rin' trees
and bonny spreading bushes . . .

From Struan, the road up Glen Errochty, the home-land of the Robertsons, leads up to Trinafour and over to Rannoch. From the pass between the two there is a glorious view up the beautiful Loch Rannoch towards Glencoe, and across the Tummel to the striking quartzite peak of Schiehallion (3,547 ft/1080 m.). The regular cone of this mountain and the consistency of its rock mass made it possible for the 18th century Astronomer Royal, Maskelyne, and, later, the Scottish mathematician Play-fair, to use it to estimate the mean density of the earth.

Kinloch Rannoch lies, oddly enough, not at the 'kin' or

head of Loch Rannoch but at its eastern outlet. There are roads on both banks, the one on the s bank leading through the Black Wood of Rannoch, once the haunt of marauders. Nowadays measures are taken to protect from hybridisation the sturdy and ancient Scots pines, descended from the original Caledonian forest. The roads reunite at the head of the loch to continue beside the tumbling River Gaur up into the great wilderness of the Moor of Rannoch, once a snow-basin feeding glaciers and now a desolation of peat-bog and lochans. The road ends at Rannoch Station, in the middle of nowhere, on the West Highland Railway to Fort William, and there is no option for the motorist but to return and enjoy the views down Loch Rannoch and the Tummel in reverse. The Hydro-Electric Board collects the waters of Loch Rannoch and of distant Loch Ericht, connected by a tunnel to Loch Garry, to feed the Tummel Bridge power station. The Board has, on the whole, been a sensitive

respecter of the countryside and the Rannoch-Tummel valley gives a unique vista of loch and mountain of very great beauty, best seen from the high wooded crag of the Queen's View at the E end of Loch Tummel. The Forestry Commission maintains an interesting Information Centre here, with an exhibition showing, as well as forestry development, the history and archaeology of the Tummel valley. A short distance up in the forest is a reconstituted medieval Highland farm or clachan. The roads on either side of Loch Tummel continue downwards past Loch Faskally to Pitlochry (q.v.).

Auchindoun Castle   Moray   Grampian 7 C3   (AM)
The grim stronghold of Auchindoun, perched on a steep, green hillside above the River Fiddich, is well seen at a distance from the A920 Dufftown to Huntly road, about 1½ miles out of Dufftown, but it is better approached by a short walk across fields from the A941 road to the

The Queen's View, Loch Tummel

Cabrach. It presents a bold picture, the shattered keep standing three storeys high above the lofty, square curtain wall. Two concentric grass dykes indicate that this was probably the site of a Pictish fort. Some castle was here from the 11th century, but the present ruined building was designed in the 15th century by James III's master mason, Cochrane, and came into possession of the Gordon family in 1535. The notorious Adam Gordon, sixth son of the rebellious Earl of Huntly, came from Auchindoun. Captured at Corrichie (q.v.) but released, he continued the Gordon vendetta against the Forbeses, defeating them at the skirmish of the Craibstone outside Aberdeen in 1571, and it was he or his followers who, in the same year, burnt the unfortunate Lady Forbes at Corgarff (q.v.) on Donside. Some 20 years later in 1592, Auchindoun was in turn burnt by Willie Mackintosh, in revenge for the Earl of Huntly's part in the murder of the Bonny Earl of Moray, despite the ballad's warning 'Gin ye burn Auchindoun, Huntly will head you'.

So there it stands, peaceful enough among the green fields and the sheep, a grim reminder of the feuds of earlier days, now shored up by the AM. Given the designs of the Gordons upon her, Mary, Queen of Scots, was wise not to visit Auchindoun on her progress through Moray in 1562. On the other hand, Queen Victoria noted the romantic ruin in her diary when she spent the night in Glen Fiddich Lodge in September 1867.

Auchterarder   Perthshire   Tayside 1 C3   (*pop.* 2,446)
Before the town was by-passed in 1980, the harassed motorist using the A9 between Dunblane and Perth was apt to remember Auchterarder as no more than a mile-long stretch of traffic hemmed between two rows of not very prepossessing houses. This is not a fair judgment, for Auchterarder was burnt twice, once by the Jacobite troops retreating from Sheriffmuir in 1715 and again in 1745. Situated as it is on the main route through Strathearn north of the Ochil Hills, Auchterarder had its historic moments. It became the main burgh of the ancient earldom of Strathearn in the 12th century, and is still the centre of the area, though smaller in population than Crieff (q.v.). James VI jokingly maintained to an arrogant English subject, who boasted of the number of drawbridges in some fine English city, that one of his Scottish towns had 50 drawbridges: the removable planks put out across the central burn in the long street of Auchterarder have since vanished.

Of the attractive little glens which descend from the Ochil Hills, the most considerable is GLEN EAGLES — nothing to do with the bird of prey, but derived from the Gaelic *eaglais*, a church. St Mungo's Well lies below the A823 road through the glen, and nearby St Mungo's Chapel, dating from 1199, was restored in 1925 as a family memorial to the extraordinary Haldane family — naval officers, evangelists and Liberal statesmen. They came from Gleneagles House at the mouth of the glen. Gleneagles is, of course, best known for its enormous hotel

and its three world-famous golf-courses, which are a couple of miles to the N, across the A9 and the main railway line, with its trim, elegant station.

Beyond the A823, NE from Gleneagles Hotel, is Tullibardine, a well-known name in Scottish history, though not many Scots could pinpoint the area. A Murray from Moray acquired the territory by marrying an heiress of the Strathearn family in 1320. His descendants became Earls of Tullibardine under James VI and later married into the great Stewart family of Atholl (q.v.). There is no castle now to be seen, but Tullibardine Chapel, founded as a collegiate (i.e. teaching) religious establishment in 1446, is an interesting pre-Reformation red sandstone building, well preserved as an AM. The open-work timber roof, the traceried transept windows and heraldic detail are noteworthy.

The Strathallan Air Museum, a famous collection of vintage aircraft, has unfortunately been closed for financial reasons, but may re-open.

River Avon (*pron.* A'an)   Moray   Grampian 7 A6
Sir Henry Alexander, Provost of Aberdeen and a connoisseur of mountain scenery, reckoned the Avon to be the most perfect glen in Scotland. In his Scottish Mountaineering Club *Guide to the Cairngorms* he wrote 'There is not a single dull passage, and every phase of Highland landscape is presented, from the wild and barren grandeur of Ben Macdhui to the luxuriant beeches of Delnashaugh, under whose shade the river flows deep and dark to meet the Spey . . . Perhaps not the least attractive scenes are those of the middle reaches, where the hills are friendly rather than fearsome, where groves of silver birches break and soften the valley-side, where the alder dips its branches in the singing water and where the oyster-catcher sweeps and cries above the shingle'. In May and June, the glen below Tomintoul is luxuriant with another beauty: the bird-cherry trees (*Prunus padus*) are covered with masses of cream blossom which foam beside the Avon and up into the side-glens.

Save in sudden spate, the water of this river runs marvellously clear over many-coloured stones. The clarity and purity of the Avon has been praised by many writers. One was Timothy Pont, the 17th century map-maker (*see* Introduction). The river is, in fact, surprisingly deep, which justifies the jingle 'The water of A'an it rins sae clear, T'wad beguile a man o' a hundred year'. So clear, indeed, that in 1906 it tempted the Aberdeen Water Board to put up a proposal to tap it, despite the fact that the nearest point is over fifty miles from the city. Fortunately, the plan was frustrated by a group which favoured the water of the River Dee, nearer if not so clear, but the issue was only settled after an appeal to the House of Lords.

The source of the Avon is as exciting as that of the Dee (q.v.). The lingering snowfields on the plateau between The Cairngorm itself and Ben Macdhui give rise to a stream which falls in a twisted tangle over granite slabs

Loch Avon from slopes of Ben Macdhui

for 1,000 ft (300 m.), to run out through a green meadow below the Shelter Stone past moraine humps into the wild and remote Loch Avon. This is no longer so remote since the Cairngorm chairlift has made access from The Cairngorm summit (some 1,500 ft above the loch) much easier - the descent, that is, not the return! Emerging from the east end of Loch Avon, with its beaches of red granite sand, the Avon runs rattling down a series of steps to the Fords of Avon. Here it is crossed by the old droving track, Lairig a' Laoigh, from Nethybridge to Braemar, a less rugged alternative to the Lairig Ghru, but when the river is in spate the Fords of Avon are cold and swift and there is no footbridge.

The Avon continues eastwards along a treeless glen, as clear as crystal over huge pink granite slabs and boulders, below the long crest of Ben Avon with its succession of prominent tors, to Inchrory and the dramatic Linn of Avon. The Linn itself is a constriction of rocks through which the river pours, loud and foaming, over a ten-foot drop where, year after year, salmon perform their miracle of leaping. Below the white water is a wide, quiet pool before the river is pressed into a long cleft where ancient Scots pines cling to the sides, and, in season, the brooms blaze a brilliant yellow.

The shooting lodge of Inchrory, built in 1847, is now only in use in the sporting season, but the area was formerly the meeting-place of the drove roads from Donside, Braemar and Tomintoul, and the centre of extensive summer pastures. The Don rises just over a low saddle to the E, and geologists maintain that the Avon (eating back through the friable limestone) has captured the original headwaters of the Don, for at Inchrory the Avon turns to flow N through gentler reaches, sometimes wide and shallow rushing over the stones, sometimes deep and running silent, the haunt of oyster-catchers and curlews. Five miles (8 km.) below Inchrory, the Avon is joined at Delnabo by the Water of Ailnack, which has worn a remarkable steep-sided canyon, and runs out into the wide water-meadows below Tomintoul village (q.v.).

About a mile below Tomintoul, the river is again constricted under the double-arched Bridge of Avon, built in 1754 as part of Caulfeild's military road from Coupar-Angus to Fort George. It was damaged by the severe frosts of 1979 and the road is now carried by a temporary Bailey bridge. For a further 5 miles, the Avon flows through a wide strath, below the rounded Cromdale Hills to the w. These beautiful reaches are the delight of the angler, tantalised by the gin-clear water in his attempts to lure the numerous and easily visible salmon to his fly. At the ruined tower of Drumin, a strategic point well selected by the Wolf of Badenoch, the Avon is joined by the Livet (*see* Glenlivet) and flows on to Delnashaugh, and out into the Spey by Ballindalloch Castle.

From Tomintoul, upper Glen Avon is only accessible on foot (or by car with special permission) above the locked gate at Birchfield.

Ballater   Kincardine and Deeside   Grampian 4 D2
Ballater is a pleasant, tidy and dignified little town on the River Dee, at the terminal of the former 'Royal Deeside' railway from Aberdeen. This reached Ballater in 1863 and was used by the Royal Family on their visits to Balmoral until it was closed a century later. An extension westwards to Braemar was started but was vetoed by Queen Victoria, who considered it would spoil the peace of Balmoral. The permanent way now gives a pleasant short stroll to the Gairn Bridge. The Dee is spanned by the solid Royal Bridge, opened by Queen Victoria in 1885, replacing two other stone bridges swept away by floods; the first in 1799, the second, Telford's of 1809, by the 'Muckle Spate' of 1829.

Ballater is a newcomer among Deeside towns. The original settlement was at Tullich, where the road through the Pass of Ballater joins the A93 to Aberdeen. The first 7th-century church was founded by St Nathalan on the 'tulach' or knoll where the pre-Reformation ruined church now stands in its graveyard (with some interesting Pictish stones). Tullich was granted Royal Burgh status in 1295, deriving its importance from the fact that it stood at the point where the Deeside route intersected the old track which came down from the Mounth, crossed the Dee by ferry a mile downstream from the Ballater bridge, continuing to Donside across the shoulder of Culblean Hill.

Tullich, now barely a hamlet, was replaced by Ballater: a far cry from Cheltenham and Bath, but all three developed in response to the 18th-century fashion for watering-places. About 1760, an old woman found that bathing in a spring at Pannanich, some 2 miles away on the s bank of the Dee, was good for her skin disease. The local Jacobite laird, Col. Francis Farquharson of Monaltrie, was captured at Culloden in 1746 and exiled. On his return he learnt of and decided to exploit the old woman's discovery. In 1770, in addition to building a lodge at the spring itself (now the Pannanich Wells Hotel), he set about developing the present site of Ballater, adjacent to his own seat at Monaltrie House. He died in 1790, but the work was completed by his son, William Farquharson (1753-1828), to whom the monument on a low hill near Tullich was erected in 1830. The Farquharsons, father and son, chose well, for the combination of the River Dee, the woods to the s and the rocky hump of Craigendarroch to the N make Ballater a most attractive holiday centre.

Craigendarroch ('the hill of oaks'), easily climbed in a brief half-hour, gives superb views not only up and down Deeside but also directly into the precipitous north corrie of Lochnagar (q.v.). To the N of Craigendarroch is the rocky defile of the Pass of Ballater, now used as a short-cut to avoid Ballater town, but once of strategic importance to the Farquharsons, who guarded the bridge over the River Gairn.

Two attractive side-glens join the Dee near Ballater: Glen Gairn from the NW, Glen Muick from the s. The GAIRN rises on the desolate south flanks of Ben Avon, flows through open moorland past the deserted shooting lodges of Loch Builg and Corndavon, to the scattered hamlet of Gairnshiel, with its tiny white-harled church set in a pine wood. Gairnshiel (some 6 miles / 10 km. from Ballater) is the scene of the charming reminiscences, *The Hills of Hame*, of Amy Stewart Fraser, whose father was minister here in more populous days. A sight, not to be missed by a collector of bridges, is the great rising arch of the bridge at Gairnshiel, built high to avoid the floods, as part of the Blairgowrie to Fort George military road of 1754.

If Glen Gairn is unmistakably Scottish then GLEN MUICK, in its lower reaches at least, has reminders of Switzerland. The E bank road climbs through birch and fir forests, past the foaming Falls of Muick (*pron.* Meck — Gaelic for 'gleaming'), to emerge in a wide, open basin. A mile or so on is the Spittal of Muick (once a 'spital' or hospice for travellers across the Capel Mounth) just short of the sparkling waters of Loch Muick. Motor traffic stops here by the deer reserve. To the N is the Balmoral estate, with a walking route to Lochnagar (q.v.). To the s, two rough tracks provide short but steep routes out of the Loch Muick basin over the Capel Mounth into Glen Clova. Across the open glen, at the foot of Lochnagar, is the shooting lodge of Allt-na-Guibseach on the Balmoral estate. Half way along Loch Muick, on the steep NW shore, is a small plantation; behind it, a path leads steeply up the rocky slope to a fine waterfall. In the wood is Glas-allt-Shiel, a cottage built in 1869 for Queen Victoria, who loved to make this her refuge in the late autumn days when the stags are belling. From the w end of Loch Muick, which can be reached on foot along either shore, there is a rough path leading up beside the torrent, which foams down over rocky shelves from the Dubh Loch, set between the sheer cliffs of Lochnagar to the N and Broad Cairn to the s.

Ballindalloch Castle   Moray   Grampian 7 B3
Ballindalloch (no loch, since 'dalloch' comes from 'davoch', an ancient land measure) is set in pleasant open parkland, where the River Avon joins the Spey. Since the 18th century it has been the home of the Macpherson-Grant family, who combine in their name the two great clans of the Upper (Macphersons of Badenoch) and the Middle Spey (the Grants). The early castle of 1562 (a typical Z-plan with a round tower to the NW and a square one to the SE) was successively extended until 1845 without spoiling the general effect. In 1602, a wide circular stair-tower was added to the middle of the w front; it rises a storey higher than the rest of the building and is crowned by a cap-house with an attractive little oriel window. House and grounds are normally open on one day in April, when the daffodils are at their best.

The main approach to the castle used to lead off the A95 under the tall beech-trees (unusual for these parts) overhanging the Avon, and then through a picturesque baronial gatehouse, designed by Thomas Mackenzie in

1850. The old road then turned sharply across a narrow bridge, which has, in recent years, been over-spanned by the modern bridge carrying the A95. It is worth pausing at the w end to walk down some steps onto the old bridge. A short distance N, below the A95 towards Aberlour, the attractive white-harled church of Inveravon (the parish kirk for Glenlivet (q.v.)) stands out on a terrace site over the Avon, accessible by a narrow track. There are three interesting Pictish cross-slabs in the graveyard.

Balmoral   Kincardine and Deeside   Grampian 5 C2
Balmoral, the Scottish home of the Royal Family since Queen Victoria first fell in love with it in 1848, has none of the blood-stained associations of so many Scottish castles, and is above all a private home where the Queen and her family can relax. When they are not in residence, the gardens (but not the house) are open to the public, usually up to the end of July, for a small fee in aid of charity.

Balmoral — the name could derive from the Gaelic *baile mor al*, a place plentiful in young animals — was in Gordon hands from 1484 till 1662, when it was sold to the Farquharsons of Inverey. In 1798 that property-financier, the Earl of Fife, acquired it and, in 1830, let it to Sir Robert Gordon, brother of the 4th Earl of Aberdeen, later Prime Minister (*see* Haddo). One of his guests, the son of Sir James Clark, Queen Victoria's physician, praised the bright, dry climate of Deeside while the Queen and his father were enduring persistent rain and mist at Ardverikie on Loch Laggan. As a result, the Queen and

Balmoral Castle from the west

Prince Albert visited Balmoral, and were enchanted with it. On Sir Robert Gordon's sudden death, they took a lease of the old Balmoral house (of which a picture can be seen at Haddo) from 1848 to 1852, when Prince Albert purchased the estate. With characteristic energy, he set about designing the new Balmoral. He engaged William Smith, the city architect of Aberdeen, but the Prince Consort's own ideas clearly had a major influence on the building. 'Balmoral has an institutional look inherent in the Prince Consort's search for perfection and too-deliberate study of the local vernacular as applied to castellated architecture', Hubert Fenwick shrewdly observes in his *Scottish Castles*. Nonetheless, Balmoral is a fine building, far superior to the many Scots-baronial revivals that have been perpetrated in its name.

The castle consists of two separate blocks of buildings connected by wings with a massive square tower 80 ft high; a round balustraded turret on one corner brings the total height to 100 ft while small conical turrets decorate the other three corners. The finely dressed ashlars of the light-grey, almost white, granite from the Invergelder quarry on the estate give Balmoral a much less heavy appearance than some other granite buildings. The finely carved coats of arms on the walls represent the Royal Arms of Scotland, six crests connected with the House of Saxe-Coburg, Saint Andrew for Scotland, Saint George for England and Saint Hubert for hunting. One bas-relief shows Malcolm Canmore presiding over 11th-century Highland Games. It is a great attraction of the Braemar Gathering nowadays that it is attended by the Queen and a family party.

The extensive grounds, with huge conifers planted as part of Prince Albert's original plan, stretch away towards Lochnagar and hold many memories of Queen Victoria and her family, recorded in her diary *Highland Leaves*. The various cairns recall marriages or deaths in the Royal Family, the most prominent being the 35 ft high cairn on Creag an Lurachain to the memory of 'Albert, the great and good ... raised by his broken-hearted widow Victoria R. August 21 1862'.

Across the River Dee, CRATHIE CHURCH is the place of worship of the Royal Family when in residence in Balmoral, and the s transept is reserved for them, with an entrance through the Queen's Porch. Crathie has been a place of Christian worship since the 6th century, and the pool opposite Balmoral known as Polmanire is traditionally where St Monire baptised his converts. The first substantive church (ruins visible in the old church-yard beside the Dee), dates from the 15th century. This was replaced by a new kirk in 1804, in which Queen Victoria and her family worshipped until the present church was constructed in 1893-5 on exactly the same site. Marshall Mackenzie, who built Marischal College in Aberdeen, was the architect. The style is basically 19th-century Gothic with a spire-capped tower above the crossing. Inside, the church contains a number of interesting features: the hexagonal pulpit incorporates 18 different kinds of Scottish granite; fixed round the moulding are marble pebbles collected by Princess Louise on the shores of Iona; the communion table, the gift of King George V and Queen Mary in memory of King Edward VII, is also of marble from Iona. The rose window in the w wall was presented by the descendants of the Revd John MacInnes, minister of Crathie from 1715 to 1748, who saved the lives of some of the rebels of the 1745 rising, and travelled to London to plead successfully the cause of Francis Farquharson of Monaltrie. The prominently displayed nine regimental badges of the Royal Guard regiments include the Scots Guards, the Black Watch, the King's Own Scottish Borderers, the Gordon Highlanders, the Royal Highland Fusiliers, the Argyll and Sutherland Highlanders and the now disbanded Cameronians.

Banchory   Kincardine and Deeside   Grampian 5 F2 (*pop. 2,355*)
Banchory, a pleasant town on a site of considerable antiquity, is now an expanding dormitory suburb of Aberdeen, 18 miles distant. There is a distillery to be visited, but of lavender-water, not whisky. A plaque in the High Street commemorates the great fiddler and composer Scott Skinner (1843-1927), known as The Strathspey King.

St Ternan came over the hills from Fordoun in the 5th century to found a monastery here, in a forest called, in Gaelic, the *ban choire* (the white circular place). This ancient site by the Dee, still a burial-ground, was used for successive places of worship until 1824. In the 18th century a circular watch-tower or mort-house with fireplace and belfry was built to defeat the 'Resurrectionists', who pursued their ghoulish trade of body-snatching to supply the Medico-Chirurgical Society of Aberdeen. The lairds were the Burnetts of Leys, who built their splendid castle of Crathes (q.v.) nearby, and, as they also owned the smaller castle at Muchalls (q.v.) over the hill in the Mearns, Sir Thomas Burnett arranged for both his properties to be included in the former county of Kincardine. This curious salient of the old county has, since the Regionalisation Act of 1975, been absorbed in the district of Kincardine and Deeside.

Banchory-Ternan, as the parish is sometimes called to distinguish it from Banchory-Devenick in Aberdeen, lies opposite the point at which the Cairn o' Mount road comes down to the Dee, through the narrow defile of the Feugh. This is here spanned by an 18th-century three-arched bridge, and an accompanying footbridge, from which, in season, the salmon can be watched leaping the falls. A local poet, David Grant, wrote a rollicking poem on how the Feugh came down in flood in the 'Muckle Spate' of 1829.

To the west of the Feugh defile is Scolty Hill, crowned by a chimney-like monument to General William Burnett of Banchory Lodge, who fought with Wellington. To the E of the Feugh is the historic Douglas fortress of

Tilquhillie (a four-storey, Z-plan tower of 1546) where the Regent Morton found shelter with John Douglas. Norman Douglas (1868-1952), author of *South Wind* and *Old Calabria,* was born in Tilquhillie (now unoccupied).

The broad vale of Feughside, presided over by the strange rock tower of Clochmaben, is the home of the Farquharsons of Finzean and figures in the landscapes of Joseph Farquharson, R.A.

Banff   Banff and Buchan   Grampian 8 E1 (*pop. 3,723*)
Banff has a special 18th-century flavour of its own — a wintering town for the gentry, from which the bustle, but not the elegance, has departed. The Banff Preservation Society sees to it that the tone is preserved. The Royal Burgh itself is much older, having been a member of the Northern Hanseatic League of trading towns in the 12th century, receiving a charter from Robert the Bruce in 1324. Of the old fortified castle nothing remains except a postern-gate on the High Street at the back of the pleasant 18th-century mansion called The Castle, built in 1750 for a Findlater earl to designs by William Adam.

The two main streets run at the top and the foot of the slope parallel with the shore and are joined by steep, narrow lanes. First impressions are of a pleasant jumble of 17th-century roofs and 18th-century Greek columns and delicate steeples. High Street, with attractive 18th-century groups of houses, contrasts with Low Street, the more important thoroughfare, with the Town House (its fluted spire, with unusual oval openings, designed by James Adam about 1765), the pleasantly Georgian Fife Arms (though built as late as 1843), leading to the Plainstones, a widening of the street at its west end. Here is the 16th-century Mercat Cross (on a 17th-century shaft) and a cannon captured at Sebastopol in the Crimea in 1855. It was probably on this site that James Macpherson, illegitimate son of Cluny Macpherson and a gipsy woman, a notorious freebooter and also fiddler, was hanged in 1700. He played the famous 'rant' as he marched to his execution, inspiring Burns (who visited Banff in 1780) to write:

Sae rantingly, sae wantonly, sae dauntingly gaed he;
He played a spring and danced it round below the
    gallows tree.
Legend has it that his reprieve was deliberately delayed until too late. Also to be noted are the episcopal church of St Andrew (by Archibald Simpson 1833), the Trinity Alvah church in Grecian style and the large parish church (1790) of St Mary's, with its classic steeple, a plaque within commemorating the Norwegian Brigade which wintered at Banff in 1941-2.

Ironically, Banff is nowadays probably less well-known than that other Banff at the gateway to the Canadian Rockies, so named by George Stephen (later Lord Mountstephen), a distinguished son of Banffshire (*see* Dufftown). In addition to this connexion with Alberta, Banff has a link with Argentina, for one of the Fife family, the good Earl James (1776-1857), campaigned with the Spanish

The mouth of the River Deveron at Banff

guerrillas in the Peninsular War and became a companion of San Martin, the liberator of Argentina. Down by the harbour, now largely silted up, was the old ruined parish church, but only the burial-aisle of the Ogilvies, Lords Banff, is now standing. Nearby is also High Shore, an interesting group of 17th-century houses, the first of which is a miniature tower-house with crowstep gable and angle-turret.

On the s edge of the town, the Information Bureau is housed in a Greek Doric temple, formerly the lodge to Duff House, that opulent monument to Duff extravagance, built by William Adam for the 1st Earl of Fife. Modelled, it is said, on the Villa Borghese in Rome, it took from 1735 to 1740 to build, cost the owner £70,000, and led to a lawsuit between him and the architect. The facade is a fine specimen of Scottish baroque, resembling that of Hopetoun, but so tall that it might almost be a baroque tower-house. The building was handed over to Banff and Macduff Town Council in 1906 and is now maintained as an AM. The interior is being slowly restored after being used by the Army in the last war. A mile or so up the Deveron River is the mausoleum of the Duff family.

The estuary of the Deveron is spanned by a fine seven-arched bridge built by Smeaton in 1779, which survived the floods of 1829 and was widened in 1881. On the other side is the thriving fishing port of MACDUFF (*pop.* 3,708), the name given in 1783 by the 2nd Earl to the village of Doune. His commercial instinct was indeed sound, for Macduff has prospered as Banff's harbour silted up. Macduff's harbour was extended in 1966. The steep streets and the busy waterfront at the foot of Doune Hill, crowned with its Italian-looking church of 1805, contrast

with the slightly passé dignity of Banff across the estuary. The open-air swimming pools at Tarlair, cut out of the rocky cliffs, are close to the earlier Well of Tarlair, a spa frequented by the gentry.

Three miles sw of Banff is the carefully restored 16th-century castle of Inchdrewer, deserted since 1713 when the 'wicked Lord Banff' was murdered in his bed, and the castle burnt to conceal the evidence.

Banff Coast Banff and Buchan Grampian 8 E1-G1
The coastline E from Macduff contains much of interest to geologist, painter, photographer, fisherman, bird-watcher or just plain scrambler along cliffs. Less well-known than the so-called Banffshire Riviera round Cullen, it divides into three sections. First, E from Macduff, the B9031 runs inland but with views over the fields which drop away to jagged cliffs. Where the road crosses the first of several 'dens' or rocky-sided ravines, there, on a greensward ledge half a mile to the N, is the roofless St John's Chapel, itself dating from 1513, but commemorating a much earlier victory, by the then ruler of Buchan, over the Danes in 1004. It overlooks to the E the safe haven of Gamrie Bay, with the twin fishing villages of Gardenstown (founded by the local laird Alexander Garden of Troup in the 18th century) and Crovie, facing w under the outlying promontory of Troup Head. Huddled on the sea-shore, they are only accessible by steep zigzag roads. Gardenstown has a modern housing development at mid-level; Crovie is the more picturesque and remote of these two quaintly situated villages, popular with artists.

The second section of the coast is the great promontory of Troup Head itself. The road cuts diagonally across its base to the ravine of the Tore of Troup, which comes to the sea at Cullykhan Bay. The cliffs of Troup Head drop sheer to the water from a height of 300-400 ft (120 m.) and provide wonderful stances for watching the antics of skuas, fulmars, puffins and kittiwakes. On the summit of the small promontory N of Cullykhan Bay are the remains of a Pictish fort, and the promontory itself is penetrated by a deep cleft, giving access at low tide to the Devil's Kitchen. A little to the W another cleft, known as Hell's Lum, the haunt of cormorants, spouts water and spray in rough weather. In spring the steep grassy slopes are thick with primroses, thrift and red campion; the vernal squill, scurvy-grass and sea purslane are also to be found.

Pennan village huddles deep below the road and is reminiscent of North Devon, while the hill country behind, with wide-open expanses of gorse, bracken and heather, is more like Exmoor than Scotland. The explanation is not far to seek: at Pennan a wide band of Old Red Sandstone comes to the surface, a continuation of the belt through Strathmore and the Howe of the Mearns. East of Pennan sheer cliffs continue to the little glen of Aberdour. The old church, roofless, but with burial aisles for local Leslies and Bairds, lies well below the early-19th-century planned village of New Aberdour, past which the B9031 runs. On the shore is the Well of St Drostan, a companion of St Columba. A mile to the E

Kittiwakes at Troup Head

along the coast is the site of the castle of Dundarg, on a red sandstone promontory. Only ruined foundations remain of this 'red fort', laid low during the 'herschip' (devastation) of Buchan in 1308. It was re-fortified by the French when they came to support the Scots against the English in 1547 at the time of the War of the Rough Wooing (1544-7).

In its final section, this exciting coast runs into the flatter, open country of Buchan proper, with low cliffs. Here are the ruins of the twin castles of Pittullie, held first by Frasers and then by Cumines, and of Pitsligo, both just inland from the fishing village of Rosehearty. Pitsligo was the more important of the two. Its Forbes laird was created Lord Pitsligo in 1633, and his grandson was a dedicated follower of the Jacobite cause, both in the Fifteen and, at the advanced age of 67, in the Forty-Five. His subsequent adventures included living on his own estate in shabby disguise and taking refuge in the seacave known as Lord Pitsligo's Cave (blocked as a precaution against invasion in World War II).

Bannockburn Stirling Central 1C5 (NTS) (*pop.* 5,899)

The scene of the most celebrated battle in Scottish history is now mostly overlaid by the modern village of Bannockburn. It was here that, on 24 June 1314, Robert the Bruce destroyed the English forces under Edward II and established Scotland as the independent nation she was to remain for nearly 400 years, up to the Act of Union in 1707. The sharp dip taken by the main A9 from Falkirk to Stirling as it crosses the little River Bannock gives a glimpse of the steep-sided, boggy stream-bed that brought about the downfall of the English. There is a vivid reconstruction at the National Monument up at the Borestane, where Robert the Bruce set up his standard on 23 June 1314. The NTS acquired the immediate surroundings in 1930 to stop them being built over. In 1964, on the 650th anniversary of the battle, Queen Elizabeth unveiled a fine bronze equestrian statue of The Bruce (by Pilkington Jackson). The NTS now have an information centre and, in 1967, added an ingenious audio-visual presentation, *The Forging of a Nation.*

The death of Edward I in 1307 brought a slow improvement in Scotland's fortunes in her struggle for independence, since Edward II was not the brilliant soldier his father had been. Gradually, Robert the Bruce and his followers forced the surrender of the English garrisons of Perth, Edinburgh and elsewhere, but in 1313 the key fortress of Stirling still held out. Robert's impetuous brother, Edward Bruce, struck a bargain with Sir Philip Moubray, the English commander of Stirling, that, unless relieved by an English army, he would surrender the fortress one year later, that is by Midsummer Day 1314. This arrangement forced on Robert Bruce the pitched battle which his guerrilla strategy had been at pains to avoid. Edward II's huge army of 22,000, with its heavily armoured cavalry, came marching from Edinburgh towards Stirling on 23

The Bruce statue, Bannockburn

June 1314. Bruce's army was only about 8,000 strong, of which 5,000 were spearmen, trained to fight in a tight mass as a shield-troop or 'schiltron', and only 500 lightly armed horsemen. Knowing that he must take advantage of the terrain, Bruce based his troops on the higher ground towards the hills, then thickly wooded, to the west of the Borestane, so that the English would be manoeuvred into the boggy ditches and pools of the little River Bannock. The incidents of the battle are too well known to be recounted in detail here: how the English advance guard under Gloucester and de Bohun moved against Bruce on the evening of 23 June; how Bruce smote and slew Bohun with his mighty axe; how the English forces spent the short summer night in the muddy bottom of the Bannock Burn, their armoured war-horses badly bogged; how the Scottish 'schiltrons' went for those horses, dismounting the English knights and throwing them into disorder; how the 'little folk', including townsmen from Stirling and clansmen from the Highlands (Duncan the Stout from Atholl among them), poured down from the hills to complete the rout of the English; and finally how Edward II fled first towards Stirling

where he was refused entry, and then SE, hotly pursued all the way to Dunbar, where he found a little boat to take him to Berwick.

Scotland's triumph was complete and The Bruce was confirmed as a great leader, but it took another 15 years before the independence, so nobly expressed by the Declaration of Arbroath of 1320, was finally recognized by England in the Treaty of Northampton of 1329. Ironically, Bannockburn makes a brief reappearance in history when Prince Charles Edward, on his way north from Derby to defeat at Culloden, spent from 4 January to 1 February 1746 at Bannockburn House. There, he made the acquaintance of Clementina Walkinshaw, who later became his mistress in Rome, the mother of his only child and the companion of public drinking bouts in his declining years, perhaps 'of all the long line of royal mistresses the least attractive', as the historian Sir Charles Petrie acidly observes.

Bannockburn emerged as a weaving village in the late 18th century and, being in the Lowlands, the weaving of tartan cloth was not forbidden as it was in the Highlands after the Forty-Five. William Wilson of Bannockburn kept patterns of the cloth supplied to his customers who were listed by number, rather than as clans. Copies of his correspondence and the attached samples are now preserved in the Museum of Tartans at Comrie (q.v.). Between Bannockburn and Stirling is the busy road-junction of St Ninian's, dominated by the tall, handsome clock-tower. The adjoining church, used as a powder-magazine by the Jacobites, was blown up by Cumberland's troops on their march northwards in 1746.

Ben Avon   *see* **Cairngorms (Eastern)**

Ben Lawers   Perthshire Tayside 1A1 (NTS)
Ben Lawers (3,984 ft/1214 m.) is a most interesting mountain from both the geological and the botanical points of view. It forms part of the Tay limestone outcrops which bring sweeter soils and greener vegetation than the usual acid rocks of the Highlands. The folding of the strata, and subsequent erosion, have brought the friable calcareous schists to the upper parts of the mountain. Here the weather conditions have favoured the growth of a unique arctic-alpine flora which has fired the enthusiasm of botanists from Victorian times onwards. The first impression of Lawers is of smooth, green slopes, of a greenness unlike the sedgy peat-bogs of the Western Highlands or the heather and blaeberry cover of the east, more reminiscent of those lush middle-level pasturages of the Swiss Alps, with the expectation of jangling cow-bells and brilliant flowers. This is not so far wrong, for in the 18th century the settlers on the N bank of Loch Tay brought their cattle (but not their sheep) up to summer grazing between the 1,500 ft (450 m.) and 2,700 ft (820 m.) level. Remnants of their shielings, or summer huts, are still to be traced. The absence of sheep meant that the flowers were not eaten down and, although any

expectation of sheets of blue gentian will be disappointed, these green slopes do produce in June a wealth of saxifrage (some seven varieties over the whole range), moss campion, the green and yellow flowering *Alchemilla alpina* (lady's mantle), hawkweeds, mountain pansy and the devil's-bit scabious. The lower crags and the crannies in the streams are the home of species such as *Dryas octopetala* (mountain aven). Higher and rarer are the Alpine forget-me-not, the boreal fleabane and the small snow gentian *Gentiana nivalis*.

Thanks to the generosity of P. J. Unna, the NTS was able in 1950 to purchase 8,000 acres of the southern watershed of Ben Lawers and to place the vegetation under strict protection. At the car-park 1,500 ft (450 m.) up on the side road from Loch Tay over to Glen Lyon, the NTS have set up a well designed Visitor's Centre to provide information on the history, geology, flora and fauna of the mountain. Here is the start of the well-beaten trail leading up over the grass slopes to the rocky summit of Ben Ghlas (3,668 ft/1118 m.) and thence along the broad ridge to the final summit of Ben Lawers itself. For the less energetic, a marked Nature Trail leads up the burn and out under the crags where a good sample of the middle-level flowers is to be seen.

The flora of Ben Lawers, unique in Britain except for small areas of Caenlochan at the head of Glen Isla, and in upper Teesdale, are to be found in similar conditions of soil and climate, some at lower levels in the Arctic, more at higher levels in the Alps and Pyrenees. Their main enemies are now man and sheep: with adequate measures of protection, this unique heritage should now be preserved from both.

Ben Macdhui   *see* Cairngorms (Eastern)

Bennachie   Gordon Grampian   8 E4

        The Mither Tap of Bennachie
        The sailor's Landmark frae the sea.

This jingle not only gives the correct pronunciation of Bennachie but also shows how strikingly this relatively modest peak stands up above the fertile farmlands of the middle Don to be visible out in the North Sea beyond Aberdeen. Bennachie - a mountain massif in miniature — is a heather-clad ridge of pink and grey granite some 5 miles long from W to E, the highest point being the rounded Oxen Craig (1,733 ft/528 m.), but the most spectacular the Mither Tap (1,698 ft/518 m.), a shattered granite tor weathered into bizarre shapes. Other weird granite outcrops occur over the range. The lower slopes of Bennachie have been afforested by the Forestry Commission, which has organised a small visitor centre on the Don side of the hill, and, near the village of Oyne, a picnic ground called Back of Bennachie after the nostalgic song of the exile, 'Would I were whaur Gadie rins, at the back of Bennachie'. The Commission has also unobtrusively marked some of the walking trails. Bennachie is a great favourite with Aberdonians and many children have had

their first taste of hill-walking here.

The Mither Tap, easily ascended from the NE by the so-called Maiden's Causeway, gives a wide view over Buchan and away to the Cairngorms. The Mither Tap is crowned by an extensive hill-fort, next highest after Tap o' Noth. A recent aerial survey, followed by excavations to the N of Bennachie, across the little River Urie, have established that a large Roman camp, not a mere marching camp, was built here in the time of Agricola and that, in all probability, the legions assembled here in A.D. 84 to do battle with Calgacus and his Caledonian hordes. In consequence, there is little doubt that the elusive Mons Graupius after which the battle was named turns out to be Bennachie. It is justifiable to picture the ranks of Caledonians mounting 'up the sloping hillside in close-packed tiers' (as Tacitus relates) and perhaps even to visualise the Mither Tap hill-fort as Calgacus's headquarters. Be that as it may, it is both convincing and satisfying that this Aberdeenshire landmark (at the heart of the modern Grampian Region) should have figured in Agricola's battle 19 centuries ago, rather than the distant and less striking mountains we now know as the Grampians.

Until well into the 19th century, the slopes of Bennachie were considered common land where squatters settled and built their own houses, until a court case in 1859 evicted them and divided the hill between nine lairds. The poet John Wisely, who emigrated to America, laments

        Oh ye was once a monarch hill,
        To freedom's footsteps free,
        But noo unless their honours will,
        We dare not tread on thee . . .

These lines, together with Charles Murray's nostalgic

        But Bennachie! Faith, yon's the hill
        Rugs at the hairt when ye're awa'!

testify to the affection in which the hill is held. It is good that the amenities are now cared for by the 'Bailies of Bennachie', an organisation founded in 1973.

Near the NE foot of the hill is a well-preserved Pictish stone, the Maiden Stone (AM), with a variety of incised symbols including a so-called 'elephant'. Visible from the A979 near Oyne is Harthill Castle, a 17th-century Z-plan castle which remained as a ruin since the 18th century, when the owner, finding his debts too much for him, burnt it down and went off to London to die a pauper. Harthill, beautifully set against the background of the north slopes of Bennachie, has been lovingly restored by an American couple. The delicate mushroom-coloured harling, the unusually imposing entrance gate to the barmkin, or domestic buildings enclosure, and the turrets, carefully re-slated with local slates, stand out as noteworthy features of this courageous venture in restoration.

Ben Rinnes   Moray Grampian   7 B3

For all its modest height, the prominent peak of Ben Rinnes (2,755 ft/840 m.) dominates the landscape of Banffshire and Moray, far more so than the remote Cairngorms, half as high again. Shattered granite tors, called *scurran* (plural of *sgurr*), form the twin summits, the more easterly being the higher. Ben Rinnes is easily ascended on foot from the Dufftown to Glenlivet B9009 road, either by the Land Rover track on the s flank of the hill or by the broad E ridge. There is on a clear day a far-reaching panorama, from Cullen by the sea to the Cairngorms in the s, from the sharp point of Bennachie to the E to the broad whaleback of Ben Wyvis beyond Inverness in the w, as well as across the Moray Firth to the distant hills of Sutherland and Caithness.

Eastwards to the distilleries of Dufftown, puffing their blue but agreeable fumes into the clear air, stretches the ridge of the Meikle and Little Convals, the latter with a large but incomplete hill-fort.

Blair Atholl   Perthshire   Tayside   3 H4
Motorists speeding along the A9 catch no more than a glimpse of the great white-harled building that is Blair Castle. It commands a strategic point on the routes to the Highlands: in ancient times the Drumochter Pass, now used by railway and A9, was long, lonely and desolate. Two ancient routes, one more direct and one more

sheltered, converge at Blair: one due s from Kingussie by the Comyn's road (or its variant the Minigaig), the other from Deeside by Glen Tilt (*see* Introduction: Communications).

So it was tempting in 1269 for John Comyn (or Cumming) of Badenoch to encroach southward into the territory of David de Strathbogie, Earl of Atholl, while he was away in England, and to start building a castle at the junction of these two routes. David won his case before Alexander III, but it did him and his successor little good, as they joined the English in opposition to Robert the Bruce and both their Atholl and their Huntly lands fell forfeit to the Crown in 1314. However, Cumming's tower remained, and the N tower of the present castle block, remodelled in Victorian days, stands on its foundations.

Blair Castle went through turbulent times and its architecture reflects its history, from medieval tower to Georgian mansion to remodelled Scots baronial castle. In 1457 James II gave Atholl to Sir John Stewart of Balvenie (*see* Dufftown). There were Stewart earls in Atholl until 1625, when the succession passed to the Murrays of Tullibardine, a family favoured by James VI for their support in the Gowrie Conspiracy (*see* Perth and Scone) and Blair has remained in Murray hands to the present day.

Blair Atholl Castle, with Ben Vrackie and the Pass of Killiecrankie

The Stewart earls enlarged the castle southwards, with the 15th-century square tower and the Great Hall of 1530, and entertained Mary, Queen of Scots, to a stupendous hunt on her northern tour in 1562. The first Murray earl was an ardent Royalist in the Civil Wars, and the Atholl men were out with Montrose in 1644 when he raised the Royal standard at Blair. In 1653 the castle was stormed by Colonel Daniel, one of Cromwell's commanders. In 1689 the 1st Marquis of Atholl, who was a supporter of William of Orange, retired to take the waters at Bath. At the instigation of 'Bonnie Dundee', his steward held the castle for King James: the Duke's son besieged it, not too vigorously, for King William. 'Bonnie Dundee' was buried in Old Blair Kirk, as a tablet records, after he had been killed in the moment of victory at nearby Killiecrankie (q.v.). In the Fifteen, the family was again divided: the eldest brother, William, and two others joined the Jacobite cause and went into exile. The second brother, Lord James, succeeded as 2nd Duke (1690-1764), loyal to the Hanoverians. In 1745 Prince Charles Edward stayed briefly at Blair on his way southwards but, when the castle was in the following year occupied by Hanoverian troops, Lord George Murray, the Prince's chief of staff, found himself bombarding his own home. The Atholl military tradition continued with Atholl Highlanders raised in the 18th century as a British regiment, and to this day the Duke has a ceremonial bodyguard.

The 18th-century reconstruction of the castle that followed under the 3rd Duke (1729-74) was a reflection of the times: prosperous and English. The two upper storeys were demolished, turrets and parapets chopped off; the building remodelled to look like a plain Georgian mansion known as Atholl House, and the village removed from Old Blair to the new site on the road. The estates improved under the management of subsequent Dukes, who set about afforesting the Atholl hillsides. From some of the seedlings of European larch, brought from the Austrian Tyrol by James Menzies (see Glen Lyon), there sprang the extensive larch woods of Atholl. Some of the original larches still stand in 'Diana's Grove', one 143 ft high.

Queen Victoria, who spent three weeks at Blair in 1844 and described it as 'a large, plain, white building', set the fashion for the next change with her enthusiasm for everything Scottish. The 6th Duke employed the architect David Bryce to remodel his great-grandfather's Georgian mansion into something approaching its original state by restoring turrets and crowstep gables, imposing the square, English-style castellations on the towers, and replacing the Georgian entrance by the Scots-baronial tower through which the castle is now entered. Queen Victoria paid a second brief visit in October 1861 on her third 'great expedition', when she returned to Balmoral by the Glen Tilt route, fording its tributary, the Tarff, in spate.

From the gates, a long avenue of lime trees leads up to the castle, which is full of treasures, well set out and illustrated in the official handbook. There is a fine collection of arms, including the helmet and breast-plate of 'Bonnie Dundee', though the bullet-hole in the latter may be a fake. There are three portraits by John Hoppner of the 4th Duke and his wife and their son who died, like Byron, in the cause of Greek independence. A charming conversation-piece by Zoffany shows the 3rd Duke and Duchess with their children beside a river, fishing, plucking fruit or making posies. The Tullibardine Room in the Cumming Tower is dedicated to the Jacobite Atholls. There is also a superb collection of Sèvres, Wedgwood and other porcelain, and a museum of family treasures.

Blairgowrie Perthshire Tayside 4 C6 (*pop.* 5,960) Blairgowrie (Gaelic for Field of Goats) and Rattray (Fort of the Hunter) are situated on opposite banks of the River Ericht, where it breaks through the Highland Boundary Fault into the farmland of Strathmore. The twin burghs are now a single municipality. Blairgowrie has no fewer than three castles: the ruined Glasclune 2 miles away on a hill to the NW; Newton situated high above the town; and Ardblair, a mile W on the A923. Newton (not open to the public) is an early 17th-century Z-plan castle with a round tower and watch chamber on one corner and a square tower on the other corner of the three-storey main block.

Ardblair, white-harled, stands in trees on a little promontory overlooking the chain of small lochs south of Blairgowrie: they used to be more extensive than at present, and the castle was correspondingly better defended. Ardblair is a pleasant L-shaped fortified house, built on two sides of a small courtyard entered by a fine arched gateway. The present house dates from the 16th century when the lands were in possession of the turbulent Blair family, one of whom in 1554 murdered the Drummond of Newton. (A Green Lady is said to haunt both castles since this episode). In 1792 Ardblair passed to the Oliphants of Gask and is now in the hands of the Blair-Oliphants. They were fervent Jacobites, one being aide-de-camp to Prince Charles Edward. Many Jacobite relics are now housed in Ardblair, also mementoes of Lady Caroline Nairne (née Oliphant) (1766-1845) who wrote popular Jacobite songs such as *Charlie is my Darling* under the pseudonym of Mrs Bogan of Bogan. Ardblair can be visited by arrangement.

RATTRAY has only one castle, Craighall Rattray, perched on a crag in the wooded gorge of the Ericht. A Rattray who survived Flodden (1513) took refuge here and in due course it became the family home of the Rattrays, sometimes claimed as the model for 'Tullyveolan' in Walter Scott's *Waverley* (but see Grandtully).

The Ericht provided water-power for flax and jute mills here in the 19th century, the population of the two towns increasing from about 1,000 in 1790 to nearly 4,000 in 1840. The mills lie idle now. Prosperity depends on something different — the raspberry crop. A local solicitor noticed the quality of the local wild raspberries and started to grow raspberries as a crop in 1898. Climate, soil and altitude combine to provide excellent growing conditions and Blairgowrie claims to produce raspberries in competition with Oregon. A fair number of Strathmore farmers devote some part of their acreage to raspberries, largely destined for the jam factories of Dundee.

Bog o' Gight   *see* **Fochabers**

Braemar   Kincardine and Deeside   Grampian   4C2
Now a popular holiday centre, Braemar has traditionally been a strategic point. The military road, now the A93 from the south over the Cairnwell Pass (2,199 ft/670 m.), converges on Deeside with the old tracks from Atholl by way of Glen Tilt and from Speyside by Glen Feshie. The village originally had two names: the predominantly Catholic settlement of Auchendryne on the w bank of the Clunie Water and Presbyterian Castleton on the east bank. In her *Leaves from a Highland Diary* Queen Victoria correctly refers to Castleton, as the two settlements were not united under the name of Braemar until 1870. The castle in question is not, however, the obvious Braemar Castle, half a mile to the E on the A93, but the remains of a 14th-century fortress, Kindrochit — the head of the bridge — visible from the bridge over the Clunie. It was already in ruins when John Taylor, the Water Poet, passed this way in 1618. The Earl of Mar replaced it in 1628 with the present Braemar Castle. This was burnt and taken over in 1689 by the Farquharsons of Invercauld, and by the English forces after the Risings of 1715 and 1745. As an important strong-point on the new military road from Blairgowrie to Fort George, built in the 1750s, Braemar Castle was, like Corgarff (q.v.), adapted to English requirements. This was done by adding, to what is basically a traditional tower-house, English-style crenellations and battlements, and by surrounding it with an eight-pointed, star-shaped wall, pierced for musketry in the manner of the French military engineer, Vauban. Sadly, the architect of this Anglification, which gives Braemar the look of a sham castle, was John Adam (1721-92), the eldest of the Adam brothers. The castle continued in military use until 1831 for the control of marauders and whisky-smugglers. It was then returned to the Farquharsons and is now regularly open.

Braemar was where the Earl of Mar, after taking a quick look at the new Hanoverian court of George I and disliking what he saw, raised the standard of rebellion in favour of the Old Pretender in September 1715. He did so under cover of assembling the nobles and their followers for a hunt. Some of the lesser lairds were reluctant to supply their contingents but, on the whole, Deeside was firmly Jacobite. The rebellion fizzled out after the battle of Sheriffmuir (q.v.), owing to the vacillation of the Earl of Mar, or Bobbing John, and the uncharismatic nature of the Old Pretender, James Edward Stuart.

Braemar is famous for its Highland Gathering, initiated in 1832, first attended by Queen Victoria in 1848, and now regularly by Queen Elizabeth and members of

Braemar Castle

the Royal Family. The Gathering, which attracts overseas competitors, takes place in early September in a beautiful setting. There is the traditional array of pipers and dancers, as well as the usual 'heavy' events, including the tossing of the caber. The tradition of Games can be traced back to Malcolm Canmore, who used this method of selecting the strongest and fastest warriors.

A good view-point, easily reached on foot, looking right into the eastern Cairngorms (q.v.), is the great sprawling hump of Morrone (2,819 ft/860 m.) with its aerial mast for mountain rescue teams, to the SE of Braemar. There is a view-point indicator at the foot of Morrone, and a nature reserve with fine examples of natural birch wood. A good all-day excursion is to ascend Lochnagar (q.v.) (3,789 ft/1155 m.) starting from Auchallater farm, 2 miles s of Braemar on the A93, and up over the Stuic to the summit. It was in Braemar that Robert Louis Stevenson began writing *Treasure Island* which he tried out on a local boy. He had come over from Pitlochry to 'pass a good deal of my time between four walls in a house lugubriously known as "the late Miss McGregor's cottage"'.

Breadalbane   Perthshire   Tayside   1 A2-C1
Breadalbane, Gaelic *braghaid Albainn*, the Upland of Alba, is the E slope of Drum-Alban, the great dividing ridge of Scotland N of the Forth. Breadalbane was also the title taken by the Campbells of Glenorchy, as they extended their lands from Argyll into Glen Dochart and Glen Lyon,

and right down to the E end of Loch Tay. As the jingle has it

> From Kenmore to Ben More
> The land is a' the Markiss's.
> The mossy howes, The heathery knowes,
> An' ilka bonny park is his.

The uppermost reach of the Tay, Strathfillan, gives easy access from Glenorchy into Breadalbane. The area of this guide-book begins at Killin at the W end of Loch Tay, now a popular holiday village but once the site of the grimmest of the seven Campbell castles — Finlarig. Its ruins stand neglected and unsignposted in a thick patch of wood down a side-road across the River Lochay, as the A827 swings north out of Killin. The three-storey tower built by Black Duncan of the Cowl (probably in 1609, as the heraldic arms above the door suggest) adjoins a sinister beheading-pit where gentry had the privilege of having their heads cut off, rather than swinging from the gallows that once stood near the holly tree. There is a more recent chapel and mausoleum nearby and the graves of the last Marquis of Breadalbane and his wife, who died in the 1920s.

The characteristics credited to the Campbells of Glenorchy are acquisitiveness, cruelty and longevity. They pushed the Macgregors and Macnabs out of their lands in the 17th century, and carried out 19th-century-style evictions in Glen Quaich. Created Earls of Breadalbane in 1677, several of them lived to a great age. Yet they also showed foresight and taste: they were early pioneers of afforestation, and they improved and developed their estates; Colin Campbell was the patron of the portrait painter George Jamesone; in 1774 the 3rd Earl built the road along the N bank of Loch Tay; in 1801 the 4th Earl had the old castle of Balloch, at the E end of Loch Tay, entirely rebuilt by the English architect William Atkinson (who also rebuilt Scone). For Queen Victoria's visit in 1842 the 2nd Marquis had Taymouth Castle, as Balloch was renamed, refurbished and 'Gothicked' by David Bryce, with lavish interior decorations; the Queen found her reception 'princely and romantic'. The glory has now departed and, after being used for various purposes including a school, Taymouth Castle is now vacant.

The historian Macaulay called the 1st Earl 'cunning as a fox, wise as a serpent, slippery as an eel', for his part in the negotiations with the Highland chiefs that led to the massacre of Glencoe in 1692, which was carried out by a kinsman, Campbell of Glen Lyon. Whatever the faults of its rulers, Breadalbane is a lovely land and its heart is Loch Tay, 15 miles (24 km.) long, which fills a 500-ft-deep glacial trench under the southern flanks of Ben Lawers (q.v.). The main A827 road runs on the N bank, rather high above the loch; if time allows, finer views are obtained by following the narrow, winding road on the S bank, or, better still, braving the steep road which climbs S out of Kenmore towards Glen Quaich, to enjoy one of the finest views in Scotland — above the fifth steep bend, from a grassy alpine ledge with a few old scattered larches, one

looks W over the glittering blue waters of Loch Tay to the snow-flecked summits of the Ben Lawers massif.

Brechin Angus Tayside 5F5 *(pop. 6,578)*
Now that the busy A94 trunk road from Perth to Aberdeen by-passes Brechin, some peace has been restored to this small cathedral town. Though the roads from Montrose, Arbroath and Forfar still converge near the centre, the attractive, steeply sloping High Street and the cathedral precincts are spared the brunt of the traffic. The best view of the group of old red sandstone buildings — castle, cathedral, round tower and older part of the town — is to be had from the Arbroath road, as it enters the town after crossing the River South Esk. The old High Street houses are gable-ended like those at nearby Montrose, and some of the closes and wynds are being attractively developed.

Kenneth II (971-95) 'gave the great monastery of Brechin to the Lord'. The Culdees followed the Celtic rite here for about 150 years until David I turned the establishment into a Catholic bishopric for this part of Angus. The Culdees left us the Round Tower (AM) restored in 1960. This remarkable belfry and landmark of Brechin, built between 995 and 1012, is a clear sign of the Irish influence brought by the Scots to the land of the Picts. The Brechin round tower, older than that of Abernethy (q.v.), follows the Irish style of construction, 86 ft from ground level to the foot of the octagonal cap (which adds another 20 ft);

Round Tower and Cathedral, Brechin

the walls are $3\frac{1}{2}$ ft thick at the base but taper to $2\frac{1}{2}$ at the top so that the interior diameter remains at a constant 8 ft. The narrow door, 6 ft above the ground, is flanked by two ecclesiastical figures with heraldic beasts below and Christ with his feet uncrossed (as in Ireland) above.

The cathedral (now the parish church of Brechin, the Bishop of the Episcopal Church residing at Dundee) did not survive so well as the Round Tower. Completed in the Pointed Gothic style about 1200, the church was ransacked by Edward I in 1303 and after the Reformation suffered serious neglect, so much so that an engraving of 1790 shows the chancel as roofless. The square tower with its spire was constructed in fits and starts between 1200 and 1400, and has survived better than the chancel. In 1806, the edifice suffered a burst of ill-judged restoration: the shallow bays known as the N and s transepts were torn down, the walls heightened and the nave widened. In 1900 a much more sensitive restoration was carried out under the direction of Dr Honeyman of Glasgow: the transepts were restored, the N one becoming a side-chapel known as the Queen's Aisle. Within, there is much modern stained glass, ranging from 1901 to 1978, including a war memorial window by Douglas Strachan and a fine recent window in the Queen's Aisle by Gordon Webster. There are three remarkable stones: two Pictish cross-slabs, one called the St Mary near the chancel, the

other the Aldbar Stone, in pink sandstone, with King David slaying the lion; the third the Brechin Hogback - a long, recumbent stone fashioned with a dragon-like head at one end and a rump at the other, almost certainly shaped by Scandinavian immigrants in the 11th century.

Brechin Castle nearby, rebuilt in 1711, is the seat of the Earl of Dalhousie, the head of the family of Maules of Panmure. Sir Thomas Maule held the castle against Edward I in 1303. The Bishops of Brechin had a charming summer palace — referred to by Bishop Meldum in 1512 as 'Palatium Nostrum' — at Farnell, 4 miles s of Brechin, an ecclesiastical tower-house, now in private hands.

Brodie Castle Moray Grampian 6H2 (NTS)
Brodie Castle, between Forres and Nairn, was acquired in 1978 by the Secretary of State for Scotland and in 1980 entrusted to the NTS, who are setting out to make it a major attraction. The Trust has refurbished it (though some of the interior work has still to be completed), while preserving its character as a family home, and has arranged the display of the wide-ranging Brodie collection of pictures.

The clan of Brodie has held these lands 'beyond all human memory', possibly back to, or beyond, the time of Macbeth. Though the family records were burnt, there is documentary evidence that the Brodies received their lands from Malcolm IV in 1160 and that Michael, Thane

Brodie Castle

of Brodie, had his charter confirmed by Robert the Bruce in 1311. In the Civil Wars, Sir Alexander Brodie (1617-80), a fanatical Presbyterian, led a party to mutilate the carvings in Elgin Cathedral (q.v.) and to destroy the paintings. As the castle of a leading Covenanter, Brodie was inevitably the target for Royalist attacks, and was burnt in 1645 by Montrose's troops under Lord Lewis Gordon. Brodie's diaries contain interesting political sidelights on the period, and he was one of the Commissioners sent to The Hague in 1650 to invite Charles II to come to Scotland. In the 18th century, another Alexander Brodie developed the estate, laying out the formal gardens, but at such a cost that, in 1774, it had to be sold. The Earl of Fife bought it and restored it to his son-in-law, the 21st Brodie. Despite straitened circumstances, the 19th-century alterations were set in hand by William, the 22nd Brodie, who himself married a wealthy heiress. His cousin Elizabeth became the wife of the 5th and last Duke of Gordon (died 1836) and many of her possessions are to be seen in the castle. The present head of the clan, the 25th Brodie of Brodie (who is correctly addressed as 'Brodie' *tout court*), continues to reside in part of the castle.

The delicate pale ochre harling of the exterior gives an apparent uniformity to the castle. The oldest part, dating from about 1560, is a strong rectangular tower, resembling Drum (q.v.), with three main floors and, above, a sentry-round parapet supported on elaborate corbelling and decorated with a great number of cannon-like waterspouts. At ground level there are arrow-slits and splayed gun-loops; and these continue into the two diagonally-opposite wings added in the 17th century to form a Z-plan castle. The staircase tower, impressively corbelled out at first-floor level, in the angle near the entrance, is capped by a steep, conical turret. In the 17th century a further wing was added on the w side; the considerable extensions on the E are by the Victorian architects William Burn and James Wylson, both pupils of Smirke.

The low, vaulted chambers on the ground floor include the kitchen, and a low pillared entrance leads to the pleasant library in the 19th-century E wing. Stairs lead up to the dining room, added by Alexander the Covenanter in the 1650s, with its elaborate, deeply recessed plaster ceiling (probably 1670), one of the most remarkable in Scotland, but coloured (controversially) a deep brown; it shows the crown of Scotland, a pelican and a unicorn. Off this room is the charming blue sitting room, with its cobalt-blue flock wallpaper. Here, the fine plaster ceiling is left white; its centrepiece is the fist clutching the three arrows of the Brodie crest, executed so as to stand free, suspended from the ceiling. Over the window is the monogram of Alexander Brodie and his wife, Elizabeth Innes.

Adjoining the dining room is the former High Hall, now known as the Red Room (the red wallpaper has still to be restored), housing a wooden, 17th-century Flemish altar-piece over the chimney. This opens out into the large, well lit, 19th-century drawing room, with some fine Louis XVI marquetry furniture, and interesting pictures, notably of Charles I by van Dyck, of Jane, 4th Duchess of Gordon, by Romney, and of William Brodie with his brothers and sisters by John Opie. The top floor is reached by climbing the turnpike stair in the turret at the corner of the Red Room. In addition to two tastefully reconstructed bed-chambers, the other rooms are used to house the 19th-century and modern paintings collected by the 24th Brodie. In a lobby on the first floor are various relics, including Prince Charles Edward's broadsword and the robe worn by Queen Adelaide at the coronation of William IV in 1831. It came to Brodie through the Duchess of Gordon, who was Mistress of the Robes at the time.

The formal 18th-century layout of the gardens, designed by Switzer, with avenues radiating from the castle, has been much overlaid by Victorian tree-planting, but the great western avenue of limes and copper beeches remains a glorious sight. By the E entrance to the grounds is a well-preserved Pictish Class II stone, an incised cross on one side and on the other symbols, including a pair of dolphins, the peculiar 'elephant' and a double-disc. Known as the Rodney Stone, it was discovered in 1781 and set up to commemorate Admiral Rodney's capture of the French fleet off Dominica in the West Indies the following year.

Buchan Coast   Banff and Buchan   Grampian 8H4-H3
Much of the SE coast of Buchan, from the mouth of the Ythan (q.v.) to the lighthouse at Boddam, is a fittingly rugged edge to a bleak and treeless interior. The undulating fields plunge abruptly in 150 ft cliffs of pink granite to boiling seas and screaming gulls below. There is sand only at Cruden Bay and where the Ythan runs to the sea by Forvie Sands. Elsewhere, little coves with steep access from the cliff top used to provide opportunities for smuggling, but nowadays nothing more than occasional fishing or rock-climbing goes on.

The shifting sand-dunes of Forvie, like those of Culbin in Moray and Rattray beyond Peterhead, have engulfed a considerable hamlet; only the remains of the church are visible. To the N is the pleasant fishing village and summer resort of Collieston, perched above a cove known as St Catherine's Dub. The St Catherine was a Flemish vessel, wrecked here in 1594, carrying arms to support the revolt of the 'Papist Earls', Erroll and Huntly — and not, as is sometimes thought, a Spanish galleon from the Armada of six years earlier.

Just along the coast, reached by high cliff path, or down a farm track, is a jagged fang of masonry on a dramatic headland. This is all that remains of the Old Castle of SLAINS, destroyed, like the Gordon castle at Huntly, under the personal supervision of James VI after the Battle of Glenlivet (1594). The present Countess of Erroll, chief of Clan Hay, has built herself a modern home inside the ancient castle.

The Bullers of Buchan

The 9th Earl of Erroll, nothing daunted when his short exile ended in 1597, chose another cliff-top site on Bowness, 5 miles to the N, for his New Castle of Slains. This stands where the sands of Cruden Bay give way to the pink Peterhead granite. Slains is now a sprawling, roofless ruin, enlarged several times from the original tower which still stands, growing out of the vertical cliff. Here the Errolls lived in great state, entertaining, among others, Dr Samuel Johnson, who asserted that, if he had to witness a storm, Slains was a place he would willingly do it from. Boswell, however, could not sleep for the roar of the waves and the fear of ghosts. This vast pink granite pile, now approached across the fields from Cruden Bay, was sold in 1916 and dismantled in 1925. Bram Stoker may have derived some inspiration for Dracula's castle when he stayed at Cruden Bay.

Cruden Bay is another pleasant coast resort with a golf-course laid out in the sand-dunes, although not enjoying the elegant fame it did when the Great North of Scotland Railway sited a pretentious hotel here. The little fishing haven of Port Erroll was built by a 19th-century earl as a substitute for the dangerous open bay below the New Slains Castle. Recently, the pipe-line from the Forties oil-field was brought ashore here through the sandy bay, causing no more damage to the amenities than a remote pumping-station.

A mile N along the coast are the Bullers (or 'Boilers') of Buchan, visited by Dr Johnson and Boswell from Slains. From the cluster of cottages beside the road, a path leads to the 150 ft-deep, spectacular cauldron in the granite cliffs, 'a rock perpendicularly tubulated' wrote Dr Johnson, joined by an arch to the open sea which, when rough, spouts up inside this great blow-hole. A separate narrow track — not for those inclined to giddiness, but followed safely by the ponderous Doctor (who also entered the Buller by boat) — leads round the edge and has provided hair-raising travellers' tales. Sea-birds, kittiwakes, guillemots and the occasional puffin, abound in the intricate maze of caves, stacks and 'yawns', caused by the sea eroding the joints of the pink granite. North beyond Long Haven, the cliffs are cluttered with quarries, oil and radar development and the southward expansion of Peterhead as far as the old village of Boddam. This lies on the most easterly point of the Scottish mainland, separated by a bridge over a narrow strait from the tiny island of Buchan Ness, where Robert Stevenson built the lighthouse in 1827, and the Prime Minister, Lord Aberdeen, sought retreat from the cares of state in the 1840s.

Buckie Moray Grampian 7 C1 (*pop.* 7,919)
Buckie, the largest centre of population in the former county of Banffshire, straggles along the coast between Portgordon to the w and Portessie to the E. The older houses, some built with their gable-ends to the sea to allow the boats to be drawn up on the open shore between them, others glistening with bright coats of paint, line the narrow strip between the escarpment and the sea, clustering round the burn which flows into the Moray Firth by the old Seatown. The mid-19th-century settlement, reflecting the prosperous days of the herring trade, is up on the terrace above the scarp, centering on the great twin spires of the Catholic St Peter's Church, almost a cathedral, which serves as a reminder that this region of Enzie is still strongly of the 'Old Persuasion'.

Though an ancient Gordon place, Buckie has expanded only in the last 175 years. When the poet Burns visited Buckie in 1787, it had no more than 14 boats and a population of 700, but the herring boom, with sales of cured herrings as far away as Russia, brought a four-fold increase in population by 1840. The herring market was subject to fluctuations and the prosperity of 1840-80 collapsed in the 1890s. By this time, the little harbour at Buckpool, built in 1855, had been replaced by the big new harbour started by Gordon of Cluny in 1872 and improved in 1932. This harbour, equipped with modern facilities, is the centre of Buckie and the home of fishing boats which range out to Shetland and round to the West Coast, and, as recent tragedies have sadly made widely known, down to Cornwall for the mackerel.

The other little harbours along this coast are either disused or serve for yachting, while once-busy villages, like Portgordon, founded by the 4th Duke of Gordon in 1797, are dormitories for fishermen whose boats are moored in Buckie.

Bow Fiddle Rock, Portknockie

Buckie has kept up with the times: its fishing boats evolved from the characteristic Moray Firth 'skaffie', with sharp wedge-like bow and broad beam (a mere 20 ft long) to the remarkable Zulu (brought into service in the year of the Zulu War, 1874) with a 60 ft keel. This was the last of the sailing vessels, to be replaced in 1900 by the steam drifter and seine-netting. Today's diesel-engined boats can be adapted for either flat fish or herring fishing. These types of boat can be inspected in the fine Buckie Maritime Museum, where representations of life among the fisherfolk and the history of fishing are also to be seen, as well as the paintings of Peter Anson, who wrote about and painted the fishing ports of the North-East.

The fishing community has traditionally kept very much to itself, cherishing its special nicknames and its superstitions; this exclusiveness was only broken down by the advent of steam, with its need for engineers and other outsiders, as well as by the development of modern technology and communications. Even today the Buckie fisherfolk regard themselves as apart from the farmers of the Banffshire hinterland. The neighbouring picturesque little harbour of Findochty (*pron.* Finechty) is a port of some antiquity, later developed by a colony of fisherfolk from Fraserburgh, and now a tourist resort and dormitory village for Buckie. There is a pleasant statue on the waterfront of a fisherman gazing out over the Moray Firth. Eastwards from Findochty, the coast becomes more rugged, with the much-photographed Bow Fiddle Rock, an isolated rock arch off Portknockie, another abandoned harbour with some gaily painted houses. Beyond this headland are the sands of Cullen Bay.

Burghead Moray Grampian 7 A1
Burghead, 7 miles N of Elgin, is a place of considerable antiquity, occupying a promontory jutting out into the Moray Firth just where the sandstone cliffs of Hopeman abut on the great sandy bay stretching W to the mouth of the River Findhorn. The tip of the peninsula is the site of an ancient Pictish fort, probably the *alata castra* (winged camp) of Ptolemy's map. The Norsemen made use of the place from the 9th to the 11th centuries, and called it Torfness. Thanks to the mapmaker, William Roy, we have an 18th-century plan of the fort as it existed before the S half was destroyed to make way for the present village built in 1805-9. This development did, however, reveal the remarkable 'Well' (key available at nearby house), an early excavation deep under the summit mound of the promontory. The ancient steps and entrance arch were renewed and it is now possible to descend to this sizeable underground pool and speculate on its origin. It seems inadequate as a water supply or a public bath; it is nothing to do with the Romans; but may well have been an early Christian baptistery. On the mound above the Well can be seen the basket on a pole where the 'Clavie' — a barrel filled with tar — is ceremonially burnt each year on 11 January - the survival of an ancient fire festival, probably of Scandinavian origin.

Some fine Pictish carvings of bulls were unearthed in the 1809 excavations: two are in the Elgin Museum and one each in the National Museum of Antiquities in Edinburgh and in the British Museum. A small museum was opened in 1979 to illustrate Celts, Picts and Vikings from 2500 B.C. to A.D 1300. Burghead's little harbour is frequented by fishing boats and yachtsmen, but the land approach to the town is spoilt by the huge modern building storing the malting barley imported for the many distilleries of the district. That apart, the view across the wide Moray Firth to the hills of Sutherland and Caithness is superb.

Cairngorms (Eastern) Grampian 4A2-B2
The eastward extensions and the southern flanks of the great Cairngorm plateau are much less visited than the northern glens and ski-slopes accessible from Aviemore and Glenmore Lodge in the Highland Region (*see* Bartholomew's *Scottish Highlands*, p.94). Of the four Cairngorm summits that top the 4,000 ft (1200 m.) mark, two, Cairntoul (4,241 ft/1292 m.) and Ben Macdhui (4,296 ft /1,309 m.) — only a few feet lower than Ben Nevis — fall entirely within the Grampian Region, and of the other two — Braeriach (4,248 ft/1295 m.) and The Cairngorm (4,084 ft/1245 m.) — only the northern slopes come within the Highland Region. The great plateau of Beinn a' Bhuird and Ben Avon, the largest area continuously over 3,000 ft (900 m.) in the British Isles, is entirely in the Grampian Region. The uniformity of these heights is an indication of the great level ice-cap that once covered the whole area. Glaciers flowing down from it

gouged out the N-s defile of the Lairig Ghru and the W-E trough of Loch Avon. Nowadays, the Cairngorms mostly present smooth whale-backs to the W and N, but glacial action has scooped out the impressive E-facing rocky corries that are the wild and secret places of these formidable hills. They may seem innocent enough on a fine summer's day, but at other seasons a tearing wind, freezing temperatures and driving snow can rapidly bring Antarctic conditions, and danger for the ill-equipped.

Tomintoul and Braemar are the only major centres for visiting this side of the Cairngorms, and motorable roads open to the public do not penetrate far into the massif. The private road up Glen Avon from Tomintoul to Inchrory is closed by a locked gate at Birchfield. The reward for long approach marches is considerable, for up here on the high, rounded slopes of the tops the hill-walker will find solitude and exhilaration. After struggling through deep heather and sometimes bog, he emerges at about 2,400 ft (730 m.) onto crisp, short heather. This, in turn, gives way to arctic lichen and mosses, springy underfoot, alternating with stripes of fine, granite gravel. Occasionally there is a splash of bright yellow, green and red moss where streams break from the melting snow-beds. This is where the dotterel breeds in summer, and the ptarmigan live all the year round, changing their plumage from winter white to speckled brown and grey - still perfectly camouflaged as the snow melts. In spring, there are wide areas between the stripes of gravel where the ground is pink with the tiny azalea *Loiseleuria procumbens*, flattened to the ground by snow and searing winds.

BEN MACDHUI is accessible from Linn of Dee by way of Glen Derry and the steep pull up to Loch Etchachan, at just over 3,000 ft (915 m.) the highest loch of this size in Britain, frozen over for half the year. This route continues over the windswept plateau to the spot at which a large cairn and view indicator mark the rather featureless summit. The indicator shows that, on a fine day, one can see from the Lammermuirs in the s to Caithness in the N, from Ben Nevis in the W to the North Sea in the E, and even distant peaks in Torridon and Sutherland are sometimes to be identified. To the W, beyond the deep gash of the Lairig Ghru, is the high ridge linking Braeriach to the right with Cairntoul to the left, encircling the wild Garbh Coire into which the infant Dee drops dramatically.

Both North Top (3,924 ft / 1196 m.) and South Top (3,860 ft / 1177 m.) of Beinn a' Bhuird stand out when seen from Invercauld, below Braemar, as do some of the fearsome crags in the E-facing corries between the tops. Up there, too, is the Laird's Blanket — a snow-patch lingering on well into summer. Divided from the North Top by the conspicuous gap of The Sneck (the shortest walking route from Braemar to Tomintoul), the long summit ridge of Ben Avon stretches away to the E, crowned by a series of granite towers, resembling the tors of Dartmoor. BEN AVON (3,842 ft / 1171 m.) figures early in literature, for it is mentioned in the *Moneylesse Perambulation of John Taylor,*

alias the King's Majesties Water Poet. John Taylor, a London waterman, touring Scotland in 1618 for a wager in the footsteps of Ben Jonson, describes how he saw — from Braemar — 'Mount Benawne, with a furr'd mist upon his snowie head instead of a nightcap; for you must understand that the oldest man alive never saw but snow on the top of divers of these hills, both in summer as well as in winter'.

Cambuskenneth Abbey Stirling Central 1C5 (AM)
Even more than neighbouring Stirling, the ruined Abbey of Cambuskenneth (in a wide loop of the River Forth) is the heart of Scotland. North-westwards, when the air is limpid after a shower, Ben Lomond and Ben Ledi stand out clearly beyond the rock of Stirling Castle; south- eastwards, when the smoke of Falkirk factories and the Grangemouth refinery are blowing away, the castle rock of Edinburgh can be seen beyond the Forth.

The 'bend in the field of Kenneth' probably marks some 9th-century battle between Kenneth MacAlpin and the Picts. The site was selected in 1147 by that devout Norman king, David I, to plant a colony of Augustinian monks from Arrouaise (near Arras in Picardy), who also established houses at Jedburgh, St Andrews and elsewhere. The monastery prospered with the tithes from the rich lands of the Forth estuary, but, as a result of its proximity to the royal court at Stirling, it also became involved in politics, despite papal admonitions. Edward I passed by in 1303. Robert Bruce held a meeting of his nobles here in 1308 and in 1326 assembled the first parliament to include seats for burgesses as well as tenants-in- chief.

The abbots, notably Patrick Pantler (1470-1519) and his relative David, included scholars, lawyers and envoys to the courts of England and France, active in politics and foreign affairs. The abbey had its setbacks too: it was pillaged of its valuable books and ornaments while David II was away losing the war with England in the 14th century; the belfry was struck by lightning; and, of course, the Reformation mobs of 1559 did their worst to the buildings. James VI appointed an Erskine Earl of Mar as Commendator, thus entitling him to the abbey's revenues without much other responsibility, temporal or spiritual, and the buildings remained with the Erskines of Mar until they were bought by the town of Stirling in 1709. Cambuskenneth passed to the Crown in 1908 and is now cared for as an AM.

The foundations show a large cruciform church of the 13th century, a chapter house, cloister and refectory with a lavatorium for washing hands before meals. The detached belfry, in pointed Gothic style of the 13th century, common enough in Italy, is seen in Scotland in a few places, such as Muthil, Dunning and Dunblane, though in this last the tower was later joined to the cathedral. At Cambuskenneth, the roof was originally saddle-backed, like Muthil, but this has been replaced by a flat roof with a stepped battlement and a circular stair in one corner, surmounted by a cap-house.

Cambuskenneth Abbey

Cambuskenneth is linked with the strange death of James III in 1488 at Sauchieburn, close by across the Forth, near Bannockburn. Attempting to quell a revolt by his nobles, in which his own son, later James IV, took part, the King lost his nerve, fled prematurely from the battle, dropped the sword of Bruce in a ditch and was thrown from his horse. A peasant gave him refuge but one of his enemies came in and stabbed him to death. James and his Queen, Margaret of Denmark, were buried under a slab of blue Tournai stone in the abbey church. Fragments of this stone and some bones were discovered near the high altar and, on the assumption that they belonged to her Stuart ancestors, Queen Victoria had them re-buried in a new tomb.

Castle Campbell Clackmannan Central 1D4 (AM)
A Bunyanesque allegory, a Highland fortress in a romantic glen, or simply a nobleman's convenient residence, Castle Gloom (as it was called until the name was altered to Castle Campbell by royal proclamation in 1490) lies above the town of Dollar (which could be punned as dolour or woe) between the burns of Care and Sorrow. The site is superb, on the s-facing slopes of the Ochil Hills astride a narrow neck of land between the two burns, looking out over the Firth of Forth to the Pentland Hills.

The 'lands of Dollar or Glume' were held in 1465 by the Stewarts of Lorne. The three Stewart daughters married Campbells, and the estate was in 1481 acquired by Colin Campbell, 1st Earl of Argyll, when the high affairs of state required a residence nearer than distant Inveraray to the King at his capital of Stirling. After being James III's ambassador to England and to France — renewing the Auld Alliance — Argyll became in 1483 Lord High Chancellor of Scotland, and was continued in that office by James IV. Archibald, the 2nd Earl, was killed at Flodden in 1513. The 4th Earl was the first person of his rank and dignity to join the Reformed faith, as the result of a visitation in 1556 by John Knox, who preached in Castle Campbell, but probably not from the rocky knoll known locally as 'John Knox's pulpit'. He is more likely to have instructed his noble convert in the oratory in his castle. The constancy with which successive generations of Campbells adhered to the Protestant cause had important political consequences, for them and for Scotland.

Archibald, the 8th Earl and 1st Marquis of Argyll (1607-61), supported the Covenanters in the Civil Wars while his former friend James Graham, the great Marquis of Montrose, joined the Royalist cause. At the end of his brilliant Highland campaign of 1645, Montrose swept with his 'bloody Irishes' from Fife across Kinross to his last victory at Kilsyth. On the way they devastated the lands of Dollar and Muckart but, contrary to the general belief that Castle Campbell was then destroyed, Montrose's wild men probably did no more than hurl insults at the hated house of Campbell, while the Marquis dined with the Earl of Mar in Alloa. The destruction of the castle came nine years later in rather different circumstances. By 1653, Castle Campbell was garrisoned by English soldiers under General Monk, who records that 'some small parties of the enemy ... burnt Castle Campbell' in July 1654. Be that as it may, the castle ceased at this period to be a stronghold of the Campbells, for the 8th Earl was executed in 1661 for his part in proclaiming Cromwell as Lord Protector, while the 9th Earl went into exile. In 1685, he joined Monmouth in the abortive rebellion against James II of England and in 1688 he, like his father, was executed.

Castle Campbell then inevitably fell into disrepair, and was in a tumbledown state by 1880, when some renovation was carried out. In 1948 the owner, Mr J. E. Kerr, offered the castle and glen to the NTS who, with help from Dollar Academy and elsewhere, restored the amenities of the glen, making access to the castle a pleasant walk up from Dollar. The castle itself is now under care as an AM.

The buildings date from three periods. The massive 4-storey square keep with its crowstep cap-house (late 15th century), 60 ft high, dominates the rest. Access to the great hall on the first floor was originally only by the narrow stairs in the thickness of the wall: the outside wheel-stair tower was added later. The hall has a convenient prison, with a pit below it, in the SE corner. The

Castle Campbell

Castle Fraser

large courtyard (entered by a gateway from the N side) was added in the 16th century. The range of buildings on the s side rests on vaults which face the garden terrace below. In the early 17th century, the more comfortable set of lodgings was added on the E side, between the tower and the s range; access to the upper floors of this block was by two wheel-stairs, one at either end of the courtyard face. The northern and the grander of these circular stairs is cleverly devised to fit into the re-entrant angle of the main tower, thus providing access at different levels to tower and residence alike. At courtyard level, between the two stairs, is the most attractive feature of the castle — a little arcaded loggia which, Fenwick considers, 'in refined design and workmanship recalls the Great Hall at Stirling Castle'.

Castle Fraser Gordon Grampian 8 F5 (NTS)
Of all the castles of Mar, Castle Fraser is the grandest with the possible exception of Fyvie. It has neither the compactness nor the perfection of Craigievar, and the defensive character of the tower-house has, by this time, been subordinated to the ornamental. In 1575, Michael Fraser set about designing his castle on an entirely new site, where no previous castle had stood, some 15 miles (24 km.) w of Aberdeen. He made use of the traditional Z-plan: a main rectangular block with a square tower at one corner (the Michael Tower) and a round one at the diagonally opposite corner. After Michael's death in 1588, his son had rather more grandiose ideas, enlarging his father's plan both in size and in height. This later work makes Castle Fraser more magnificent than its contemporaries: the corner turrets are carried up through two floors instead of one, the cable mouldings, the stone cannons and, in particular, the huge heraldic blazon high on the N side above the original main entrance testify to his love of display.

By 1636 the building was complete, including the two low wings enclosing the entrance courtyard (one of these now houses an informative 'Castles of Mar' exhibition set up by the NTS). Originally these were the servants' quarters and are much more of a piece with the castle itself than the usual huddle of buildings which, in an earlier age, clustered inside the barmkin wall. The master masons Bell and Leiper, of whom so little is known beyond their marks on the stone, worked here.

Castle Fraser was spared most of the ravages of the Civil Wars, though Montrose did 'spoil' it in 1644. The first Lord Fraser, created a peer by Charles I, later joined the Covenanters. Subsequent lairds were Jacobites and renounced the title. The redoubtable Miss Elyza Fraser ruled in the castle from 1792 until 1814, while her male relations were fighting in the Peninsular War, of which a number of relics are preserved, including Col. Charles Fraser's cleverly articulated wooden leg.

The present entrance is through the low door on the s side of the main block into the lower Servants Hall. The kitchen is at the base of the Michael Tower, and a wide

staircase mounts to the High Hall — a splendid room; thanks to its high windows, it is light and airy despite the thick walls. The main entrance (now blocked) originally led directly into the hall through its N wall; it was approached by an imposing double staircase from the courtyard below, under the great heraldic blazon. Next door is the dining room, where mementoes of the Peninsular War are to be seen. Opening off this is the charming Peacock Parlour, or smoking room, with a portrait of Charles I painted on glass. From here it is worth climbing the steep stairs to the top of the big round tower, both for the view of the country and to see the overall plan of the castle. The cap-house on the stair-head, with its ogee-shaped lead roof, and the balustrades round the top of the tower, are probably of French inspiration and may represent the Fraser ambition to out-do neighbouring Midmar, a slightly earlier castle of very similar design. From half-way down the tower a passage leads over the hall to the so-called Worked Room, formerly the laird's study, and now a bedroom where bed-hangings and curtains are of embroidery worked by Miss Elyza Fraser and her companion. The tiny closet discovered in the sw corner of this room was reported to Sir Walter Scott and inspired his description of the 'laird's lug' in *The Fortunes of Nigel*; he does not seem to have ever visited Castle Fraser himself. It is now thought that the closet was a hiding-hole, or strong-room for documents and valuables, especially as, in the adjoining room in the Michael Tower, there is a spy-hole which enables a hidden watcher to survey a large part of the High Hall.

In 1921 Castle Fraser was acquired by Lord Cowdray, whose son, the Hon. Clive Pearson, did much careful restoration work. Lord Cowdray's grand-daughter Lavinia and her husband, Major Michael Smiley, made the castle over to the NTS in 1976. From documents in the Charter Room, Mrs Smiley has compiled a delightful booklet entitled *Life at Castle Fraser 150 years ago*.

Caterthuns, White and Brown Angus Tayside
5 E4 (AM)
Five miles NW from Brechin, the by-road to Glen Lethnot crosses the ridge separating the West Water from Strathmore. The Brown Caterthun is to the E; the White Caterthun to the w. Of the numerous Iron Age hill-forts (500 B.C.–A.D. 100), these two are the largest. The Brown Caterthun (934 ft/285 m.) has no fewer than six lines of defence enclosing a wide area of the hill-top: except for the innermost, these are of heather or turf, and hence the description of 'brown'. The outermost ring encloses a vast area of about 330 yds by 300 yds, with eight entrances.

The Brown Caterthun was at some stage abandoned in favour of the White Caterthun (978 ft/302 m.), so-called because its ring of stones shows up white on the hill-top. Approached by a grassy track westwards from the road, the White Caterthun is an oval enclosure about 170 yds long by 70 yds wide. When upright, the surrounding wall may have been an amazing 40 ft thick and outside it is another concentric wall about 20 ft thick. The tumbled stones of both now spread over 100 ft, obscuring the entrance in the south-east corner.

Whatever guesses one may hazard about the size of the population and the organisation involved in assembling this vast mass of stones, there is no doubt that the man who selected this hill-top had an eye for a view, if only for the practical purpose of observing the approach of an enemy. Up here, on a clear day, you can see E to the town of Montrose, between its basin and the North Sea, NE far into the Mearns, N into the Braes of Angus, and sw down the length of Strathmore to the Tay and beyond, with a hint of Dundee over the Sidlaw Hills.

Clackmannan District   Central   1 C5

With a population of 47,600 in an area of 55 square miles, the 'wee coonty' of Clackmannan enjoys all the advantages of a neat, compact and self-contained community, with no necessity to spend its revenues on lengthy roads to distant villages. Moreover, its towns are on the flat alluvial lands between the winding estuary of the Forth, giving access to the sea, and the steep south-facing scarp of the Ochil Hills, their picturesque, deep-cut glens providing water and power. What geologists term the Ochil Fault runs in a straight line from Blairlogie in the W to beyond Dollar in the E, making an extra-ordinarily abrupt change from the steep, almost precipitous hills, with their modest summits in Dumyat Peak (1,373 ft/419 m.), Ben Cleuch (2,328 ft/710 m.) and King's Seat, to the flat valley of the River Devon. The name of 'Hillfoots', given to the towns and villages of Menstrie, Alva, Tillycoultry and Dollar, is very apt.

Before the Kincardine road bridge was built across the Forth in 1936, Clackmannanshire commanded the through route from Fife to Stirling — not always to its advantage, for the French troops brought in by Marie de Guise retreated this way from St Andrews in 1559 (with some looting en route), and Montrose's 'Irishes' wreaked havoc in Alloa, while their leader was dining with the Earl of Mar in Alloa Tower. This 13th-century tower was the birthplace of 'Bobbing John', the Earl of Mar who started the 1715 Rising. It is still the residence of the Earls of Mar and Kellie. Alloa is now a thriving industrial town of some 14,000 inhabitants, and has replaced Clackmannan as the county town. Like Alloa, Clackmannan has a prominent rectangular tower, in this case ascribed to Robert the Bruce and now under restoration as an AM. The earliest part is late-14th-century, and there are later additions. Clackmannan old town has its charm, with restored houses, its imposing Tolbooth and the Mercat Cross beside the Clach Mannan, or Stone of Mannan — a pre-Celtic pagan deity whose name survives in Slamannan and the Isle of Man.

DOLLAR (probably from Gaelic dol-lar, the ploughed meadow) has nothing to do with the 'dolour' associated with the 'lands of Glume' of Castle Campbell (q.v.) which

The Mannan Stone and Belfry, Clackmannan

lies up the steep glen behind. In contrast to the industrial towns of Alloa and Tillycoultry, Dollar is largely concerned with education and is noted for its famous Academy, built in 1818 by the Greek Revival architect William Playfair, who designed the Academy and National Gallery in Edinburgh.

With all the advantages of scenic beauty, natural resources, thriving industry and good communications it is no wonder that Clackmannanshire was able to maintain its identity as a District under the regionalisation arrangements of 1975. Small is, if not beautiful throughout, at least administratively satisfying.

Claypotts Castle   Angus   Tayside   2 G1   (AM)

Claypotts is in strong contrast to the elegant tower-houses of Aberdeenshire or the Mearns, though built at much the same period — the late 16th century. This ungainly building now finds itself incongruously situated at a busy crossroads 5 miles E of the centre of Dundee and in the middle of a modern housing estate.

The 'Tower Fortalice and Mannor Place' of Claypotts is a well-preserved Z-plan tower-house, built primarily for defence — and defence, moreover, against and by the new-fangled firearm, unlike the four-square 'keep' towers of the bow and arrow era. Two squat round towers at the diagonally opposite corners of the central keep cover all approaches and make awkward corners for attackers. The original tiny windows, the rough, massive stonework and the parapet walks, all emphasize the essentially defensive character. So do the wide-splayed gun-ports at ground level, one pointing straight at the round stair tower which has had to be deeply channelled to allow the free passage of shot. Three storeys up, a pair of quaint rectangular 'cottages', corbelled out to the square, perch awkwardly on the round towers, and a similar structure, also with its own crow-stepped gable, crowns the main tower. These garrets, or watch-chambers, are quite unlike the fanciful superstructures of Craigievar or Crathes. The only external concession to ornament is the Renaissance dormer window with pilasters and fan-shaped tympanum on the sw tower. Within, however, more provision was made for comfort than in the earlier rectangular keeps: the private rooms are larger and lighter and the garderobes or latrines were closed off. The original windows, shuttered and protected by iron grilles, were replaced by the present sash windows in the late 17th century.

The lands of Claypotts were in the hands of the Strachan family in the early 16th century. The English invasion of 1547 led to the occupation of nearby Broughty Castle for two years, and Claypotts may have been involved in the fighting. Perhaps it was this, and the general uncertainty of the times, that induced John Strachan, fearful for the safety of his seven children, to build Claypotts. Though work began in 1569, as indicated

on the s tower, and was not completed until 1588, according to the date on the N tower, the castle seems to have been planned and built as a whole. John Strachan died in 1593, and eight years later Claypotts was sold, first to the Grahams of Ballunie and then to a Claverhouse ancestor of 'Bonnie Dundee'. The latter rarely visited Claypotts, and, after 1689, all his lands were forfeited to the Crown. In the 18th century they passed to the Douglases, and through them to the Earls of Home, to whom Claypotts still belongs, though placed under care as an AM in 1926.

Comrie Perthshire Tayside 1 B3 (*pop. 2,000*)
Comrie (from the Gaelic *comar*, the meeting of the waters) justifies its name, for the Lednock from the N and the Water of Ruchil, flowing down Glen Artney from the sw, join the Earn at this pleasant village favoured by holiday-makers and retired people. Until the mid 18th century, Comrie was the important last stage for drovers coming from the West Highlands to sell their cattle at the Crieff Tryst, or later at Falkirk. Comrie's trim white church (1805) with a stumpy spire, in the main street, is now a youth centre. The Gothic building to the w is the present kirk for Comrie and Strowan.

The little suburb known as The Ross was the centre of a flourishing weaving trade which specialised in tartan until it was suppressed after the Forty Five. The Museum of Tartans in the main street of Comrie, maintained by the Scottish Tartan Society, entertainingly presents the

Claypotts Castle

largest collection of records relating to tartans and Highland dress, including a library of prints, maps and details of every known tartan. In the 18th century, patterns of tartan cloth were numbered and supplied to Highland gentlemen for themselves, and as a kind of uniform for their retinues, even for their slaves in the West Indies. It was not until Sir Walter Scott, on the occasion of George IV's visit to Scotland in 1822, urged the clan chiefs to get their tartans sorted out that the meticulous association of tartans with clans became part of Scottish tradition. An 8 ft-high portrait of Queen Victoria's famous man-servant, John Brown, dominates the 'Balmorality' corner of the museum, which recently acquired his kilt and accoutrements. Behind the museum is a reconstructed 18th-century weaver's cottage and a garden with wild plants for the identification of the original vegetable dyes.

The rocks of the Highland Boundary Fault, following the line of Glen Artney and on past Crieff, are still settling gently, giving Comrie its unusual reputation for earthquake tremors. None of these have been of great severity, though the biggest one in 1839 damaged some walls. Earthquakes have been recorded at irregular intervals since 1789. Local seismological enthusiasts, a shoemaker and the postmaster, studied the shocks in the 19th century, measuring 7,300 tremors in the 1830s. In 1869, they built a strange little 'earthquake house' (which still stands on the outskirts of The Ross) to contain their elementary seismograph. Their work continued until it was taken over by the more sophisticated seismological centre at Eskdalemuir in Dumfrieshire.

The little burgh was dominated by the Dundas family. The tall Melville Monument of 1812 on the hill to the N does not allow Comrie to forget Henry Dundas (1742-1811), Viscount Melville, whose ruined mansion of Dunira lies under the wooded hills to the w of the monument. For nearly 30 years he managed Scotland so effectively by the exercise of patronage and by his control of the Scottish Members of Parliament that he became known as King Harry the Ninth, and his rule as the Dundas Despotism. He resigned in 1803 on accusations of corruption. His last public act was to build the new road from Comrie to Lochearnhead 'to the full breadth required by law and in the best possible direction' at his own expense.

From the w end of Comrie a road winds up below the Melville Monument, leaving the De'il's Cauldron — a waterfall accessible on foot from Comrie — below on the right. The road continues up the open Glen Lednock, passing the water-slide of Rollo Spout, spreading like a fan over the rock, to end at the Hydro-Electric dam of Loch Lednock.

The road sw from Comrie follows the Water of Ruchil up Glen Artney, made famous by the first canto of Scott's *Lady of the Lake*, where the stag which led Fitzjames to Ellen's Isle 'deep his midnight lair had made, in lone Glen Artney's hazel shade'. The motor road ends by Glen Artney Lodge, where the glen divides: an easy walking route leads w over to Callander; another follows the wide upper glen past the E slopes of Ben Vorlich (3,224 ft/985 m.) down to Loch Earn at Ardvorlich (*see* Loch Earn).

Corgarff Castle Gordon Grampian 7 B6 (AM)
On the s side of the 2,090 ft (635 m.) Lecht Pass from Tomintoul to Strathdon by the A939 there is a spectacular view-point just before the last steep descent to the hamlet of Cockbridge. The ring of summits, from The Cairngorm on the right, past the long, tor-strewn ridge of Ben Avon to Lochnagar, encircles the white-harled tower of Corgarff standing out boldly in the valley of the Don below. One melodramatic journalist described it early this century as a 'grim monster brooding over a desolation'; it was then a stark grey, half-roofed building. Despite its sinister history, Corgarff in its recently restored state scarcely justifies this shudder of horror today.

Originally belonging to the Earls of Mar, the land passed in 1453 to the Elphinstones, one of whom built this castle keep in 1537. In 1571, it was in the hands of the Forbes, and when her laird was away Lady Forbes moved here for safety with her family and servants. The terrible tragedy that followed was popularised by the ballad *Edom o' Gordon*. A marauding party of Gordons from Auchindoun (q.v.), whether or not under the leadership of Adam Gordon ('who reck'd not sin nor shame'), burnt the tower to the ground, and all 24 inhabitants perished in the flames. The 'grund-wa' stone', removed by the treacherous Jock of the ballad to introduce the fire, was the moveable stone blocking the lower end of the chute from the garderobe. According to the ballad, Lady Forbes' younger son besought his mother to 'gie owre your house, for the reek it smithers me', but his mother replied 'I winna gie up my house, my dear, to nae sik traitor as he'. The Forbes laird returned to find 'baith lady and babes burnt'.

Corgarff came back into the hands of the Earls of Mar in 1626. Montrose made use of it in his marches through these hills in 1644-5. Burnt in 1689 by the Jacobites, it was used as a rendezvous for some of Mar's forces in 1715. The Hanoverian Government took it over to deny it to the Jacobites, who were nonetheless back in occupation in 1745. They left in a hurry before the troops of Lord Ancrum, who found 'no living being within the house but a poor cat sitting by the fire'. A strong-point on the military road to Fort George, Corgarff was garrisoned until 1831, first for hunting down rebels, and later to control whisky-smuggling over the Ladder Hills from the Braes of Glenlivet to Perthshire and the Lowlands.

Despite this troubled history, Corgarff's stark tower survived more or less intact. In 1748 two wings or 'pavilions' were added to the tower and, as at Braemar Castle, the whole enclosed by the zigzag curtain-wall with slits for muskets, adequate to repel marauders but no defence against artillery.

The officers' rooms on the first floor, the men's barracks above with their box-beds, accommodating 21

Corgarff Castle

out of the 45 men of the garrison (the rest presumably being on patrol), the vaulted cellars used as prison or stores and the cobbled courtyard are all well displayed. This successful restoration was initiated by the owners, Sir Ernest and Lady Stockdale, in 1972 and carried out by the AM in whose care the castle now is. Some would dispute, however, whether the white harling is historically the correct protection for the original rough rubble-facing.

Corrichie, Battle of   Kincardine and Deeside
Grampian   8 F6
The Hill of Fare (1,545 ft / 471 m.) is a broad moorland hill N of Banchory (q.v.), the first to loom above the lower land to any traveller westbound from Aberdeen. Its SE flank is breached by a little burn — the Burn of Corrichie. Where it crosses the B977, the Deeside Field Club have erected a tall granite stone commemorating the battle that took place on 28 October 1562 on the hill above. For Mary, Queen of Scots, the battle was the tragic end of what had started as a peaceful royal progress through the North-East, a pleasant part of her domains governed by the powerful Gordons, Earls of Huntly, Catholics like herself. In August 1562 Mary set out from Stirling, accompanied by her elder half-brother James, the illegitimate son of James V, and travelled by way of Glamis to Aberdeen with the plan of continuing to Inverness. The insolent behaviour of the good-looking fourth son of the Earl of Huntly, Sir John Gordon, was a foretaste of what was to come. He had been involved in a scandal with Lady Ogilvie of Findlater and had twice escaped from jail. Now he was casting strong hints that he was a suitable consort for the Queen herself. John Gordon and his horsemen harried the royal party across the Garioch and he later

admitted he had a plan to abduct the Queen. Mary wisely by-passed his father's castle of Huntly in Strathbogie, and headed for Darnaway, the Moray castle near Nairn where James was invested as Earl of Moray, and given some Gordon lands as well.

On her return, she was again pursued by the ambitious (or amorous) John Gordon, but was back in Aberdeen unscathed on 22 September, after calling on the Bishop of Moray in his palace at Spynie by Elgin. In Aberdeen, Mary and Moray decided that Gordon disobedience must be punished. Emissaries were sent to Huntly Castle to demand its surrender, but the Earl and his sons had taken to the hills, where guerrilla warfare might have continued indefinitely. However, Lady Huntly, encouraged by a witch's prophecy that the Earl would lie in Aberdeen without a wound on his body, egged on her husband to take the offensive.

Huntly marched on 27 October southward through Echt to camp near the stone circle of Cullerlie. Meanwhile, Moray had marched out from Aberdeen and camped within striking distance at Garlogie. On 28 October, after a preliminary skirmish, Huntly's forces retreated up the east flank of the Hill of Fare. Moray moved his main force westwards, along what is now the B977, to the Burn of Corrichie, turning up into the hill to outflank Huntly on the flat eastern summit. Confusion and treachery played their part, and the Gordons were driven down to be slaughtered in the upper basin of the Corrichie burn which, according to the ballad, 'has run this day with bleid'. The tradition that Mary watched the battle from the spot marked Queen's Chair on the map is not substantiated. Huntly and two of his sons were taken prisoner, but dramatically, at the moment of capture, the corpulent earl 'bristit and swelt, spake nae word bot decessit' — in other words, had a stroke and died. His body did lie in Aberdeen that night, as the witch had foretold, and it was embalmed to stand trial for treason, by the grisly custom of the day, in Edinburgh. His son Adam Gordon (of Auchindoun) was reprieved, to become the villain of the burning of Corgarff (q.v.) 9 years later. The presumptuous John was clearly destined for immediate execution in Aberdeen. According to Antonia Fraser, Moray compelled Mary to watch the 'heiding' of John Gordon by the Maiden (an early form of guillotine) in order to dispel rumours that the Queen had some affection for him. But the executioner bungled the job and Mary broke down in tears, thereby lending colour to John Knox's accusations that she was John Gordon's lover and providing material for the ballad-writer:

For Huntley's stalwart son
Wis heidit on Heidin' hill . . .
Cruel Murry gart the waeful quine luke out
And see her lover and liges slain.

Coxton Tower   Moray   Grampian   7 B1
Just S of the A96, two miles E of Elgin, is the diminutive Coxton Tower, a miniature but perfect example of a

tower-house. Medieval in concept and built to withstand any attack short of artillery, the Coxton Tower was completed as late as 1644 by Sir Alexander Innes, who considered a tower-house the only safe and suitable residence for a laird. Before the stone forestair was built, the only access to the first floor was by a wooden ladder that could be drawn up from within.

The square tower stands nearly 60 ft high on four floors, each floor being vaulted in alternate directions - a solid form of construction to enable the walls, a mere $4\frac{1}{2}$ ft thick, to withstand the weight of the building above, all of stone with little or no timber. The high pointed roof rises between two crowstep gables; two of the corners are topped by stumpy over-sailing turrets with conical helmets: a third carries a square open turret with miniature battlements and machicolations. The windows are diminutive and, like the doorway, most are protected by solid iron yetts (grilles). Communication between the four rooms, on top of one another, was originally by means of hatches in the floors and ladders. The Innes coat of arms with the date 1644 appears over the first-floor entrance, with 'R.I.' for Robert and 'A.I.' for his grandson Alexander.

Only stubborn devotion to the traditional and primitive building arrangements of the previous 300 years could have inspired this highly inconvenient residence for a gentleman of the mid-17th century, when some degree of comfort and security were to be

Coxton Tower

expected. As late as 1708, the 4th laird, who fought at Killiecrankie, was still using the tower and still climbing in by ladder. His successor, alas, a 'weak and indolent man much given to the bottle', sold the tower in 1714 to the Duff banking family. It came into the hands of the present owner's family in 1910. Access is by appointment.

Craigievar Castle Gordon   Grampian 8 E 5 (NTS)
Some 25 miles w of Aberdeen, Craigievar (a corruption of the 'rock of Mar') enjoys no great strategic position. Architecturally, it is the most perfect and the least altered of that wonderful group of Aberdeenshire 17th-century tower-houses that flourished between the end of the troubles of the Reformation and the beginning of the Civil Wars (say, 1570-1639). With turrets and gables topping a sturdy tower, but nonetheless spacious within, Craigievar justifies Stewart Cruden's claim that it has 'a Scottish place in the front rank of European architecture. . . . Quite perfect . . . it is the apotheosis of its type'.

The Mortimer family sold the estate in 1610 to William Forbes, the younger son of the Forbes from neighbouring Corse Castle (now a ruin), some 2 miles to the N, and brother of the Bp Patrick Forbes of Aberdeen. William, whose episcopal brother backed his initial venture with God Almighty as his bondsman, prospered in the Danzig trade, earning his nickname of Danzig Willie. He was a good example of a cultured laird who, having made his fortune, was wise enough to use it, with the help of the master mason 'I. Bel', who also worked on Castle Fraser (q.v.), to create another architectural masterpiece.

The building and interior decorations were completed in 1626, just after Charles I came to the throne, and four years before Danzig Willie's death in 1630. His grandson, known as 'Red Sir John', succeeded in 1648, and thereafter Craigievar's lairds, who married into the Sempill family and later inherited the title of Lord Sempill, enjoyed a peaceful existence, though an intruding Gordon was once forced at sword point out of an upper window, and Gilderoy, the local marauding Macgregor, raided it from his hide-out at the Burn o' Vat. Since 1963 Craigievar has been in the care of the NTS.

This lovely building, rising sturdily yet gracefully from its terrace, is harled a pale apricot colour, setting off the pinkish dressed granite of the exposed courses. Bell's mastery lies in the skilful blending of foreign and native Scottish influences. The basic L-plan of the house, a rectangular tower-house, with a jutting wing and a square tower set in the re-entrant angle, is purely Scottish. But the upper three storeys of this six-storeyed building are a glorious cluster of crowstep gables, conical turrets and ogee helmets, recalling nothing so much as the distant silhouette of Bruges. This was the period when it was thought safe enough to start the transformation of a traditional laird's fortalice into a gentleman's comfortable residence, while retaining the tower-house design. Nonetheless it was as well to be secure, and Danzig Willie's mansion has only one strongly fortified entrance — a

Craigievar Castle

heavily studded door backed by a strong iron yett or grille. Higher up the building, architectural tricks could be played; for instance, those stone cannon projecting from below the turrets could not possibly fire anything — they are only gargoyles to carry off the rainwater. Craigievar also illustrates the dispute over the merits of the angle turret, which dominated castles in the 16th century, and those of the more attractive gable which gained in popularity as the need for defensive turrets receded. At Craigievar, the plump, two-storey turrets are the main theme on the s face; round the corner, a crowstep gable fills the short w wall; but surprise comes on the N where half a gable and half a turret share each of the corners; and the whole is topped by a renaissance balustrade and two ogee-helmeted turrets quite unrelated to the conical turrets.

Once past the fortified entrance door, a single flight of stairs rises to the right (instead of the traditional spiral stair, which was more easily defended). Above the Great Hall, the spiral stairs, in fact vertical corridors, are ingeniously contrived, providing for the inhabitants (and now for the visitor) one way up, and another way down,

The Great Hall, Craigievar Castle

by the so-called secret stair. On the first floor is the Great Hall, architecturally a completely medieval room, with groin-vaulting and a minstrels' gallery, but superbly decorated in Renaissance plaster-work. The Gothic fireplace is dominated by a huge plaster display of the royal arms of the United Kingdom; it is the finest thing of its kind in Scotland, even outdoing the Gordon fireplace at Huntly (q.v.). The plaster-work of the ceiling shows the initials of Willie (M.W.F.) and his wife Marjorie Woodward (M.W.), and a series of medallions cast in moulds of biblical and classical figures — Joshua, David, Alexander the Great, and even that inglorious Roman

emperor Jovian (Iovinianus, in the medallion) who succeeded Julian the Apostate. This intricate plaster-work, using identical moulds in various combinations, became fashionable at this time. Peculiarities of the moulds, such as a reversed letter 'D', can be traced in other ceilings, for instance at Glamis.

The narrow spiral stairs lead first to the Queen's Bedroom, so named by the 1st laird in the hope of a royal visit; then to the nursery floor. On the fifth floor is a long gallery used in early days as a baronial court, then as a fashionable drawing room, and now housing a display of family documents. Above this, by climbing to the roof, one can see the juxtaposition of turret and gable on their own level, and enjoy the view over the peaceful Aberdeenshire countryside.

To avoid disappointment, remember that Craigievar is only open in the afternoons after 2 p.m., and then only on certain days of the week, according to season.

Craigston Castle Banff and Buchan Grampian 8 F 2
Five miles NE of Turriff, Craigston is a remarkable place - remarkable for its unusual architecture and for the extraordinary literary figure whose works are enshrined in the library. From the W front of the substantial five-storey rectangular keep there project two equally tall gabled wings, the gap between them being bridged at fourth-floor level by an arch 36 ft up, surmounted by an ornate balcony (the porch at the foot is a later addition, obscuring the original doorway). The balcony is supported on a rich and varied series of corbels, topped by animal-headed water-spouts. The bays of the balcony are decorated with five roundels showing armoured knights, a gloomy-looking piper and a figure of David with his sling. One striking feature of the facade is the manner in which the long horizontal quoins (or corner-stones) are left in the original red sandstone to stand out against the white-harled walls. Another is elaborate corbelling at the corners, which looks as if it were

intended to support turrets that were never built. The library runs along the whole floor above the arch, and the gabled roofs of the two wings are joined above the balcony by a flat-topped balustraded belvedere. The low, two-storey wings to N and S were added in the 18th century.

As the panel to the right of the porch so precisely states, Craigston was built between 14 March 1604 and 8 December 1607 by Sir John Urquhart, Tutor of Cromarty, whose armorial bearings appear in the left-hand panel. He was tutor to his nephew, Sir Thomas Urquhart of Cromarty, father of that other Thomas Urquhart (1611-1660), the eccentric translator of Rabelais, a writer on trigonometry, the chronicler of his own genealogy and the inventor of a new language. His *Trissotetras*, though using obscure terms, 'published for the benefit of the mathematically affected', is well in advance of his time. His Rabelais runs to 200,000 words as against 130,000 of the original French, for instance increasing the famous Rabelaisian list of animal noises from 9 to 71. In the genealogy, he claims to be 153rd in descent from Adam and 146th from Eve, dating Noah's flood to 2893 B.C. And his *Logopandectics, or Introduction to a Universal Language* invented an impossible new language with 11 cases, 4 numbers, 4 voices, 7 moods and 11 tenses! His output was fantastic, written at a speed that kept pace with the

Craigston Castle

printer, and his memory remarkable in being able to reproduce manuscripts lost in the confusion after the Battle of Worcester in 1651. Thomas Urquhart had supported his unwarlike monarch in this disaster, but, nine years later, he is said to have died of laughing on hearing that Charles II, then in exile in France, was to be restored to the throne.

In the last quarter of the 17th century, Craigston passed out of the direct Urquhart line and came into the hands of the acquisitive Patrick Duff, whose wife Mary Urquhart bore him 23 out of his total of 36 children. But in 1739 her brother Captain John Urquhart (1696-1756), known as The Pirate, was able to buy back Craigston with the fortune he had made as a privateer on the high seas - a respectable way of making money in the 18th century. He has left a list of 'Dangers Escaped' which include numerous adventures at sea, and not being killed at Sheriffmuir in 1715, though this led to his exile, and 'Blissings received'. A most interesting character, his portrait by Trevisani hangs in the Great Hall, together with that of his comrade-in- arms James Keith, who later became a Prussian field-marshal.

Another delight of Craigston is the set of early-17th-century carved oak panels with vigorous, if somewhat unimaginative, portraits of traditional heroes, including Scander Beg, the 15th-century Albanian national hero, the six Kings James of Scotland, Biblical figures including David, Joshua and 'Judasma' (or Judas Maccabeus) and representations of the six Virtues — similar to the subjects to be seen on the painted ceilings of Crathes (q.v.). These panels are inserted in the shutters and doors of the original Great Hall, now divided into ante-room and dining room.

The present Urquhart, owner of Craigston, is justifiably proud of his castle and its possessions. He allows visitors by appointment.

Crathes Castle Gordon Grampian 5 G2 (NTS)
Less ambitious than Castle Fraser, less architecturally perfect than Craigievar, Crathes is nonetheless a most satisfying place, both for the wealth of its internal decorations and for the glory of its gardens. Situated about 2 miles E of Banchory (q.v.), Crathes rises among the trees on the N bank of the Dee. The strong lower walls, the single entrance and the formidable yett all emphasize the continued need for defence, but the relative peace and growing prosperity of the latter half of the 16th century allowed the laird and his master masons, probably the Bells who also worked at Midmar and Castle Fraser, to give full play to their architectural fancies in the upper storeys. Closer inspection shows that no sentry could effectively mount guard in these corner turrets, which are now little studies or garderobes, that those projecting stone cannon are just water-spouts, and that the machicolations which once supported the battlements have become no more than a line of ornamental corbelling. Even the projecting dormer window above the front door is not for pouring boiling oil on unwanted visitors but for hauling goods to the top floor. The roof-line, less spectacular than at Craigievar, is nonetheless a fascinating array of crowstep gables, corbelling, turret, chimney and even a pair of little cottages at the corners. The impressiveness of the tower-house is somewhat marred by the low 18th-century wing through which the present-day visitor enters. This, together with a Victorian addition burnt down in 1966, was the residence of the Leys family until Crathes was made over to the NTS in 1952.

In 1323, Alexander de Burnard was appointed by Robert the Bruce Royal Forester, one of the two guardians of the royal hunting forest outside Aberdeen, the other being Irvine of Drum (q.v.). The family, who adapted their name to Burnett, first chose as their residence an island-site in the Loch of the Leys (now drained), and became known as Burnett of the Leys (rhyming with days). It was not until 1553 that Sir Alexander Burnett decided to move from this rather damp residence and to start building the fine castle which took more than 40 years to complete. The slowness of the work was due less to the brief interruption of the tranquil life of Deeside by the Battle of Corrichie in 1562 than to the deaths of two Burnett lairds in quick succession. The laird who lived to enjoy this splendid creation was Sir Thomas Burnett (d. 1653). Though nominally a Covenanter, he kept on good terms with Montrose and Huntly and prevented his lands from being overrun by either side in the Civil Wars.

The interior of Crathes has a number of unusual features, including the famous painted ceilings. The High Hall on the first floor is well lit by the big Renaissance window in the s wall; before this was broken out there was a third window in the w wall where the fireplace now stands. The walls are stripped back to the original stone, but may have once been decorated with moulded plaster work, as in Craigievar. Five of the family portraits in the Hall are by the Scottish 'Van Dyck', George Jamesone of Aberdeen (1586-1644), and include Sir Thomas Burnett, the 1st Baronet; the sixth portrait is by Peter Lely of Gilbert Burnett, Bishop of Salisbury from 1684 to 1715, who chastised Charles II for his immorality and made a successful comeback with William of Orange. The great treasure in the High Hall is the Horn of the Leys, of fluted ivory with four bands of gilt and three crystals, given by Robert the Bruce as a token of the grant of his lands. Above the High Hall, reached by the winding main stair, is the laird's room, now furnished as a Victorian bedroom, but formerly used as his study, where the laird interviewed his visitors. A private stair (used by present-day visitors on the way down) also communicates to the Hall below.

In the next rooms are the painted wooden ceilings, a form of art rare in England, deriving from the painted vaults of pre-Reformation churches of Scandinavia and Germany. Examples in churches in Scotland are to be seen at St Mary's Church by Grandtully (q.v.) and at

Delgatie Castle (q.v.). By the Civil War, the fashion for painted ceilings had given way to plaster-work ceilings, as at Glamis, Craigievar and Muchalls. The Crathes ceilings therefore date from soon after the completion of the castle, say 1600. With their firm black lines and vivid coloured figures, they are among the best of their kind. In the first of the three rooms are the Nine Nobles — three pagan heroes, Hector, Alexander and Julius Caesar; three Old Testament heroes, Joshua, David and Judas Maccabeus; and three Christian, King Arthur, Charlemagne and Godfrey de Bouillon. Next comes the Green Lady's Room, named from the ghost of an unfortunate young girl and her child, said to have been murdered by her lover: and it is true that a baby's skeleton was found in this very room. Here, inscriptions on the beams are quotations from the Bible or moral maxims such as 'Flie sone all naughtie companie, From fools no freindship crave, Keep fellowship with such as be Both wittie, sane and grave'.

The main stairs continue upwards to the Long Gallery, where the ceiling is not painted but beautifully panelled in oak. The armorial shields down the centre represent the arms of contemporary Burnetts, Hamiltons, Setons and other families. A narrow stair leads down again, first to the Green Lady's Room, then to the Laird's Bedroom (adjoining his study) with its great four-poster bed, carved with the date 1597 and numerous heraldic devices. Part way down a side-door leads to the Muses Room, the last of the rooms with painted ceilings. This is equipped as a music room, where the seven virtues of Temperance, Fortitude, Wisdom, Justice, Faith, Hope and Charity adorn the ceiling beams. The stair ends in the Stone Hall on the ground floor.

The garden is virtually six separate, though interlocking, enclosures with names such as the Trough, Rose or Fountain Gardens, and also the Camel Garden built round two humps, covering in all about six acres. The arrangement of hedges, walls and borders gives a delightful intimacy, as well as practical shelter for the plants. The gardens are open throughout the year, even when the castle is closed, but are at their best between May and September. The great yew hedges of the formal garden near the castle date from 1702, but the effective development took place in the 1930s. Then the happy partnership of Sir James Burnett, with his interest in roses, trees and shrubs from all parts of the world, and of Lady Burnett, with her flair for the juxtaposition of colours and textures of flowers and foliage, created this series of remarkable gardens, on the lines of Hidcote Manor in the Cotswolds, or Sissinghurst in Kent. The NTS Handbook to Crathes gives a detailed description with a list of plants of special interest. One should not miss the Pool Garden, the White Border and, especially, the diagonal June border, a tapestry of lupins, poppies, iris and asphodel lining both sides of a path leading from a charming doocot, with its own little garden of heathers and azalea, towards the great bulk of the castle. Since the NTS took over, a

Crathes Castle

delicious Golden Garden has been laid out as a memorial to Lady Burnett.

Crathie   *see* Balmoral

Crieff Perthshire Tayside 1 C3 (*pop.* 5,603)
A pleasant little town with steep streets climbing up the scarp of the Highland Boundary Fault, Crieff overlooks Strathearn. Previously known as Drummond, being associated with the Drummond family, now Earls of Perth, the town was, like Auchterarder, destroyed by the Jacobite army retreating in 1715 after Sheriffmuir. The ancient name of Crieff was then restored, derived from *crubha cnoic* (hilltop in the trees), the Knock of Crieff (911 ft/278 m.) which rises behind the golf-course. This is a fine view-point with an indicator.

Crieff was an important centre for the Earls of Strathearn, who held an outdoor court here at which a fair number of Highland miscreants were condemned to the 'kindly gallows tree'. For well over 100 years, the Crieff tryst was the most important market for the sale of cattle driven over the hills and down the glens from as far away as Skye. It had declined in importance by 1770 in favour of Falkirk, more accessible to English buyers. Crieff, now the second largest town in Perthshire, flourishes on light industry, which includes the well-known Strathearn glass factory, and on the tourist trade.

There is not much of antiquity to be seen in the town. The old cross of the Regality of Drummond stands at the corner of the town hall, which, in 1842, replaced the old jail of 1665; the 'jougs' or stocks at its foot were in use until 1816. Across the street is a 10th-century Celtic cross-slab, known as the Cross of Crieff, but probably brought from an adjoining village. The bridge over the River Earn dates from 1690 and was only partially demolished by the Jacobites. The A822 leads from it s past a remarkable geological feature, a volcanic dyke of greenstone, like a long wall rising out of the fields, known as Concraig. The first Drummonds were Knights of Concraig and the remains of the 15th-century castle are nearby. All that is left is the keep, now maintained as an armoury museum, the rest having been damaged by Cromwell's men in 1651, and again in 1715 by the Countess of Perth herself, to deny it to the Hanoverians. The well laid-out Italian-style gardens (open to the public) are in the formal style of Pitmedden and Edzell, with an elaborate sundial. West of Crieff, near Monzievaird, is the tall obelisk commemorating General Sir David Baird (1757-1829), who fought against Tippoo Sahib of Mysore and won the battle of Seringapatam in 1792. Three miles s of Crieff is the 18th-century village of Muthil (formerly Moot-hill), largely destroyed, like Auchterarder, by the Jacobites after their defeat at Sheriffmuir in 1715. The saddle-back 70 ft-high tower, mainly 12th century with foundations dating back to the 9th century, and the ruined nave and choir are all that remain of the pre-Reformation church, rebuilt in 1430.

The Howe of Cromar   Gordon Grampian· 7 D6
Cromar is perhaps the most perfect of the hill-encircled basins, or howes, of the North-East. The Howe of Alford and the Howe of the Mearns are further from the high hills and have been used as through routes since time immemorial. Cromar is sheltered on the w by the great hump of Morven (2,861 ft/872 m.), the last high easterly outlier of the Cairngorms, of which Byron so light-heartedly wrote 'When I roved a young Highlander o'er this dark heath, And climbed thy steep summit, oh Morven of snow!'. To the N are the Donside hills and to the s the hillocky Muir of Dinnet. Cromar is best approached from the N by the A97 from Donside, or from the NE by the A974 from Aberdeen. Either road, as it tops the rim of the Cromar basin, discloses a stupendous view over Deeside, from the A97 southwards into the purple hills of the Mounth, or westwards into the high Cairngorms beyond Braemar.

It is a place of great antiquity: there is a recumbent stone circle at Tomnaverie (AM), and the descent from the Slack (slochd or gap) of Tarland by the A974 passes, at CULSH (AM), a well-preserved example of a Pictish earth-house, souterrain, or weem, which is worth a brief visit. After groping (with a torch provided at the neighbouring farm) into the curving, stone-lined, dead-end tunnel, one

is left puzzling whether this was store-house, refuge, stable or dwelling-place.

Cromar (one of the parts of the old Earldom of Mar, others being Bramar (q.v.) and Midmar (q.v.)) centres on the pleasant little village of TARLAND. The 'big hoose' was formerly the residence of 'We Twa', the well-known Marquis of Aberdeen (Viceroy of Ireland and Governor-General of Canada) and his wife. As Alastrean House, it is now an R.A.F. Rest Centre, established by the MacRobert Trust which also manages the superbly well-farmed lands of Cromar. The Trust was established in memory of the three sons of Sir Alexander and Lady MacRobert, killed in service with the R.A.F. between 1938 and 1941.

To the sw, among the birch-clad hillocks of the Muir of Dinnet (now a Nature Reserve — see Dee), which is in fact the terminal moraine of the former Deeside glacier, are the two 'kettle-hole' lochs of Davan and Kinord. To the SE of the Howe is Coull, with a castle ruined long ago by Wallace. This was the seat of the once-powerful Durward family, the 'door-ward' of Scotland, of whom Alan Durward (d. 1268) was Regent during the minority of Alexander III. The Durward rule extended over the hills to the E, out of the Howe into the adjoining hollow of Lumphanan. Here is the great Peel of LUMPHANAN (AM), the Durward stronghold before Coull, described as a 'first-rate and rare example of a shell-keep, i.e. enclosure castle on a mound, protected by a wall round the summit, earthworks and ditches round the base'. The term 'peel' derives from the wood paling protecting the defenders, which, in the 12th century, developed into a stone wall.

Nearby, in Lumphanan Wood — not, as Shakespeare's play alleges, at Dunsinane (q.v.) — Macbeth met his death. Having escaped the noose closing round Dunsinane, he fled over the Mounth to regain his homeland of Moray, but was intercepted here by Macduff who killed him in a hand-to-hand battle hereabouts. A Macbeth's Cairn on the hill to the N of the modern village of Lumphanan is of prehistoric origin, and not the grave of Macbeth, who was buried with other Scottish kings on Iona.

Culbin Sands   see **Findhorn**

Culblean   see **Dee**

Cullen   Moray Grampian 7 D1
Cullen, 'the pearl of the Banffshire coast', is an attractive seaside resort on the Moray Firth. A mile of golden sand, with the isolated rock pillars known as the Three Kings, stretches w to Portknockie. To the E, Cullen Bay is overlooked by Castle Hill, beyond which the fearsomely jagged coast extends towards Portsoy. The town of Cullen is in two parts. Down on the shore are the painted fisher-cottages (now mainly holiday homes) and the twisting lanes of the Seatown (the 'Seton' of George Macdonald's novels). The upper town, with spacious square and broad main street, was sited here in 1822 by the Earl of Seafield, who objected to the village of Old Cullen

Findlater Castle

being so close to his great house half a mile away. The two parts of the town are divided by the nine arches of the spectacular railway viaduct on the coastal branch (opened in 1884, closed in 1964) of the former Great North of Scotland Railway. The viaducts (there are in fact three) were built because the old Countess of Seafield refused to have the trains run near Cullen House. There is a fine view through the largest arch over the Seatown onto the sandy bay, with its white rollers.

The history of Cullen is closely bound up with the Earls of Seafield and Findlater, whose family name is Ogilvie. In 1445, an early Ogilvie fortified the rocky point 2 miles E of Cullen on which now stand the ruins of Findlater Castle. This can be reached by a short walk across the fields from the Barnyards of Findlater, past a well-preserved doocot, to the edge of the cliffs. Below, in a dramatic position, the ruined walls cling to the cliffside, while the sea-birds scream above the rocks. The Ogilvies, involved on the Gordon side at the battle of Corrichie (q.v.) in 1562, did not become Earls of Findlater until 1638. By the early 16th century, they had abandoned the exposed castle and moved to lands they had acquired at Deskford, 4 miles inland from Cullen. The old church at Deskford (AM), now roofless, contains various Ogilvie monuments of which the most interesting is a decorated sacrament-house or aumbry of 1551, with angels and scroll-work, now protected by a glass shield, donated by Alexander Ogilvie and Elizabeth Gordon, his wife.

In 1600 the Ogilvies began work on Cullen House — an L-plan tower-house, extended in the 18th century by Robert Adam and, less happily, by David Bryce in the 19th century. The 4th Earl, Chancellor of Scotland, who became Earl of Seafield in 1701, goes down in history for his remark that the Treaty of Union with England (1707) was 'the end of ane auld sang'. The magnificent collection of portraits, the 17th-century armoury of guns and pistols, the Grinling Gibbon carvings and many other treasures were, sadly, dispersed by auction in 1976 and the house, previously open to the public, stands closed and neglected.

Cullen Auld Kirk, which was in the middle of the old village before its removal in 1822, is an interesting building. A solitary rounded arch dates the original construction back to the 12th century. Robert the Bruce's second wife, Elizabeth de Burgh (for eight years a prisoner of the English), died here, and her 'interior parts' are said

The doocot, Barnyards of Findlater

to be buried in the church. Most of the building dates from the period 1536 to 1543. It was enlarged in the 18th century to its present cruciform shape. Making use of the Fishermen's Loft, the Believers' Loft (from which the pulpit could not be seen), the pretentious Laird's Loft and the pumphels or box pews, it was possible to accommodate 800 worshippers. The aumbry, carved in Moray sandstone with two angels holding the monstrance on high, is very similar to the one at Deskford. It was also donated by the pious Alexander Ogilvie whose stone effigy lies in an alcove under an ornate stone canopy. The aumbry was, until 1877, screened from Presbyterian eyes by the marble monument eulogising the Chancellor Earl, now on the N wall.

The alcove in St Anne's Aisle stood empty from 1792 to 1967, but once more contains the effigy of John Duff of Muldavit. He was the victim of a curious piece of genealogical fraud perpetrated by the Earl of Fife in a clumsy attempt, including the manipulation of dates, to prove that the 19th-century Earls of Fife were descended from Macduff, Thane of Fife! With the connivance of the Earl of Seafield, the effigy was transferred to the mausoleum of the Duffs near Banff (q.v.). With the acquisition of Duff House as an AM, the effigy was restored to its original position.

Culsh *see* **Cromar**

River Dee Grampian 4 A2-5 H1
A mile of Don's worth twa of Dee,
Unless it be for fish and stone and tree.
The abundance of salmon, the splendid craggy scenery and the well-preserved forests justify the qualities ascribed to 'Royal Deeside' in this jingle. The very source of the Dee is exciting: at nearly 4,000 ft on the Cairngorm plateau between Braeriach (4,248 ft/1295 m.) and Cairntoul (4,241 ft/1292 m.), the Wells of Dee form a patch of green in a great area of reddish granite gravel; the infant stream flows past, or under, a snowfield, which persists into summer, to plunge 200 ft over the cliffs into the Garbh Coire of Braeriach. A mile or so down it unites with another burn which has its source in the clear, mysterious Pools of Dee, among the boulders at the summit of the Lairig Ghru, that great gash through the Cairngorms. The Dee now turns southwards, taking in the Geldie burn, which only a low watershed separates from Glen Feshie. This is the ancient track from Braemar to Speyside: in 1860 Queen Victoria rode this way, and from the time of General Wade onwards it has, at intervals, been threatened with 'development' as a modern road. The next 25 miles (40 km.) of the Dee's course to the North Sea run nearly due E between the high Eastern Cairngorms and the Mounth. This highland trench was worn through the granite mass by the Ice Age glacier grinding down from the Cairngorms to its terminal moraine in the Muir of Dinnet. At the Linn of Dee, 6 miles up from Braemar, the river churns through a narrow,

spectacular cleft under the Victorian road-bridge. The road on the N bank passes Mar Lodge, the incongruous half-timbered house built as a shooting lodge in 1895 for the Duke of Fife, and continues to the Quoich Water. This clear, green-grey stream drains the whole s side of Beinn a' Bhuird, sliding over broad slabs and tumbling down falls in the picturesque Linn of Quoich.

The s bank road passes Inverey, a hamlet at the mouth of picturesque Glen Ey. One and a half miles up this side-glen is a rocky shelf known as the Colonel's Bed where the Jacobite 'Black Colonel', John Farquharson of Inverey, lay concealed after Killiecrankie (1689). Inverey boasts a monument, erected in 1934 by the Deeside Field Club, to its most distinguished citizen 'John Lamont 1805-1879, Astronomer Royal of Bavaria'. At Braemar (q.v.) the Dee is joined by the Clunie Water, which the A93 follows down from the skiing area at the Cairnwell Pass. Between Braemar and Balmoral (q.v.) is the Dee's most magnificent stretch, flowing fast and wide through the ancient Scots pines of Ballochbuie Forest on the royal estate. From the bridge by Invercauld, these pines frame the peak of Lochnagar; in the foreground is the old Invercauld Bridge built in 1753 as part of the military road from Blairgowrie by Caulfeild, Wade's successor. A spectacular five-arch bridge with massive cut-water buttresses, this is a masterpiece of 18th-century military engineering.

Downstream from Crathie Church (*see* Balmoral) one can drive all the way to Aberdeen either on the main A93 road on the N bank of the Dee or by the less frequented, but much more beautiful, s bank road, with bridges at Ballater and Banchory. On the s bank between Balmoral and Ballater are the two very different tower-houses of Abergeldie and Knock, both built in the second half of the 15th century. Abergeldie (now back in Gordon hands, after being leased to the Royal Family for the past century), recently harled a fine apricot colour, has a friendly air. The semi-circular stair tower supports a balustraded platform with an ogee-helmeted cap-house and a clock. On the top storey a handsome window has been broken out on the s side, no doubt for the view.

Knock, on a green mound near the confluence of Glen Muick and the Dee, is a grim keep, now under restoration, with a gruesome tale of a boundary feud between the Gordon owner and his Forbes neighbour. Seven Gordon sons cutting peat on Forbes land were overwhelmed and beheaded; their heads were stuck on peat-cutting spades to be discovered by a horrified servant bringing their dinner. On hearing the news the Gordon father had such a shock that he fell down his own stair and was killed.

Some miles E of Ballater (q.v.) by Cambus o' May (the 'bend in the plain') with its attractive white suspension footbridge, the Dee valley loses its Highland character, opening out into the MUIR OF DINNET, since 1977 a National Nature Reserve. Gravelly humps (or 'kames'), and small 'kettle-hole' basins filled by Lochs Davan and Kinord, mark the Muir of Dinnet as the spreading terminal moraine of the one-time Deeside glacier.

Old Invercauld Bridge across the Dee

Furthermore, the extraordinary cauldron and gorge at Burn o' Vat could only have been hollowed out of the solid rock by fierce glacial action, and not by the small stream now running through it from Culblean Hill. This strange place was the haunt of Gilderoy, the 17th-century Macgregor marauder.

On the A97 below the Burn o' Vat, a granite monolith set up by the Deeside Field Club in 1956 commemorates the battle of CULBLEAN, where Andrew de Moray (whose father was killed fighting with Wallace at Stirling Bridge) defeated the pro-English forces of David de Strathbogie on 30 November 1335. The latter were encamped near the point at which the Burn o' Vat flows into Loch Kinord. Andrew de Moray took them by surprise by advancing N of Loch Davan and descending on them from the slopes of Culblean Hill. His victory not only relieved the siege of Kildrummy, where his wife, Lady Christian Bruce, King Robert's sister, was holding out, but was the turning point in the Second Scottish War of Independence.

From Dinnet eastwards, the Highlands are left behind. The Dee flows more gently through pasture, field and forest. Gliding is practised on a broad meadow beside the A93 just w of the trim, English-looking town of Aboyne, with its broad green where the Aboyne Highland Games are held. Five miles on, at Kincardine O' Neil, the medieval hospice that adjoined the (now roofless) ancient church once served as a staging-post for travellers, including Edward I, on their way from the south to Moray. A ferry continued in use until 1812 when Thomas Telford built the fine Potarch Bridge, 2 miles SE.

Banchory (q.v.) is soon reached, and now the Dee flows on calmly past Drum (q.v.) and the pleasant western suburbs of Aberdeen, which stretch out to Peterculter. Here it is joined by the swifter Leuchar burn, which provides power for the paper-mills. Where the A93 crosses this burn, a life-size coloured figure in Highland dress is to be seen on the rocks of the little gorge. This is a ship's figure-head of Rob Roy Macgregor, who is said to have leapt the burn after a surreptitious visit to his distinguished academic relative, Professor James Gregory of Aberdeen (and some say a girl as well).

Past the Roman Catholic Blairs College, successor to the remote Scalan in the Braes of Glenlivet (q.v.), under the historic Bridge of Dee and past Kincorth, where Montrose won the first battle of Aberdeen in 1639, the Dee rolls majestically between banks of daffodils in spring. Then, almost turning its back on the busy port of Aberdeen, and thereby keeping its waters clear enough to attract salmon upstream to their spawning-grounds, the Dee reaches the grey North Sea between the little fisher-port of Footdee and Robert Stevenson's lighthouse of Girdle Ness.

Delgatie Castle   Banff and Buchan   Grampian   8 F2
Two miles NE of Turriff (q.v.) is Delgatie, a castle built, like
Slains on the Buchan coast, by the Hays of Erroll, Lord
High Constables of Scotland. Originally a 13th-century
keep two or three storeys high, Delgatie, built in red sandstone and now largely pink-harled, has been extended at
various periods. The parapeted rectangular tower of five
storeys is now 80 ft high, with an equally high gabled
house added on the w side in the 16th century. After the
'Papist Earls' Erroll and Huntly had achieved in 1594 their
brief victory over Argyll at Glenlivet (q.v.), the forces of
James VI laid siege to Delgatie. The castle withstood the
attack for six weeks, but the w wall collapsed. The Hays
went into exile, but were soon reprieved and, in 1597,
were allowed to rebuild Delgatie on condition that the
walls were no more than an arrowshaft thick. This
reconstruction and a further addition of 1720 resulted in
the magnificent long drawing room which now occupies
the whole of the w side. In the 17th century, low wings
were added — the chapel to the w, the kitchen to the E.

From the lower hall within the porch, a broad spiral
stair leads to the relatively small upper hall, where a fine,
ribbed, groin-vaulted ceiling suggests the hand of the
master mason of Towie Barclay. The central boss bears
the Erroll arms in colour and there are a number of
heraldic devices, as well as the pious slogan carved on the
lintel of the fireplace: 'My hoyp is in Ye Lord 1570'. Mary,
Queen of Scots, spent three nights here after the Battle of
Corrichie (q.v.) and her portrait, attributed to the French
painter Clouet, hangs in the room she slept in. In the
upper hall there is a portrait of Sir William Hay, the
experienced soldier who was chief-of-staff to Montrose
throughout his later campaigns. They were both
executed in Edinburgh in 1650 but after the Restoration
of 1660 were given a state funeral and now lie side by side
in St Giles. The Hays were Jacobites in 1715 and in 1745
and, as a result, Delgatie was forfeited. It was acquired by
the Duffs in 1777.

Among the delights of Delgatie are two rooms with
painted ceilings. One is the so-called Tulip Room; the
tulips painted on the walls were obliterated in the 19th
century, but the removal of a false ceiling revealed beams
dating from 1592 bearing old Scottish proverbs taken
from a *Treatis of Morall philosophye containing sayings of the
wyse* of 1567. On the next floor is the Painted Room (a
bedroom with a four-poster bed), with similar beams
bearing proverbs and also gaily-coloured designs with
humorous faces, which may be caricatures of
contemporaries, stewards and others, at the castle.

Delgatie was occupied by the Army from 1940 to 1945,
and was in a derelict condition when acquired in 1951 by
the present owner, Captain Hay of Hayfield. He is, among
other accomplishments, a skilled master mason, and in
the past 30 years has done much to restore and enhance
the fabric of the castle and its immediate surroundings.
Besides various Hay family portraits, there is a collection
of armour, including Eastern weapons, a Genoese cross-
bow of 1350 and some fine early Scottish arms. Access is
by appointment only.

River Deveron   Banff and Buchan   Grampian   7 C4-E1
Less well-known than its sister rivers of Grampian
Region, Spey, Don and Dee, the Deveron — the Dabrona
of Ptolemy's map, or *dubh-aran* in Gaelic — is a delightful
river throughout its length, and a great favourite with discerning salmon fishermen. As the Black Water — an
English back-translation of *dubh-aran* — the Deveron
rises in the peaty hills surrounding the remote, windswept basin of the Cabrach, north of Glenbuchat and east
of Glenlivet. Once the refuge of persecuted Catholics,
who called it the Siberia of Scotland, the Cabrach is now
largely deer-forest with a few sheep farms tucked under
the pointed peak of the Buck of Cabrach (2,368 ft/722 m.).
Edward I and other medieval travellers took this direct
route through the Cabrach from Balvenie (*see* Dufftown)
to Kildrummy. Nowadays, as the A941, it makes a fine
excursion, though sometimes blocked by snow in winter.

Not far from the isolated but popular Grouse Inn, the
Deveron leaves the line of the A941, flowing away NE,
accompanied by a pleasant by-road, past sheep farms,
with a fringe of hazels and birches softening the heathery
uplands. Here is Beldorney Castle, a Gordon fortalice of
the mid 16th century, where John Gordon hid in a secret
chamber after Culloden, while the 'Chevalier de
Johnstone', Prince Charles's aide-de-camp, mingled with
the servants in the kitchen. A later laird was caught nos-
ing round French dockyards and shot as a spy at Brest in
1769. Nearby is the site of the Wallakirk, dating from the
8th-century Pictish missionary St Moluag (or Wallach):
there is no kirk now, but a peaceful cemetery approached
by a wide green sward.

At the Haugh of Glass, the Deveron turns E with the
first of the major twists and curves that characterize this
elusive river, to merge just by Huntly Castle with the
N-flowing Bogie. The map suggests that the Deveron
might then have headed straight for the sea at Portsoy,
but not a bit of it. When the Isla, flowing in from Keith on
the N, joins the main stream, the Deveron swerves away
to the E through a most attractive wooded reach. Fine
views are obtained from the B9117 by-road, which starts
from Rothiemay, where James Gordon the mapmaker
(1615-86) was minister, and where the self-taught
astronomer James Ferguson (1710-76) is commemorated
by a monument. The B9117 joins the A97 Huntly to Banff
road at the fine bridge of Marnoch (1806), guarded by the
picturesque crowstep gable tower of Kinnairdy Castle,
the home of the brilliant Gregory family, a dynasty of professors of medicine, chemistry and mathematics between
the late 17th and mid 19th centuries.

From Marnoch to Turriff, the winding eastward course
of the Deveron is difficult to follow except by an
ingenious use of by-roads and a good map, but the effort
is worth-while for the delight of wooded slopes and curving stream. At Turriff, by some quirk of geology, the

Deveron turns N towards the Moray Firth instead of, as it did at some much earlier date in geological time, continuing E to join the Ythan's course to the North Sea. Once past the wooded slopes of Forglen and the ruined castle of Eden, the Deveron is joined by the Burn of King Edward. This is nothing to do with Edward I or any other king, but a corruption of the Gaelic *kinneddar*, head of the land. Between Kirkton of Alvah and Mountcoffer Wood, the Deveron makes a last twist through a steep wooded gorge, spanned by the picturesque single-arched Bridge of Alvah (1772), high over a deep pool. It finally runs through the policies of Duff House to join the Moray Firth between the twin towns of Banff and Macduff.

Dollar   *see* **Clackmannan District**

River Don   Gordon   Grampian   7 B6-8H5
> River Dee for fish and tree;
> But Don for horn and corn.

Compared with the aristocratic splendours of Deeside, the Don is a more workaday river. The opulence of its farmlands, waving with corn or dotted with splendid Aberdeen-Angus beef cattle, signals the difference. The geologists put it more prosaically, contrasting the 'acid, bouldery outwash of Deeside with the more fertile and less acid argillaceous soils of Donside'. The Don may be a less sensational river but, for those prepared to leave the main roads for the lanes of Aberdeenshire, it springs a number of surprises in its course, alternating between close gorge and open reach.

The Don's original headwaters were captured by the more romantic Avon (q.v.). So, instead of rising in the snow-fields of Ben Macdhui and flowing through Loch Avon, the Don's source is in the boggy hills to the east of Inchrory. The quiet stream flows E past the sinister castle of Corgarff (q.v.) to be joined by the little Cock Burn at Cockbridge, where the A939 drops steeply down from the Lecht Pass. A mile or so further E, the A939 breaks off to the S, bearing its coach-loads and crowds over the hills to Braemar, while the B973, becoming the A97 at Deskry, winds on down through a succession of quiet localities — Lonach, Roughpark and Bellabeg — known collectively as Strathdon. Lonach — the war-cry of the Forbes clan — gives its name to the Highland Games held at Bellabeg where, in late August, the Forbes, Wallace, Gordon and other warriors parade with their spears in full Highland panoply. The games, founded in 1823, take pride in 'preserving the Highland garb'. At Bellabeg, the Water of Nochty joins the Don, just by the Doune of Invernochty — a huge earth mound, the motte of an early-12th-century castle belonging to the Earls of Mar, guardians of the passes from the Mounth into Moray. This section of the Don offers lanes leading up enticing side-valleys, leading nowhere in particular, towards the Ladder Hills to the N or the lower slopes of Morven on the S — places of great peace and beauty. The longest of these side-glens is Glenbuchat (q.v.), its entrance guarded by the Castle of Glenbuchat (AM).

At Glenkindie, the Don shakes itself free of the hills and flows through fertile farmland, bending away from the A97, which goes through a gap to the medieval castle of Kildrummy (q.v.). At this point the Don gives its first surprise, turning sharply from N to E, and breaking its way through a wooded defile (shared with the A944 to Aberdeen) to emerge into a little hill-encircled plain, the Howe of Alford (*pron.* Afford). Here the Great Montrose, after his astonishing marches back and forth through the hills of Banffshire and Moray, defeated his Covenanting adversaries under General Baillie in July 1645. Montrose took his stand S of the Don, causing his opponent to advance through the river (the bridge was not built till 1810) and across a boggy stretch of land.

The wayward Don wanders away from the main road, passing Castle Forbes, a granite castellated work by the 19th-century architect Archibald Simpson, who left his indelible mark on Aberdeen. The Don next enters its most attractive reach, winding for 5 miles under the S wooded flanks of Bennachie (q.v.), Aberdeen's favourite mountain. A pleasant minor road, known as My Lord's Throat, follows the river most of the way, past the Forestry Commission's information centre, to emerge into the open country near the ruined castle of Pitfichie (under restoration), and to pass by Monymusk (q.v.). Thereafter, the last 20 miles of the Don's course are more prosaic, but still pleasant. It first heads NE past the granite quarries of Kemnay to Inverurie (q.v.), where it is joined by the River Urie at Port Elphinstone (*see* Introduction: Communications).

Two miles downstream, the royal burgh of Kintore boasts a dignified grey granite Town House of 1740, with a clock-tower and curving external stairs. The ruined tower of Hallforest Castle to the SE was a residence of the Keiths, Earls Marischal of Scotland, until 1639.

Across the Don from Kintore and beyond a low hill lies Balbithan House, built in 1560 by a Chalmers who, when a cannon-ball from Hallforest fell into the coutyard of his home nearer the Don, vowed he would build a new castle where 'neither friend nor foe could find him'. He succeeded in doing just that, and the result today is a dignified old house surrounded by long-established gardens, a pleasant and peaceful place. The long W wing was added in 1630, and both wings raised to three storeys. In the early 19th century, the top floor was removed and the second-storey ceilings raised, so that the corner turrets seem set disproportionately high. The turret corbelled out over the front door rests on a carved stone mask. The present owner has carried out much careful restoration, and allows visitors by appointment.

For its last 5 miles, the Don flows more swiftly, providing power for paper-mills and other industry, past the suburb of Dyce, rapidly developing round the busy Aberdeen airport. Just by St Machar's Cathedral in Old Aberdeen, the Don springs its last surprise — a steeply-wooded gorge spanned by the ancient Brig o' Balgownie

Doune Castle

— before flowing under Telford's Bridge of Don out through sand-hills to the North Sea.

Doune Stirling Central 1 B4

Doune, now a large village, lies where the A84 from Stirling to Callander crosses the River Teith to join the A820 from Dunblane. As the Dun of Menteith, it was the centre of an earldom, but it has declined in importance since the 15th century, when its great red sandstone castle stood for the power of the Dukes of Albany. Even in the 19th century, as the big, gaunt church indicates, Doune's population was greater than at present. Doune was also famous for its pistols. In 1626, one Thomas Cadell introduced their manufacture and Doune pistols continued to be made by three generations of Cadells, until after Prince Charles Edward had occupied the place in 1745. This dangerous trade was then banned, and replaced by the more innocent one of textile-weaving. The fine bridge across the Teith, now widened, was built in 1535 by Robert Spittal, the wealthy Stirling tailor who supplied clothes to suit the expensive tastes of James IV's widow, Margaret Tudor, sister of Henry VIII.

Doune Castle is the last and the best preserved court-yard castle (castle of *enceinte*) in Scotland, built by the powerful Robert, Duke of Albany (1339-1420), who was Regent for Robert II during his last years, continued effectively to rule during the reign (1390-1406) of his lackadaisical brother Robert III, and took no active steps to ransom the young King, James I, during the 18 years of his detention by the English. About 1395, he set about building Doune, as a castle fit for the de facto ruler of Scotland, who could no longer count on the unswerving loyalty of his tenants but has to fall back on the uncertain services of professional mercenaries for his protection. The massive remains seen today are a complex keep-gatehouse built in two self-contained parts, one a residence (capable of independent defence) for the duke, his family and household, the other a lower block for the standing garrison whose loyalty could not be guaranteed. There was no communication between the two (the door joining the two halls is modern), the entrance to the court-yard being underneath the 'lord's hall' which had its own water-supply in the corner-tower, and from which the portcullis could be controlled. Access to the 'retainers' hall' was only through the courtyard. The outer walls of both buildings form the northern and strongest section of the perimeter wall. The rest of the extensive curtain wall surrounding the five-sided courtyard is, with its sentry-walk, the requisite 40 ft high. This height was required because a scaling-ladder more than 40 ft long is too heavy to manhandle and anyway wobbles when placed up against a wall. All these defensive works were designed to impress the King's subjects with the power of the Dukes of Albany, father and son, Murdoch having succeeded his father in 1420. Not surprisingly, when James I did eventually return to Scotland in 1424, he had Murdoch smartly executed.

More than a century later, Doune Castle came into the hands of James Stewart (1560-92) who married the daughter of the Earl of Moray, Regent for his half-sister Mary, Queen of Scots. On Moray's assassination in 1570, the good-looking James Stewart of Doune took the title of Earl of Moray and became the darling of the Protestant faction. This exacerbated the family feud with the Catholic Gordons who had been defeated by the Regent Moray at Corrichie (q.v.) 30 years earlier. In 1592 the Earl of Huntly lured the 'Bonnie Earl of Moray' from Doune to Donibristle in Fife and murdered him there. So, as the ballad sings,

O lang will his ladie Look frae the Castle Doune
Ere she see the Earl o'Moray
Come soundin' through the toun.

Doune, captured by the Jacobites in 1745, remains in the hands of the Earls of Moray to the present day, and is open to the public. The Doune Gardens are a mile or so w of Doune off the A84. Here, in 1802, the 10th Earl of Moray built himself Doune Lodge, alongside the little Buchany Burn, which has been incorporated into a series of gardens including a walled garden, a rose garden, a shrub garden and a pinetum, with some outsize conifers. Large, vivid splashes of colour from roses or rhododendrons are part of the theme. The gardens were rescued from war-time neglect in 1968, and are now open to the public in season. To the E of the Buchany Burn is the Motor

Museum, housing the Earl of Moray's collection of vintage cars.

Drum Castle Gordon Grampian 8 F6 (NTS)
Situated in lovely parkland on a low ridge (*drum* being Gaelic for a ridge) some 10 miles w of Aberdeen, Drum Castle harmoniously juxtaposes a massive 13th-century keep with a Jacobean mansion. In 1323 Robert the Bruce granted the lands of Drum to Richard de Irwin (or Irvine), who thus shared the Royal Forest, and it seems also the title of King's Forester, with Burnard of the Leys (*see* Crathes). He was no doubt expected also to guard the crossing of the Dee. The castle and lands remained in the hands of the one family of Irvines for 653 years, until ceded to the NTS in 1976. On the whole, they enjoyed a peaceful existence, though the castle was 'pitifully plundered' by Argyll's Covenanters in 1644. The 3rd laird, Sir Alexander de Irwyne, fell at Harlaw (q.v.) in 1411 and his successor was invited to take up the special office of Captain-General of the City of Aberdeen. The s transept of St Nicholas Church, containing effigies of himself and his lady, is known as the Drum Aisle. The stone canopy from their tomb is preserved in the little Chapel of Drum, near the castle.

The blunt, four-square tower, with its rounded corners and rectangular crenellations round the battlements, makes no pretence to L- or Z-plan, which it antedates by almost two centuries. The walls are 12 ft thick at the base, narrowing to 9 ft higher up. A spiral stair leads to the magnificent Upper Hall, now the library, which occupies the whole area of the second floor, and the height of the former third floor as well. The big E window was broken out in 1845. The impressive barrel-vault of the Hall is decorated with armorial bearings showing the connexions of the Irvines with Keiths, Gordons and other great families.

The Jacobean mansion was added in 1619 so as to marry with, but not to surround, the old tower. The present entrance is at the foot of the tall turret in the sw corner of the garden front. This leads to a fine vaulted and flagged passage running the entire length of the ground floor and also through a yett or grille up a straight stair to the drawing and dining rooms above. These are pleasantly furnished with 18th-century furniture and *objets d'art*; on the walls hang portraits of members of the Irvine family, two by Raeburn and one by Reynolds, also a view of Castlegate in Aberdeen, painted in 1812 by Hugh Irvine, the artist of the family. The north facade of Drum, with its Victorian gallery, corbelled and turreted entrance gateway and courtyard, was added in 1875 by the 'Scots-baronial' architect David Bryce, whose contribution here

Drum Castle

harmonises suprisingly well with the tower and the mansion built respectively 550 years and 250 years earlier.

Drum figures in the ballad *The Laird of Drum*, which concerns the 11th Laird. At the age of 63 he married as his second wife a shepherd's daughter, aged 16, one Margaret Coutts, who, despite her pretty protest —

> But set your love on anither, kind sir,
> O set it not on me,
> For I'm too low to be Lady o' Drum,
> And your miss I'd scorn to be

— turned out to be an effective widow-administrator of the estate.

Drumminor *see* **Strathbogie**

Dufftown Moray Grampian 7 C3
Nowadays Dufftown, on the little River Fiddich, means whisky and the home of Glenfiddich. Indeed, the jingle that

> Rome was built on seven hills
> Dufftown stands on seven stills

is certainly outdated as the next distillery goes up. There is a pleasant whiff of roasting malt on the air. The town is a point on the Whisky Trail and a visit to a distillery is always of interest. Certain of the distilleries on the Trail have organised Visitor Centres, and give a welcoming dram.

Dufftown was founded in 1817 by James Duff, Earl of Fife, to give employment after the Napoleonic Wars. The four main streets converge on the battlemented Town House tower, built in 1836, with its ogee-roofed lead belfry on stilts. Formerly the jail and other municipal offices, it now houses the Tourist Information Bureau, and a small historical exhibition. Nineteenth-century and modern Dufftown is pleasantly laid out, but has little of interest to the visitor, save the Stephen Hospital which was founded in 1889 by Lord Mountstephen, who was originally George Stephen, born at Croftglas in neighbouring Glenrinnes in 1829, and educated in Dufftown. Lord Mountstephen, together with his friend Donald Smith from Forres, later Lord Strathcona, were the chief promoters of the Canadian Pacific Railway.

The long ecclesiastical and military history of the place is to be found in MORTLACH parish church and in Balvenie Castle, both well worth a visit. Mortlach Church is one of the oldest places of Christian worship in Scotland, founded by St Moluag, a contemporary of St Columba, in 566. In the year 1010, Malcolm II 'ramscuttered' an army of Scandinavian invaders nearby, and fulfilled his pious vow to extend the church by three spears' length. The Mortlach 'Battle Stone', down by the River Dullan, commemorates this event. The present Mortlach Church, last renovated in 1930, is an unusual T-shape. In addition to the well-preserved 'Elephant Stone' dating from A.D. 500, it contains a number of other stones of the 16th and 17th centuries, a recumbent effigy of Alexander Leslie of Kininvie (d. 1549), a tablet to Field Marshal Sir

Donald Stewart, 1824-1900 (who served in the Indian Mutiny, Abyssinia and Afghanistan), and some interesting stained glass windows. Three of these, 'Faith, Hope and Charity' are by Cottier of Paris and one by Douglas Strachan. A pair of windows commemorating Lord Mountstephen and another family, the Kemps, is unusual in featuring a C.P.R. wood-burning steam locomotive, and a group of Malayan rubber-tappers, respectively. The octagonal watch-house to the E was provided for relatives to keep watch by night when body-snatching was prevalent.

Medieval strategists could scarcely overlook the military value of a point where the direct route (now the A941) from Kildrummy (q.v.) through the Cabrach and down the Fiddich Glen past Auchindoun (q.v.) converges with two other important routes to run together down to the Spey and into Moray. Hidden in beech trees behind two prominent distilleries is the splendid castle of Balvenie (AM), a courtyard castle of the 13th century. First mentioned in the account of Edward I's return journey from Moray in 1296, it was then in Comyn hands, but after the 'herschip' (devastation) of Buchan in 1308, when Robert the Bruce dispossessed the Comyns, it went to the Douglases. After the defeat of the Black Douglas rebellion in 1455, Balvenie passed to the Stewarts of Atholl, who retained it until the 17th century and were responsible for the Renaissance renovation of the SE wing, making it more of a 'palace' than a stronghold. In the 17th century Balvenie Castle changed hands frequently; in 1644 it provided a few days' rest for Montrose and his men after his near-shave with Argyll at Fyvie, and in 1649 it fell to 'the old, little, crooked soldier', General Alexander Leslie, and his Covenanters. Later the Duffs of Braco acquired Balvenie as they did so many other properties — in payment of debts. The Duff of the day remained neutral in the Rising of 1715 and the castle was untouched. It was occupied by Government forces for the last time in 1746.

The spacious rooms in the Atholl wing, with its grand circular staircase and other spiral stairs, though now open to the sky, suggest a more comfortable way of life than the dark cellars and kitchens and 7 ft-thick walls of the medieval fortress. On the E wall the yellow freestone has been removed to build the Atholl wing, and replaced by the local grey limestone, for Dufftown lies on an outcrop of the Tay limestones (as the busy Parkmore quarry on the Keith road clearly indicates).

Duffus Castle Moray Grampian 7 B1 (AM)
Some 4 miles N of Elgin, the motte of Duffus (AM), which carried a wooden stockade before the cumbrous, top-heavy stone castle was built on it, rises out of the flat Laich of Moray (q.v.), resembling, it is said, a 'boss on a buckler' but now, alas, set somewhat askew. For the huge, three-storeyed stone keep has partially subsided on the NW side, together with part of the curtain wall. The lower bailey was separated by a ditch from the keep for extra protection should the bailey surrender. The whole castle

was — and still largely is — surrounded by a water-moat.

Freskin the Fleming was entrusted about 1160 with the task of defending this outpost in Moray. Styling himself de Moravia, Freskin founded the house of Moray. In 1290 the English Commissioners sent to meet the unfortunate Margaret, Maid of Norway, the Norwegian princess who was the only undisputed heir to the Scottish crown when Alexander III fell from his horse and was killed, stopped at Duffus on their way north to Orkney; and again on their 'dolorous return' with the news that the poor little Maid had died on her journey. In the War of Scottish Independence that followed, Reginald le Cheyne, who had inherited Duffus, took the English side. In the mid 14th century, the castle passed to Nicholas Sutherland, who probably built the stone castle we see today. One of the Sutherland lairds landed with Charles II at Garmouth (*see* Spey) in 1650 and, in return for financial support, was given the title of Lord Duffus. The castle was deserted in the 17th century, sold in 1705 to the Dunbar family, and became an AM in 1926.

A short distance to the N is the roofless but well-preserved ruin of St Peter's Kirk, or Duffus Old Church, founded in 1226, with an interesting groin-vaulted porch built in 1524 by a Sutherland. There is also a Sutherland burial-aisle at the foot of the former tower and St Peter's Cross, a typical medieval Mercat Cross.

Dull   *see* Fortingall

Dunblane   Stirling   Central   1 B4

Motorists hurrying along the A9 from Stirling to Perth pass close to the Queen Victoria School for the Sons of Sailors, Soldiers and Airmen, with no more than a distant glimpse of an imposing cathedral. It is well worth turning aside to visit this attractive little town on the E bank of the Allan Water. The main street leads up into a cathedral close, with a group of 17th-century houses, well restored and now the Scottish Churches' House. The crowstep gabled house of 1687 with an open forestair is Bp Robert Leighton's Library, founded by his nephew just after the bishop's death to house his 1,500 books. The Cathedral Museum is on the ground floor of the former Dean's House, built in 1624.

The present-day glory of Dunblane is the cathedral. There has been a place of worship here since St Blane came from Ireland about 600, but attacks by Danes in the 10th century destroyed whatever buildings there may have been then. The oldest part of the present building is the prominent tower, now a belfry and perhaps earlier a place of defence. It stands apart from the church, though now connected with it, and is in the tradition of a separate campanile as at Muthil and Cambuskenneth. The lower four storeys, of red sandstone and Norman in style, were built about 1100. The upper two storeys were added later and the parapet about 1500. It was Bp Clement (1233-58) who, with encouragement from the pious Gilbert, 3rd Earl of Strathearn (*see* Fowlis Wester) and funds from the

Duffus Castle

pope, built most of the fabric of the cathedral as we now see it, in particular the choir and the beautifully proportioned lady chapel (or chapter house) with its cross-vaulted groined roof and bosses. The nave was complete by the mid 14th century. Decay and neglect following the Reformation led to the roof of the nave collapsing, but services continued to be held in the choir, and the episcopal church of the 17th century was re-established under the rule of the saintly Bp Robert Leighton who tried, unsuccessfully, to reach a compromise with the Presbyterians.

The splendid Gothic architecture of Dunblane excited the admiration of John Ruskin who, in *Architecture and Painting* says 'He was no common man who designed that Cathedral of Dunblane. I know not anything so perfect in its simplicity, and so beautiful, as far as it reaches, in all the Gothic with which I am acquainted'. Whether under Ruskin's inspiration or not, the roof was restored in 1893 and further restoration carried out by Sir Rowand Anderson, who also designed the pulpit, the Keir Memorial, and the screen dividing choir and nave. The high lancet windows, in Early Pointed style, carry stained glass of the present century, some of it of high quality, notably the baptismal window by the font, the memorial windows of World War I, both by Douglas Strachan, and the magnificent 'Benedicite' south windows of the choir, the work of Louis Davis. Among the figures and elements praising God in this window are St Margaret of Scotland, St Francis of Assisi, William Blake and St Blane, while 'Chaos', which praises cold and heat, includes the names of the five members of Scott's expedition of 1912 who reached the South Pole.

Dunblane Cathedral

The six intricately carved wooden stalls, erected by Bp Chisholm in 1486, stand at the w end of the nave. Under blue slabs of Tournai stone in the choir lie the three Drummond sisters of whom the eldest, Margaret, was secretly married to James IV. They were probably poisoned in 1501 by the faction that wished the king to marry Princess Margaret of England, Henry VII's daughter, which James obligingly did in 1503 — a first and unsuccessful attempt towards the Union of the Crowns. The w door is of interest — deeply recessed with a series of pointed shafts and arch-mouldings, flanked by a pair of pointed blind arches. Above the door, visible only from the outside, is a small lozenge-shaped window, much praised by Ruskin.

At the top end of the High Street is the low-lying Balhaldie House, once the town house of the Macgregors and Drummonds, where Prince Charles Edward held a ball on his journey south in September 1745, a happier memory than the usual, more melancholy, recollections of the Prince.

Dundee Tayside 2 G2 *(pop. 194,732)*
Of all Scottish cities, Dundee is perhaps one of the best endowed by nature, and, from time to time, the worst blighted by man. The site is superb: here the Tay estuary narrows and Angus looks over to Fife, the Sidlaw Hills come down to the sea, and a broad slope rises from the

water's edge to the sharp volcanic peak of Dundee Law (571 ft / 174 m.). Yet this favoured site has not always been to the town's advantage. It has tempted invaders from the time of the Viking raids across the North Sea; it suffered the several incursions of Edward I and his successors; it was besieged by the English in 1547 during the War of the Rough Wooing, it was sacked in 1645 by Montrose, occupied and pillaged by General Monk on behalf of Cromwell in 1651, and attacked again by Graham of Claverhouse, 'Bonnie Dundee' himself, in 1688.

Dundee's reputation as a great commercial centre of Scotland has had its ups and downs too, but so long as trade looked across the North Sea it made very effective use of its position on a major eastward-facing estuary. There was rivalry between Dundee at the mouth of the estuary and Perth at the first bridgeable point, and the early charters of the two cities gave rise to some knotty legal conflicts: at one point, the Dundonians triumphantly record 'as to privileges of the Water of Tay . . . quhairfore we put to silence to yim of Perth . . .' Dundee had the stranglehold, being able to control shipping through the narrows. Between the early 14th and the end of the 16th centuries, Dundee's trade flourished with Flanders (through the Dutch port of Campvere, modern Veere, on the island of Walcheren, where the splendidly decorated Scottish houses are still to be seen) and also with the Baltic and Russia, through Danzig, Königsberg and Riga. By

1600, Dundee was the second most important town in Scotland, but the decline which set in with the development of trans-Atlantic trade to the American colonies through the growing port of Glasgow was accentuated by the devastation of the city by General Monk in 1651. This marked the end of Dundee's initial period of prosperity and, by 1655, a traveller could write of Dundee's former grandeur that it was 'sometime a town of riches and trade, now much shaken and abated'.

A century of poverty followed before technical ingenuity and commercial skills brought a new prosperity to Dundee. This all stemmed from the fishing; when the other east coast fishermen went to fish the North Sea, the Dundee men went whaling in the Arctic Ocean, while their womenfolk kept themselves by spinning the local flax and weaving it into cloth, including sails for the Royal Navy. After the disaster of 1651 there was no money to provide more than the coarsest and cheapest flax, but by the end of the 18th century a market was found for coarse bags in the American plantations.

In 1822, the East India Company sent home from Bengal a sample of a new fibre called jute, too brittle to handle until it was found that whale-oil added to the batching process made possible its manipulation and manufacture to meet the growing demand for sacks. When the linen bounty ceased in 1832, Dundee was well placed to become the centre of the jute industry, and the

familiar gunny-sack, and the even more familiar linoleum, became the basis of its new fortune. The population jumped from 35,000 in 1836 to 130,000 in 1886, with appalling consequences for the city's housing which are still being set right today. This was a terrible price to pay for the city's splendid but restricted situation: tenements crowded round the centre and the docks, while the wealthy jute barons built their pretentious villas out at 'Juteopolis' along the road to Broughty Ferry.

After the independence of India and Pakistan in 1947, Dundee could no longer compete in the cheaper end of the jute market, but local skills, particularly of the city's womenfolk, brought a new prosperity, with cash registers, watches, cookers and a multiplicity of modern products. So the old jibe of 'jute, jam and journalism' turned to cash registers, carpets, cameras, computers and cake; spinning and ship-building might also have been included. The old whaling trade, dating back to the 12th century, built its own ships, and the great Antarctic explorer, Robert Falcon Scott, turned to Dundee for his stout ice-resistant ships, *Discovery* and *Terra Nova*. The jam comes from James Keiller who, in 1913, started large-scale production of a product known to Dundee from the distant past as 'murmblade'. Journalism is represented by the powerful publishing house of D. C. Thomson, producing the *Dundee Courier* and a wide range of popular magazines, including the admirable *Scots Magazine*, first

Tay Road Bridge and Dundee Law

Pictish souterrain or earth-house, Carlungie

published in 1739, which is to be found wherever there are Scots the world over, even in remote Patagonia.

The earliest inhabitants evidently thought the mouth of the estuary a good place to live: the prehistoric midden of a fishing community was found in the Stannergate, the hinterland of Dundee has plenty of Pictish symbol-stones and Pictish earth-houses are to be seen at Ardestie, Carlungie and Tealing. Dundee enters recorded history with the charter given by William the Lion about 1180, and the foundation of the Church of St Mary's by his brother David of Huntingdon. A century later, William Wallace went to school here and struck the first blow for Scottish independence by dealing summarily with young Selby, son of the English governor of Dundee. When Wallace himself became Military Governor of Scotland, with Dundee as his base, he supported Alexander the Skirmisher (whose name was contracted to Scrymgeour) as Constable of the city — a post which was confirmed as hereditary in the Scrymgeour family by Robert the Bruce. The ancient castle of Dundee, down in the centre of the town, was demolished as being too vulnerable to the English, and the Scrymgeours made their fortified residence at Dudhope on a terrace below Dundee Law. From here, they carried on a ding-dong battle through the centuries with the Provosts of the city below, occasionally taking over the office of Provost themselves. In 1482, the Church of St Mary's was enlarged and the great Gothic tower built, 156 ft high, rising above the city centre, and known affectionately to Dundonians as Old Steeple. It was restored, in the original soft local stone, by Sir Giles Gilbert Scott in 1872. The great church suffered from fire

and bombardment during the English siege of 1547, and, in the way of Scots churches in times of rapidly expanding population, became the triple kirk that it still is, though none of the three churches in the shadow of Old Steeple is older than the 19th century.

Calvinism took an early grip on Dundee, which became known as the Geneva of Scotland. George Wishart preached here in 1544, and again in 1545, a month before he met a martyr's death at St Andrews. The Cowgate, or East Port, the only remaining part of the old city wall (though built in 1591) is traditionally known as the Wishart Arch. John Knox preached here too, and the mob which sacked the Perth religious houses in 1560 set out from Dundee. A curious survival of medieval times is to be seen in the Howff, a burial ground given to the town by the Greyfriars monastery. The Trade Guilds used it as their meeting-place ('howff') until they acquired their own hall in 1778, and it continued to be used as a graveyard until the 1880s; the quaint and interesting gravestones of many famous, and not so famous, citizens are still to be seen in the centre of the city. In view of their Protestant sympathies the inhabitants were not best pleased when Catholic James II of England appointed John Graham Claverhouse, the scourge of the Covenanters in the south-west, as Provost of Dundee in 1684 and made him Viscount Dundee in 1688. The Town Council welcomed the Old Pretender to the town in January 1716 but in 1745 their successors, fearful of again backing the wrong horse and so disturbing their growing trade, were unsympathetic to Prince Charles Edward; Provost Duncan suffered the ignominy of being locked up by the Jacobite Lord Ogilvy, who took over the city for the Prince. This provost was a relative of Dundee's second most celebrated citizen, Admiral Duncan, Viscount Camperdown (1731-1804), the admiral who defeated the Dutch Fleet in the North Sea at Camperdown in 1797.

The uncontrolled population expansion of the 19th century imposed an impossible strain on the medieval town plan. The water supply, which until as late as 1835 was delivered by water carts or water caddies, was impure and unhealthy, so that those who could afford it migrated to the seaside at Broughty Ferry or to the higher suburbs, while the poor clustered in tenements near the docks. In this get-rich-quick atmosphere, there was no room for the grace and formal quality of Edinburgh's New Town or Archibald Simpson's town planning of his Granite City. The old merchants' houses were swept away: even the Town House designed by William Adam in 1734 was demolished in 1931. Not much of the Victorian architecture, civic, factory or housing, can claim even limited distinction though, with growing prosperity, better architects were employed. Since 1947, an enormous amount has been done to sweep away slums, creating a multi-level shopping complex and leaving good parking spaces in the city centre.

The railways — first the Caledonian from Perth along the coast, and later the North British across the Tay estuary from Fife — brought more prosperity to Dundee. This was scarcely interrupted by the appalling Tay Bridge disaster, when, a bare 18 months after the opening of the railway bridge, on the stormy night of 28 December 1879, a north-bound train with 75 people aboard plunged into the sea because the thirteen girders of the high span had been swept away. The story has been told many times, most recently in John Prebble's *High Girders*; the subsequent enquiry showed that critical girders were of careless and faulty construction, and the report blamed the famous engineer Sir Thomas Bouch, who later committed suicide. The bridge was back again nine years later and its graceful curve, as it comes into the Angus shore, is the subject of many paintings, in particular those of J. Mackintosh Patrick. The Tay Bridge Disaster was also recorded by Dundee's special poet William McGonagall in his own excruciating couplets and flat-footed verse:

Beautiful Railway Bridge of the Silvery Tay!
Alas! I am very sorry to say
That ninety lives have been taken away
On the last Sabbath Day of 1879
Which will be remembered for a very long time.

The Howff burial ground, Dundee

Nothing daunted, he was quick to praise the new bridge:

With your thirteen central girders which seem to my eye
Strong enough all windy storms to defy.

Since 1966, the railway bridge has been supplemented by the low, straight road bridge, not one of the more interesting bridges of Scotland, when compared (to go no further) with the new Friarton motorway bridge higher up the Tay estuary.

Dundee possesses at least four castles: Claypotts (q.v.); Mains of Fintry, a 16th-century Graham fortalice with an unusually tall watch-tower, neglected in the 19th century but now in the care of the city, in Caird Park; Dudhope, the seat of the Scrymgeours; and Broughty Castle, guarding the sea approaches. Dudhope, where the Scrymgeours rather disdainfully 'reigned' over Dundee, has been sadly neglected since the office of Constable was abolished. Starting as an oblong tower, round corners were added, also a s extension, and even an enclosed courtyard as the Scrymgeours' power waxed. When that vanished, Dudhope was used as a barracks (1796-1879) and is now a meeting place for sporting and other clubs.

Broughty Castle, on a rocky promontory at the entrance to the Tay estuary, intended as Dundee's seaward defence, has sometimes failed in this task. The massive five-storey keep with its small windows, built by the Lords Gray soon after 1490, still dominates the clutter of later structures. The 4th Lord Gray goes down in Scottish history as the arch-traitor: in 1547 he met the English invaders at St Andrews and agreed to surrender his castle at Broughty. The 2,000 English troops not only took it over, but remained there, besieged or besiegers, for two years. Gray got off lightly for his treachery, but his castle went to the Hamiltons and others, until Lord Aberdeen's Government bought it in 1855 and refurbished it for coastal defence, conceivably for defence against the Russians in the Crimean War. Now it is a museum devoted mainly to whaling relics and the history of the castle.

Dundee's other museums include the Barrack Street Museum, near the Howff, concerned with Old Dundee and the geology and ecology of East Central Scotland; the City Museum, with local archaeological and other collections (under reorganisation); and Art Gallery with works by Flemish, French and Scottish painters, both housed in the Albert Institute in Albert Square. In Camperdown Park, a fine open space centering on the Grecian-style mansion built in 1824 for Robert, the son of the victor of Camperdown, there is the Spalding Golf Museum, displaying the oldest golf club, dating back to 1680.

A strange mixture of personalities is associated with Dundee, from Devorguilla (1209-89, mother of the ill-fated King John Balliol) who, with her husband, founded Dundee's Greyfriars monastery as well as Balliol College, Oxford, to James Chalmers, the inventor in 1834 (and acknowledged as such by no less than Rowland Hill him-

Broughty Castle

self) of the adhesive postage stamp. Others include Mary Slessor (1858-1915), the intrepid woman traveller, missionary and magistrate, who brought high standards of justice and service to the West Africans of Calabar; Patrick Blair (1616-1728), the first dissector of an elephant (which died on the road from Broughty Ferry to Dundee), and the author of *Osteographica Elephantica*; James Bowman Lindsay, who, in advance of Marconi, sent wireless signals across the Tay in 1853; and Mary Wollstonecraft Godwin, who wrote *Frankenstein*, married Shelley and lived, when in Dundee, at Peep o' Day Lane.

Dundee may have risen to be the second city of Scotland at the peak of its 17th-century prosperity, and it has since claimed precedence over Aberdeen, but it has not benefited to the same extent from the oil boom. The 1975 population estimates give the Granite City a clear lead of 15,000 over Dundee, now in fourth place. Modern construction, particularly of high-rise blocks on the outskirts of the town, has done much to alleviate the Victorian slum conditions of the centre, and Dundee is well on the way to becoming once more a fine city on a fine site.

Dunkeld Perthshire Tayside 1 D1
Many places along the Highland Boundary Fault claim the title of 'gateway to the Highlands': Dunkeld best deserves it. The River Tay breaks through a gap in the rugged wooded hills and Dunkeld has seen plenty of the

turmoil of Scottish history. In the present day, its former dignity as a cathedral city has been restored by the reconstruction of the 40 or so little houses in the street and precinct leading to the cathedral, now parish kirk. This work was carried out by the NTS and the Perth City Council. The neat and attractive result richly deserved the Civic Trust award of 1966 for an 'outstanding contribution to the appearance of the local scene'. The focal point of Dunkeld is the ancient cathedral. The remains visible today consist of the partially reconstructed 13th-to 14th-century choir forming the present parish kirk, a roofless nave (AM and under restoration), a prominent tower on the NW, and a chapter house, now the mausoleum of the family of the Duke of Atholl.

Dun Caledonia, or Fort of the Celts, has an ancient history. St Adamnan, the biographer of St Columba, founded a monastery here before 700. It was a Pictish capital, until Kenneth MacAlpin made it his own, together with Scone, in 844. One of its lay abbots, Crinan, married the daughter of Malcolm II and was the father of King Duncan, slain in battle by Macbeth in 1040. There followed a close association between subsequent kings of Scotland and the bishops of Dunkeld, who provided a distinguished line of statesmen, ambassadors, builders, poets and even a warrior, Bp William Sinclair (1312-37), who earned Robert the Bruce's gratitude by repelling an English invasion in 1317. The cathedral was a long time in

Dunkeld Cathedral

the building; the choir was completed by Bp Sinclair in 1318 and the 15th-century nave, with its massive round pillars separating seven bays and two side-aisles, was mainly built under Bp Robert de Cardeny (d. 1420), whose decorated tomb is in the s aisle. One of the last bishops was the controversial Gavin Douglas (1474–1522) who earned a year in the dungeons of St Andrews for having canvassed the pope rather than the king for his appointment: he is more famous for his translation of the Aeneid ('He gave rude Scotland Virgil's page' – wrote Sir Walter Scott) than for his attention to the affairs of his see.

The NW tower was completed only in 1501, just 60 years before the destruction of this fine medieval Scottish Gothic church by the zeal of the Reformers. The letter to the local lairds, dated 12 August 1560, has been preserved: it instructed them to take down the images and burn them, cast down the altar and purge the kirk of all monuments of idolatry; a postscript, which was plainly overlooked or disregarded, enjoined them to take good heed that neither 'windocks nor durris, be ony ways hurt or broken — eyther glassin wark or iron wark'. The subsequent removal of the leaded roof and neglect of the building brought the inevitable ruin. In addition to frequent raids from the Highlands and a visitation by Montrose, Dunkeld suffered further destruction in 1689. That was the year when the Highland force, though victorious at Killiecrankie (q.v.), lost its leader 'Bonnie Dundee' and marched down the Tay under Col. Cannon to attack the Government forces of Dutch King William under Lt. Col. Cleland. The desperate struggle, in which the zealous Presbyterian Cameronians made their name, ended in the withdrawal of the Jacobites, but only after the almost total destruction of the town and more damage to the cathedral, of which the tower had been used for defence. Cleland was killed and is commemorated by a simple stone in the sw corner of the nave. In what is now the parish kirk end of the cathedral (restored in 1908) there is a monument to Alexander Stewart, the Wolf of Badenoch, who did penance for his destruction of Elgin Cathedral in 1390, and was buried in Dunkeld. Other monuments include the Atholl coat of arms and genealogical tree, and an impressive memorial to the Black Watch.

A bridge across the broad Tay presented a problem for centuries. A difference of opinion between the Duke of Atholl and General Wade led to Wade terminating one of his roads to Inverness on the north bank at Dunkeld, while his other road from Stirling via Crieff northwards took the Sma' Glen route, crossing the Tay at Aberfeldy (q.v.) instead. Not until 1809 did Telford's graceful seven-arched bridge, which stands today, replace the age-old ferry (used as late as 1803 by the Wordsworths), and even then the tolls on the bridge provoked riots in 1879. Despite the bridge, the coming of the Highland Railway in 1840, on the other bank, led to a decline in the prosperity of Dunkeld, only restored when tourists began

to travel by car along the A9 through the town. Now, the new section of A9 opened in 1978 by-passes Dunkeld, and the visitor can enjoy the peace of the little town without the thunder of through traffic.

Across the river are three settlements; Little Dunkeld, Inver where the Braan joins the Tay, and Birnam and its wood, of which Pennant sarcastically remarked in 1769 that it 'seems never to have recovered from the march which its ancestors made to Dunsinane'. Inver is renowned as the home of the great fiddler Neil Gow (1727–1807), who played before Prince Charles Edward at Dunkeld House, was visited by Burns in 1787, painted by Raeburn, became known as the 'Atholl Paganini' or the 'King of Rant and Reel', and earned the neat epitaph:

Gow and Time are equal now;
Gow beat time, now Time's beat Gow.

His tomb and a brass plaque are at Inver Church, and the Raeburn portrait is to be seen at Blair Castle (see Blair Atholl).

A little way along the new A9, a NTS signpost points the way to the Hermitage, a romantic retreat overlooking a tumbling waterfall, built by the 3rd Duke of Atholl in 1758; it was also known as Ossian's Hall. It attracted vandals even in the 18th and 19th centuries, but was in 1952 restored by the NTS, in whose care the little building and its approaches now are. These include some magnificent Douglas firs alongside the rushing River Braan. Wordsworth was distressed at the Duke's fresco of Ossian and the glass panels reflecting the dancing waters (now no more):

What — Ossian here — a painted thrall
Mute fixture on a stuccoed wall? . . .
Illusive cataracts . . . devised out of a sick man's dream
. . . set free the Bard from such iniquity!

Dunnottar Kincardine and Deeside Grampian 5H3 Dunnottar, 2 miles s of Stonehaven off the A92 coast road, is one of the most exciting castles in Scotland, both for the striking grandeur of its situation on a nearly inaccessible promontory, and for the important part it played in Scottish history, in particular the safeguarding of the royal regalia in 1651 and the incarceration of the persecuted Covenanters in 1685. *Dun-oithir*, the 'fort on a low promontory', was the site of one of St Ninian's churches. The strategic value of the place also attracted warriors and kings, the first being Brude, King of the Picts, who made it his headquarters for the Mearns in 681. 'Le castel de Dunostre' found its way into French Romance epic in Norman times; in 1297 Wallace stormed the English garrison in what his chronicler Blind Harry called this 'snuk (promontory) within the se' and 'brynt up the Kirk and all that was ther in'. In 1336, Edward III sent a governor by sea to fortify the place, but Andrew de Moray passed that way and burnt it down. By the end of the 14th century, it had passed into the hands of the Keith family, the Earls Marischal of Scotland. The 5th Earl got into trouble with the pope for building his castle on consecrated land, but bought himself off by founding the church of Dunnottar a mile inland.

Dunnottar, the chief seat of the Earls Marischal for 250 years, was made into a magnificent residence by successive earls in the late 16th and early 17th centuries. The imposing Marischal's suite was added as late as 1645. Kings and queens, including Queen Mary, regularly visited Dunnottar and it was reckoned a safe repository, for instance for Aberdeen's documents during the Gordon-Forbes riots of 1571, as later for the royal regalia. As a leading Protestant, the 7th Earl Marischal declared for the Covenant in 1639, and was besieged in Dunnottar in 1645 by his former comrade-in-arms, Montrose. Keith, persuaded by the Covenanting minister Andrew Cant not to surrender to Montrose, was mortified to see smoke rising from his plundered lands. He was scarcely comforted by what must go down as one of the most hypocritical pieces of cant in history: 'Trouble not, for this reek will be a sweet-smelling savour in the nostrils of the Lord'!

In 1650, Charles II was entertained in Dunnottar on his way south from Garmouth (see Spey), but by the time of his defeat at Worcester in September 1651 the Crown Jewels, regalia and papers had been sent to Dunnottar for safe-keeping. As Cromwell's troops advanced, Dunnottar, defended by Sir George Ogilvy, was the only place still under Royalist control, but it was evident that, once English artillery was brought up to the heights above the promontory, the besieged garrison could not hold out long. There are several versions of what happened, but the most authentic is that, under the courtesies of the times, Anne Lindsay was allowed to visit her relative, the Governor's wife, and came out rather stouter with the royal documents, some 176 pieces, stitched in a belt round her waist, while the regalia (crown, sceptre and sword) were lowered over the walls to Christian Grainger, wife of the minister of Kinneff, posing as a gatherer of seaweed on the shore. They were stored safely under the floor boards of her husband's church at Kinneff, some 7 miles down the coast, and faithfully kept until the Restoration in 1660. After 8 months' resistance, Dunnottar surrendered in the spring of 1652, when the great tower was bombarded.

The grimmest episode in the long history of Dunnottar was still to come. In 1685, the 9th Earl of Argyll, in conjunction with the Duke of Monmouth, rebelled against the Catholic King James II of England. The Scottish rising failed and Argyll was executed; a large body of Covenanter prisoners, 122 men and 45 women, was taken for security to Dunnottar and crammed into the now notorious Whigs' Vault, where they were kept for two months in the stifling height of summer. Some 25 tried to escape by climbing down the cliffs, two dying in the attempt; the others were recaptured and subjected to torture. Those who refused to take the oath of allegiance were shipped to the Quaker colony of East New Jersey. The Covenanters' Stone in Dunnottar churchyard (see Stonehaven) gives the names of nine prisoners who died.

The 10th Earl Marischal was prominent in the Rising of 1715, with the result that his estates were forfeited and made over to the York Buildings Company, who stripped the lead from the roofs. Two centuries later, Dunnottar was sold to Lady Cowdray (of Dunecht), who repaired and restored the ruins, which are now open to the public under the auspices of the Cowdray Trust.

The crag on which these ruins stand is composed of conglomerate red sandstone, the strata being thrown almost vertical by the pressures from the Highland Boundary Fault which runs out to sea only a couple of miles to the N. The ruins themselves represent, according to Macgibbon and Ross, 'an epitome of nearly the whole history of domestic and castellated architecture in Scotland', ranging from the tall, L-shaped medieval keep to the great quadrangle with its three storeys of kitchen, dining room and drawing room, and the, once, comparatively elegant apartments added as late as 1645. The Whigs' Vault is in the basement of this latest addition (in the NE corner of the crag). As well as the main buildings, there is a chapel, a so-called priest's house, a bakehouse, a bowling green and, most spectacular of all, the strongest gatehouse in Scotland. The approach route across the low isthmus from the mainland leaves, on the right, an artificially-narrowed peninsula (known as the Fiddlehead, and pierced by a recent tunnel) and then climbs up a rough staircase, at the head of which the visitor is confronted by three grim tiers of gaping gun-ports and loopholes. This is the Curtain, 30 ft high, filling the gap between the main rock on the left and the five-storey building on the right known as Benholm's Lodging (after the Keith who owned the estate of that name). The entrance to the fortress continues upwards through a couple of vaulted tunnels or pends, but one should step aside into Benholm's Lodging to see the dark, gruesome prison, the barrack room where the escaping Covenanters were tortured, and the roundway for sentries watching for attacks. After this gloomy entrance, it is a relief to be out in the open greensward of the inner fortress and to enjoy the sound of the sea below, and the birds above, and to forget for a moment the grim history of the place.

Dunsinane   Perthshire   Tayside   2 E2
Macbeth V, v

> I pull in resolution and begin
> To doubt the equivocation of the fiend
> That lies like truth; 'Fear not, till Birnam wood
> Do come to Dunsinane'; and now a wood
> Comes towards Dunsinane.

Shakespeare got his geography right: Birnam wood is certainly visible from Dunsinane (*pron.* Dunsinnan), 11 miles (18 km.) away as the crow flies, across the wide vale of the Tay. He was weaker on his history, for Macbeth did not meet his fate here, but over 50 miles (80 km.) away at Lumphanan, N of the River Dee.

The volcanic range of the Sidlaw Hills, which form an abrupt SE edge to Strathmore, culminates in the two summits of King's Seat (1,236 ft/378 m.) and Black Hill (1,182 ft/360 m.), with Dunsinane on the W flank of the latter. There is a conspicuous hill-fort on Dunsinane, an easy walk from the A93 at Collace, with a magnificent view over Strathmore and across the Tay. When Macbeth moved S from Moray to begin his prosperous and relatively peaceful reign of 17 years as High King of Scotland, he made his residence near Scone (q.v.), the traditional crowning-place of Scottish Kings. This was probably at Cairnbeddie (*Carn-beth*), now a farm with a green mound, E of the A93 and near the hamlet of St Martin's. He may even have consulted his witches at a spot marked on the O.S. map as Witches' Stone, hidden in scrub less than a mile away, and about the same distance from Dunsinane House, built in 1830. Macbeth's Law, E of the A94, also suggests a Macbeth connexion.

Whether Macbeth was influenced by the ambivalent counsels of the witches to move up to the fort of Dunsinane Hill, believing himself safe there, or whether this was a sensible precaution as the forces of Malcolm Canmore and Macduff gathered to overthrow him, we shall never know. But it is reasonably well established that they did use the device of a 'moving grove' and that there was a battle in 1057 below the hill of Dunsinane. Macbeth did not, however, die in that battle, but, as vividly related in Nigel Tranter's *Macbeth the King*, he slipped through the closing ring to try to make his way, with a few followers, back to his own land of Moray. He knew the country well, evading pursuit by cutting over from the West Water to Glen Esk and by the Fir Mount track over to Deeside. He crossed the Dee at Dinnet, less likely to be watched than the ferry at Kincardine O' Neil; but he was unable to escape his enemies, who were waiting for him N of Aboyne. Macbeth was slain by Malcolm Canmore on 15 August 1057, within sight of the Peel of Lumphanan in Mar (*see* Cromar).

Edzell Angus Tayside 5 F4 (AM)
Where the Glen Esk routes over the Mounth from Deeside debouch into Strathmore, one would expect to find a

Edzell Castle and garden

castle but not a formal walled garden of taste and sophistication. Since 1357, Edzell (AM) was in the possession of the Crawford Lindsays, a gifted family, renowned for gallantry and artistic taste, yet tragic and feckless — in fact, the 'lichtsome Lindsays'. Early in the 16th century, the Lindsays built the fine red sandstone tower-house seen today; they entertained Mary, Queen of Scots, on her journey N in 1562. In 1580, they added the sumptuous mansion round a quadrangle (now partly ruined).

In the relatively peaceful period between the troubles of the Reformation and the outbreak of the Civil Wars (say, 1570-1639), the artistic spirit enjoyed a renaissance. Sir David Lindsay, Lord Edzell, succeeding to the estate in 1558, travelled on the Continent, principally in Germany, during his formative years. He built the magnificent mansion which, in its hey-day, with its painted ceilings and lavish furnishings, must have rivalled Crathes (q.v.). These, alas, we can no longer see, but we can enjoy the 'pleasance' or walled garden he created in 1604 to the s of the old tower. The walls of this remarkable enclosure, all in the glowing red sandstone, are divided into compartments, the chequer-board armorial bearings of the Lindsays alternating with oval or rectangular panels, portraying on the E side the Planets, on the s the Liberal Arts, and on the w the Cardinal Virtues. These are distinctively German in style. The Planets are copied from a series of engravings made in 1528 by Georg Pencz (or Iörg Bentz), a Nüremberg pupil of Dürer's; indeed, his initials 'I.B.' are faithfully reproduced on the halberd held by Mars. The Liberal Arts include Grammatica portrayed as a woman-teacher with a rod in her girdle and Dialectica accompanied by a chattering swallow, a wily serpent and two garrulous frogs.

The formal garden is the fascinating and elegant expression of taste by an educated and well-travelled Scottish gentleman. It is at its best when the beds of roses are in flower, surrounded by low box hedges meticulously cut to read 'Dum spiro spero' (the Lindsay motto), and the alcoves are gay with blue and white lobelia representing, with the red stone, the Lindsay colours. The charming pavilion in the SE corner of the garden has been preserved and the upper room restored.

David Lindsay also imported two German mining engineers, Bernard Fechtenburg and Hans Ziegler, to mine for copper and lead at the head of Glen Esk. These activities landed him in debt by his death in 1610, and the glories of Edzell faded all too soon. Although Edzell was not seriously damaged in the Civil Wars, the extravagance of the Lindsays led to the estate being sold to Lord Panmure in 1715. He took the Old Pretender's side in the Fifteen, and the estate soon fell forfeit to the York Buildings Company who, over a period of 50 years, stripped first the lavishly appointed house, then the roof and floors, and finally the avenue of beech trees. In 1764, a later Panmure bought back the estate which passed to the Dalhousie family. Since 1935, Edzell has been in the care of the AM. The custodian maintains the garden with

meticulous care, making it a place of rare beauty as well as peace.

In the 19th century the village moved from the neighbourhood of the castle to its present site on the long, straight B966. The entrance from the s is through a red sandstone arch, resembling the one at Fettercairn erected for Queen Victoria, but this one dates from 1887 and commemorates the 15th Earl of Dalhousie. The church (1818) has a curious metal belfry, but the graveyard remained near the castle. In the 18th century Edzell, like Doune, was renowned for its pistols.

Elgin Moray Grampian 7 B1 *(pop.* 16,407)
Elgin, the centre of the fair land of Moray (q.v.), is a pleasant, lively place, favoured with a dry and often sunny climate. Situated on a low ridge between the loops of the River Lossie, the town was from early days a residence of Scottish kings, and, when Edward I made it the turning-point of his triumphant progress of 1296, his chronicler called it 'bon chastell et bonne ville'. Combining the seclusion of a former medieval cathedral precinct with the elegance of 18th-century buildings, Elgin's modernisers have treated the town with care, preserving the plan of the medieval burgh. The main street, which links the castle-mound to the west with Cathedral Close to the east, widens to the old cobbled market place — the Plainstones — and is joined to parallel streets north and south by narrow wynds and pends. The steep motte of Lady Hill, once crowned by a Norman castle of which no traces remain, now carries a column surmounted by a statue of the last Duke of Gordon (d. 1836).

The easily worked Moray freestone from the quarries on the coast at Hopeman provides Elgin houses with their cream, yellow or pinkish stone facing. Two good examples of 17th-century architecture, now both public houses, are the Tower House in the main street, a round tower surmounted by a charming diminutive cap-house with crowstep gables, dated 1634; and Thunderton House, just up a wynd to the s. This, once the most splendid mansion in Moray, belonged successively to the Moray, Duffus and Dunbar families; Prince Charles Edward lodged here in 1746 just before the battle of Culloden.

A feature of the early 18th century were what were known to Dr Johnson, who lodged at the Red Lion in 1773, as 'piazzas' — an erroneous term, since 'piazza' is Italian for 'square', whereas in Elgin these are arcaded passages along a street — in fact the 'loggia' of Italy. Very few of the older type survive and those that do have been incorporated into shop-fronts. A good example may be seen at the E end of the High Street in Braco's Banking House (built 1694). This was acquired in 1702 by William Duff of Dipple at the start of the family's successful financial career that was to make his descendant Duke of Fife (*see* Keith). The city has attempted to maintain the tradition with a modern series of arcades along the N side of the main street;

St. Giles Church, Elgin

these open out into pleasant modern 'closes'. The widening of the main street is dominated by the classical church of St Giles, designed in 1828-32 by Archibald Simpson, the Aberdeen architect, in the manner of a Greek temple, with a portico of six fluted columns and a tower surmounted by a pillar and six slim columns supporting what some might call a flower-vase: in fact an adaptation of the Choragic monument of Lysicrates in Athens. It is executed in honey-coloured Moray freestone and not in Simpson's accustomed granite. His work can also be seen in the Anderson Institution 'For the Support of Old Age and the Education of Youth' at the E end of the town. This was built in 1832 from a legacy left by General Andrew Anderson (1745-1824), whose mother, a poor woman, nursed her fatherless infant in the chapter house of the ruined cathedral. Anderson went out to India as a drummer-boy in 1760, made a fortune as a nabob, and returned to benefit his native Elgin. At the W end of the town is Dr Gray's Hospital, built in 1816-19, also from a fortune made in India; another classical design, this time by Gillespie Graham, the architect of parts of Edinburgh New Town.

It is pleasant to turn from the bustle of the main street

to the green expanse of Cooper's Park, now cut across by a new road. This park approximates to the former cathedral walled precincts, of which fragments remain, the most considerable being the E gateway known as Pann's Port. Within this area were once the 23 manses of the cathedral canons, the only one remaining being the so-called Bishop's Lodging with its crowstep gables. Though it bears the date 1557 and the arms of Patrick Hepburn, bishop from 1535-1573, it was probably the Precentor's Manse, since the bishops resided at Spynie. What remains of the cathedral, justly considered the most perfect of Scottish cathedrals, is still a magnificent sight. The W facade, with its twin towers, its wide portal arched over the two entrances, and the great window above (its tracery now all gone), reminds one of the Gothic cathedrals of Northern France: Amiens, Laon, Rouen. The middle tower over the crossing was higher than the two W towers, and once supported a lantern, but this has collapsed. The two transepts are the oldest part of the cathedral. The E end, with its arrangement of ten pointed Gothic lancet windows on two levels below the wheel of the one-time great rose window, is the most impressive. St Mary's Aisle, s of the choir, contains the tomb of Bp Winchester and was the burial aisle of the Gordons of Huntly, up to the last Duke of Gordon who died in 1836. The best-preserved part is the octagonal chapter house (added after the destruction of 1390), the ribs of the roof-vault springing from a central pillar. The bosses and corbels are decorated with interesting allegorical stone-carvings; grimacing demon faces, animals disguised as humans, as well as oak leaves and grapes.

How did it come about that this fine cathedral is reduced to such a sorry state? The damage wrought by the Wolf of Badenoch in 1390 was made good: the corruption of pre-Reformation bishops, the zeal of the Reformers and the neglect of the 18th century are the true causes. To understand this, one needs to trace briefly the history of the 'Lanthorn of the North', so closely bound up with the rich province of Moray. In the 12th century, Norman feudalism and the Roman Catholic Church consolidated Moray as an outpost against the Highland marauders to the north. The early bishops of Moray covered a wide area, up into Easter Ross, but had no fixed seat. For a time, they based themselves on Birnie, probably the oldest continuously used church in Scotland, dating back to 1140. Five miles s of Elgin, Birnie is an interesting little church, with its Norman arch and its 1,000-year-old 'Ronel' Bell, a kind of oblong gong. Early in the 13th century, the bishop moved to Spynie, a couple of miles north of Elgin, and this remained the seat of the increasingly powerful bishops of Moray for the next three and a half centuries. It was not, however, a convenient place of worship for the inhabitants of Elgin and, in 1224, papal authority was obtained to erect the 'Church of the Holy Trinity juxta Elgin'. A fine cathedral, nearly as large in area as the

Elgin Cathedral

ruins we see today, was built with a constitution modelled on that of Lincoln.

Bp David de Moravia (1299-1326) played a leading part in support of Robert the Bruce during the War of Independence. Bp Alexander Bur (1362-97) was unwise enough to excommunicate Alexander Stewart, Earl of Buchan, Lord of Badenoch, son of Robert II, for neglecting his lawful wife and consorting with one Mariott Athyn, by whom he had several children. The Wolf of Badenoch took a terrible vengeance, swooping down from his island fortress in Lochindorb with his 'wyld wykked Hieland-men' to burn the 'elegant cathedral of Moray, the mirror of the land, the glory of the Kingdom'. Nor did they spare the town of Elgin. The crime nearly broke the heart of Bp Bur, who wrote a pathetic letter to the King. The Wolf in due course did penance and earned a place in Dunkeld Cathedral. Generous contributions repaired the damage and Elgin Cathedral was soon as fine as ever, indeed, enlarged by its beautiful chapter house.

James I raised the Church's lands here into the barony of Spynie, thereby greatly increasing the temporal power of Bp Winchester (1437-58) and his successors. Nor did they scruple to make use of this power. When the excommunicated Earl of Huntly threatened to pluck Bp David Stewart (1462-76) out of his 'pigeon-holes', he retorted by building Davy's Tower, a massive keep six storeys high with wide splayed gun-loops, adjoining Spynie Palace, and dared the earl to attack. With James Hepburn (1516-24), the bishopric reached the height of its wealth and magnificence. Patrick Hepburn (1535-73) was the last of the Roman Catholic bishops of Moray. Foreseeing the success of the Reformation, he set about taking over church lands for his personal use; and, barricading himself in Spynie, he defied the Reformation until his death in 1573. In 1640, the Covenanters made Spynie their local headquarters. After 1690 it was neglected and the main vault of Davy's Tower collapsed about 1760. Today, this great palace stands desolate and neglected, half a mile to the E of the Lossiemouth road, Davy's Tower shored up by scaffolding and the low ground which was once the bishops' harbour covered with scrub.

As a result of Bp Patrick Hepburn's unscrupulous expropriation of church property, no funds remained for the maintenance of Elgin Cathedral, which was never used by Presbyterians or by Episcopalians after 1560, though a Mass was said there following the Battle of Glenlivet (1594). Regent Moray ordered the lead to be stripped from the roof in 1567 and the weather brought the collapse of the choir rafters. Cromwell's soldiers shot at the window tracery — the bullet marks are still to be seen inside. In 1711, the great central tower fell; in the 18th century the building was used as a quarry and a rubbish dump. In 1825, a keeper was approved, one John Shanks, a shoemaker who died in 1841 at the age of 83. His tombstone, near the SE corner of the cathedral, tells how 'for 17 years he was the keeper of this Cathedral, and while not even the Crown was doing anything for its preservation he, with his own hands, cleared it of many thousand cubic yards of rubbish, disclosing the bases of the pillars, collecting the carved fragments and introducing some order and prosperity'. Finally, the Government stepped in, and for the past 100 years Elgin Cathedral has been well cared for as an AM.

Elgin's Museum, next door to Braco's Banking House and facing the Little Mercat Cross where the Wolf of Badenoch did penance for his crimes, is housed in an Italian-style building, with attractive internal arcading, designed for the purpose in 1842 by Thomas Mackenzie, who also built, in Tudor-Gothic style, Drummuir Castle and Milne's High School at Fochabers. The Museum has been recently thoroughly reorganized, and is worth a visit, not only for well-arranged displays of local historical interest, which include the incised stones of Pictish bulls from Burghead, an Early Iron Age log-boat, used on the Spey, as well as the round basket-work *curraghs* used by the Spey log-raft men of the 18th century, but also the well-preserved fossils of extinct fish and reptiles found in the various local sandstone quarries, which made an important contribution to 19th-century geological studies.

Errol   Perthshire   Tayside   2 F2

The 'capital' of the Carse of Gowrie (q.v.) is a pleasant village set in the rich alluvial lands N of the Tay Estuary, and a mile or so s of the Dundee to Perth road. It is famous for its early connexion with the great family of Hays of Erroll, whom we meet again at Slains (see Buchan Coast) and at Delgatie (q.v.). The legend of how the Hays came by their lands is attractive and romantic, though it rests on the dubious authority of the erratic Hector Boece. The story runs that in the reign of King Kenneth III, at the end of the 10th century, one of several Danish invasions ravaged the lands from Angus to the Tay, penetrating as far w as Luncarty (N of Perth) before battle was joined by the Scottish king and his nobles. The Scots were on the point of flight when a gigantic peasant and his two huge sons, brandishing ox-yokes, rallied the royal forces and drove the Danes from the field. Kenneth offered to reward the patriotic locals with as much land as his hawk could fly over without perching. The father wisely directed the flight to be over the fertile lands of the Carse, though whether this helpful bird really covered the parish of Errol from the

Hawkstone in St Madoes to the Falcon Stone of Rossie remains uncertain. Giving colour to the legend, the Hay crest is a falcon, supported by two men in country garb, bearing ox-yokes with the motto 'Serva Jugum'; and to this day the Hays are giants of men. Be all that as it may, the Hays did well in the 12th and 13th centuries and supported Robert the Bruce in the War of Independence. After Bannockburn, Sir Gilbert Hay was granted the hereditary title of Lord High Constable of Scotland, and given lands in Buchan, including Delgatie and Slains. In 1452, his descendant was made 1st Earl of Erroll. The 4th Earl fell at Flodden in 1513, with 87 other members of his clan. It was Francis, the 9th Earl, who associated himself with Huntly in the Papist plot with Spain against James VI, and was exiled after the Battle of Glenlivet (q.v.). The extravagance of the 10th Earl at the Holyrood coronation of Charles I in 1633 led to the estate at Errol being sold, and, after 1634, the fortunes of the Hay family lie elsewhere.

Errol Park then passed through various hands, including those of John Allen, a West Indian merchant and an 18th-century improving landlord, who reclaimed land from the Tay marshes, bringing agriculture and industry to the area and improving the small harbour on the Tay, then the only one between Perth and Dundee, now known as Port Allen. His Georgian mansion was burnt to the ground in 1874, and replaced by the present Victorian building. The village of Errol is pleasant, if undistinguished, standing on a slight elevation in the alluvial plain, one of the various 'inches' which were islands before the Tay was held back and the land drained. The large Gothic church, built in 1831-3 by the Edinburgh architect Gillespie Graham, is conspicuous enough to be nicknamed 'the Cathedral of the Carse'. Of the old church only the graveyard remains, with a burial vault of the Errol Park families.

Between Errol and the busy A85 road from Perth to Dundee stands Megginch Castle, reconstructed, so an inscription says, by Peter Hay in 1575. It belonged to the Hays until the 17th century and since then has been the home of the Drummond family. They extended it in the 19th century, preserving the original north front. This mellow castle has a well-settled look among its ancient trees, including an avenue of hollies and thousand-year-old yews. The castle gardens are open to the public in the summer.

Fasque   Kincardine and Deeside   Grampian   5 F3

Gladstonians will be interested to know that the ancestral home of the great Liberal Prime Minister has been open to the public since 1978, and that Gladstone *memorabilia* have been assembled in his former bedroom. For the rest, Fasque is no museum, but a brave attempt by the present owner, Mr Peter Gladstone, to re-create a Victorian mansion as it was in the days of opulence when there were 15 or more servants to polish the copper, mow the lawns, keep the stables, serve at table and operate the huge kitchen. There are also furniture, silk screens and other Oriental objects brought from India and Japan, including a life-size eagle built of ivory pieces, each feather a separate piece.

Fasque, meaning 'shelter', lies under the Mounth hills, 2 miles N of Fettercairn (q.v.). The red sandstone mansion was built in 1809 for Sir Alexander Ramsay of Balmain on the site of an earlier castle. He ruined himself in the process and 20 years later sold it to John Gladstone (1764-1851), 'John the Founder', a successful merchant from Leith, who made his fortune in the Liverpool Atlantic trade. He added the rather meagre porch and the central tower with its castellations, and set about improving the estate. His fourth son was William Ewart Gladstone (1809-98), the future Prime Minister whose home was at Fasque from 1830 until his father died in 1851. The great Gladstone's enjoyment of the hills and the shooting is recorded in his diaries. The principal rooms are light, airy and well proportioned. In particular the entrance hall, leading to the double curved cantilever staircase, is a delight to the eye. A sad note is struck in the room used by Helen Gladstone, a woman of similar intellectual capacity to her celebrated brother. Frustrated by their domineering father and the Victorian restrictions on women, she turned first rebel, then Roman Catholic and suffered from nervous disorders before finally recovering her sanity and, one is glad to learn, some degree of independence.

Fettercairn   Kincardine and Deeside   Grampian   5 F4
Kincardine Castle (see Mearns) is nothing but a green tree-covered mound. Fettercairn, 2 miles away, is the village where the Cairn o' Mount road slants down to the Howe of the Mearns on its way to Montrose. The Mercat Cross (carrying the standard ell measure) in the wide central square was taken from the original Kincardine: its finial, a sundial, and his initials were added by the flamboyant John, 1st Earl of Middleton (1608-74), who fought with Charles II at Worcester, escaped with him to France, rose to be Commander-in-Chief in Scotland and Commissioner to the Scottish Parliament after the Restoration. Fettercairn is entered from the W through a red sandstone archway, erected to commemorate the visit here in September 1861 of Queen Victoria, Prince Albert and her entourage; describing themselves at one point as 'a wedding party from Aberdeen', they spent the night supposedly incognito at the Ramsay Arms. They had ridden in the day from Ballater, over the shoulder of Mount Keen, and lunched at the Queen's Well by the Water of Mark. At Invermark, they were met by 'a sort of double dog-cart which could carry eight — but was very narrow inside', as the Queen describes it in her journal. The party returned to Balmoral the following day over the Cairn o' Mount, the view 'entirely obscured by a heavy driving mist'. They diverged from the South Deeside road to go

up Glen Tanar and recross the hills on horse-back to the Bridge of Muick — quite an excursion: 82 miles (132 km.) in the two days, the Queen records.

Finavon   Angus   Tayside   5 E5
No prehistoric strategist could fail to be attracted by the litle spine of rocky ridge that projects out of undulating Strathmore between Brechin and Forfar. The narrow, twisting road NW from Aberlemno winds through this miniature range. On the northern spur is the ancient hill-fort of Finavon, not large as hill-forts go, but on a superb site with views up Strathmore to the Mearns and W to Blairgowrie. There is a similar fort on the neighbouring, even more steeply-scarped, Turin Hill, a mile to the S.

To the N, the medieval tower of Finavon, 186 ft high, peers above the trees. This is an ancient stronghold of the Earls of Crawford, who saw the advantages of a strategic site where the Lemno Burn joins the South Esk, and now astride the busy modern Brechin to Forfar highway (A94). The gaunt tower (which may be visited) could tell some grim tales of this branch of the Lindsays, Earls of Crawford, who held Finavon from 1375 until the title passed to the Lindsays of Edzell (q.v.) in the early 17th century. History relates that the 3rd Earl was killed in 1446 at the 'Battle of Arbroath' — the clash with the Ogilvys over the claim to be justiciar, or lay protector, of Arbroath Abbey (q.v.), with its rich pickings. Legend has it differently: Ogilvy's sister was Lindsay's wife; both arrived wounded at Finavon; when Lindsay died, his wife smothered her own brother in revenge. Her son was the notorious 'Tiger', or 'Earl Beardie', who hanged his minstrel by hooks from Finavon tower for prophesying his defeat by Huntly at the Battle of Brechin in 1452, and committed other cruelties on his insubordinate tenants. Despite his support of the Douglases at Brechin, 'Earl Beardie' was forgiven by James II, and entertained the King at Finavon. The 16th-century earls had their troubles: one was imprisoned in his own dungeon by his son 'the Wicked Master', who was himself stabbed to death in 1542 in a drunken brawl in Dundee.

Just to the N of the A94 the big lectern-type doocot, one of the largest in Scotland, with nesting-boxes for 2,000 birds, has been restored. The western half was inaugurated in July 1979 as a museum of Angus doocots: the other half remains an active working doocot (see Introduction: Architecture).

River Findhorn   Moray   Grampian   7 A 2-1
The sources of the River Findhorn are in the peaty morasses of the Monadliath Mountains in the Highland Region. Some distance below the A9 and also below the spectacular military road crossing at Dulsie Bridge, the Findhorn flows into Moray and, for the last 10 miles (16 km.) of its course to the Moray Firth, shows a surprising variety of wooded glen and steep rocky gorge. Its waters

too, dark with peat, are quite different from the crystal-clear waters of the Avon from the granite Cairngorms.

'Randolph's Leap' at Relugas, where the Divie Burn joins the Findhorn below the B9007 to Carrbridge, is a particularly dramatic stretch of rocky gorge. The place is mis-named, for it was a Cumming and not a Randolph from Moray who leapt the 10 ft gap over the boiling black waters. When Robert the Bruce created Thomas Randolph Earl of Moray, the Cummings on the E bank of the Findhorn resented the loss of their lands on the w bank. They organized a raid on the Moray Castle of Darnaway. Foiled in this, they were pursued by Randolph's men and, in the course of the pursuit, one Alastair Cumming leapt the Findhorn.

Though the title of Earl of Moray passed through various hands, the Moray seat is still at Darnaway, a largely 19th-century castle, away in the thick forests to the w of the Findhorn (not open except on special occasions). It incorporates the famous Randolph's Hall of 1450, with its magnificent oak roof; there is the posthumous portrait of the 'Bonnie Earl of Moray', showing the wounds on his body inflicted by his murderers at Donibristle (*see* Doune).

Below Forres, the Findhorn opens out into the broad tidal expanse of Findhorn Bay, a favourite haunt of yachtsmen and wildfowl. The currents and prevailing westerly winds make the mouth of the Findhorn a strange place of shifting geography. West of the bay are the famous CULBIN SANDS, which, in 1694, overwhelmed the Kinnaird estate. Legends of bells tolling under the sands or flourishing apple-trees are to be discounted. The catastrophe did not happen at one fell swoop. The encroachment of the sand, blown by NW gales, must have occurred over a number of years, culminating in the great storm of 1694, and it was certainly accelerated by the custom of plucking marram grass for thatch (later forbidden). The afforestation of the area did not begin until 1870, and has now been completed by the Forestry Commission, using Corsican pine (resistant to the dry, salty air). There is a small exhibition on the Culbin Sands in the Falconer Museum in Forres (q.v.). One of the few sand deserts in Britain, Culbin now offers pleasant forest walks. On the way to Culbin, the gardens of Kincorth, specialising in roses, are open to the public in summer.

Fochabers Moray Grampian 7 C2
The main branch of the powerful Catholic Gordon family, who rose from Earls of Huntly to Dukes of Gordon, had two principal residences: one in Strathbogie, which became known as Huntly; the other where the coastal route through Moray crosses the Spey 5 miles from its mouth. The latter, now the village of Fochabers, was known as BOG O' GIGHT (the bog of the wind) — not to be confused with Gight Castle, the home of Byron's mother. The site of the present Gordon Castle at Fochabers dates back to the 12th century; the Old Tower which stands today was raised to its present height of six

storeys by the 2nd Earl of Huntly about 1500. Various additions were made, resulting in a rambling house which the 4th Duke of Gordon (1743-1827) found unsuitable as a setting for his beautiful bride Jane Maxwell, whom he married in 1767. This was the famous Duchess who raised the Gordon Highlanders with a shilling between her lips and a kiss for each recruit. The 4th Duke pulled down everything except the Old Tower and built a grandiose mansion with a facade nearly 200 yds long. In the course of this reconstruction, he found it inconvenient to have the old village so close to his castle, so, in 1776, following the contemporary trend for 'improvement', he founded Fochabers as a planned village in the parish of Bellie.

Fochabers is a fine example of 18th-century town-planning, though its main street now carries the busy A96 Aberdeen to Inverness traffic. The principal buildings and main square have great charm, in particular the parish church, well proportioned with pillared portico and spire, flanked by dignified grey stone houses, on the s side of the square. Fochabers owes much to John Baxter (mason to William Adam, the architect), who laid out the rectangular plan. Another benefactor was Alexander Milne, who emigrated to America because he would not have his hair cut as the duke wished. After making a fortune in Louisiana, he returned in 1846 to found Milne's High School, built in the Tudor Revival Gothic style by Thomas Mackenzie, the architect of Elgin Museum and the Victorian pile of Drummuir Castle, between Keith and Dufftown. Two present-day businessmen whose success has brought wealth to Fochabers are both direct descendants of ducal retainers. Unlike the village, which has prospered and grown, Gordon Castle fell on evil days after the title of Duke of Gordon passed to the Duke of Richmond in 1836, and these lands were, a century later, made over to the Crown. In World War II, the buildings were used by the Army and deteriorated so badly that the centre wing was demolished in the 1950s. Lt Gen. Sir George Gordon-Lennox rescued what remained and converted one wing into his own residence.

To the E of Fochabers, the A98 coast road to Banff passes through an extensive forest, developed by the Forestry Commission, with pleasant walks to viewpoints over the Laich of Moray. To the E of this wooded area is the strongly Catholic area of Enzie (*pron.* Ingie), the hinterland of Buckie and the fishing villages along the coast. The powerful patronage of the Gordon family ensured, as Peter Anson writes in his *Underground Catholicism in Scotland 1622-1878*, that 'under the reigns of James VI and Charles I, a Catholic traveller from Elgin to Aberdeen could take his choice of households where he could spend the night without molestation'. In the 18th century Catholics had to be more circumspect. After seeking various refuges in which to worship, they were in 1755 given by the Gordons a sheep-cote at Newlands by Tynet, near the road to Speymouth. The little church of St Ninian's still looks like a long, white-washed cottage in a field, with a ball-finial instead of a cross. It is said to be the oldest post-Reformation Catholic church still extant in Scotland, and became known as the 'Banffshire Bethlehem'.

Fordyce Banff and Buchan Grampian 7 D1
Three miles inland from Portsoy is the picturesque village of Fordyce, with its winding lanes, the whole declared a special conservation area. The laird's house, dating from 1592, is in the middle of the main street. This delightful little castle is an L-plan tower-house with crowstep gables, angle-turrets, and a stair-turret in the re-entrant angle, supported by an elaborate piece of corbelling, in which five plain courses alternate with six ornamental ones, all different. It was built by Sir Thomas Menzies, of the family that supplied several provosts of Aberdeen. He must have had his anxieties, for his tower-house has a multitude of triple pistol-loops under the windows, but they may have been for decoration only.

Across the way is the graveyard of St Talorgan (or Talaricanus) — the modern Tarquin — round the remains of the old kirk. These consist of a pend (or archway) framed in the soft red sandstone and supporting a priest's room above, accessible by an outside stair. The whole is crowned by a little belfry. The rather overcrowded graveyard includes a number of enclosed tombs: an Ogilvie tomb with a pair of fine decorated pointed recesses, one occupied by a recumbent stone effigy of a knight in armour, his feet resting on a dog.

Forres Moray Grampian 11 A2 (*pop.* 4,718)
The pleasant little town of Forres, the *Varris* of Ptolemy's map, is a smaller edition of Elgin, with which it shares both the fertile Laich of Moray (q.v.) and the fate of having been burnt by the Wolf of Badenoch in 1390. King Duncan held his court here when Macbeth rebelled against him. If Macbeth did not meet the three witches at the Knock of Alves, near Elgin, then he may have done so at Macbeth Hillock on the border of Moray and Nairn (but *see* Dunsinane). At all events, this is witches' country: as late as the 18th century, these unfortunate women were put into barrels and rolled down Cluny Hill as a preliminary to being burnt. The busy main street of Forres has a mildly medieval air with crowstep gables, narrow wynds and a 19th-century Tudor-Gothic Town House on the site of the earlier Tolbooth. Spiky St Laurence Church is mostly 19th-century Gothic. At the w end of the main street, on a terrace where the old castle probably stood, is a tall granite obelisk erected in 1857 to Dr James Thomson, who died helping wounded Russian prisoners in the Crimean War.

The attractive Falconer Museum (housing the Tourist Information Bureau), executed in classical style in golden Moray stone, has recently been refurbished. Founded in memory of the brothers Alexander and Hugh Falconer

in 1871, it houses a collection of local birds, fossils from the Old Red Sandstone, also orientalia, as well as an exhibit on the Culbin Sands (*see* Findhorn). Hugh Falconer (1808-65), botanist and geologist, advised the Government of Bengal on the development in India of the tea plant from China. Other items from the Orient include paintings of Indian tradesmen and their costumes by the remarkable traveller Constance Frederika Gordon-Cumming of Altyre, who spent twelve years (from 1868) travelling in India and the Far East.

The wooded Cluny Hill to the s is crowned by the Nelson Tower, built in 1806 to commemorate the great admiral. It provides a good view over Findhorn Bay to the N and over the forests and hills of Moray to the s. Just E of the town is the remarkable Sueno's Stone, a 23 ft-high Pictish monolith carved with an intricate series of strips showing horsemen, spearsmen, captives and headless bodies. Boece's interpretation that it records a victory of Sweyn the Dane over the Picts is incorrect. As it has Christian symbols on the back, it is more likely to commemorate some Pictish victory of the 9th century. On the low hills overlooking the Laich of Moray to the E of Forres are the twin towers of Burgie and Blervie, both five or six storeys high, both originally belonging to the Dunbar family, and both having had the adjoining halls demolished to build modern residences.

River Forth Stirling Central 1 A4-D6
The derivation of Forth is the longest entry in Johnston's *Place Names of Scotland*. Of the variety of interpretations, which include the obvious 'ford', a 'boundary' (between Saxon and Celt), and confusion with the Scandinavian fjord (which, in fact, is our 'firth'), the most convincing is from the Celtic *voredia* — the slow-running one. The Forth, flowing in loops and coils through deep peat moss or rich alluvial lands, is indeed a sluggish river. In its lower reaches the soil is so rich that it is rightly said that 'A crook of Forth is worth an earldom in the North'. Though scenically less interesting than other Scottish rivers, the Forth is of considerable historical interest and of strategic and economic importance. In the reign of James I, John Hardyng, the English spy, wrote of 'Foorth, that ryver principall, of right faire waye, and plentiful it all'. After rising on Ben Lomond and in the Trossachs, the Forth changes from a Highland stream to run through the flattest land in Scotland, taking some 40 miles (64 km.) to reach Stirling, over double the distance that a crow would fly, and falling a mere 37 ft on the way. In Caledonian days, the Forth valley must have been thickly forested but devastation, starting with the axes of the Romans and continuing through the centuries, reduced the oak woods to a thick blanket of peat, 6 to 12 ft deep, overlying the alluvial soil. The improving landlords of the 18th century saw the advantage of reclamation, making use of the labour of Highlanders out of work after the Forty-Five, and resettling them on the reclaimed land, where they

became known as the Moss Lairds. In particular Lord Kames, who in 1766 inherited Blair Drummond through his wife, started the work of stripping off the peat. Blair Drummond Moss is now some of the finest farmland in the country, producing the best timothy grass. Parts of Flanders Moss remain unreclaimed, and the desolate atmosphere of the peat bog as it was can be recaptured from the B822 road from Kippen to Thornhill. This road crosses the Forth near the Fords of Frew — once the only possible crossing w of Stirling, by which a skilful commander with a good guide could evade the strategic point of Stirling.

The Forth coils and winds its way eastwards at the foot of the Gargunnock Hills, to be joined just w of the M9 by its principal and faster-flowing tributary, the Teith. From this point, the castle of Stirling (q.v.) stands dramatically on its volcanic crag; guarding the ford used by the Romans and the first bridge upstream from the estuary, it epitomises over seven centuries of Scottish history. East of Stirling, the Forth, wider now and tidal as well, continues meandering through the rich carse-lands until, below the modern Kincardine Bridge by Falkirk, it becomes an inlet of the sea.

Fortingall Perthshire Tayside 3 G6
Fortingall and Garth, Coshieville and Dull trip off the tongue like Housman's Shropshire hills and though not all may agree that they are the 'pleasantest places under the sun' the number of prehistoric remains indicate that its earliest inhabitants favoured this sheltered valley, where the River Lyon (see Glen Lyon) ceases to be a mountain stream and, after taking in the tumultuous Keltney Burn, runs peacefully to join the Tay. The flat area by the junction of the rivers is known as Strath Appin, or the Appin of Dull, nothing to do with Appin of Argyll, save that both derive from the Gaelic *apuin*, abbey land. DULL comes from *Doilweem*, the Valley of the Cave. There is a close association with the biographer of St Columba, St Adamnan (or Eonan). He came from Iona in 687, founded the College of Dull for Culdee clerics, and died here in 704.

Coshieville, though now little more than an hotel, marks the point at which the Keltney Burn (a nature reserve), rushing down a steep chasm with little waterfalls, joins the flat valley of the Lyon. The Wade military road, now the B846, runs steeply up the E bank of the Keltney Burn, past the deer park of Glengoulandie, over the shoulder of the prominent conical peak of Schiehallion, and down to Tummel Bridge. The cattle drovers too came over here from Rannoch on their way to the tryst at Crieff. The Menzies held this road junction in the 14th century from their little castle of Comrie, now ruined. They must have found the Stewarts of Garth awkward neighbours and moved their residence to the newer castle of Weem (see Aberfeldy).

The grim-looking tower-keep of GARTH (now modernised and in private hands), a mile up the Keltney Burn but readily visible from the B846 up the E bank, was a stronghold of the notorious Wolf of Badenoch (see Elgin). His descendants were an unruly lot too and, in the 16th century, Garth became a place of refuge for cattle-thieves, Macgregors and other outlaws. Neil Stewart of Garth raided Weem with his 'caterans' in 1502 and carried off the unfortunate Sir Robert Menzies to the dungeons at Garth. The later Stewarts of Garth moved down from their tower to Garth House, just w of Coshieville. General Sir David Stewart of Garth (1772-1829), whose statue stands at Coshieville, served with distinction in Egypt under Abercrombie and in the Peninsular War. He also played an important part in the rehabilitation of the Highlander by his *Sketches of the Character, Manners and present state of the Highlanders of Scotland, with Details of the Military Service of the Highland Regiments*, published in 1822. These lively sketches (still very readable) caught the mood of the moment as George IV appeared in Edinburgh in a kilt and was persuaded by Sir Walter Scott to try a glass of malt whisky.

Fortingall itself was rebuilt by Sir Donald Currie in the late 19th century with thatched houses (unfortunately liable to fire) in the style of the trim village of Selworthy on Exmoor. The church contains a font used by St Adamnan, a 7th-century bell, another bell cast in Amsterdam in 1765, and a modern screen designed by Sir Robert Lorimer. The priest who died here in 1551 was James Macgregor, who started the *Chronicle of Fortingall*. Earlier, as dean of Lismore, he had made the collection of Gaelic verse dating back to the 14th century, the *Book of the Dean of Lismore*, written in a phonetic Gaelic much easier to read than the complicated modern orthography. Glen Lyon House, originally built by the Robert Campbell made infamous by his part in the Massacre of Glencoe, was largely reconstructed at the end of the 19th century. Fortingall's best-known celebrity is its ancient yew tree, variously said to be 2,000 or even 3,000 years old. Pennant measured the circumference in 1769 as $56\frac{1}{2}$ ft (17 m.). It suffered the depredations of bowmakers, when bows and arrows were in demand, and since Pennant's day of souvenir-hunters. Indeed, it is rather a sad thing, surrounded by a wall with its straggling limbs supported on piles of masonry. All that can be said for certain is that it has been there a long time. Holinshed (on whom Shakespeare drew for his historical plays) recorded the story that Pontius Pilate was born at Fortingall. His father, it is thought, was sent on a mission to the Pictish king Metallanus, who lived at Dun Geal, the Pictish fort on the hill above, and his mother could have been a local girl. The story does not hold together chronologically, but it is as durable as the yew tree.

Fowlis Wester Perthshire Tayside 1 C2
It is a fair distance from Fowlis Easter, near Dundee, to this quiet village (just N of the A85 from Crieff to Perth) on a green terrace above Strathearn. It was once a busy

centre on a main road, with a cattle-selling tryst as important as that of Crieff. The church is dedicated to St Bean, an Irish missionary who came over in the early 8th century. The present long, low, barrel-vaulted building dates from the 13th century, well restored in 1927. Within, there is a fine Pictish symbol-stone with a Celtic cross, showing robed clerical figures and, below, two monks facing a branch with twin buds at the top and seven buds below, symbolising the Earl of Strathearn and his seven sons, or else the seven churches he founded; in the top right-hand corner, Jonah is being swallowed by the whale. At the chancel end of the church is a 'leper squint' allowing lepers to watch the celebration of Mass from outside without coming into contact with the congregation. By contrast, 20th-century history has been recorded with the piece of MacBean tartan which Alan L. Bean, the American astronaut, took to the moon and back, and presented to St Bean's Church.

There is a large carved Celtic cross with intricate decoration and animals in the centre of the village. Though called the Cross of Fowlis, it was brought here from Balnacroisk, over the hill at the mouth of the Sma' Glen. The red sandstone is weathering badly and the figures are becoming indistinct.

Fraserburgh Buchan Grampian 8 G1
(*pop.* 1,606)

Fraserburgh is at the extreme NE corner of the 'cold shoulder' of Scotland. Kinnairds Head was already known to the Romans, being marked on Ptolemy's map as *Promontorium Taezalorum.* In the 10th and 11th centuries, the Vikings doubtless found it convenient to land in Fraserburgh Bay, and the various castles of the area (Inverallochy, Pitsligo, Pitullie, Philorth and Cairnbulg, as well as the castle on Kinnairds Head itself) developed from strongholds originally designed to resist these invasions. Kinnairds Head Castle existed before Sir Alexander Fraser of Philorth (whose ancestors arrived in Buchan in the wake of the Stewarts in 1375) obtained a charter in 1546 to turn the little fishing village of Faithlie, as it was then called, into a refuge for ships rounding the promontory. His son completed the 'burgum et portum de Fraser' some 30 years later and, in 1601, obtained the right to call it Fraserburgh. Nowadays, the locals refer to the place as The Broch, though there is no Celtic broch anywhere in this area. The new 16th-century burgh had great pretentions, for the charter included permission to found a university: George Keith, the fifth Earl Marischal, who founded Marischal College in Aberdeen in 1593, started Fraserburgh University in the same year, but the venture failed after just 10 years of existence.

Kinnairds Head Castle, a rugged rectangular keep of four storeys, is unique in being the base of an operational lighthouse, one of the earliest in Britain, dating from 1787. Close by is the primitive rubble-built Wine Tower (nothing to do with wine, but doubtless a watch tower), probably dating from the early 16th century. Access is in-

convenient, being only by a rope to an upper window. The Frasers moved out to the nearby castle at Philorth, which remained their home until burnt down in 1915. Philorth was also their local name, to distinguish them from the Frasers of Lovat. The title of Lord Saltoun was conferred in the 18th century and remains with the Frasers of Philorth. After the burning of Philorth Castle, the Frasers restored the ancient 14th-century fortress of Cairnbulg, now the family home of the last descendant, Lady Saltoun. Other reminders of the Frasers are in the Mercat Cross in Saltoun Square and in the statue of Lord Saltoun in a high domed tower over the Town House of 1855. The Fraser mausoleum, a curious stepped pyramid, is on the s side of the distinctive parish church in Saltoun Square.

Just as the fishing of the small ports of the Banffshire coast has been consolidated in Buckie and Macduff, so the two main fishing ports on the Buchan coast are Fraserburgh and Peterhead: and the little villages of Inverallochy and St Combs, once fierce rivals, are now dormitories for Fraserburgh fishermen. Fraserburgh has prospered, its population mutiplying four-fold since 1800. The oil-boom of the 1970s has had its spin-off in Fraserburgh, but the town has not suffered the same direct impact of the oil developments as Peterhead.

Fyvie Gordon Grampian 8 F3

Fyvie, on the River Ythan, some 25 miles (40 km.) NW of Aberdeen on the A947 to Turriff and Banff, has an important place in Scottish history. Fyvie Castle (not open to the public) is the most grandiose of the castles of the North-East, comparable with Glamis, for the lairds of Fyvie represent a succession of distinguished families — Prestons, Setons, Gordons and Forbes-Leith. Fyvie was originally the seat of the Thane of Formartine, the Celtic district between the Rivers Ythan and Don. The Norman family of Le Cheyne acquired the lands; Edward I passed by the 'Chastel de Fyvin' in 1296; Bruce stayed here for some time after defeating the Comyns of Buchan in 1308, and so Fyvie was not destroyed in the devastation ('herschip') of Buchan. The building of the castle in its present form began with Sir Henry Preston, who acquired Fyvie out of the proceeds of a ransom received from one of the Percy family captured at Otterburn in 1390. (A frieze in bas-relief inside the new entrance, set up in 1890, depicts a scene from the battle). The Preston Tower, the oldest of the towers, is at the right-hand end of the splendid pink-hearted facade of Fyvie. The Meldrum lairds (from 1433-1596) built the second, or Meldrum, Tower.

Fyvie then passed to the Setons, staunch Royalists, one of whom helped Mary, Queen of Scots, escape from Loch Leven; another was Mary Seton, Mary's faithful lady-in-waiting; and a third, who married Elizabeth Gordon, continued the Huntly Gordon line by calling his descendants Gordon. Alexander Seton rose rapidly under James VI to become Lord President of Scotland in 1593, Chancellor in

1605, and was created Lord Dunfermline. He was entrusted with James VI's young and delicate son, Charles (later Charles I), who spent some of his childhood at Fyvie. Lord Dunfermline improved Fyvie by raising the s front between the Preston and Meldrum Towers, and inserting a central double tower of two semi-drums — the Seton Tower — united 42 ft up by a high narrow arch. The result is a splendid front of unusual symmetry for the period, the two older flanking towers brought together by the Seton Tower over the entrance guarded by its stout yett and topped by three pairs of turrets surmounted by little stone figures. This entrance did not lead directly to the principal apartments, which are accessible by Lord Dunfermline's second architectural triumph, the broad, gently graduated wheel stair, reminiscent of Blois and the French Renaissance. This is away to the w wing, close to the entrance from the courtyard which was opened up in the 19th century.

In 1644, Montrose was nearly trapped in Fyvie by Argyll, but slipped away. Some bullets, said to be from the skirmish, are among the treasured relics of the castle. The courageous Seton ladies confronted the Cromwellian troops during their occupation. The 4th Earl, James, joined 'Bonnie Dundee' at the Battle of Killiecrankie in 1689, and died in exile. Fyvie was forfeited, and in 1733 came into the hands of the Gordons of Haddo, family of the Earls of Aberdeen. William Gordon (1745-1816), a Hanoverian supporter, developed the estate and built the Gordon Tower at the corner of the w wing, demolishing the chapel to do so. His son planted the beech and other hardwoods, and drained the swamp to make the attractive lake on which wildfowl now congregate.

After his death in 1847, Fyvie was neglected until bought in 1889 by Alexander Forbes-Leith, a steel magnate who had made a fortune in the United States. He lavished much care and attention on Fyvie, adding a Leith Tower, grafted onto the Gordon Tower, and making it a treasure-house of beautiful things, including numerous portraits by Raeburn of the Setons and Gordons. He was created Lord Leith of Fyvie in 1905, and the castle remains with his family.

Fyvie church is on a knoll to the E of the village — probably Christians have worshipped here since St Devenick came this way in the 6th century. St Mary's Priory was established here in 1285, but abandoned at the Reformation, the site being marked by the tall cross in a field, a short distance from the present church. This dates from 1808, but Pictish stones of great antiquity have been built into the outside chancel wall, and a number of old graves preserved, including those of Alexander Gordon of Gight (1716-61), Byron's grandfather, and of 'Tifty's Annie', the daughter of the Miller of Tifty. The ballad relates how her cruel father refused to allow her to wed the Laird of Fyvie's trumpeter 'who had the art to gain the heart o' Mill of Tifty's Annie'. She was a real person, and died of a broken heart in 1673. Within Fyvie Church there are a number of treasures, including a tablet to

15th-century Prior Thomas Cranno, and the coloured coat of arms of Alexander Seton, 1st Lord Dunfermline, dated 1603. The chancel was extended by Lord Fyvie in memory of his son, Percy Forbes-Leith, who died in 1900 during the Boer War at the age of 20. The large memorial window depicting the Archangel Michael was designed and executed by the New York glass-designer Tiffany (1848-1933) and is a fine example of the unique type of stained glass called 'Favrile', which he perfected.

The Garioch   Gordon   Grampian   8 E4
The Garioch (*pron.* Geerie) is one of those districts that give a lift to the heart: it is best approached from the surrounding hills, either from the s by the Struie road over the Correen Hills from Bridge of Alford to Clatt, or from the N by the winding road from Huntly down past Dunnideer to Insch. It is hard to forget this view over the undulating, fertile basin, whether in early summer, when the cornfields are green, or later, when the harvest is due, or, perhaps best of all, when the low autumn sun casts its light over the chequer-board of reddish-brown plough and yellow-grey stubble. To the N are the slaty ridges of Foudland, to the s the schists of the Correen Hills and the looming granite mass of Bennachie. Lying between these, the Garioch has, the geologists tell us, benefited from the weathering of the rock into extremely fertile soils.

Small wonder that this small district contains a large number of prehistoric and Pictish standing-stones, or that David II took over the 'meal girnal' (granary) of Aberdeenshire as a personal fief, or that Robert the Bruce, who fought the Buchan Comyn over this ground, kept the title of Lord of Garioch. The insignificant stream that drains the western Garioch, the Gadie Burn, inspired that most nostalgic of songs of the North-East, 'Oh! gin I were where Gadie rins, where Gadie rins . . . at the back o' Bennachie'. Many versions exist of this song, but the refrain is always the same. The Scottish soldiers at the siege of Pondicherry in 1760 (perhaps Gordons, but they might have been Leslies, for they speak of 'Thick as Leslies on Gadieside') heard it sung by a homesick lady within the walls.

The western half of the Garioch focuses on the conical hill of Dunnideer, a mere 878 ft (268 m.) high, but dominating the little town of Insch and the narrow pass of the Shevock stream. Dunnideer is crowned by the remaining high ruined wall of a medieval tower, pierced by a great window, once popularly called Macbeth's Castle; but its importance dates back to the triple hill-fort surrounding the tower. Across the Shevock burn is the 'Hill of Christ's Kirk'. *Christ's Kirk on the Green* is a poem ascribed to James I about the goings-on at an overnight fair held at the nearby suitably-named farm of Sleepytown. To the N is the Picardy Stone (AM) with a clearly incised set of enigmatic Pictish symbols. The Gadie runs past the castle of Leslie, much ruined but a good example of an L-plan tower-house with defensive features such as round turrets on each main angle, and many gunloops and shot-holes that would not be expected in a castle built in 1661. Lickley Head Castle (not open to the public) 2 miles E of Leslie dates mainly from 1629, and has been beautifully restored by the mother of the present owner.

Chapel of Garioch is a scattered parish on the NE slopes of Bennachie, with good views over the Aberdeenshire farmlands. The arched gateway to the former church still stands. Chapel of Garioch is the 'Pyketillim' where William Alexander's novel *Johnny Gibb of Gushetneuk* is set (see Introduction: North-East in Literature).

For the eastern part of the Garioch, see under Inverurie.

Garth   *see* **Fortingall**

Gight   *see* **Ythan**

Glamis   Angus   Tayside   4 D6
The Castle of Glamis (*pron.* Glahms) is justly renowned in legend, literature and history. The size and magnificence of this massive pinkish-grey structure, rising from the peaceful Vale of Strathmore, testify to the repute and standing of the Lyon family, who have held the lands of Glamis under the successive titles of Lords Glamis, Earls of Kinghorne and Earls of Strathmore from 1372 to the present day. They have had close personal links with the Royal Family from the first Sir John Lyon who, in 1376, married the daughter of King Robert II, down to Queen Elizabeth, the Queen Mother, who was brought up at Glamis. The present Earl, 17th in line, is first cousin to Her Majesty, Queen Elizabeth II.

The site of the church and village at the foot of the wooded Hunter's Hill dates from St Fergus's visitation, about 750. There was a royal hunting-lodge from the 11th to the 14th century. Though Malcolm II died here in 1034, it was certainly not in the room now known as King Malcolm's Room, with its legend of the blood-stained floor, as that was not built until three centuries later. Nor does history substantiate the legend that Macbeth, though certainly Thane of Glamis, entertained his victim Duncan in the vaulted guard-room in the present crypt known as Duncan's Hall (in fact, Macbeth slew Duncan in open combat near Elgin). Difficult though it is to disentangle history, legend and literature, there is no doubt that the lower central parts of the castle are of great antiquity, and were built into the 15th-century tower which forms the core of the Renaissance castle.

At first sight, Glamis does not resemble the traditional Scottish castle. The eye is beguiled by wings to E and W, and the cluster of turrets, gables and balustraded catwalks 100 ft above the ground. If these additions and embellishments are disregarded, the central six-storey part of the castle is a simple L-plan tower with a circular stair-tower built into the re-entrant angle. The two stout turreted towers flanking the lower extensions are all that remain of the towers and curtain walling originally surrounding a great courtyard. The flat-roofed extensions were built as part of the grandiose schemes of Patrick, 9th Lord Glamis and from 1606 1st Earl of Kinghorne, who also heightened the central block and added the lavish heraldic decoration. The work was continued after his death in 1615 by his son John, the 2nd Earl, who put in the plaster-work ceilings, but the

Glamis Castle

burden of this, coupled with the expenses of supporting the Army of Covenant against Montrose, left his successor with the enormous debt of £400,000. Patrick, the 3rd Earl of Kinghorne, who was created 1st Earl of Strathmore in 1677, paid off the debt by 'prudence and frugality' and made further additions to the castle. The 9th Earl improved the family fortunes by marrying Mary Bowes, an heiress from North Yorkshire, and assumed the name of Bowes-Lyon.

The interior of the castle contains much of interest, of which details are set out in the excellent official guide-book. The broad vaulted crypt, with suits of armour and trophies of arms, was originally the main lower hall of the 15th-century castle, above the grim dungeon below; the adjoining guard-room, with its early portraits of James V and Mary of Lorraine, is Duncan's Hall. Earl Patrick's Great Hall (now the Drawing Room) has a magnificent plaster-work ceiling (by the same team of plaster-moulders that made the ceilings at Craigievar and at Muchalls) and a huge fireplace, with caryatids merging at the waist into vase-shaped pillars. The large picture at the end of the room shows Earl Patrick — in flesh-coloured armour — with his sons, pointing to the castle as it once was, with the surrounding walls and the seven gates on the approach avenue.

The wood-panelled chapel is decorated with Biblical scenes painted by the Dutch artist Jakob de Wet, including an unusual one of Christ in a Dutch gardener's hat. The story goes that this was de Wet's revenge for being underpaid by the earl, though the practice of painting Christ in a hat was not unknown. The other side to the dispute between painter and earl was that de Wet brought in Dundee painters to do the hack-work. The Royal Apartments, beautifully arranged and furnished, are those used by the late King George VI and his consort, Queen Elizabeth, the Queen Mother, who still visits her old home.

There is a Dutch garden on the terrace and a more elaborate Italian garden beyond. The intricate sundial in the forecourt, with facets for all months of the year, was erected by Earl Patrick in the 1670s. The wider expanse of grounds and the grand approach, with its lectern doocot, were the result of landscape planning by 'Capability' Brown, much to the annoyance of Sir Walter Scott, who believed that the seven gates and the outer battlements should have been preserved to keep the romantic look of 'Macbeth's Castle'.

In the village of Glamis, the NTS have converted a charming row of one-storey, 17th-century cottages as the Angus Folk Museum, housing a collection of farm and domestic implements, attractively displayed. There are such interesting objects as flaughter spades for cutting turf, leisters (for spearing salmon), a student's mealie scoop, crusie lamps and fir-candles, also a pair of decorated snuff-boxes from Laurencekirk in the Mearns. The prize exhibit is a reconstructed kitchen of the last century, complete in every detail.

Pictish stone (front) at the manse in Glamis

In the garden of the manse nearby there is a beautiful Pictish stone, 9 ft high, artistically carved with intricate decorative cross on one side and fish and serpent symbols on the other.

Glenbuchat Gordon Grampian 7 C5
The stark ruin of Glenbuchat Castle (AM) stands boldly in a bend of the River Don on a ridge of the prominent Hill of Newe, dominating both the track over the Ladder Hills from Glenlivet and the main route down Deeside. The remains are of both historical and architectural interest, and the area is associated with the exploits of that sturdy Jacobite 'Old Glenbucket' (Glenbucket was the correct spelling in his day, but over-sophisticated Victorians 'Gaelicised' it to Glenbuchat).

The castle was built in 1590 by John Gordon and his wife Helen Carnegie, whose names figure, with their motto 'Nothing on Earth remains bot (= without) Faime', over the doorway. Subsequent Gordon lairds quarrelled over the succession and, in 1701, the castle passed to a less unruly branch of the family, of whom the most famous was John Gordon of Glenbucket, known for his devotion to the Jacobite cause. He may have been present at Killiecrankie (1689) as a young lad; he was certainly heavily involved in the Earl of Mar's call to arms in the Rising of 1715, and he fought at Sheriffmuir; when the Old Pretender fled abroad, Glenbucket was imprisoned in Edinburgh. In 1738 he sold the Glenbucket estates to Duff of Braco (later Earl of Fife) and the castle was in Fife hands until 1883. 'Old Glenbucket' retired to his farm at St Bridget's, close to where Tomintoul (q.v.) was founded some 40 years later. From there he made visits to Paris and Rome to concert arrangements with the Jacobites in exile, for the 1745 Rising. He joined Prince Charles Edward with a contingent of 300 men, was appointed to his Council in Holyrood, fought in the campaign in England, and his 'much crouched figure' was seen at Culloden in 1746. His farm at St Bridget's was burned and he took refuge at nearby Croughly. Chased from there, the old man, now 70, made his way to Peterhead, took ship to Norway, crossed the mountains to Sweden, rejoined the Jacobite court in exile, and finally died, broken by age and suffering but undaunted in spirit, at Boulogne in 1750. The Hanoverian forces had good reason to fear the little old man, and George II was said to wake from a nightmare crying: 'De gread Glenbogged is goming'!

Architecturally, Glenbuchat Castle is a fine example of a Z-plan tower-house. Square towers are built at diagonally-opposite corners of the main keep, with emphasis on defence rather than ornament. The gunloops, including one in the sw tower slanting to cover the entrance, are here for real; in this remote glen there

was no pretence as in the softer and safer country round the opulent tower-houses of Crathes or Craigievar. A curious feature is that the stair turrets in the re-entrants of the towers, instead of being built out on projecting corbels, are carried on *trompes*, or flying arches. This was a French technique, popularised by the architect Philibert de l'Orme, who built the 16th-century Tuileries for Henri II. The fact that Sir Robert Carnegie, father-in-law of the John Gordon who built Glenbuchat, was ambassador to the French court at this time may explain how this French architectural trick found its way here to a remote Scottish glen.

A short distance up Glenbuchat, under the Hill of Newe, is the charming Kirk of St Peter, first built in 1473, reconstructed in the 17th and 18th centuries. It has a belfry with a Dutch bell dated 1643, and box pews with room for tables. The present owner of the estate resides in a lodge at Badenyon, 4 miles up the glen, and the site of the home of the Gordons before they built the castle in 1590.

A pleasant circuit may be made up to Badenyon by the Water of Buchat, returning to Strathdon by way of the Water of Nochty. At the head of this glen is the ruined farm curiously known as 'Duff Defiance' from a Duff who came over the Ladder Hills from Glenlivet and defiantly set his lum to reek in the land of the Gordons.

Glenbuchat Castle

Glen Clova and **Glen Prosen** Angus Tayside 4 D4
Glen Clova is the finest of the Angus glens, even if the middle section, a typical U-shaped glacial trench forming a flat fertile strath with roads on both banks, may seem tedious to those impatient to reach the wildness of the upper glen. So it may have seemed to Charles II when he escaped from those Covenanting sermons in Perth (q.v.) and spent the night at Cortachy (leaving his Euclid and Prayer Book behind). He was recaptured by his zealous supporters halfway up the glen, having spent a second night in a hut, 'on an old bolster on a serge-mat, over-wearied and fearful'!

The focal point of the glen is Milton of Clova, with a tiny, well kept kirk and a scrap of castle wall, lying under the steep slope leading up to a hanging corrie with its loch, Loch Brandy (*bran-dubh* or 'raven-black'). Four miles on, the motor road comes to an end at Braedownie, where the glen divides. Up the right-hand fork is the start of the Capel Mounth (Mounth for horses); a mere 2,250 ft (685 m.) high and only 6 miles to shelter at Spittal of Glenmuick, it is the lowest and shortest of the passes to Deeside. Left-handed from Braedownie is Glen Doll (*pron.* Dole, meadow), thickly blanketed for 500 ft (150 m.) or so up the lower slopes by Forestry Commission plantations mostly of Norway spruce. Above the enveloping trees, there is the gladdening sight of a high circuit of crags and wild upper corries. There is rock-climbing here and some hard walking over the plateau, either to the head of Glen Isla, or over the high and exposed Tolmount, a 3,000 ft (900 m.) pass into Glen Callater and so down to Braemar, 18 miles distant. The Tolmount (preserved as a right of way by court action in the 1880s) is not to be undertaken lightly, or in doubtful weather, for several walkers have met their deaths in recent years in the snow-storms that can sweep this exposed, featureless plateau.

Parallel with Glen Clova to the west is little Glen Prosen, afforested in the lower section but opening out into birch woods and moorland higher up. About 2 miles up, by the E bank road, below the Airlie Memorial Tower, there is a fountain erected in memory of Captain Robert Scott and Dr Edmund Wilson of the Antarctic expedition of 1912-13. The two explorers met here to discuss plans for their ill-fated adventure.

The Prosen stream and the little Carity Burn join the South Esk a short distance below the Ogilvy castle of Cortachy (*see* Airlie). Hard by where the waters meet is another and older Ogilvy castle, Inverquharity. A massive L-shaped, five-storey, 15th-century keep in vivid red sandstone, it has been recently restored and converted to modern use. A good sight of it may be had from the by-road leading s from Prosen Bridge towards Forfar.

Glen Eagles *see* **Auchterarder**

Glen Esk and **Glen Lethnot** Angus Tayside 5 E4
Glen Esk is the longest and most varied of the Angus glens. It is joined by Glen Lethnot below Edzell, and both streams flow into the North Sea near Montrose as the River North Esk. Glen Esk's emergence into Strathmore provides some spectacular scenery just N of Edzell. Starting from the Gannochy Bridge on the B966, a walk for 2 miles through the grounds of The Burn — a late-18th-century mansion and now a university study centre — follows the edge of a chasm where the river foams through a narrow cleft in the Old Red Sandstone conglomerate. It forms dark pools where salmon wait before leaping the fall — or otherwise climbing the fish ladder roughly hewn in the rock — to reach the calmer stream above. The actual line of the Highland Boundary Fault can here be identified as a sill of rock across the bed of the river. Higher up, the path is hewn out of the rock above a second gorge, before re-joining the road up at Glen Esk. Continuing up Glen Esk, the twisting 16 miles (26 km.) of the road give delightfully changing views of the shingly reaches of the river, the birch woods on the lower slopes and, above, the heather-covered hills. Nine miles up is The Retreat, an excellent Highland folk museum, improbably housed in a white-harled shooting-lodge. It contains local relics, arms, tools, and household utensils, in rooms set up for various periods with costumed figures. A couple of miles further up is Tarfside, the principal hamlet of Glen Esk, where two roughly parallel Mounth roads take off over the hills for Aboyne on Deeside, one by the headwaters of the Feugh, the other (the Fir Mounth) by Glen Tanar. The tall monument on the nearby hill was erected by the Earl of Dalhousie in 1866 and is curiously dedicated 'in memory of 7 members of his family already dead, and of himself and two others; when it shall please God to call them hence'.

Four miles further on, the motorable road ends at Lochlee Church, severe and Presbyterian, dating from 1803, just short of Loch Lee itself. The scenery becomes abruptly wilder and here is the grim keep of Invermark, which once held this outlying point for the Lindsays of Edzell. Down Glen Mark (that is, from the NW) came Queen Victoria, having crossed the high shoulder of Mount Keen (3,037 ft/926 m.) on her ride from Ballater to Fettercairn in September 1861. The spot where she drank, at the foot of the steep descent into Glen Mark, is commemorated by a granite canopy in the form of a crown over the Queen's Well.

The next glen to the w is the shorter and gentler Glen Lethnot, of which the lower stretches are known as the West Water, which joins the North Esk below Edzell. Its winding course mimics that of its bigger neighbour, Glen Esk. From its upper reaches, known as the Water of Saughs, a good mountain walk follows the stream to its source near Muckle Cairn (2,700 ft/820 m.) and down past the deep, glacier-cut corrie of Loch Brandy to Milton in Glen Clova (q.v.). From the middle reaches, a track leads N through the narrow gap of the Clash of Wirren to Tarfside in Glen Esk. This was a section of the Whisky Track, by which the produce of the illicit stills of Deeside and further north was conveyed to thirsty consumers in Strathmore. In the 18th century, as the Priest's Road, it was used by the Episcopalian priest from Tarfside who served both communities, walking over to minister to his Jacobite flock in Glen Lethnot, much to the annoyance of his Presbyterian colleagues who, in both glens, were of Hanoverian sympathies.

Glen Gairn   *see* **Ballater**

Glen Isla   *see* **Airlie**

Glenlivet   Moray   Grampian   7 B4-5
Glenlivet and its Braes have until quite recent times been considered remote, and its inhabitants benefited from this remoteness, spiritually in the 18th century by serving as a refuge of Roman Catholics, and materially in the 18th and 19th centuries by the production of whisky, first for smuggling and later legally. Historically part of the Gordon lands, Glenlivet gives its name to the battle that took place in October 1594 (*see* Introduction: The Stuart Kings). The actual battle-ground is on the upper edge of a large area afforested by the Forestry Commission, s of the B9009 from Glenlivet to Dufftown.

In the 18th century there were perhaps 200 illicit stills in the Glenlivet area, serving first the domestic needs of the inhabitants, the surplus being carried by smugglers over the Ladder Hills as far as Montrose and Perth. In 1824 George Smith of Glenlivet decided to steal a march on his competitors by trading legally, and in the result 'The Glenlivet' is known the world over (*see* Introduction: Whisky).

Close by the distillery is the stark, ruined tower of Blair-findy, where the 2nd Marquis of Huntly (son of the victor of Glenlivet) was held by Covenanters in 1648 after his capture in December 1648 at Delnabo near Tomintoul, and before his execution in Edinburgh in 1649. Higher up Glenlivet are two more distilleries, one an undistinguished group of buildings at Tomnavoulin, the other at the end of the Braes road at Chapeltown. The latter, completed in 1974, won an architectural award, skilfully combining, in a modern idiom, a medieval saddle-back tower with the pagoda-like turret characteristic of many distilleries.

The secret refuge in the Braes for Roman Catholics of the 18th century lies a mile or so beyond Chapeltown at the remote seminary of Scalan (Gaelic for a 'turf-roofed shelter' on the summer pasturages). Being in the territory of the powerful Catholic Duke of Gordon, this was a safe area for members of the Catholic faith, save for raids by the British soldiery after the Risings of 1715 and 1745. The 2nd Duke agreed that Scalan should be a college for Catholic priests, and over 100 priests were trained here between 1717 and 1799. Set in a bowl of the heather-clad Ladder Hills, 'this popish seminary of learning, the only one in Scotland with six priests and a bishop' (as a 1751

In a Speyside distillery

record describes it), provided a secluded retreat. With increasing tolerance towards Catholics, it was possible for the seminary to be moved nearer Aberdeen in the 19th century, first to Aquhorthies, and later to Deeside, where it now flourishes as Blairs College.

An early contribution to this increased tolerance of Catholics was made by one of Scalan's distinguished pupils, the Abbé Paul Macpherson (1756-1846), to whom there are two tablets in the Chapeltown church. In view of his close connexion with the Scots College in Rome, the Abbé Paul was engaged by British authorities in 1812 to take a message to Pope Pius VII, then imprisoned by Napoleon in the fortress of Savona, to warn him to be ready to escape when the British forces arrived. In the event, the plot failed, as the Pope was moved to France and was freed in 1813. After re-opening the Scots College in 1820, Macpherson returned to Glenlivet to build up chapel, presbytery and school, later dying in Rome at the great age of 90.

There is another Catholic church at Tombae, in the side-glen of the Crombie Water leading up to the Suie, as the NE branch of the Livet is known. In the upper Suie, one can watch the birds, fish for trout in the stream and walk for hours under open skies with a sense of space and height, up into the treeless Blackwater Forest, with its huge herds of red deer.

Glen Lyon   Perthshire   Tayside   3F6–G6
Glen Lyon's claim to be, with 33 miles (53 km.), the longest glen in Scotland can be challenged by the 40-odd miles of Glen Avon (from Ben Macdhui to Ballindalloch), but length is a foolish criterion by which to measure the striking and very different beauty of these two marvellous glens. The headwaters of Glen Lyon have been trapped in reservoirs for the Hydro-Electric scheme and cannot be compared with the austere solitude of Loch Avon. But the narrowest section of Glen Avon is less impressive than the entrance to Glen Lyon, where the rushing torrent roars down between high crags to debouch in the little plain of Fortingall (q.v.). This dramatic gorge, of special beauty in spring when the beech trees are in early leaf and the daffodils bloom, more closely resembles the entrance to an alpine valley than any other glen is Scotland. Here are the narrows over which the unfortunate 16th century Macgregor chief Gregor Roy leapt to escape pursuit by men of the ferocious Black Duncan Campbell of Glenorchy, only to be caught in the end and executed at Finlarig.

Higher up, Glen Lyon broadens into wide Alpine-style meadows bordering the now more tranquil stream, and there are a number of scattered settlements dotted up the peaceful valley. Some of the side-glens provided relatively easy routes for cattle-raiders or other marauders into and out of Glen Lyon. Traces of twelve or more stone rings, of which the best preserved is near Cashlie in the upper glen, below the Hydro dam, mark the fortified homesteads of a prehistoric people who found safety here. The theory has been advanced that this was once the central stronghold of the Picts. There are 'testing-stones' to be seen (and lifted, if you can) near Camusvrachan, and the Bhacain, or Dog Stone, near Cashlie, said to have been used for tethering the legendary stag-hound, Bran, or else the hunting-dogs of the early Scottish kings. St Adamnan, the biographer of St Columba, spent some time in Glen Lyon, living at Milton Eonan (a corruption of Adamnan) and banishing the plague. A handbell attributed to him is in Glen Lyon Church, and another in Fortingall.

The glen centres on the twin hamlets of Innerwick and Bridge of Balgie, where a side-road heads s towards the gap of Lochan-na-Lairig, over the western shoulder of Ben Lawers, and down past the Visitor Centre to Loch Tay. The road continuing up Glen Lyon passes, in a couple of miles, Meggernie Castle, no longer the sinister stronghold of Mad Colin Campbell, but a white-harled, tall, square tower with turrets at each corner, with a modern residence adjoining. Mad Colin, the son of Red Duncan, began the castle in about 1570; he abducted the Countess of Erroll in 1585 and brought her here. It remained in Campbell hands for another century, but after the Massacre of Glencoe (1692) at which Robert Campbell, great-grandson of Mad Colin, was the infamous army commander, Meggernie passed into the hands of the Menzies family.

The beauty of Glen Lyon is enhanced by the ancient spreading larches, part of the collection of seedling European larches introduced into Scotland in 1736 by James Menzies, known as Old Culdares from the name of his former farm. He brought them from the Austrian Tyrol, where he spent some of his time in exile between the Fifteen and the Forty Five. Meggernie has its peculiar ghost, the wife of a Menzies laird who murdered her in a fit of jealousy, and cut the body in two for easy disposal. The lower half was safely buried, but the upper half never reached the graveyard and is said to haunt the castle. The magnificent trees around Meggernie, which include limes and beeches, as well as larches, are of course due to that great tree-planter Old Culdares, but the fine stand of Scots pines is part of the ancient Caledonian forest. The tradition of tree-planting continues with the Forestry Commission's recent afforestation of the NW slopes of Ben Lawers.

The road up the glen continues into barer, more open spaces, until the uppermost hamlets of Cashlie and Pubil are reached, and we are in Hydro-Electric country. The public road here comes to an end, though there is a private way out to Glen Lochay and Killin for the Hydro Board and the local inhabitants.

Glen Muick   *see* **Ballater**

Glen Shee   Perthshire   Tayside   4 B3–B4
Not so long ago, Glen Shee was famous for the Devil's Elbow, the dangerous zigzag bend where cars were liable to stall on the final ascent to the Cairnwell Pass (2,199 ft/670 m.). The Devil's Elbow now lies obliterated beneath a broad highway. Before that, the sturdy but narrow bridges, particularly the hump-backed one still at Spittal of Glenshee, studded the route of Caulfeild's military road from Blairgowrie by Braemar and Tomintoul to Fort George.

Nowadays, Glenshee means a 25-mile (40 km.) drive by A93 from Blairgowrie, with the possibility of skiing on the slopes above the Cairnwell Pass. The nearest accommodation is at Spittal, 5 miles down the treeless glen. The ski areas extend from the large car-park on the pass to over 3,000 ft (900 m.) on the tops. There is a chair-lift, also a number of ski-tows, and an artificial ski-slope for the final descent to the foot of the lift when snow is scarce. Hang-gliding is also becoming popular here. The half-dozen pieces of modern sculpture by the car-park, including a gentleman sitting in an armchair contemplating the heights ('Tommy', in black fibre-glass by Malcolm Robertson), are part of a plan by the Scottish Sculpture Trust to popularise sculpture in open places. More pieces are to be seen at the Carrbridge Landmark Centre. ('Tommy' has recently been joined by a lady).

To the E, over the hump of Glas Maol (3,504 ft / 1,068 m.), the old Monega track crosses from Braemar to Glen Isla, passing close to the Caenlochan Nature Reserve, where, as on Ben Lawers (q.v.), the soil and rock formation favours the growth of an arctic-alpine flora.

Gordon District Grampian 7 C5-8 G5
It may seem strange that the small village of Gordon in Berwickshire should, in the reorganization of local government in 1975, have given its name to a new district in the heart of old Aberdeenshire. The connexion is the powerful family of Gordon, which was encouraged by Robert the Bruce in the 14th century to move into Strathbogie (q.v.) to occupy lands confiscated from the Comyns of Buchan. Their northern seat was first at Huntly (q.v.) — also a Berwickshire name — but was later moved to the Bog o' Gight (modern Fochabers (q.v.). As controllers of the approaches to the fertile land of Moray and the valleys of Don, Dee and Deveron, and as protectors of the prosperous city of Aberdeen, the Gordons became indispensable to the rulers of Scotland, earning the nickname of Cock o' the North. Despite the Gordon revolt put down by Queen Mary and the Earl of Moray at Corrichie (q.v.) in 1562, despite the disloyalty shown by the 'Papist Earls', Erroll and Huntly, in the affair of the Spanish Blanks (*see* Introduction: The Stuart Kings), leading to the Battle of Glenlivet in 1594, despite exile and the destruction of the palace of Huntly, the Gordons, although usually Catholic, managed to bounce back into favour. They rose from being Earls of Huntly to Marquises of

Aboyne and Dukes of Gordon in the 18th century, recruiting the Gordon Highlanders with the famous shilling in the Duchess's lips, and furnishing a distinguished line of Gordon generals, not only in Britain, but also to Prussia and Russia. Whatever was afoot 'in Bogie, Deveron, Don and Dee', the Gordons seemed, as the saying went, to 'hae the guidin o't'.

Subsidiary branches of the Gordon clan were the Gordons of Haddo (q.v.) (including the 19th-century Prime Minister Lord Aberdeen), the ill-fated Gordons of Gight (ancestors of the poet Lord Byron) and that prototype of a devoted Jacobite, Old Glenbucket himself.

The modern Gordon District, with its headquarters at Inverurie, does not cover all the former Gordon lands but, extending as it does from the Lecht Pass at the head of the Don to the city boundaries of Aberdeen, it includes the historic districts of Strathbogie, Formartine and the Garioch, as well as Midmar. The modern administrator has chosen the name well.

Gordonstoun Moray Grampian 7 B1
Gordonstoun, 5 miles N of Elgin, lies in the rich green and wooded Laich (lowland) of Moray, a surprise to those who might expect Kurt Hahn's rugged style of education to be based in equally rugged country. As is well known, in 1934 he brought from Germany his inspiring principle of combining individual outdoor activities to develop character with sound book-learning, to produce a balanced citizen.

Gordonstoun House

Against the odds, his vision and leadership established a new school in the abandoned mansion of Gordonstoun. The school has its own fire-brigade, and its mountain-rescue and coastguard teams, which are to be seen not only practising but also engaged in real rescue work on the nearby rocky Hopeman coast. This educational experiment rapidly gained impetus. His Royal Highness, Prince Philip, and his sons, Prince Charles, Prince Andrew and Prince Edward, were all educated at Gordonstoun.

The school has three fine buildings; the 17th-century mansion of the Bog of Plewlands; the Round Square, now housing class-rooms and school library; and the modern school chapel, St Christopher's, built with the help of the MacRobert Trust in 1950. Bog of Plewlands was owned by Ogstouns from 1240 to 1473. From 1473, the estate was in the hands of the Innes family until acquired by the Marquis of Huntly in 1616, and the name changed to Gordonstoun. The two wings, with their angle-turrets, were added at this time. In 1642, the Gordons of Gordonstoun developed it. Sir Ludovick drained the bog to form the present lake. Legends of witchcraft circulated about the 'Wizard Laird', Sir Robert (d. 1704), evidently a gifted scientist ahead of his time, who designed a sea-water pump taken up by Pepys for use by the Royal Navy. It was he who built the remarkable Round Square in 1690, intending this farm-block as a 'scientific sanctuary for his soul', allegedly so that the devil could not drive him into a corner. Legend has it that the devil got him in the end, escaping across the still un-drained Loch of Spynie to Birnie Church. His widow built the interesting Michael Kirk, half a mile to the E of the house, including a stone panel giving the genealogy of the Gordons of Gordonstoun. Their son, 'Bad Sir Robert', reconstructed the main house in its present classical form in 1729. He is said to have made use of the caves in the Hopeman cliffs, known as the Laird's Stables, for smuggling. He also built several large doocots on the estate (some still to be seen), hoping thereby to get rid of his wife as the building of a doocot supposedly caused a death in the family, but she survived him!

Carse of Gowrie Perthshire Tayside 2 E2-F2
Gowrie was one of the five ancient Celtic districts which, together with Atholl, Breadalbane, Menteith and Strathearn, made up the great county of Perth. In those days, Gowrie covered the whole area N of the Tay Estuary up to the Highland Boundary Fault, including, of course, Blair (town of) Gowrie (q.v.). The Carse, from the Scandinavian 'kjerr', or marsh, is the 18 mile-long (29 km.) strip of alluvial land north of the Tay Estuary between Kinnoull Hill near Perth and the outskirts of Dundee. Nowadays, 'Gowrie' denotes just the Carse and the slopes of the Sidlaw Hills behind, but no further. Certainly, it is a fertile, sheltered and pleasant country, perhaps, with Moray, the most coveted land in Scotland N of the Forth.

In 1628, that colourful traveller William Lithgow, 'lug-less Will' (who lost his ears, surprisingly enough, in Lanark before setting out on his *Rare Adventures and Painful Peregrinations*) described the Carse as an 'earthly paradise', though he considered 'the inhabitants defective in affableness'. Pennant, in the 18th century, passed a witty but uncharitable remark about the 'carles or churls of the Carse'. Nonetheless, many of Scotland's great families –Hays, Drummonds, Blairs, Grays, Ogilvys, Lyons and others – have their connexions with the Carse. Even Cumberland, when given Gowrie House in Perth (q.v.) for his use, asked, grumbling, whether the lands of Gowrie went with it. More prosaically, the Carse now supplies much of the fruit for Dundee's jam industry.

Perhaps over the ages the Carse has been too prosperous, for of the string of castles between Dundee and Perth, only a few, like Megginch and Kinfauns, have survived. Others have been heavily restored or replaced by opulent Victorian mansions which, if not without dignity and solidity, scarcely reflect Scottish traditions in architecture. Before the land was drained, the villages clustered on the higher ground, the so-called 'inches' (islands). Most of the traffic was by boat along the estuary, with a poor road along the foot of the hills, until the coming of the Perth-Dundee turnpike road in 1790, of the Caledonian Railway in 1847, and of the two great bridges, first rail and recently road, across the E end of the Tay estuary at Dundee.

The views, melancholy or sparkling according to season, across the Tay to the s shore have attracted artists from Sir John Millais, who painted 'Chill October' (now in Perth Art Gallery) on the station platform at Kinfauns, having his easel blown over by passing trains and receiving advice from the porter, to J. Mackintosh Patrick, with his appealing landscapes of the country round his native Dundee. Perhaps Lady Caroline Nairne (1766-1845), who wrote *Charlie is my Darling* and other Jacobite songs, best caught the spirit of the Carse with her poem which begins:

A lassie wi' a brave new gown
Cam' ower the hills to Gowrie,
As oh the scene was passing fair
For what in Scotland can compare
With the Carse of Gowrie.
The sun was setting o'er the Tay
The blue hills melting into grey
The mavis and the blackbird's lay
Were sweetly heard in Gowrie.

The Grampians 4 A3-5 H1
'The Grampians' covers on the map the ill-defined mountain mass N of the Highland Boundary Fault and s of the Great Glen. The modern regional administrator took this name in 1975 for the new Region of Grampian, with its headquarters at Aberdeen, and severely, if illogically, limited it to those parts of NE Scotland E of Nairn and N of Montrose, to include the former counties of Aberdeen-

shire, Banffshire, Kincardineshire and Moray. Though this includes the second highest mountain in Scotland (Ben Macdhui) and much hilly country, a large proportion is not mountain at all.

No great harm is done, since the word Grampian is anyway a bit of a ghost-name. By some slip of a medieval copyist's pen, perpetuated by the historian Hector Boece, Mons Graupius, the name of the battle in which, as Tacitus tells us, Agricola defeated the Caledonian forces under Calgacus in 84 A.D., was transmuted to Mons Grampius. As 'Grampios Montes', the name first appeared on Blaeu's maps of Scotland in his Atlas Novus of 1654. The site of the battle of Mons Graupius has long been disputed by scholars and has ranged from Comrie as far as Keith (*see* Introduction: From Stone Age to Romans, and also Bennachie).

The most clearly defined part of the mountain mass of the Grampians is the southern watershed of the Dee, which was well-known to Bruce's chronicler Wyntoun, and to subsequent ages, as the White Mounth, because of the lingering snows on the summit range, or simply The Mounth. This was the main obstacle to N–S travel in medieval times. The westerly pass of Drumochter, now used by the railway and the A9, was long, dangerous and desolate. Much better to use the shorter, sharper, even if higher, passes leading directly from the southern glens to Deeside, for instance up Glen Tilt from Blair Atholl over an imperceptible watershed to Braemar, even over the high Monega Pass from Glen Isla or the desolate Tolmount from Glen Doll, which both converge on Braemar.

Further E, the Capel (or horse) Mounth led from Glen Clova (q.v.) into Glen Muick. From the head of Glen Esk, another fine route goes by Glen Mark, nearly over the top of Mount Keen (3,077 ft/938 m.) and down to Deeside. Taylor, the Water Poet, came this way in 1618 on his *Pennilesse Pilgrimage*: he found that his 'teeth began to dance in my head with cold, like virginals' jacks', and he experienced a Scotch mist: 'so friendly a dew that it did moisten throrow all my clothes'. It was also used by harvesters from Tomintoul seeking work at the Brechin Fair, by whisky-smugglers until the mid 1800s, and by Queen Victoria on her 'Second Great Expedition' in 1861 (*see* also Angus Glens).

All these are walking or riding routes. The first motor-road crossing E of the A93 by Glenshee is the B974 from Fettercairn to Banchory giving, at the Cairn o' Mount, one of the finest views from any road in Scotland. On the summit is the sprawling cairn of stones that gives the pass its name. Northwards is Deeside and the mixture of farm and moorland that is Aberdeenshire; s over the Howe of the Mearns is the North Sea, on a clear day glittering in the sun, when Fife can also be seen across the Firth of Tay. Westwards, Lochnagar looms above the peaty plateau at the head of the Angus glens. Though only 1,488 ft (454 m.) above sea-level, the Cairn o' Mount, highly exposed to the winds of the North Sea, was never a popular crossing.

Even nowadays, it is sometimes closed by drifting snow.

East of Cairn o' Mount, the Grampians are less formidable. The Cryne Corse, probably used by Edward I, crossed from Drumlithie in the Mearns, below where the tall Durris television mast now stands, to Deeside. The modern Slug road goes through a narrow gullet (or 'slochd') from Stonehaven to Banchory. Most easterly of all, the now abandoned, gently undulating Causey Mounth heads straight from Stonehaven to Aberdeen's Bridge of Dee, somewhat to the w of the busy A92.

Grandtully Perthshire Tayside 3 H5 (AM)
Two or three miles down Strathtay are the church and castle of Grandtully. A rough farm road, signposted to St Mary's, Grandtully (AM), leads up from the A827 to the long, low white-harled church tucked away behind farm buildings. It was established in 1553 (just before the Reformation) by Sir Alexander Stewart as an outlying place of worship for the priory of Dull. In 1636 Sir William Stewart, Sheriff of Perth from 1630–34, enlarged the church and installed the remarkable timber waggon ceiling, of which half has been well restored. The 29 brightly painted wooden panels are a profusion of scriptural texts and arms of the local landowners, interspersed with bunches of fruit, vases of flowers and stoutish cherubim blowing trumpets and waving quill pens. To inspire such a splendidly baroque ceiling at the outset of the Civil War in this rather remote place smacked of liturgical arrangements closer to those of Charles I than of the dour Covenanters. St Mary's continued to be used for worship up to the 19th century, and in 1954 became an AM.

Grandtully Castle, not open to the public, can be seen from the road up to St Mary's, and, when the trees are not in leaf, from the A927. Dating from the 14th century, it was given a turreted look by its Stewart owner in 1626; an unusual feature is the big round stair tower set boldly in the middle of one wall, rising higher than the principal roof and capped with a 17th-century ogee helmet. Its strategic position made Grandtully a useful headquarters for various commanders, including Montrose in 1644, Mar in 1715 and Lord George Murray in 1745. Sir Walter Scott, in a footnote to *Waverley*, admits to having 'been informed that the House of Grandtully resembles that of the Baron of Bradwardine' (that is to say, what Scott calls Tullyveolan) more than any other.

Haddo House Gordon Grampian 8 G3 (NTS)
Haddo, since 1978 in the care of the NTS, is quite different from the tower-houses of Aberdeenshire which, for all their delightful exuberance, are basically places of defence. Haddo, a Palladian mansion built by William Adam in 1731 for the 2nd Earl of Aberdeen, represents the prosperous 18th century. It is a welcoming house set in undulating wooded grounds that might be in Sussex. Under the enthusiastic guidance of June Gordon, Lady Aberdeen, and of her husband, the late Marquess, Haddo House has become a famous centre for music, attracting

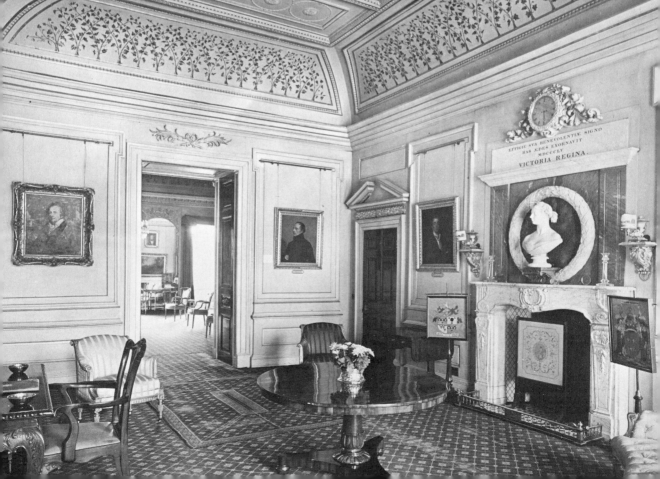

eminent musicians and singers to a successful series of concerts and operas organized by the Haddo Choral Society and given generous support by the oil companies. Performances are usually held in a purpose-built hall.

The two wings of the house converge on the centre block which is approached by curving flights of stairs to the first floor terrace. The courtyard is thus an ideal setting for open-air opera when the weather is kind. The original front entrance was on the upper terrace, opening straight into the ante-room, an approach more suited to Naples than to Aberdeen; only in 1880 was the present covered entrance made at ground level. The inner rooms are sumptuous yet friendly, containing many reminders of the Aberdeen family, including a bust of Queen Victoria presented after her visit in 1857. In the ante-room are portraits of the 4th Earl (the Prime Minister), of Pitt, his guardian, and of contemporary friends and politicians, Castlereagh, Wellington, Peel and Guizot. The phrase 'entente cordiale' originated in correspondence between Aberdeen and Guizot. The drawing room looks out onto the formal gardens now part of the NTS country park. The cedar-panelled library in the N wing is a magnificent setting for its books, with green and white Wedgwood decorated mantelpieces. The dining room has portraits of the 1st Earl, Chancellor of Scotland under Charles II, and of the 'Wicked' 3rd Earl.

This Wicked Earl was a successful 18th-century businessman, who liked to refer to himself as 'Us' and kept three brown-eyed mistresses, one at Cairnbulg near Fraserburgh, one at nearby Ellon and one in faraway Devon. He disposed of much of the original Adam furnishings, and raised a flourishing family of illegitimate Gordons, whose children were later to become distinguished generals and admirals. His heir was the unfortunate Lord Haddo (1764-91), whose portrait hangs on the Grand Staircase and who was killed in a riding accident at nearby Gight on the River Ythan (q.v.). It was his son George, the 4th Earl (1784-1860) who headed the Coalition Government of 1852-5, which let Britain slide into the Crimean War. As Prime Minister, Lord Aberdeen has been unjustly blamed for this. His achievements in foreign affairs are more significant: as a young ambassador in Vienna in 1813-14, he arranged the terms on which the Great Powers were to meet at the end of the Napoleonic Wars and as Foreign Secretary from 1814 to 1851 he was responsible for the conclusion of the war with China and the settlement of the Columbia River dispute with the United States, which put the name Aberdeen on the map in places as far apart as Hong Kong and the Oregon Territory of the United States. He was a supporter of Catholic Emancipation and of free trade, and it is to his activity at Haddo (after the neglect of the Wicked Earl), during his happy times of leisure at home,

Haddo House

Ante-room, Haddo House

that estate and mansion owe their present ordered beauty.

The 6th Earl took to the sea, becoming an ordinary seaman under the name of George H. Osborne, liking nothing so much as service in a small American vessel. He was lost at sea in 1870, and was succeeded by the flamboyant 7th Earl who was twice Viceroy of Ireland, and Governor-General of Canada. He added the Gothic revival chapel, designed by G. E. Street in 1882, with a stained glass Burne-Jones window. In 1916 Lord Aberdeen was created Marquis of Aberdeen and Temair and, together with his wife Countess Ishbel, wrote their story in the well-known book *We Twa*. They moved to the House of Cromar (q.v.) by Tarland from 1920 until his death in 1934.

The family tombs are in the church at the nearby village of Tarves, and the prominent tower known as the Prop of Ythsie was built as a memorial to the 4th Earl, the Prime Minister.

Harlaw Gordon Grampian 8 F4

On high ground on the E bank of the little River Urie there is a curious-looking tower, well seen from the A96 a couple of miles NW of Inverurie. This rough, tapering hexagon, with projecting spikes on the upper storey and a pyramidal roof, all in red granite, was built in 1911, 500 years after the event, 'To the memory of Provost Robert Davidson and the burgesses who fell here in A.D. 1411'.

The Battle of Harlaw reflects the troubled state of Scotland during the minority and absence of James I who, from 1406 to 1424, was a prisoner of Henry IV of England. Donald, Lord of the Isles, with some encouragement from Henry IV, thought this a good occasion to move eastwards and, after capturing Inverness, to promise his men the plundering of Aberdeen. The burghers of Aberdeen thought otherwise: they enlisted Alexander Stewart (by then Earl of Mar), son of the notorious Wolf of Badenoch, to lead a hastily assembled force of Keiths, Forbeses, Leslies, Irvines and Gordons, together with some of the good burghers themselves, headed by Provost Robert Davidson, who, as noted on the tower, fell in battle. The fight raged all the day of 24 July 1411, and both forces fought themselves to a standstill by nightfall. The Highlanders made for home and Aberdeen was saved. The traditional ballad laments what was probably the bloodiest battle ever fought between Scots:

The Cronach's cried on Bennachie
And down the Don and a',
And Heilan' and Lowland may mournful be
For the sair field of Harlaw.

Provost Davidson, whose tomb and effigy are in Collinson's Aisle in St Nicholas Kirk in Aberdeen, was the last head of a municipality to die leading troops in battle. Aberdeen learnt that lesson, and henceforward, it is said, their provosts were prohibited from leaving the city in their official capacity. In the following year, they appointed the Earl of Mar as the

Huntingtower (the old House of Ruthven)

official Captain and Governor of the city. On his death in 1435, the office devolved on Sir Alexander Irvine of Drum, passing subsequently to the Gordon Earls of Huntly.

Huntingtower Perthshire Tayside 1 D2 (AM)
Huntingtower, 3 miles NW of Perth, or the House of Ruthven (*pron.* Rivven), as it was called before 1600, is an interesting example of two nearly identical rectangular towers of different sizes set at a slight angle to one another, with a gap between. This gap gave rise to the tale of the Maiden's Leap, related by the English 18th-century traveller, Pennant. The daughter of the house, warned that she was likely to be apprehended with a suitor of whom the family disapproved, took a flying leap across the 9 ft-wide, 60 ft-high gap to regain her own bedroom in the other tower, where her mother duly found her. However, doubtless not wishing to take another leap, she eloped with her lover the next day. In the late 17th century, the towers were linked up. The great hall, on the first floor, has an early example of a painted wooden ceiling of about 1540, simple but colourful patterns with a few grotesque heads, by no means as fine as those at Crathes (q.v.). The second floor room has a fine fireplace and a built-in garderobe. The W tower, also with three storeys, a garret and a look-out roof, is enlarged by a 'jamb' or wing set on the south-west corner. The garret was equipped as a doocot to provide fresh pigeon-meat for the inhabitants.

In addition to the maiden's spectacular leap, Huntingtower was the scene of an historic and more sensational event — the kidnapping of a king. The Ruthvens had been a distinguished Perthshire family since the 13th century, and the second Lord Ruthven was a much respected provost of Perth in the mid 16th century. His son Patrick and his grandson William were implicated in the murder of Queen Mary's Italian favourite Rizzio in 1566. William, the 4th Lord Ruthven, was one of the lords who forced Queen Mary's abdication at Loch Leven Castle in 1567, became Treasurer of Scotland during the minority of James VI, and was created Earl of Gowrie in 1581. In August of the following year, the young king, just 16 years old, was returning from a hunt in Atholl when he was met by the Earls of Gowrie and Mar and other noblemen, and persuaded to enter the House of Ruthven. Gowrie and the others supported the Protestant cause, and wanted to extricate the King from the power of Regents Lennox and Arran. James VI was detained for 10 months, being obliged to sign proclamations, one declaring that he was a free agent, another setting out the wickedness of the previous Government. The young King burst into tears, provoking the stern words from one of his captors: 'Better bairns greet (weep) than bearded men'. James never forgot nor forgave: Gowrie was executed at Stirling in 1585, and, though the estates were inherited by his sons, the King's final revenge on the family waited for 18 years. In 1600, the 3rd Earl, Gowrie's grandson, and his brother were killed at Gowrie house in

Perth (q.v.) in mysterious circumstances: their dead bodies were tried for treason, the estates forfeited to the Crown, the surname of Ruthven abolished by Act of Parliament and the castle's name changed to Huntingtower. Needless to say, since Ruthven (red river, or red crag) is a common place-name in Scotland, the prohibition did not last for long.

Huntingtower subsequently passed into the hands of the Murrays of Tullibardine and through them to the Atholl family, giving rise to the jolly rhyme:

Blair in Atholl's mine, Jeanie,
Little Dunkeld is mine, Jeanie,
Saint Johnston's Bower (Perth) and Huntingtower,
And all that's mine is thine, Jeanie.

Huntly Gordon Grampian 7 D3 *(pop. 3,645)*
Huntly in Strathbogie (not to be confused with the Huntly Castle of the Grays in the Carse of Gowrie) stands at what was, in medieval days, the important strategic point where the little River Bogie joins the Deveron (q.v.). Huntly Castle (AM) was one of the chain of fortresses — Kindrochit (Braemar), Kildrummy, Balvenie (Dufftown)

and others — guarding the route to the fertile but often disaffected province of Moray. The conical, flat-topped motte just W of the present castle, marks the peel, or palisaded enclosure, of 12th-century Norman Strathbogie. Robert the Bruce was brought here for safety in 1307, when he fell sick during his campaign against the Comyns of Buchan. David de Strathbogie rebelled against Bruce before Bannockburn (1314) and forfeited his lands, which were granted to Sir Adam Gordon of Huntly in Berwickshire, but the name was not confirmed as the 'Castle of Huntly' until 1506.

The Norman motte-and-bailey was transformed to the fine 'palace' (from the Latin 'palatium' meaning a horizontal hall-house, as opposed to a vertical tower-house) whose ruins are to be seen today. An early-15th-century tower (the Auld Wark) stood on the foundations now visible to the NE of the motte: its grim dungeons form the basement of the present 'palace'. The 4th Earl of Huntly determined to transform this gloomy house into a residence comparable with the splendid châteaux of France, which he knew well, and between 1551 and 1554 he rebuilt it from the basement upwards.

Huntly Castle

On the occasion of the visit in 1556 of Marie de Guise, Regent for her daughter Mary, Queen of Scots, the magnificence of the entertainment made the French ambassador suggest to the Queen Mother that Huntly's wings should be clipped. Six years later, in 1562, the forces of Mary, Queen of Scots, persuaded by her half-brother the Earl of Moray that Huntly's independence should be checked, defeated Huntly at the Battle of Corrichie (q.v.). He died of apoplexy on the field. Huntly Castle was pillaged and its rich loot found its way to Aberdeen and Edinburgh. The 5th Earl set about restoring his hall, but involvement in the 'Affair of the Spanish Blanks' led to his short-lived victory over Argyll at the Battle of Glenlivet (q.v.) in 1594, and his castle was 'cast down' by James VI. Borrowing a large quantity of powder from Aberdeen, the King personally supervised the work of destruction carried out by his engineer, William Shaw. The Auld Wark was destroyed, but the damage to the palace was probably not very extensive.

Huntly's disgrace was short-lived; by 1597, he was back again and, two years later, promoted Marquis. The restoration of his palace-mansion was, according to the bold inscription on the south front, completed by 1602. The magnificent row of oriel windows is modelled on the Château of Blois on the Loire. These, together with the charming, smaller oriel projecting from the big round tower on the same level, are a reminder of vanished glories. So, too, is the most splendid heraldic doorway in the British Isles, which stands above the entrance to the smaller round tower, in the NE corner. This long vertical 'frontispiece', in red sandstone from Turriff, must have looked splendid when fresh and emblazoned in colour. It is still a fine piece of heraldic symbolism: the arms of Gordon and Lennox are at the bottom, under the royal arms of James VI and his Queen, in turn surmounted by a compartment showing the five wounds of Christ and above that a circular panel of the Risen Christ in glory. Both the latter were defaced by a Puritan army captain during the Covenanters' occupation of 1640. The great mantelpiece in the upper hall is also an outstanding example of an armorial fireplace, portraying the arms of Huntly and Lennox.

The glories of Huntly's palace lasted less than 40 years. The 2nd Marquis supported the King in the Civil Wars, when the castle changed hands repeatedly. Huntly himself, captured at Delnabo near Tomintoul, was brought to Edinburgh for execution in 1649, saying bravely 'you may take my head from my shoulders but not my heart from my sovereign'. After the Restoration of 1660, the Gordons, promoted Dukes in 1684, moved to the Bog o' Gight, later Gordon Castle, near the modern Fochabers (q.v.). Huntly Castle fell into decay and was used as a quarry by all and sundry including, regrettably, the widow of the 3rd Duke of Gordon who, in 1752, built Huntly Lodge (now the hotel across the bridge from the castle) out of the stones. The castle became an AM in 1923.

Huntly town is laid out on the typical grid-iron plan of the 18th century, with a busy square at the centre, in which are to be found two standing stones. The road N to the castle runs through an arch, under a clock-tower surmounted by an attractive ogee-shaped helmet. This and the flanking buildings formed the original Gordon Schools (now expanded to Huntly Academy), founded in 1839 by the widow of the 5th Duke of Gordon. Three miles to the SE, just off the A96 at Bogside of Adamston, is the interesting museum of agricultural implements and other farming items collected by Mr McCall Smith since 1972 — well worth a visit.

Innerpeffray Perth Tayside 1 C3
The oldest public library in Scotland, in continuous use since 1691, is surprisingly tucked away at the end of a farm-road leading down to the River Earn from the B8062, half way between Crieff and Auchterarder. Its interesting collection of 3,000 books is housed in a beautifully proportioned room with wide windows, built in 1750 by Archbishop Hay Drummond, when Archbishop of York, to house both his own library and the original books hitherto kept by David Drummond, 3rd Lord Madertie (Montrose's brother-in-law), in the loft of the neighbouring chapel.

The library carries a number of rare books, well displayed in cases with descriptions in a fair italic hand. They include some rare bibles, such as the 'Breeches' Bible of 1599 (in which Adam and Eve made 'breeches' of fig leaves), the 'Treacle' Bible of 1602 (with 'treacle' for the 'Balm' of Gilead) and the Great Montrose's personal bible in French, inscribed with his own quotations. There is a 1577 edition of Holinshed's Chronicles from which Shakespeare drew material for his historical plays, including Macbeth, and early editions of Fabyan's *Cronycle* (1533) and Boece's *History and Cronikles of Scotland,* translated from Latin by John Bellenden in 1540. Probably the earliest Scots vernacular prose work, this last is a fine example of 16th-century Scottish printing. James VI's works, including his famous *Counterblast to Tobacco* ('a custom loathesome to the eye, hatefull to the nose, and dangerous to the lungs'), are there in a first edition of 1616, and a first edition (1550) of Gavin Douglas's translation of the Aeneid. The library is well cared-for by a private trust.

The neighbouring chapel of St Mary (AM) is an interesting pre-Reformation collegiate foundation of 1508, on the site of an earlier 14th-century chapel, of which the primitive altar has been restored. Within, there are some areas of brightly-coloured frescoes, in particular on the ceiling under the tiny loft in which the original library was housed. There are Drummond memorials on the walls, a leper squint, a confessional and the graveyard is a Drummond burial place.

The Library, Innerpeffray

Recumbent Stone Circle, Loanhead of Daviot

Inverurie Gordon Grampian 8 F4 (*pop.* 5,437)
East of Bennachie (q.v.) and 'just whaur creeping Urie
joins its mountain cousin Don' (as William Thom the
weaver-poet has it), lies Inverurie, formerly 'capital' of the
Garioch (q.v.) and now the chief town of Gordon District
(q.v.). The medieval burgh developed round the
important junction where the roads to Huntly, Banff and
Fraserburgh respectively still branch. In the 19th century,
it was the headquarters of the Great North of Scotland
Railway: the former locomotive works are now an
industrial estate. The town takes pride in its historical
museum.

The country round is certainly full of history. There are
very fine stone circles at Loanhead of Daviot (AM) to the
N, at Aquhorthies to the W, as well as standing stones elsewhere, in particular the Brandsbutt Stone (AM), once
broken but now re-assembled, with incised Pictish
symbols. The Bass of Inverurie on the outskirts of the
town is a conical, 60 ft grass mound, with a lower mound
(the Little Bass) to the east. (Both were originally joined
together.) They are excellent examples of the motte, the
high mound on which David of Huntingdon's wooden
peel stood in the 12th century, and the lower bailey for
the domestic establishment. The modern cemetery at the
foot of the Bass has a variety of Pictish stones, including
one with a trotting horse.

On the hill across the Don to the S, in the year 1307,
Robert the Bruce lay sick in camp but, stirred to action by
raids from the rebellious Comyn Earl of Buchan, he led
his army to the decisive victory at the Hill of Barra (on the
road to Old Meldrum), destroying the power of the
Comyns and devastating the province, in what became
known as the 'herschip of Buchan'.

Downstream from the Bass of Inverurie is the
interesting ruined church of Kinkell. In addition to an
aumbry (alcove for holding the sacrament) of 1528, there
is the impressive grave slab of Gilbert de Greenlaw, who
fell at nearby Harlaw (q.v.) in 1411. This shows the main
elements of a nobleman's armour of the time: a conical
basinet on his head, a chain-mail habergeon reaching to
below his hips, mail chausses on his legs and, at his side,
his single-handed sword with its typical quillons (cross-
guard, separating hilt from blade) pointing towards the
tip of the sword. These items of armour can be seen in
Provost Skene's House in Aberdeen.

Keith Moray Grampian 7D2 (*pop.* 4,177)
Keith is the centre of the farming district of Banffshire
and the home of several distilleries and woollen mills.
The Keith Agricultural Show in the first week of August is
the great event of the local farming year. Otherwise, it is a
busy rather than an exciting place, with little to attract the
visitor except, down in the old town by the River Isla,
among the distilleries, the Auld Brig, with steps up to the
crown, much painted by artists, and a fragment of early
castle. The New Town, laid out in 1750 by the Earl of Findlater on the gridiron plan which served as a model for
subsequent planned villages, is dominated by the dome of
the Catholic Church of St Thomas, built with a donation
from Charles X of France, who presented the 'Incredulity
of St Thomas' by the French painter Dubois. Keith was
the home of John Ogilvie, the only recent Scottish saint
and martyr; he was hanged for denying royal supremacy
in 1615, beatified in 1929 and canonised in 1976. His statue
outside St Thomas is by a monk from Pluscarden (q.v.).

The puzzling appearance of the name Fife in these
parts, far from the Kingdom of Fife, marks the meteoric
rise of the Duff family of bankers. The most successful was

William Duff (1693-1763) of Braco, a farm just east of Keith. In 1718, he took over from his father William Duff of Dipple (near Fochabers), the banking house which the latter had created at Elgin by buying up land available as a result of the bad harvests at the end of the 17th century, and of the failure of the Darien venture. William of Braco increased his fortune by buying up estates forfeited after the Fifteen and Forty-Five, including Balvenie Castle (see Dufftown). By 1735, he was Lord Braco and in 1759 Viscount Macduff, 1st Earl of Fife, having built the ruin-ously expensive Duff House at Banff (q.v.). The 2nd Earl tried to establish his descent from the Macduff Thanes of Fife of Macbeth's day, even though this line expired with the Dukes of Albany in 1424. The 3rd Earl fought in Spain in 1811 alongside San Martin, the liberator of Argentina; he founded the western suburb of Fife-Keith in 1817 and became the friend and adviser of George IV. In 1889, the 6th Earl (1849-1912) married Princess Louise, daughter of the Prince of Wales (later Edward VII) and was created a Royal Duke — naturally of Fife — thus achieving a record rise from farmers to Dukes in fewer than 200 years.

Kildrummy Castle Gordon Grampian 7 D5 (AM)
From the 13th century Kildrummy Castle has

commanded the approaches from the s to the fertile but often unruly province of Moray. The castle is set to the w of the River Don (q.v.) at the foot of a wooded defile where a gap in the Aberdeenshire hills leads from Mar N into Strathbogie (q.v.). In the previous century, the Doune of Invernochty, 10 miles up Donside had guarded the route. Alexander II (1198-1249), encouraged by the Bishop of Moray to build a stronghold half way between Brechin and Elgin, perceived the strategic importance of the Kildrummy site. This remarkable courtyard castle (or castle of *enceinte*), the most northerly of its kind, with curtain walls and five tall towers, is modelled on Alexander's French father-in-law's massive castle of Coucy in France, N of Paris. Edward I stopped here on both his journeys into Moray in 1296 and 1303, and it seems probable that his architect, Master James of St George, who built Edward's castles in North Wales, added the two drum towers of the gatehouse (of which only the foundations remain). Of the five great towers, only two now project above the curtain wall: in the N corner near the chapel, with its three fine lancet-windows, is the Warden's Tower, standing above the strongest corner of the defences where the wall drops steeply down into the ravine below. Two-thirds of the

Kildrummy Castle

way along the w front is the Snow Tower, the original donjon or keep. Between the Snow Tower and the Warden's Tower are the remains of the Great Hall, the solar — or private suite of the lord — and the kitchens, with a small postern gate beside the Warden's Tower permitting a rapid exit into the ravine. This straight western section of the curtain wall is flanked by curving sections on N and S which come together at the gatehouse, enclosing a large cobbled area. The ruins were tidied up when the castle was taken over as an AM in 1951.

Kildrummy has figured prominently in Scottish history. In 1306, after his defeat at Methven, Robert Bruce sent his wife and her ladies here under the charge of his brother Nigel. They were besieged by Prince Edward (later Edward II) and would have held out but for the treachery of Osborn the Smith who, in agreement with the English, set fire to part of the castle, in return for 'as much gold as he could carry'. Nigel Bruce was killed, the ladies, after escaping, were captured, and Osborn got his gold: the English poured it, molten, down his throat. Restored in 1333, Kildrummy was defended by Bruce's sister Christian against English forces under David de Strathbogie of the Balliol faction. Hurrying northwards to her defence in November 1335, her husband, Andrew de Moray, defeated Strathbogie and his men on the hill of Culblean (see Dee). Kildrummy became the traditional fortress of the Earls of Mar, who were frequently in dispute with the Crown and also with Alexander Stewart, son of the Wolf of Badenoch, who abducted and forcibly married the Countess of Mar in order to acquire her lands. Its troubled history continued into the 17th century, when it was occupied by Cromwell's troops in 1654, and fired in 1690 to forestall Dutch King William. In 1715 it was used by the Earl of Mar to rally forces for his ill-fated rising. On its failure, Kildrummy was forfeited, fell into disuse and was exploited as a quarry until restored in the first part of the 20th century.

The steep wooded ravine to the w of the castle encloses an interesting garden, principally rhododendrons and azaleas, open to the public in season. The 13th-century castle replaced an earlier small motte-and-bailey about 1½ miles NE, where the present kirk of Kildrummy stands, attractively set on a green mound overlooking the Don, with numerous ancient gravestones. Dating from 1805, it is a curiously nondescript building: the saying goes that 'you could make a kirk or a mill of it'.

Killiecrankie   Perthshire   Tayside   4 A5

The most picturesque section of the A9 is the point between Pitlochry and Blair Atholl, where the valley of the Garry, just before its junction with the Tummel, contracts to a narrow gorge through which road and rail thread their way. This is the Pass of Killiecrankie, and the scene of the historic battle of 27 July 1689. On the one side were the Highland forces under Col. John Graham Claverhouse, created Viscount Dundee by King James II of England and VII of Scotland shortly before he went

into exile, and on the other the troops supporting the Government of William and Mary under General Hugh Mackay (1640-92). After raising the Jacobite standard on Dundee Law, 'Bonnie Dundee' (as he was known to his own side, but 'Bloody Clavers' to the Covenanters he had hunted down ten years previously) set out to recruit the Highland clans. By 25 July he was in Badenoch, but on hearing that Mackay, with 4,400 men, was moving N from Dunkeld, Dundee marched his Highlanders — some 2,400 of them — to Blair Atholl (q.v.). The Marquis of Atholl, a supporter of King William, had discreetly retired to take the waters at Bath, so Dundee persuaded the Duke's steward, one Patrick Stewart, to hold the castle for King James.

By the morning of 27 July, Mackay's advance troops had emerged from the N end of the Killiecrankie defile to flat, level ground alongside the Garry, but they were badly sited below the shelf which runs above the valley floor. Meanwhile Dundee, knowing that he must manoeuvre his inferior force into a superior position, had led his men up Glen Fender and down the little glen to the E of the Hill of Lude, in order to take Mackay from above. The Government forces had no chance to make use of either their cavalry or of that new-fangled weapon, the bayonet, which had then to be plugged into the muzzle of the musket. The Highlanders, charging down from above, completely routed them. 'In the twinkling of an eye', Mackay reported 'our men and the enemy were out of sight, being got down pell mell to the river where our baggage stood'. Wordsworth wrote in 1803:

> Like a whirlwind came
> The Highlanders, the slaughter spread like flame;
> And Garry, thundering down his mountain road,
> Was stopp'd, and could not breathe beneath the load
> Of the dead bodies.

The Highlanders lost 600 men, but their most grievous loss was 'Bonnie Dundee' himself who, conspicuous in his silver and buff coat, fell mortally wounded from a musket bullet. He died in the inn at Old Blair, and was buried in the kirk there.

As King William was one of the first to appreciate, the loss of Dundee's leadership was fatal to the Jacobite cause. 'Armies are needless', he said to the panicking Whigs,'the war is over with Dundee's life'. Colonel Cannon, the routine soldier, followed up the victory of Killiecrankie as far as Dunkeld (q.v.), but failed to overcome the resistance of Cleland's Cameronians there. Within a year, Mackay has subdued the Highlands — at least, until the next time. The mound where the officers of both sides were buried is surmounted by a monument erected in 1950 to Ian Campbell Younger of nearby Urrard, killed in Malaya. The battle can be followed in detail in the attractive little museum built by the NTS in 1964. Tracks lead down through the oaks into the gorge, where there is the famous Soldier's Leap.

Kincardine   see The Mearns

Kinross Perth and Kinross Tayside 2 E4
One a tiny county in its own right, and before 1426 part of
Fife, Kinross lost its administrative identity in the
Regionalisation scheme of 1975 and has been swallowed
up in the Tayside Region. Perhaps the new M90, which
sweeps in a great curve through the district of Kinross on
its way from the Forth Bridge to Perth, made the
amalgamation inevitable.

Even from the M90, some idea can be gathered of the
unity of this oval plain in a shallow bowl between the
Ochils to the N, the Cleish Hills to the SW, the Lomond
Hills of Fife to the E and, on the S, Benarty Hill dominating
Loch Leven (q.v.), itself the focal point of the district.
Kinross town, now by-passed, popular among anglers, is
proud of its 16th-century Tolbooth, restored in 1771 by
Robert Adam, whose father William Adam had acquired
the estate of Blairadam nearby.

Kinross House, with its fine Renaissance exterior,
described by Defoe as this 'most beautiful and regular
Piece of Architecture', was built for himself between 1685
and 1690 by Sir William Bruce (1630-1710), Master of
Works to King Charles II, for whom he had restored and
enlarged Holyrood Palace in Edinburgh. This spacious,
well proportioned house in the French style is in strange
contrast to the tower-houses of only a few decades
before. The gardens of Kinross House (open to the public
on certain days) are in the French formal style of Le Nòtre
(as at Holyrood), which also inspired Pitmedden (q.v.). The
vista was deliberately sited to have Loch Leven Castle in
full view.

At the N end of Loch Leven, and to the E of the village
of Milnathort, is the interesting Burleigh Castle, belonging since 1446 to the Balfours of Burleigh, and now an
AM. It consists of two towers joined by a gateway: one is
a standard rectangular 15th-century keep; the smaller
is unusual, being circular at its base but corbelled out at
the second floor to form a square-gabled watch-
chamber.

In the undulating country to the W of the loch are three
private castles. Tulliebole, just a mile E of where the River
Devon makes its great bend at Crook of Devon, was built
in 1608 by an Edinburgh lawyer, John Halliday, who
seems to have turned a traditional keep into a turretted,
castellated mansion; in 1705 it passed to the family of Lord
Moncrieff, in whose hands it still is. Aldie Castle stands tall
and white-harled about 2 miles to the S as the crow flies.
The tower was built in 1464, the turrets at three of the
corners and the cap-house added in 1585. Later came the
wings, turning a strong fortalice into the pleasant 'House
of Aldie'. Its present owner has lovingly restored what
risked becoming a ruin. Cleish Castle, standing out
against the wooded background of the Cleish Hills, dates
from the 16th century and was restored in 1840, luckily
before the 'Balmoralising' period of Bryce and others.

On the E side of Loch Leven are: Scotlandwell, said to
have been a well since Roman times; Kinnesswood, the
home of the meteorologist Alexander Buchan (1829-1907)

who gave his names to the annual cycles of cold and
warmth; and Portmoak, an airfield for gliders.

Kirriemuir Angus Tayside 4 D5 *(pop. 4,138)*
Kirriemuir is a pleasant little town of some antiquity on
the northern edge of Strathmore near the point at which
Glen Clova and Glen Prosen emerge from the hills.
Kirriemuir suffered not only from the continual feuding
between Lindsays and Ogilvys in the 16th century, but
also for its allegiance to the Stuart cause in the 1640s, and
again in 1715 and 1745. Later, the independence of mind
and intense personal convictions of Scottish weavers
involved Kirriemuir in the arguments of the various
Secession factions of the Scottish Kirk, and as a result of
their agitation against the Industrial Revolution, large-
scale manufacture did not replace hand-loom weaving
until the 1860s.

The red sandstone houses separated by narrow wynds
and steep streets cluster irregularly round the kirk with its
tall steeple; this was the way of weavers' settlements, the
houses seemingly dropped down in haphazard fashion,
but in reality reflecting the strong individuality of the
weavers, who did not want their front door to face
another's. Kirriemuir's most famous citizen, James
Matthew Barrie, playwright and author, was born in a
weaver's house at 9 Brechin Road in 1860. Outside the
white-washed cottage (preserved by the NTS as a
museum) is the quaint little wash-house which was
Barrie's first theatre at the age of seven, and later the
inspiration for the 'Wendy-house' of *Peter Pan.* Within the
cottage, two rooms are devoted to Barrie relics, from his
mutch or baby-cap to the leather jerkin of the first Peter
Pan. The source of inspiration of *A Window in Thrums* was

Peter Pan at Kirriemuir

a small cottage, still to be seen at the junction of the Forfar and Glamis roads, with a small isolated window looking northwards over the town. 'Thrums' are in fact loose threads of flax used to repair a fault in weaving and not, except as a projection of Barrie's fantasy, an alternative name for Kirriemuir. The museum includes the original letter from Captain Scott (who was Barrie's god-son) written in 1912 from the last camp in Antarctica. This inspired Barrie's address on 'Courage' to St Andrews University.

Leith Hall   Gordon   Grampian   7 D4   (NTS)
Leith Hall, not a spectacular tower-house like Craigievar, nor a noble castle like Fyvie, is a graceful country house, added to by succeeding generations of a family in continuous residence for over 300 years. Now under the care of the NTS, it is a well-chosen setting for portraits of the Leith-Hay family and relics of their part in the Peninsular and other wars of the 19th century. The house stands four-square round a central courtyard, with few pretentions to defence beyond an entrance gate and some angle-turrets.

The Leith family, originally ship owners from Edinburgh (deriving their name from the port of that city), moved up to Aberdeen where they prospered and furnished the city with two provosts, one succeeding Provost Davidson who was killed at Harlaw in 1411. It was not until 1649 that James Leith decided to build a house on the lands recently acquired by his father in this NW corner of the Garioch, just over the watershed into Strathbogie.

The original building is the present N wing — a modest construction compared with the opulent castles built in the previous 80 years or so, but reflecting the troubled 1650s. The square rectangular block — three storeys high — was ornamented only by traditional angle-turrets and by the arms of the founder and his wife over the gateway. James Leith lived in peace and comparative security to see the end of Stuart rule in 1688. His son, grandson and great-grandson, all called John, found life harder, what with the hungry years at the end of the 17th century and the family's Jacobite sympathies in 1715 and 1745. The second John married in 1730 Mary Hay of Rannes (on the Banffshire coast) but died soon after, leaving as laird during the Forty-Five a young son whose uncles and Rannes relatives were out with Prince Charles. In 1756 the third John married Harriot Stuart, and together they added the two storeys of the E wing and reconstructed the s wing. He was mysteriously shot in the street in Aberdeen in 1763, leaving Harriot to manage the estate and bring up three sons, of whom the eldest died young in 1776, while the two others, Alexander and James, became distinguished generals. Meanwhile, an unexpected stroke of good fortune had come from their great-uncle, Andrew Hay of Rannes, a seven-foot giant who had been exiled after the Forty-Five and returned home in 1763. Being without children, he sold his Rannes estate in 1789 to free

Leith Hall from debt on condition that the family should bear the name of Leith-Hay. This generous act enabled Alexander to do much for the estate of which he was the laird for 62 years (1776-1838). The estate prospered by following the example of Monymusk over enclosures and the rotation of crops. Alexander also added a third storey to his father's E and s wings and the family moved from their living quarters in the N wing to the similar s wing, thus gaining a southern aspect without having to look out on the bustle of the courtyard. At the same time, the w side of the courtyard was closed by a simple line of imitation battlements.

Meanwhile, James had been active in the Peninsular War, first in Moore's retreat to Corunna, then under Wellington in a succession of battles, but playing a particularly prominent part in storming both the castle at Badajoz (1812) and the citadel at San Sebastian (1813) where he was severely wounded, with his nephew Andrew nearby as his aide-de-camp. Knighted for services to Lord Melbourne's Government, Sir Andrew later devoted himself to the estate, which prospered with the improvement of communications, particularly the arrival of the Great North of Scotland Railway in 1854. Of Sir Andrew's five sons, the eldest, Alexander Sebastian, saw service in the Crimean War and in the Indian Mutiny. The other four sons emigrated to Australia, but a nephew, Charles, returned to succeed Alexander Sebastian as laird on the latter's death in 1900. In 1939, the 300-year association of house and family came tragically to an end with the death of Charles, and four months later the accidental killing of his only son. Mrs Leith-Hay, considering that this part of the valuable heritage should not be lost to Scotland, entrusted the house and estate to the NTS.

The w wing is open to the public, the other sections of the house being let to tenants to assist in the upkeep. From the visitors' entrance in the NW corner a stair leads up to two small bedrooms, providing an attractive setting for a display of china (in the turret), needlework and furniture. Across the stair-head and above the w entrance is the so-called Music Room; this is in fact a museum, containing a number of interesting family relics, including such curiosities as the personal jewellery of the last King of Oudh — trophies from the Indian Mutiny; a sash belonging to Napoleon, given to Andrew Leith-Hay by the wife of his prisoner, General Gazan, after the battle of Vitoria; and a large powder horn engraved with maps of the Hudson and Mohawk valleys, dating from the British campaign of 1758 against the French in North-East America. A huge pair of silk stockings testifies to the size of the gigantic Andrew Hay of Rannes; the writing-case given him by Prince Charles Edward, and a miniature of the Prince, are also here together with the lengthy pardon signed by George III in 1780. In the passage at the s end of the Music Room hang large pictures of Balaclava and the siege of the Residency at Lucknow and, over the door to the library, one of the

Leith Hall

storming of San Sebastian in 1813. In the turret of the library is the costume of a Red Indian chief, acquired by Alexander Sebastian in Canada. A stair leads down to the dining room, well furnished with good examples of Scottish craftsmanship.

The extensive s-facing gardens sloping up the hillside behind the house were created by the Australian Charles Leith-Hay and his wife. The NTS has reconstituted various gardens, with their broad herbaceous borders, including a rock garden in a small quarry. There is a view westwards towards the prominent knob of Tap o' Noth with its hill-fort.

Loch Earn Perthshire Tayside 1 A3
Loch Earn, running E and w, 6½ miles (10 km.) long but no more than a mile wide, is the effective start of the River Earn, collecting the waters of Glen Ample, Glen Ogle and other streams into this deep trough along the Highland Boundary Fault. Loch Earn is popular with the sailing fraternity and recently water-skiing has been developed at Lochearnhead at the west end. Historically, the interest of the area lies in the centuries-long conflict between Highland and Lowland, but in modern times it has become a useful line of communication. The rugged rock mass of Dundurn, a mile from the E end of Loch Earn, stands 300 ft (90 m.) high above the level strath. It was probably the principal stronghold of the Picts w of the Tay. The Romans, from their outpost at Dalginross by

Comrie, no doubt kept an eye on Dundurn; and during the Scottish-Irish invasion of Pictland Dundurn was attacked in A.D. 683.

St Fillans, at the E end of Loch Earn, is a relatively recent creation. It is named after the Celtic Saint Faolain the Leper who, around A.D. 500, preached the gospel from Dundurn, where his chair is to be seen in the rock. Before 1800, the few cottages on the shore were known as Port of Lochearn, but in 1817 the Drummond landlord offered sites on the estate for development, and so the little village grew up, now extended in summer by a large caravan park on the s bank of the loch. The great bulk of Ben Vorlich (3,231 ft/985 m.) with its narrow summit ridge, and its attendant peak of Stuc a' Chroin, dominates the s side of Loch Earn. From ARDVORLICH on the loch-side, a straightforward, if consistently steep, track leads to the top in about 3 hours, and the view is well worth-while.

Ardvorlich House is the home of the small sub-clan, the Stewarts of Ardvorlich, who settled here about 1580. They had an unhappy history, being at one time classed, possibly not without justification, with the outlawed Macgregors as cattle-thieves and marauders. But nothing they may have done could compare with the horrible tale of the Macgregors who murdered the King's forester, Drummond-Ernoch, brother-in-law to the Stewart of Ardvorlich of the day. Drummond-Ernoch had caught some Macgregors poaching while he himself was hunting deer intended for James VI's wedding-feast in 1589. The Macgregors, vowing revenge, killed him, cut off his head and took it to Ardvorlich. While enjoying the hospitality of the lady of Ardvorlich, they stuffed the mouth of her dead brother with bread and cheese while she was out of the room. On her return, the poor lady, then pregnant, was so horrified that she rushed up into the hills and there gave birth to a baby who later became the 'Mad Major' James Stewart, one of Montrose's captains. In addition to killing every Macgregor he could lay hands on, the obsessed man ended by stabbing to death his own friend and fellow-officer Lord Kilpont — a story which Sir Walter Scott uses in *A Legend of Montrose*, James Stewart being the original of Allan MacAulay. Ardvorlich was attacked from farther afield too, for a stone near the bridge on the lochside marks the spot where the bodies of seven Macdonalds of Glencoe were buried, 'killed when attempting to harry Ardvorlich Anno Domini 1620'.

The small wooded island off St Fillans was the place of refuge of the Neish tribe, a sub-clan of the Macgregors. Early in the 17th century they were rash enough to raid a party of Macnabs carrying Christmas supplies from Crieff back to their home in Killin on Loch Tay. The Chief Macnab swore vengeance and sent his twelve sons over the hills carrying a boat, to cross the water to surprise the Neishes on their island. The Neishes were all slain except one boy, who swam ashore and is presumably the ancestor of all the MacNishes of the present day. The Macnabs not only took the head of the chief Neish back to their father, but also carried their boat part of the way back up Glentarken, where the remains were to be seen as late as 1854. Iain Macnab, the leader of the band, died fighting for Charles II at Worcester in 1651.

Loch Leven   Perth and Kinross   Tayside 2 E4
This nearly circular loch, celebrated among anglers for its pink-fleshed trout, has had its ups and downs. The English dammed the outlet in 1335 to try to force Sir Alan Wypont out of Loch Leven Castle on the island, and the area of the loch remained considerably greater until the level was lowered, first by Sir William Bruce in 1685 to provide land for the garden of Kinross House, and again in the 19th century when a third island appeared. The largest island is St Serf's (from Servatius), where that saint had his cell, and where, as Prior, Andrew of Wyntoun (1355-1422) wrote his *Orygynal Cronikil of Scotland*.

The lowering of the loch has enlarged Castle Island to some eight acres, a good deal more than Mary, Queen of Scots, had to walk about on when she was imprisoned here. The Douglas of Lochleven family built, in the 14th century, the massive oblong keep, five storeys high, with forbiddingly small windows. In the 15th century, they added the extensive courtyard wall, enclosing most of the island as it then was. At the SE corner, communicating with the keep only along the curtain wall, is the small round tower in which Mary, Queen of Scots, was con-

Loch Leven Castle on its island

fined. There are rooms on the three upper floors and the first floor has a diminutive oriel window, from which Mary must have looked hopefully s across the loch towards Edinburgh.

The story of her imprisonment here from 17 June 1567 until her escape on 2 May 1568 has been told many times and is an incident in Sir Walter Scott's *The Abbot*. After first her own troops, and then Bothwell, deserted her at Carberry Hill, Mary became the prisoner of the nobles who committed her to the custody of Sir William Douglas in his castle of Loch Leven. Her jailer's mother, Lady Margaret Douglas, was the Margaret Erskine who, as mistress of James V, was the mother of Mary's illegitimate half-brother James, Earl of Moray. Lady Margaret was Mary's implacable enemy, no doubt because she grudged her the crown that might have been her son's. Moray visited Mary in Loch Leven to force her abdication and to extort from her the royal jewels, ostensibly for the infant James VI, though some found their way to Moray's wife. It was a grim time for Mary: she was sick, her child, probably Bothwell's, miscarried and she was daily taunted by Lady Margaret. When the spring came, however, her thoughts turned to escape. She used her wiles to good effect on George Douglas, her jailer's handsome younger brother, who became her devoted admirer. He not only connived at her escape, but conveyed messages to the lords of the Queen's party. Young Willy Douglas, a cousin, also gleefully helped Mary to leave the island, boring holes in all the boats but one, purloining keys and, according to one story, arranging a pageant so that Mary was escorted to the boat in disguise. On the mainland Mary was met by the resourceful George Douglas with horses stolen from the laird of Lochleven's stables. They rode swiftly southwards, crossed the Forth to join the Hamiltons, Setons and others who saw advantage in the Queen's party. The account of their defeat at Langside, Mary's flight into England, and of her 20-year imprisonment and execution by Elizabeth I belong elsewhere. Loch Leven Castle is now an AM and is accessible by ferry from Kinross Town.

At the s end of the loch is the Vane Farm Nature Reserve, the first nature centre opened in Britain, with displays devoted to the local geology, wildlife and botany. The loch is, during the autumn and winter months, a favourite feeding ground for wild geese, duck and other water-fowl, and the reserve is under the care of the RSPB.

Loch of the Lowes Perthshire Tayside 4 B6
The Loch of the Lowes (to rhyme with 'cows'), just over the hill E of Dunkeld (q.v.), is the biggest of three 'kettle-hole' lochs, formed by large lumps of ice sitting on the valley floor as the glaciers retreated after the Ice Age, their basins kept free from the sand and gravel deposited round them by the meltwater streams. The juxtaposition of water and forest, and the changing levels of the loch, provide just the environment, in particular the reed-beds, needed by nesting water-fowl. The osprey, too, needs tall trees as observation posts, close to water for its prey of fish. The Loch of the Lowes is now one of the two places in Britain (the other being Loch Garten on Speyside) where from a well-organized hide, a pair of ospreys can regularly be observed mating and hatching their chicks under properly protected conditions. The osprey nests in other places, but these are well-kept secrets, lest vandals loot the eggs.

The Loch of the Lowes is under the care of the SWT. In addition to the hide, there is a Visitor Centre with an exhibition on the ecology of the loch.

Lochnagar Kincardine and Deeside Grampian 4C3
Lochnagar (3,789 ft/1155 m.) is no loch, but a fine mountain south of the Dee. Byron is to be thanked for the rejection of the ancient and more appropriate name of White Mounth. His well-known lines bear repetition:
England, thy beauties are tame and domestic,
To one who has roved o'er the mountains afar:
Oh for the crags that are wild and majestic!
The steep frowning glories of dark Lochnagar.
The little *loch-nan-gabhar* (loch of the goats), which lies cradled at the foot of the precipitous cliffs of the N-facing corrie, has given its name to this southern outlying massif of the Cairngorms. The summit tor and cairn (*Cae Carn Beag*), seen as a sharp peak from the Invercauld Bridge of the Dee on the Braemar to Balmoral road, lie some way back from the edge of the corrie.

This magnificent mountain, made popular in song and poem, was visited by Queen Victoria in 1861. Its precipitous N-facing crags are tempting to the expert rock-climber, and in winter provide severe ice-climbs. That great climber and versifier Tom Patey could ironically maintain that the Karakoram peaks
Masherbrum, Gasherbrum, Distegal Sar:
They're very good training for dark Lochnagar.
The ascent of Lochnagar from the A93 by way of Loch Callater has been noted under Braemar (q.v.). This was the route followed by Queen Victoria in 1861. A shorter, more attractive route takes about 3 hours from Spittal of Glen Muick (*see* Ballater). After following a track to the head of Glen Gelder, overlooking Balmoral, the path climbs steeply to the edge of the crags, which can be followed all the way round to Black Spout gully, giving precipitous views down to the little loch over 1,000 ft (300 m.) below. The granite here is weathered into gigantic blocks, giving the appearance of having been put together by some Brobdignagian architect. By whichever route, Lochnagar is a splendid excursion and, given good visibility, the view extends far beyond the snow-flecked plateau and steep corries of the main Cairngorm range to the N. The indicator placed on the summit by the Cairngorm Club shows that Morven in Caithness, Ben Nevis, Ben Lomond and the Pentland Hills beyond Edinburgh are all, on occasion, visible.

Lumphanan *see* **Cromar**

The northern corrie, Lochnagar

Lunan Bay Angus Tayside 5 F5

Lunan Bay is a 4-mile stretch of sands between Boddin Point, s of Montrose (q.v.) and the great cliff of Red Head N of Arbroath (q.v.). Where the Lunan Water winds into the bay is a charming little kirk and, on a nearby bluff, the grim ruin of Red Castle. This formidable and rather sinister 15th-century tower replaces an earlier stronghold built as a defence against Danish invaders. William the Lion may have lived here while supervising the construction of Arbroath Abbey. There is an awesome 25ft-deep pit prison where malefactors were confined. In the 16th century the castle came into the hands of Cardinal Beaton, who also owned nearby Ethie. Later it became a manse and then a Customs look out post. Cardinal Beaton, when Abbot of Arbroath, must have been fond of the area. Ethie, a square, pink-harled 15th-century tower, now in private ownership, was a home for Marion Ogilvy, his wife or mistress, and their seven children. He added to the original keep and, after his murder at St Andrews in 1546, his ghost, according to legend, was seen in the Cardinal's chamber at Ethie. Sir Walter Scott drew on both Ethie and Red Castle for his imaginary castle of Knockwinnock in *The Antiquary*.

Macduff *see* **Banff**

The Mearns Grampian 5F4-G3

The Mearns is the affectionate (and ancient) name used for the former county of Kincardine, now part of the District of Kincardine and Deeside. Legend has it that Oengus (Angus or Aeneas) and Mearnia were brothers of Kenneth II who divided the rich inheritance of Strathmore between them. Alternatively, the name can be prosaically derived from the Gaelic *am mhaoirne* meaning 'Stewartry'. Nonetheless, situated just where the important Cairn o' Mount crossing debouches into the Howe of the Mearns, Kincardine Castle was once an important place. The Picts had earlier realised its value, with their Green Castle at the mouth of the glen below Finella Hill. Finella was the courageous Mearns princess who in 994 revenged the death of her son by murdering Kenneth II hereabouts, according to legend, by means of a booby-trap whereby arrows were fired when the victim grasped the bait of a golden apple — an ingenious girl, if this is true! Finella was finally run to earth at Denfinella on the coast near St Cyrus. The early Scottish kings enjoyed the hunting (as shown by the great Deer Dyke) but the fact that three of them were killed nearby could account for its decline in popularity as a royal capital. The castle was demolished in 1646 and only a wooded mound, a mile or so NE of Fettercairn, is now to be seen. Nor was

Kincardine much of a success as a county town, which was transferred to Stonehaven in 1606. The 'castle' of Drumtochty in Strathfinella is a 19th-century affair, by Gillespie Graham (1777-1855), the architect of part of Edinburgh New Town.

It is the Howe of the Mearns that is the heart of the place: a wide fertile basin where the rich till of Old Red Sandstone is turned to a creamy red by the plough. Its landscape has been evocatively described by Leslie Mitchell (1901-35), writing under the pseudonym of Lewis Grassic Gibbon in *Sunset Song,* the first volume of his trilogy *A Scots Quair.* The history of the Mearns is sketched in the opening chapter of the second volume *Cloud Howe.* The third volume, *Grey Granite,* is set in the city of 'Duncairn', neither Dundee nor Aberdeen but, as the author whimsically declares, the city the Mearns would have built had the inhabitants foreseen the requirements of his novel.

It is simple to pass rapidly through the Howe of the Mearns by the A94 through the rather uninteresting little town of Laurencekirk, planned and built in the 18th century by the improving Lord Gardenston who, according to Boswell, was 'as proud as if he had founded Thebes'. But it is pleasanter to turn aside to hunt out the churches and castles (many in private hands) tucked away in the folds of the hills. Among the latter is the fortified farm-house of Monboddo, recently restored by the present owner. This was the home of James Burnett, Lord Monboddo (1714-99), the learned but eccentric 18th-century judge who, in his *Origin and Progress of Language,* advanced the theory that men were descended from monkeys, and was credited with the belief that humans were born with tails. But, as a more modern versifier points out

Though Darwin now proclaims the law
And spreads it far abroad-o,
The man that first that secret saw
Was honest old Monboddo.

Dr Samuel Johnson said in his bluff way 'Other people have strange notions, but they conceal them. If they have tails, they hide them. But Monboddo is as jealous of his tail as a squirrel'. Notwithstanding his views, the good Doctor allowed himself to be persuaded by Boswell, who was 'curious to see them together', to spend a night in August 1773 at Monboddo, and the two learned gentlemen enjoyed a long, intellectual conversation reported in detail by Boswell.

The castles (ruined and restored) of the Mearns are too numerous to describe in detail. There is Inglismaldie (Church of St Magdalen), in its plantation on the River North Esk; there is Lauriston, now a ruin in a wooded ravine, up from the coast near St Cyrus; there are Hallgreen, overlooking Bervie Bay, and the tall, 15th-century keep of Benholm Tower, the home of the Keith who was Governor of Dunnottar (q.v.). There are Thornton, well preserved, and Fiddes, well restored, as well as Fetteresso, now a shell but after Dunnottar the

residence of the Keiths and where, in 1715, the Old Pretender was proclaimed king.

The two summits of the long hill of Garvock, E of Laurencekirk, are crowned respectively by an ancient cairn to the N and, on the S by the (modern) Johnston's Tower, the name of Lord Gardenston's estate. Together with the lower bleak hills to the N of the Bervie Water, which flows to the sea at Inverbervie, Garvock cuts off the Howe from the sea. These hills are a lava intrusion giving the poor clay soils on which Grassic Gibbon's 'John Guthrie' toiled away at 'Blawearie'; this farm can be identified as Bloomfield, on one of the by-roads between the A94 and Arbuthnott Church where Grassic Gibbon is buried. Somewhere in these hills took place the gruesome episode involving the conscientious, if officious, Sheriff Melville of Kincardine. James I expressed the wish that the tiresome 'Sheriff were sodden and suppit in bree'. Five of the local lairds, led by David Barclay of Mathers, are said to have done just that, boiling the unfortunate sheriff down to a soup, which they all then supped. The remnants of Barclay's castle, the Kaim of Mathers, are to be seen on a narrow promontory near St Cyrus, but most has been eroded by the sea. The Melville family came from up the glen at Glenbervie with its 16th-century castle and its 19th-century kirk which stands big and gaunt just where a signpost points down a lane to the old churchyard. Here, under a small canopy, are the grave-stones of James Burnes of Brawlinmuir and William Burnes of Bogjordan, great-grandfather and great-grand-uncle of the poet Robert Burns. His father William Burness (the spelling varies) farmed at Clochnahill 5 miles to the W before he left for Ayrshire in the mid 18th century; a memorial cairn stands on the A94 by the entrance. James Burnes, a cousin of the poet, was the father of the famous Alexander Burnes who, in 1832, travelled from India through Afghanistan to Persia in disguise. In 1839, when Political Resident in Kabul, he was murdered by an Afghan mob. Close by is Drumlithie, the 'Segget' of Grassic Gibbon's *Cloud Howe* — an old weaving town set down higgledy-piggledy. The slim round tower, in imitation of Abernethy and Brechin, dates only from 1770 and was intended as a bell-tower to regulate the weavers' working hours. Westwards from Glenbervie the little town of Auchenblae is celebrated for its associations with St Palladius (an Irish saint whose bones were brought here by St Ternan), who gave his name to the various 'Paldy Fairs'.

The Mearns coast northwards from Inverbervie to Dunnottar and Stonehaven is a wild succession of cliffs, headlands and little smugglers' coves. The only cliff-top villages are Catterline, beloved of artists, and Kinneff. In the church of Kinneff, the regalia of the Crown of Scotland were devotedly kept in secret for Charles II by the minister's wife, after she had smuggled them out of Dunnottar (q.v.) under the noses of Cromwell's soldiers. There is a monument in the church dated 1738 commemorating the event. The big headland just NE of

Inverbervie is called Craig David, for here, in 1341, at the King's Step, Bruce's son David II landed to take up his kingdom. The rugged coast, the bleak open hills which are the home of hard-working farmers, the fertile Howe and its little towns, and the great sweeps of wild, uninhabited moorland, heather-covered in the w and N but afforested to the E, last outposts of the Mounth, all these make up the compact province of the Mearns — as it were, a Scotland in miniature.

Meigle see Aberlemno

Melgund Angus Tayside 5 E5

There is a signpost to Melgund 5 miles out of Brechin on the road to Aberlemno, but nothing to indicate that a rather elegant and remarkable castle stands, desolate and neglected, in the corner of a field. At first glance, it looks like a standard L-shaped, 15th-century keep, extended for more gracious living in the following century, as at Edzell, but closer inspection shows that the masonry is all of a piece and that the same elaborate corbelling continues over both sections of the building. The main hall is not, as at Edzell and elsewhere, on the first floor of the four-storey keep, but in the two-storey extension. The amenities are those of the mid 16th century, with a big kitchen and plenty of bedroom accommodation. This is because Cardinal David Beaton, Archbishop of St Andrews and Chancellor of Scotland (1494-1546) built this castle for his 'chief lewd' Marion Ogilvy, daughter of the first Lord Ogilvy of Airlie. The cardinal may have been legally married to Marion, but demoted her to mistress when he embarked on a career as an ecclesiastic. She bore him seven children, one of the daughters being married over the hill at Finavon to the Earl of Crawford's son. Melgund passed to the Gordons of Huntly, to the Maules, the Morays and finally the Earls of Minto, whose heirs still bear the title of Viscount Melgund.

Menstrie Clackmannan Central 1 C5

This small Clackmannanshire town has a remarkable connexion with Canada; from its 16th-century castle, well restored in the 1950s, sprang the idea of the colonisation of Nova Scotia. Sir William Alexander (1577-1640) came from the west following the Earl of Argyll who took over Castle Campbell (q.v.) near Dollar. Alexander was a distinguished author and poet of the early 17th century, much in favour with James VI and tutor to his eldest son, Prince Henry (who died before Charles I came to the throne). Inspired by the vision of a New Scotland in America, alongside New England and New France, Alexander obtained in 1621 a charter from the King, making him hereditary Lieutenant-General over a considerable area of eastern Canada, covering not only modern Nova Scotia but also New Brunswick up to the St Lawrence, including the Gaspé peninsula. As a barrier against the French, this idea appealed to the English

Government, but the first two parties of settlers failed to establish themselves, leaving debts and bringing protests from the French. King James then accepted Alexander's advice to raise money by offering the title of baronet with 30,000 acres in the new colony to each subscriber in return for a considerable sum in hard cash and a promise to send out settlers. An Anglo-Scottish company was formed to take over Nova Scotia. Led by Alexander's son, the settlers occupied Port Royal (later Annapolis Royal) but they failed to take Cape Sable or to hold Cape Breton Island. In 1632 Charles I surrendered the settlement to the French who held it until 1713. While their representatives and settlers were being subject to trials and tribulations in Canada, the titular baronets themselves found it difficult to follow the ancient custom of 'sasine', that is handing over earth from the new land granted as a token of allegiance in return for the freehold. So a piece of Scottish earth in the moat of Edinburgh Castle was deemed to be Nova Scotia for this purpose — a legal fiction which was made reality some 300 years later when, in 1953, the Premier of Nova Scotia deposited a handful of Nova Scotia earth in Edinburgh Castle.

Misguided Sir William Alexander, though made Earl of Stirling and Viscount of Canada, spent his whole fortune on the venture and died in debt in 1640. The Crown continued to make money out of selling baronetcies in a non-existent colony until the Union of Parliaments in 1707. Menstrie Castle fell into disrepair and, by 1956, the building was under serious threat of demolition, particularly in view of the urgent need for modern housing. Fortunately, opinion was rallied in favour of the 16th-century castle, with its long facade, its crowstep gables and jaunty pepper-pot turrets, and a proposal to transplant it to Halifax (Nova Scotia) was abandoned. A happy compromise between the rival claims of history and housing was evolved by making the castle the centrepiece of a new housing complex, providing several new flats in the castle itself, and setting aside two large rooms, one as a library, the other as the Nova Scotia Commemoration Room, which were opened in December 1963.

In the Commemoration Room are displayed colourful shields bearing the coats of arms of the 107 Nova Scotia baronetcies still extant, out of the 280 granted. There are large portraits of James VI, rather unusually corpulent, and of Charles I. Maps show the location of the estates in eastern Canada from which the baronets took their titles. The moulded plaster ceiling includes the motifs of both the Scottish thistle and the Canadian maple leaf. The flag of Nova Scotia flies outside on a flagpole donated in 1973.

Midmar Gordon Grampian 8 F6

The great Celtic province, and later Scottish earldom, of Mar covered all the lands between the Dee and Don and more besides. The power of the Earls of Mar, based on Kildrummy (q.v.), passed to the Gordons of Huntly and what was left of Mar was fragmented after 'Bobbing

John', Earl of Mar, raised the standard for the unsuccessful insurrection of 1715. Some of these fragments are to be recognized in Braemar, Cromar, Craigievar (the 'Crag of Mar') and the scattered parish of Midmar, which lies on the northern slopes of the Hill of Fare, astride the pleasant A974 road from Aberdeen to Tarland.

Midmar Castle is architecturally one of the most interesting of the Aberdeenshire Z-plan castles. Probably built by George Bell, of the same family of master masons who designed Castle Fraser and Crathes, Midmar is a good generation earlier, about 1575. One of the towers of the Z-plan is square and turretted, the other circular, six storeys high, crenellated and with an ogee-helmeted caphouse. The latter is a rougher, earlier version of Castle Fraser's more elegant round tower, while the crowstep gables and rectangular turrets recall the more elaborate skyline of Craigievar (q.v.). As Midmar Castle is tucked away in a wooded glen at the foot of the Hill of Fare, and had no exciting history, it has been well preserved through a succession of owners. The present owners do not allow access, but the castle can be seen fairly well (according to season) from the A974.

Midmar has two churches, one roofless with some interesting gravestones beside a green motte just to the s of the A974, the other, dating from the late 18th century, a few hundred yards up a side-road to the N, with a splendid prehistoric stone-circle (seven upright stones and one recumbent one) close beside it in the graveyard. The area has a number of other interesting stone circles, in particular an even larger one at Sunhoney Farm, half a mile to the E of the church. There is another well preserved circle, with eight boulders surrounding eight cairns, probably of the second millenium B.C. (preserved as an AM), at Cullerlie, 1 mile s of the A974 at Garlogie crossroads. To the E of Midmar is the dome-like hill of the Barmekin of Echt, crowned by a large circular Pictish fort, with five concentric rings of fortifications. It is a strong place, with a fine view, N to the Mither Tap of Bennachie, E over Loch Skene to the outskirts of Aberdeen.

The large house in the wooded grounds to the E of the Barmekin is Dunecht, built in the early 19th century by William Forbes, enlarged in 1880 or so by the Earl of Crawford, and now the property of Lord Cowdray. The pair of huge gatehouses, resembling improbably tall tower-houses with side turrets, strike the traveller coming W on the A944 road from Aberdeen to Alford, after passing Loch Skene.

Montrose Angus Tayside 5 G5 (*pop.* 9,959)
Montrose sounds French, but the name comes from the Gaelic *moine t' ros,* the moor on the peninsula. The town is situated between the North Sea to the E, the outflow of the River South Esk to the s and the wide tidal basin to the w. Draining at low tide, the basin and its reed-beds are the haunt of wildfowl and a gathering point for the pink-footed geese on migration. Despite this constricted site, Montrose has a spacious, prosperous air, thanks to two factors; first, its trade with the Low Countries and with Scandinavia across the North Sea — a trade which was supplemented by extensive smuggling after the Act of Union of 1707 — and, second, its 18th-century function as a watering-place for the Angus landed gentry, many of whom built their town houses here. Dr Johnson, sparing in his praises of Scotland, was prepared to find Montrose 'well-built, airy and clean'. The irregular central square — through which the traffic of the A92 flows unremittingly — has very much the look of a Flemish Groot Plaats, as in Mechlin or in Aalst. The square, wider to the N, is divided into two halves by the projection of the Town House, with an arched loggia below it, and dominated by the flying-buttressed spire of the Steeple, attached to, but not part of, the parish kirk. The Steeple was built in 1832 by Gillespie Graham, the architect of Edinburgh's Moray Place. The southern half of the square is presided over by an 1825 statue of Sir Robert Peel, who turns his back on Castelsted House, the town house of the Grahams, now in use as offices. James Graham, the 1st and Great Marquis of Montrose, is said to have been born here in 1612, but it is more likely that he was born at the now-ruined castle of Old Montrose, west of the tidal basin.

Montrose was spared many of the tribulations of Scottish history. Since Wallace destroyed the English-held castle in 1297, the most stirring events were probably the frequent clashes between smugglers and excise men in the 18th century. The campaigns of Montrose's most distinguished citizen passed his own town by. The Old Pretender re-embarked here for France in 1716 after his short, ill-fated stay in the North-East, and Cumberland stayed briefly in 1746. Reforming zeal was brought from the Continent in the late 16th century by the French Protestant Pierre de Marsiliers, who taught at Montrose Academy, numbering among his pupils those ardent Presbyterians, George Wishart who perished at St Andrews and Andrew Melville who reminded James VI that he was but 'God's sillie vassal'.

Recently, Montrose has added involvement in oil-connected industry to its shipping, fishing, distilling and other industries. Nonetheless, it remains a popular holiday centre, with access inland to the Angus glens (q.v.) and seawards to a low but rocky, rugged coastline, with coves favoured by smugglers and beaches where semi-precious 'agates' are to be found. Southwards from the South Esk are: the lighthouse at Scurdyness, the Elephant Rock with a natural arch forming the trunk, and Boddin Head with its lime-kiln, at the northern point of the golden sands of Lucan Bay (q.v.). Inland, at Upper Dysart farm, is a lean-to lectern-type doocot. Northwards from Montrose, the River North Esk is spanned by a fine bridge built in 1775 which still carries the A92. Further N, the crumbling cliffs have claimed as victims a fair-sized village, Miltonhaven, and most of the castle of Kaim of Mathers. St Cyrus, the modern village, has retreated to the cliff-top, but the tangle of cliffs and 'dens' along the saltings left when the North Esk changed its course in 1879 form the national nature reserve of St Cyrus, with interesting plant species.

Monymusk   Gordon Grampian 8 E5

Monymusk, on the lower Don just s of Bennachie (q.v.), is a village with a long ecclesiastical tradition dating back to the Culdees who, under Norman influence in 1170, became amalgamated with incoming monks of the Augustinian order. The square-towered church, though restored, is an attractive building with a good modern stainedglass window showing a Culdee priest preaching to the Picts, with the peak of Bennachie in the background. The Monymusk Pictish Stone is housed in the church entrance.

Monymusk is also famous for the Monymusk Reliquary, a beautiful little house-shaped casket of the 7th century, said to contain a bone of St Columba (the 'Brecbennoch'), which is to be seen in the National Museum of Antiquities in Edinburgh. Made of bronze-silver plates with an enamelled hinge for a strap, it was given to Arbroath Abbey by William the Lion in 1211, on condition that the monks served in the army. Abbot de Linton of Arbroath did carry it at Bannockburn in 1314, but transferred it the following year — with its obligation — to Monymusk Priory.

The Monymusk estate was bought in 1712 from the Forbes family by Sir Francis Grant (Lord Cullen) whose son, Sir Archibald Grant, was an enlightened agricultural pioneer, leading the way in the rotation of crops, the enclosure of fields and the cultivation of the turnip. He also had an eye for afforestation, planting 50 million trees in 50 years to our great benefit today.

The Laich of Moray   Moray Grampian 7 A1-C1

Ancient Moray, or Moravia (Gaelic *moireabh,* probably 'settlement by the sea') spread its boundaries wider than the present district of Moray centred on Elgin. The prize of Moray was always the Laich or lowland — the 'girnal' (granary) of Scotland — that wonderfully fertile region which stretches along the coast between the Rivers Spey and Findhorn. Blessed with a dry climate, it is 'brightened every year', observed James Gordon the cartographer, 'with forty days of greater clearness than the whole vicinity'. The Romans never quite reached it; the Vikings raided it between the 9th and 10th centuries and had a base at Torfness (Burghead); the Picts defended it against them until they were absorbed by the Scots; consolidated under Macbeth in the 11th century, the Laich was important and rebellious enough to earn visits from the English King Edward I in 1296 and again in 1303; its independent prelates originated the Scottish War of Independence; it gave rise to a breed of strong personalities in the Earls of Moray and the Prince Bishops of Elgin (q.v.), who were often in conflict with king or Reformed Kirk. The Laich's ecclesiastical associations date back to the foundation in 1159 of Kinloss Abbey (now an ivy-clad ruin) by the pious Queen Margaret and her son David I, and to the charming little 12th century church of Birnie, a few miles s of Elgin. These, and other ecclesiastical foundations like Pluscarden (q.v.), were originally intended by the Normans as means of absorbing or converting the Celtic Culdee church to the Roman rite. The palace of Spynie is a remarkably well fortified building (*see* Elgin) for a bishop's palace.

The broad sweep of the Laich is bounded on the N by three different coastlines. To the E are the shingle beaches between the mouth of the Spey and the promontory sheltering the fishing port of Lossiemouth, founded by the burghers of Elgin in 1698 and increasingly developed as Loch Spynie silted up. Lossiemouth was the birthplace of Ramsay Macdonald, who lies buried in Spynie Churchyard. Next, westwards for 5 miles, from the prominent Covesea Lighthouse (built by Alan Stevenson in 1844) as far as the promontory of Burghead, the fields drop unexpectedly away in a line of 200 ft-high cliffs of yellow sandstone. At Hopeman, these have long been quarried to provide the easily worked Moray freestone. Here are the Painted Cave with Pictish inscriptions, the wind-eroded pillar of Gow's Crag, and a cliff walk, dazzling and scented in June with sheets of yellow gorse in full bloom. The third section, from Burghead westward, is a broad arc of sandy bay stretching to the mouth of the Findhorn, the dunes tethered from invading the farmlands (as the Culbin Sands did in the 17th century) by the Forestry Commission's plantation of Roseisle, where there is a picnic area. Inland, the light fertile soil and slight rainfall (only 36 in. a year) provide those rolling acres of wheat which justify the name of 'granary of Scotland'. In earlier days, the area was not so large, for the Loch of Spynie extended from about Duffus Castle eastwards to the River Lossie, providing the bishop with a convenient harbour. The draining of the loch was begun by Telford in 1808 but not completed until 1880. An area roughly corresponding to the rich farmland thus gained was, however, taken over by the Air Ministry after World War II: the almost total absence of fog makes the two airfields of Kinloss and Lossiemouth invaluable to the R.A.F. in their task of defending Britain.

As in Angus, the rich farmlands of Moray provide plenty of grain for pigeons, and so the doocot is a feature of the Moray landscape (for more on doocots, *see* Introduction: Architecture).

A low, wooded ridge runs through the Laich w of Elgin: the prominent York Tower was erected in 1827 on the Knock of Alves by a member of the Forteath family (whose burial vault is here) to mark the point at which the 18th-century Duke of York (brother of the Duke of Cumberland) decided that his visit to the Highlands had gone far enough.

To the s the Laich is bounded by a low, indeterminate range of hills culminating behind Forres in the Knock of Braemoray (1,493 ft/455 m.). On clear days there are stupendous views to be had from the roads crossing these hills — across the Laich and the Moray Firth over to the Black Isle, to the blue hills of Sutherland, with the big hills of Morven and Scaraben prominently on the Caithness border.

Mortlach   *see* **Dufftown**

Muchalls Castle   Kincardine and Deeside
Grampian   5 H2
Of the smaller castles of NE Scotland, Muchalls takes pride of place. Standing high about a mile inland from the coast N of Stonehaven, Muchalls is a real gem, not least because it has been so little altered since its completion in 1627, and is lovingly furnished and cared for by the present owner, who allows access by arrangement. The original castle (of which little remains except the underground vaulting), derives from the Fraser who was one of Robert the Bruce's nobles. Andrew, the last Fraser heir to Muchalls, was a cantankerous young man who, in 1614, attacked his neighbour as a result of a quarrel over who should pass through a door first. The laird, Andrew's father, had to play a heavy fine and, in 1619, the property passed to Alexander Burnett of the Leys, who had just completed his magnificent castle of Crathes (q.v.) across the hills on Deeside. He began work on Muchalls which, as the inscription over the gateway to the coutyard records, was 'Ended be Sir Thomas Burnet of Leyis his sonne 1627'; though the Burnetts do not appear to have lived there for long, or, indeed, at all after 1700. The two main blocks are set in the familiar L-plan with angle-turrets on the crowstep gables and a semi-circular stair-case tower in the re-entrant angle. The curtain-walling completing the other two sides of the courtyard has been preserved intact; triple gun-loops are to be seen on either side of the gateway, though the general effect was probably more ornamental than defensive.

The ground floor is roofed by plain groin-vaulting. The Great Hall above is the chief glory of Muchalls. As at Craigievar, there is a superb plaster-work ceiling, perhaps the best of them all, displaying the coat of arms of the Burnett family, four medallions of biblical and classical heroes and with three hooks for hanging lamps. There is also a huge sculptured mantelpiece dated 1624, with the royal arms of Scotland as borne after the Union with England in 1603, the collar of the Thistle being inside the Garter. All armorial bearings stand out in their bright colours against the white background. Two other rooms on the same floor, the drawing room and the laird's study, have equally fine ceilings and heraldry. The laird's bedroom above has a 'lug' or listening channel connecting with the Hall below. There are the usual tales of a secret staircase (now blocked), a Green Lady, and a passage to a smuggler's cove, the 'Gin Shore', the last un-sportingly blocked by a Lord Justice General who occupied Muchalls at the end of the 19th century.

Muir of Dinnet   *see* **Dee**

Old Deer   Banff and Buchan   Grampian   8 G2
As early as A.D. 520 St Drostan founded a Celtic monastery at Old Deer, probably in the bend of the Ugie where the parish church now stands. In 1218 William Comyn, the first non-Celtic Earl of Buchan, replaced it with a Cistercian monastery, bringing a few monks from Kinloss but, for the rest, obliging the local Culdee monks to adopt the Roman rite and the Cistercian habit. Some of the early abbots found the climate too bleak for them and retreated to their mother-house at Melrose. The monastery suffered a set-back after 1308, when Bruce defeated the Comyn Earls of Buchan, the last battle being fought at Aikey Brae, just south of the abbey. Nonetheless, the foundation prospered until after the Reformation, when a branch of the Keith family, who had gained control of the abbey funds, diverted them to their own personal gain. In 1590 one of them, Robert Keith of Benholm, had to be dislodged from the abbey by his kins-man the Earl Marischal in person. Post-Reformation decay reduced the abbey buildings to ruins. In 1809 the owner, James Ferguson of Pitfour, tidied up the ruins and in 1930 they became an AM.

Though only the foundations of the abbey are now visible, they represent the most complete plan of any monastery in Scotland. There are the great abbey church, the adjoining cloister, chapter house, the dormitory (over the parlour) with its rere-dorter and flushing drain behind; also the abbot's house. The renown of Old Deer stems from the Book of Deer, a precious 9th-century Latin manuscript (now in Cambridge University Library), with the Gospel of St John, various other extracts from the Bible, and, most interesting, examples of Gaelic notes of the 11th and 12th centuries written in the margins, describing the gifts conferred on the monastery by the mormaers (Celtic predecessors of the earls) of Buchan.

The improving landlord James Ferguson of Pitfour (1734-1820) drove turnpike roads through Buchan, planted hawthorn hedges and afforested the bare hills of his estate. He also founded the planned villages of Fetterangus, Mintlaw and Stuartfield. The more pretentious aspects of the Pitfour estate — the lake, the Grecian temple — were due to the efforts of his successor, Admiral Ferguson, who also built himself a mausoleum (now destroyed) in the abbey church. The neighbouring estate of Aden House is a country park.

Perth   Tayside   2 E2   (*pop.* 43,030)
Where a river broadens out into an estuary open to sea-going ships, one is likely to find an important and prosperous town. So it has been with 'St John's town at the mouth of the Tay', the medieval name of Perth. The 16th-century historian Boece reckoned that the city must be on the site of the Roman camp of 'Bertha', itself a name invented by the chronicler John of Fordoun. The

The Fair Maid's house, Perth

Roman camp is 2 miles up the Tay where it is joined by the River Almond, but the name Perth has stuck. St John's Church has been its principal church since the 12th century, and 'St Johnstone' is the name of the Perth Football Club. Perth still has a harbour but it has, over the centuries, lost out to Dundee. Perth's importance as a river crossing has been at the mercy of the frequent floods of the Tay: bridge after bridge was swept away in the 500 years of Perth's records until the graceful, seven-arched, 18th-century bridge by Smeaton, taking nearly seven years to complete (1766-72) was built at the N end of the town. It is now supplemented by the modern Queen's Bridge which continues the line of South Street across the Tay.

Perth is proud of its reputation as the ancient capital and as the Fair City. Certainly, the Stuart kings favoured it, even if James I had the misfortune to be assassinated there in 1437, but their capital, once it ceased to be wherever the king held court, came to rest at Stirling, before it moved to Edinburgh. The proximity of Scone (q.v.), where Scottish kings were crowned, gives Perth another claim to this honour. Many of its medieval buildings were torn down and replaced in the 19th century. Since 1967, the Perth Civic Trust has been active in preserving its architectural heritage, and in restoring Perth's claim to be a fair city. It is the situation of the city, which put Prince Albert in mind of Basel, that really justifies this claim. It is indeed a fair and spectacular view of Perth that greets the traveller from the south as he tops the crest of Moncrieffe Hill and looks over the winding Tay, the spires

of the town, the green open spaces of the North and South Inches, across the Tay to Kinnoull Hill, with its sham Rhineland tower, and N to the distant Highland hills. It impressed even the Romans, who compared the Tay with the Tiber. This low ridge between Earn and Tay is now a skein of motorways: one leads to the bold new Friarton Bridge (opened in 1978) spanning the estuary, completing rather than spoiling the prospect. While the rectangular layout of the old town may have suggested the site of the Roman camp, it is in fact due to the constraints of a peninsular site, up against the river to the E and separated from the two Inches (or islands, as they were then) by branches of the main stream. These two open spaces, N and s of the city, add enormously to the attraction of a town which was, until the late 18th century, tightly confined within medieval walls. The North Inch was in 1396 the scene of the extraordinary conflict known as the Battle of the Clans (described by Sir Walter Scott in *The Fair Maid of Perth*), between 30 men from Clan Chattan, largely Macphersons, and 30 men from Clan Kay, mainly Camerons, in the presence of King Robert III. The purpose of this disgraceful gladiatorial contest, from which only one Cameron and eleven of Clan Chattan emerged alive, is obscure; it may have been an attempt to assert royal power over the Highlanders, or it may just have been a tournament that got out of hand. More civilised sporting contests now take place in the splendid domed Bell's Sporting Centre, built in 1968 on the edge of the North Inch by the Gannochy Trust.

Not surprisingly, Perth has had its share of Scottish history, but nine floods, seven sieges, five plagues, sundry assassinations and an excess of religious fervour have done little to affect its prosperity through the ages. St John's Church was founded in 1126, and for a time housed the heart of good King Alexander II. The present church dates largely from the 15th century — a cruciform building with a square, battlemented central tower, surmounted by a short spire. In 1559, John Knox preached his inflammatory sermon to purge idolatry here — perhaps not surprisingly, in view of the 40 altars then in the church. In 1644 Montrose confined 800 Covenanters in the church after his victory at Tibbermore outside Perth. When a crowned captive of the Covenanters in 1651, Charles II yawned his way through interminable sermons, and escaped for a couple of nights to Cortachy and Glen Cova (q.v.) in Angus. Like St Nicholas in Aberdeen, St John's was divided, first into two kirks in 1598, and then into three in 1773. Its unity has now been restored and the north transept is a war memorial to the dead of World War I. The stained glass in the east window is by Douglas Strachan. Perth's medieval prosperity led to the establishment of four monasteries and ten religious houses. Blackfriars monastery was the scene of the assassination of James I in 1437, despite the courageous effort of Catherine Douglas (known as Barlass) to hold off the attackers by inserting her arm in place of the door-bolt. In the orgy of reformist frenzy that followed John Knox's sermon at St John's on the theme 'Thus shall Babylon be cast down', all these religious foundations were destroyed, their altars and ornaments scattered.

Perth, too, was the scene of the Gowrie Conspiracy of 1600, that puzzling incident when James VI, enticed into Gowrie House by an improbable tale of a man with a pot of gold, cried 'I am murdered! Treason!' from an angle-turret. He was rescued by two of his nobles, who killed the King's supposed assailant, Alexander Ruthven, and his brother the Earl of Gowrie, a popular Provost of Perth and the younger son of the King's captor at Huntingtower (q.v.) 18 years previously. James was in debt to Gowrie and had long nursed the idea of vengeance on the Ruthven family. The King's subsequent actions, including un-characteristic generosity to the town of Perth, raised suspicions that the conspiracy was a put-up job by James, but recent historical opinion inclines to the view that there was a genuine plot by the Ruthvens, possibly using the contemporary constitutional trick of kidnapping rather than murdering the king, with a view to forcing reforms on him. The king's vengeance was terrible: the dead bodies of the Ruthvens were put on trial in Edinburgh, the name of Ruthven expunged 'for ever-more', the House of Gowrie handed over to the City of Perth, and the Gowrie palace at Scone given to the Murrays, who had helped keep off the townsfolk. Eighteenth-century engravings show Gowrie House to have been a fine medieval building overlooking the Tay. It was given to Cumberland in 1746, who sold it to the Government: and in 1805 it was demolished to make way for the County Buildings.

Virtually the only medieval house remaining in the city, and that much restored in 1894, is the Fair Maid's House, formerly the Glovers' Hall, now a curio shop. The heroine of Walter Scott's *Fair Maid of Perth* was the daughter of Simon Glover — hence the name of the house. The old houses of the nobility have vanished but there are still a few interesting medieval corners and 18th-century shop fronts to be seen in the centre of the city. There are also narrow wynds, or 'vennels' as they are called here, to peer into or wander through, with names like Meal Vennel, Horner's Lane, Ropemaker's Close, Cow Vennel.

Nineteenth-century Perth is more rewarding. Marshall Place, the pleasant row of Georgian houses fronting the South Inch, was designed in 1801 by Sir Robert Reid, whose work is to be seen elsewhere in the town. The church in the centre of the row, with the interesting closed-crown steeple (as at St Giles, Edinburgh and King's College chapel, Aberdeen), supporting an elegant spire, is not, as is often believed, St John's, but St Leonard's-in-the-Fields, dating from 1885. An extraordinary archi-tectural essay is the Tourist Information Centre, housed since 1968 in the restored Old Waterworks (or Round House) at the east end of Marshall Place. This classical rotunda had on its first floor a circular

reservoir in front, and a classical-style engine and boiler house behind, the chimney being concealed in the elegant, 110 ft-high stone column, with a classical vase on top. This ingenious and handsome building was com-pleted in 1832 by the versatile Dr Adam Anderson, Rector of Perth Academy, in response to long-standing complaints about the pollution of the city's water supply. He acted as planner, architect, engineer and chemist for the whole project. The doctor, as a good Latinist, composed the motto 'Aquam Igne et Aqua Haurio' (I draw water by fire and water), now in gilt letters over the main door. The pumping station continued in use until 1965. The modern Art Gallery and Museum houses exhibits of the city's display of equipment used in the early days of whisky manufacture (Perth is the head-quarters of two major whisky firms, though not much is distilled in the neighbourhood). There are pleasant Georgian houses bordering this corner of the North Inch from Atholl Crescent to Barossa Place (named after a battle of the Peninsular War), in particular the Old Academy (in Rose Terrace) by Sir Robert Reid. On the w side of the city are St Ninian's Cathedral, a Butterfield building of 1849, and the City Mills. The Lower Mill houses a water-wheel, 16 ft in diameter, built in 1808, and the wooden wheel and water-leat (or lade) of the Upper Mill have been made into a feature of the hotel to which it has been converted. On the busy corner of County Place stands a tall four-storey block, now white-harled, with distinctive quoins crowned by a cupola. This is the James VI Hospital, founded in 1587 out of funds from the destroyed monastic foundations, but not in fact built until 1750. Finally, enthusiasts for railway architecture should not miss the curving platforms and resilient iron columns of the old Caledonian Railway station.

On the northern outskirts of Perth is Balhousie Castle, possibly older than the town itself, but the 1478 tower-house has been lapped about by the Victorian extensions of the Hays of Kinnoull. Since 1962, it has housed the Regimental H.Q. and the extensive and faithfully con-served Museum of the famous Black Watch (Royal High-land Regiment). Their interesting historical relics date back to Fontenoy, their first major engagement overseas, in 1745; to Ticonderoga in North America in 1758; and continue through the Peninsular and Waterloo campaigns of Wellington, the African wars of the 19th century, to the regiment's glorious record in two World Wars. Across the Tay to the E, a short distance along the road to Dundee, is the charming Branklyn Garden, developed by Mr and Mrs Renton for 40 years before their deaths in 1966-7. Bequeathed to the NTS, it is open to the public, and should be visited in spring or summer. The collection is in the main of alpine plants, but there are lovely rhododendrons, meconopsis, and other gardeners' delights. Behind Branklyn is the steep slope of Kinnoull Hill, a pleasant recreational area of forest, bequeathed to the town by Lord Dewar. The summit, with a view-point indicator, gives a wide-ranging

The Rotunda and former Water Tower, Perth

panorama. This westernmost outpost of the Sidlaw Hills plunges precipitously to the Tay below, and is crowned by a foreign-looking tower, built by an Earl of Kinnoull to emulate the castles of the Rhine.

Peterhead Buchan Grampian 8 H2 (*pop.* 15,050)
Thrusting out into the North Sea at the most easterly point of Scotland, Peterhead is situated where the red granite cliffs of the s Buchan coast (q.v.) give way to wide, sandy bays and dunes north-westwards to Rattray Head and Fraserburgh. The trim and thriving town has had a relatively short but interesting history since 1593, when George Keith, the great 5th Earl Marischal of Scotland, founded the small village of 'Peter Ugie' on the island promontory of Keith Inch, on lands ceded at the Reformation by the Abbey of Deer (*see* Old Deer). The Keiths were both Protestants and Jacobites and in the 1715 Rising the 10th Earl Marischal, George Keith, and his brother James supported the Old Pretender who landed at Peterhead on 22 December 1715. After Sheriffmuir, the Keith brothers sought service abroad with the King of Prussia. James became a Prussian field-marshal and was killed at Hochkirchen in 1758, and George became a trusted adviser of Frederick the Great. A replica of the statue to Field-Marshal Keith in Potsdam was given to Peterhead in 1868 by Wilhelm I of Prussia. It stands in Broad Street, in front of the old Town House of 1788 which, with its tall steeple, clock and bell, was built by John Baxter, the architect of Fochabers (q.v.). At the foot of Broad Street is the square parish kirk of 1804, with a slender steeple. The rest of old Peterhead, with its solid

red granite houses and its windswept green at the top of the town, has a certain charm, perhaps reflecting the period in the 18th century when the town was not only a fashionable spa for the former Jacobite gentry, but also in the ownership of an Edinburgh girls' school — the former Merchant Maiden's Hospital, now known as the Mary Erskine School — which purchased it in 1728 as a result of the forfeiture of the Keith estates.

Since the end of the 18th century, Peterhead's interests have been first whaling and then oil. They centre round the various harbours, the older ones between Keith Inch and the mainland, enlarged by Smeaton in 1773 and by Telford in 1818; and the big modern harbour, designed to provide refuge for shipping from the North Sea, and now invaluable for the oil industry. Peterhead's reputation as the main whaling centre of Britain began in the Napoleonic Wars and lasted exactly 100 years, until 1893, when the last whaler put out from the port. The trade fluctuated with the demand for whale oil (for lighting, until paraffin came in) and for whale bone, and with the availability of whales in Arctic waters. The skills of Peterhead whalers at sea and of the associated trades on land built up the town's wealth, making it more important than Aberdeen as a whaling port. But, failing to adapt to the new harpoon-firing techniques, the steam-driven whaler and the need for long voyages to the Antarctic, Peterhead lost its supremacy to the Norwegian whalers and to the ship-builders of Dundee, who continued with whaling expeditions up to 1909. Harpoons, blubber-knives, ship models and other relics of the Arctic whaling trade are to be seen in the Arbuthnot Museum.

With the discovery of North Sea oil in the 1970s, the town and harbour became the hub of the off-shore oil and gas industry of NE Scotland, being one of the major areas servicing the oil exploration, production and pipe-laying industries, as well as supplying materials to the derrick barges and the production platforms out in the North Sea.

South of the town is H.M. Prison, a grim set of buildings squeezed between the A952 and the shore of Peterhead Bay. The tall tower on the hill above celebrates the repeal of the Corn Laws. Further s are the oil service base, the new Hydro-Electric Power House and the pink granite quarries, creating noise and dust, but peace may still be found beyond Boddam, on the rugged s Buchan coast.

North of Peterhead is the little River Ugie with two ruined castles; Inverugie, the original home of the Keiths, and Ravenscraig. Beyond the stream are long stretches of sand dunes, interrupted only at St Fergus, where the gas pipe-line from the Frigg Field comes ashore and a large gas installation occupies the flat land. Further N, Rattray Head and the enclosed Loch of Strathbeg are interesting relics of a once flourishing burgh and a former port, dramatically sealed off by a sudden storm in 1720, when a small ship was trapped inside the loch. Now there is a wide expanse of sand-dunes between the sea and the land-locked loch (a sea-plane base in World War I and now a Royal Naval wireless station). Efforts have been made to preserve the numerous wild-fowl and wading birds.

Pitcaple Castle   Gordon   Grampian   8 F4
Pitcaple, just N of the A96 between the Garioch and Inverurie, is a fine 15th-century Z-plan castle, which belonged to the unruly Leslies from 1457 to 1757. Since then, it has been the home of the Lumsden family. The castle is generally open throughout the summer. The two large round towers on opposite corners of the main block are capped by sharply-pointed turrets, as is the 19th-century wing, giving the whole building a French look. This is the result of an 1830 renovation by a laird who wished to copy French château architecture. Being on the road from Inverness to Aberdeen, Pitcaple was frequently visited by royalty — James IV; Mary, Queen of Scots, who planted a thorn tree in 1562 (which lasted for 300 years and was replaced in 1923 by a red maple, planted by another Queen Mary, grandmother of Her Majesty Queen Elizabeth II); and Charles II, who stayed here after his landing at Garmouth in June 1650. Only a month earlier, the tragic figure of the Great Montrose, after his betrayal by Macleod of Assynt, had spent the night here as a captive — labelled 'James Graham, traitor to his country'. The Lady of Pitcaple, a relative, lodged him in what is now known as Montrose's Room. This has a little shaft in the thickness of the wall, which she offered him as a secret means of escape. 'Rather than be smothered in that hole, I'll take my chance in Edinburgh', replied Montrose, who was executed there a few days later.

Pitlochry   Perthshire   Tayside 4 A5   *(pop. 2,599)*
A thriving tourist centre through which the busy A9 from Perth to Inverness passes — at least, until the by-pass is open — Pitlochry offers facilities for fishing, sailing on Loch Faskally, pony-trekking and golf, as well as a wealth of beautiful scenery, combining the thickly-wooded glens with the wild, open hills behind. Though the town is of no great antiquity, the finely-carved Pictish cross-slab just across the Tummel at Dunfallandy (with a cross, beasts and angels on one side and a horseman and symbols on the other) indicates that the Picts were hereabouts in the 8th century. The medieval settlement was up on the s-facing plateau at Moulin, centred on Black Castle, a ruin dating back to the 14th century. General Wade's military road of 1729 linked Dunkeld with Dalnacardoch, where it joined his 'main' road from Crieff to Inverness, but it did not do much for Pitlochry. More important were Queen Victoria's first visit to Blair Atholl in 1844, when she admired the Falls of Tummel (now largely submerged in Loch Faskally), and the coming of the Highland Railway in 1863. The Victorian visitors came in crowds to admire the romantic splendours of the Pass of Killiecrankie (q.v.) and the glories of the Tummel Valley, or to climb the heights of Ben Vrackie (2,760 ft/841 m.) as a respite from

taking the waters at the imposing Hydro Hotel. Robert Louis Stevenson spent part of a summer at Kinnaird Cottage up above Moulin ('a sweet spot'), writing *Thrawn Janet* and some of the *Wrecker* tales, before moving to Braemar.

Pitlochry is fortunate to have its Festival Theatre, with a repertoire of drama throughout the summer season. Started in a tent in 1951, the theatre has outgrown its present accommodation and a fine new theatre is due to open in 1981, just downstream from the dam. Pitlochry is also the centre of the Hydro-Electric scheme for the Central Highlands. The imaginative way in which it has been carried out has enhanced rather than, as was once feared, detracted from the scenic and other tourist attractions of the Tummel Valley. The 50 ft-high dam, built in 1953 just below Pitlochry, has created the beautiful Loch Faskally, its banks clothed in a mixture of conifers and deciduous trees, the latter especially fine in their autumn foliage. Beside the dam is an enclosed 'fish-pass' where the salmon can be seen passing through ponds as they move up-river, or leaping out of the water in the large pool below the dam. This is a fascinating and very popular spectacle, but it does not really compare with the sight of a huge fish jumping a fall on a remote mountain river. The exhibition rooms and the vast power house hall are also great attractions. On the west bank of Loch Faskally is the imposing Cluny Arch. Commemorating the Hydro-Electric scheme, it is a copy of the arch through which the waters collected from Lochs Errochty and Ericht debouch into Loch Faskally. A mile or so above Pitlochry, at the foot of the Pass of Killiecrankie (q.v.), the B9019 strikes off across the Garry to Tummel Bridge. On the w side of the bridge a pleasant walk leads round the promontory (property of the NTS) between Tummel and Garry at the head of Loch Faskally. The track continues to the Coronation footbridge (coronation of George V), over the narrows of the Tummel and so back to Pitlochry by the w bank of Loch Faskally. To go eastwards from Pitlochry is to leave the thickly-wooded glens of Garry and Tummel for wide-open moorland country. The A924 leads over Moulin Moor, south of Ben Vrackie, into Strathardle; at its head is the Kindrogan Field Centre, offering courses in geology, wildlife and other nature studies. A branch road leads over to Glen Shee, with its skiing areas at the Cairnwell Pass.

Pitmedden   Gordon   Grampian   8 G4   (NTS)
About 20 miles N of Aberdeen, the great formal garden of Pitmedden House is one of the many surprises to be found in this so-called 'cold shoulder of Scotland'. In 1952, the NTS undertook the painstaking task of re-creating, from a kitchen garden, the 17th-century garden originally laid out by Sir Alexander Seton, Lord Pitmedden. This required historical and horticultural research by Dr Richardson, Inspector of Ancient Monuments, and the devoted practical gardening skills of Mr George Barron, for 25 years until his retirement in 1977.

Pitmedden House and estate were acquired in the

The Great Garden, Pitmedden

early 17th century by the staunchly Royalist Seton family. The 3rd laird, John Seton, was killed defending the royal standard at the battle of the Brig o' Dee in June 1639, and his two young sons were entrusted to the care of their relative, the Earl of Winton, who had already begun to develop his garden in East Lothian. The elder, James, was killed at Chatham fighting the Dutch in 1667. The younger, Alexander, who inherited Pitmedden, had meanwhile pursued the more peaceful career of lawyer, becoming in 1677 a Lord of Session under Charles II. In the reign of James II of England, as Lord Pitmedden, he opposed measures to re-establish Roman Catholicism and his judicial career came to an abrupt end. With evident satisfaction, he retired to Pitmedden, refused re-appointment under William and Mary, and set about composing his great garden, being disturbed neither by the Union of 1707 nor the Rising of 1715, until his death in 1719. Already by Tudor times, the tradition of the Italian formal Renaissance garden had reached England, as to be seen at Hampton Court, and in Scotland by 1604, as at Edzell (q.v.). Parkinson's *Paradisi in Sole Paradisus,* or *Garden of Pleasant Flowers,* published in 1629, gave designs for 'knots' (the elaborate geometric patterns set in rect angles), and his friend John Tradescant, later Charles II's famous gardener, collected plants for English gardens. Even Cromwell employed French gardeners and Charles II, in his exile, admired Le Nôtre's formal gardens. After

the Restoration, Charles II, with the help of William Bruce, created the formal garden at Holyrood and this, together with recollections of his youth at Winton, was the inspiration of Alexander Seton's garden at Pitmedden. As the plaque on the entrance gate shows, he began it in 1675: 'Fundat 2 May 1675', with the initials 'S.A.S.' (Sir Alexander Seton) and 'D.M.L.' (Dame Margaret Lauder, his wife).

Pitmedden House stands on a terrace overlooking the three acres of sunken, walled garden. At the N and s ends of the terrace are two delightful ogee-helmeted 'thunder-houses' or pleasure pavilions, of which the northern one contains a small exhibition on the formal garden. Against the terrace wall are high, sculptured box hedges, sheltering many roses. Ahead, as one descends the stone steps from the terrace, is an avenue of immaculately-trimmed formal beds, laid out in patterns of densely-planted flowers, each separate bed outlined in tiny box hedges and enclosed in smooth grass paths. The SE bed carries the motto 'Tempus Fugit' and centres on an intricate sundial with 27 facets. The NW parterre is the most elaborate, with the St Andrew's cross and Scottish thistle composed round the Seton arms ('S.A.S.' and 'D.M.L.' figure again), bearing the date 1675 and two mottoes. One is 'Sustento sanguine signa' (I bear the standard with my blood) referring to John Seton's death at the Brig o' Dee; the second, 'Merces Haec Certa Laborum' (This sure reward of our labours), records Alexander's modest but more enduring claim to fame. The other two beds follow conventional patterns. The beds are laid out each year in May, with 30,000 annuals raised at Pitmedden, and outlined with 8 miles (13 km.) of nine-inch-high box hedge. On the E and N walls, wide and beautifully-tended herbaceous borders create a vivid tapestry of flowers in the best informal tradition, inspired by the late Lady Burnett of Crathes (q.v.). The N wall is clothed with many climbing shrubs and fruit trees trained *en Espalier.* The garden is open to view at most times of year, but is at its best in August and September.

Pluscarden Abbey   Moray   Grampian   7 A2
Set in the peaceful vale of St Andrew 6 miles (10 km.) w of Elgin, under a wooded hill, Pluscarden Abbey is a 13th-century monastery which suffered neglect rather than deliberate destruction at the Reformation, but is now being carefully restored by 20th-century Benedictine monks who have re-created a deeply religious community.

There was probably a hermit's cell here even before Alexander II founded a priory in 1230. The community then, like those of the similar foundations of Beauly in Ross and Ardchattan in Argyll, stemmed from the French parent house of *Vallis Caulium* in Burgundy, and the old Scottish name of Kail Glen for the vale of St Andrew was no more than a translation from the Latin. The priory was damaged in Edward I's invasion of Moray in 1303 and burnt by the Wolf of Badenoch in the course of his raid on

Forres and Elgin in 1390. In 1454, it was amalgamated with the declining priory at Urquhart, 5 miles NE of Elgin, and the Urquhart Benedictines took over Pluscarden. Alexander Dunbar, the last Prior of Pluscarden (1533-60), foreseeing the Reformation, followed the unscrupulous example of Bp Hepburn of Elgin and diverted priory lands to his own family. Consequently, after 1560, there were no funds to maintain the monastery and the buildings gradually fell into decay and passed through various hands, including the Fife family, to the 3rd Marquis of Bute in 1897. He put the work of preservation in hand. In 1943, his son, Lord Calum Crichton-Stuart, gave the land to the Benedictine community of Prinknash in Gloucestershire, who established a new community in Pluscarden in 1948, and set about the work of restoration. In 1974, the monastery became an independent abbey.

The N and S transepts of the great cruciform abbey church have been roofed and work has begun on the choir. The rose window of the N transept glows with the reds, yellows and blues of fine stained glass, executed at Pluscarden in 1960 in contemporary style. The E side has been roofed to give a small public chapel and a view through into the lady chapel. The choir (being re-roofed) is on a grand scale, with a splendid E window, with four lancets, triple light, aureole and trefoil openings topping one another. The cloister is extended to the S by the restored chapter house, library and refectory, where the monks live, and not therefore open to the public. The Benedictine monks welcome visitors who come to see what they have accomplished, not only by way of restoring the buildings, but also in forming a religious community where artistic and creative work, in particular wood-carving, glass-staining and the illuminating of manuscripts, have their place in addition to music.

Portsoy   Banff and Buchan   Grampian   8 E1

Portsoy is a pleasant fishing town turned holiday resort. It exists on two levels, the more modern part on the flat ground above, with steep streets leading down to the little harbour. Portsoy harbour was built as a safe haven by the Ogilvies of Boyne in 1692 and enlarged in 1825-8. Southey called it a 'neat, thriving place' in 1819. Nowadays, Buckie and Macduff attract the fishing vessels and no more than a few lobster-boats and yachts continue to be based at Portsoy. The 17th- and 18th-century warehouse buildings round the harbour have been well restored. Many of the former gentry's houses in the upper town and the old fisher-cottages lower down have been harled and whitewashed. Thanks to the efforts of local conservationists, Portsoy is a most attractive place.

One warehouse near the harbour is used by the Portsoy marble craft-shop, which produces articles made from the local vein of green or red serpentine. This revives, in a minor way, the flourishing trade in 'Portsoy marble' organised by Lord Boyne, who succeeded in having the import of foreign marble banned. Much of the export was to France and two chimney-pieces in

Versailles are made from this serpentine.

Walks along the not very high, but jagged, cliffs provide lessons in geology as the veins of gneiss, hornblende-schist, serpentine, quartz and granite come down to the coast within a few hundred yards of one another. One can go westward to the fishing village of Sandend, or eastward to the Burn of Boyne. Little remains of the old stronghold of the Craig of Boyne, which was built on the cliff-girt promontory. The so-called 'new' Castle of Boyne is in a wooded hollow a short distance up the Burn from the sea. It looks impressive — a four-storey structure with four round towers — but defensive castles of this type went out of fashion long before this was built, probably by Alexander Ogilvie, laird of Portsoy, who married one of Mary, Queen of Scots' 'Four Maries'.

Rattray   *see* **Blairgowrie**

Restenneth   Angus Tayside   5E5   (AM)

Restenneth Priory, a couple of miles E of Forfar on the B9133 road to Montrose, incorporates the only piece of Pictish masonry of which there is an authentic outside record, unlike their carved stones and hill-forts of which no chronicle has survived. The 70 ft-high square tower,

Restenneth Priory, near Forfar

surmounted by an octagonal broach spire, rises from the ruins of an Augustinian priory church on a low promontory in what was one of the chain of shallow lakes round Forfar, now mostly drained.

Over on the s side of Dunnichen Hill (sw of Restenneth) Brude Macbile, the High King of the Picts, stemmed the encroachment of the Anglians from Northumbria by defeating Egfrith at the Battle of Nechtansmere on 20 May 685, as recorded by the Venerable Bede. Brude's successor Nechtan thought it wise to accept technical advice from the Northumbrians, both over the calculation of the date of Easter (the Celtic Culdee Church differed from the Anglian, which followed the Roman tradition) and also, in 710, for the construction of a church at Restenneth 'after the manner of the Romans'. The lowest section of the tower was thus probably built for a Pictish king by masons from Wearmouth in Northumbria: the rounded arch of the small door on the s side, built from a single block, is typical Anglo-Saxon work. The upper levels of the tower were built at various subsequent periods, most of the tower itself being pre-Norman; the octagonal spire probably dates from the 15th century.

Soon after 1150, Augustinian canons from Jedburgh Abbey were encouraged to set up a priory here. They respected the ancient tower, incorporating it in their church as a bell-tower and landmark, widening the older

South front of Scone Palace

building. The choir to the E ends in a fine pointed Gothic chancel. To the w, only the foundations of the nave remain, its roof indicated by the diagonal line across the face of the tower. Church and cloister were burnt by Edward I in 1305, but restored under Robert the Bruce.

St Vigean's   Angus   Tayside   5 F6
St Vigean's, its kirk on top of a steep conical mound, is a place of considerable antiquity, a mile or so N of Arbroath (q.v.) in the little valley of the Brothock Water. It was inhabited in the Bronze Age, Christianity was established here by the Irish colonising saint St Fechin (as in Ecclefechan) in the 7th century, and the original of the present church was consecrated in 1242. In medieval times, it was the parish kirk for many of the inhabitants of Arbroath, because the monks of the abbey there did not normally conduct services for the public. The church was sensitively restored in 1871-2 by Rowand Anderson, preserving as much as possible of the original red sandstone. Within, the double N aisle with its low arches is very pleasing, while, outside, the tower and belfry make a unique effect.

Round the foot of the hillock is a series of charming and well preserved one-storey cottages. A pair of these houses contain an excellent museum of Pictish symbol stones (*see* Aberlemno).

On the hill to the w is the Royal Marine Commando establishment, with considerable helicopter activity.

Scone   Perthshire   Tayside   2 E2
Scone (*pron.* 'Skoon') is probably the most historic spot in Scotland's destiny, though not the most sacred (that distinction rests with Iona). Scone is the place where Scottish kings were crowned from Kenneth MacAlpin in 843 to Charles II in 1651 (including the hasty coronation of Robert the Bruce in 1306). It is now the private seat of the Earl of Mansfield. Open to the public in summer, Scone Palace, as well as being interesting for its historical associations, displays a wealth of fine furniture and *objets d'art*.

The famous Stone of Destiny, an oblong block of red sandstone, which may have been a portable Celtic altar, was installed at Scone by Kenneth MacAlpin. It was used as a royal seat for coronations until removed by Edward I of England in 1296, unless, as legend has it, the monks substituted another stone and concealed the original, perhaps in Dunsinane. The Stone, genuine or not, has remained in Westminster Abbey ever since, except for a brief period in 1951 when it was removed and brought to Scotland by enthusiastic nationalists. The Moot (or meeting) Hill is the artificial mound in front of the present palace, where the early Councils met and the nobles declared allegiance to the King. Religious and political developments went hand in hand. The Celtic church at Scone was absorbed or replaced in 1120 by Alexander I's foundation of a priory of Augustinian monks, elevated to an abbey in 1164, with links to the important bishoprics of

St Andrews and Moray. But John Knox's inflammatory sermon in 1559 in nearby Perth spelt disaster for the abbey: even though he himself tried to prevent its destruction, a maddened crowd from Dundee sacked and burnt the abbey and bishop's palace.

Temporarily held by the powerful Gowrie family between 1581 and the murky conspiracy of 1600 (*see* Perth), Scone then passed to the Murray family, two of whose members happened to be in Perth when King James VI was held prisoner in Gowrie House, and helped to fight off the angry townspeople. Sir David Murray of Gospetrie (portrait in the ante-room) was created Lord Stormont and Lord Scone in 1604, and it is from the Murrays that the present Earl of Mansfield is descended. His most distinguished ancestor, created 1st Earl of Mansfield in 1776 (taking this oddly English title from his wife's home), was Lord Chief Justice of England for over 30 years, twice Lord Chancellor, and an early champion of the abolition of the slave trade. His silver-tongued eloquence pleaded for fairness to Quakers and Roman Catholics alike, so much so that his London home was looted in the No Popery Riots of 1780, though his country house at Kenwood on Hampstead Heath (now under the care of the NT) was saved. The famous portrait of him by Joshua Reynolds hangs in the drawing room in Scone. The 3rd Earl of Mansfield decided to build an imposing palace in place of the old Gowrie-Stormont house, built from the abbey ruins. He commissioned an English architect, William Atkinson, who carried out the work between 1802 and 1808. The resulting palace, built of the local red sandstone, is, with its square castellations and Tudor-style shallow boss-and-rib vaulted ceilings, more in line with Strawberry Hill Gothick than any Scottish castle. However, the lovely setting of the palace and the accumulated treasures within more than make up for any sense of disappointment at the exterior.

The porcelain collections – the Worcester service laid out in the dining room, the Meissen, Sèvres and Derby displayed in the library, as well as an armorial set sent to China for painting and firing – are a delight for the connoisseur. So are the 17th- and 18th-century French, Italian and other ivories. The drawing room contains some beautiful French 18th-century furniture, twelve chairs with needlework panels of artistic and mythological subjects, as well as a Louis XVI writing table, in marquetry, made by the cabinet-maker Riesener for Marie Antoinette. The Ambassador's Room is dominated by the 18th-century four-poster canopied bed, presented by George III to the 2nd Earl of Mansfield on his appointment as ambassador to the French Court (1772-8) and bears the Royal coat-of-arms and cipher 'G.R.'. The charming painting by Zoffany (1734-1810) is of the ambassador's daughter, Lady Elizabeth Murray, probably at Kenwood. The Inner Hall emphasises animals: in addition to two brown bears shot in Russia, there are some elephant skulls and David Teniers's painting of monkeys and dromedaries. The Long Gallery has an ancient floor of bog-oak 168 ft long, cleared for Prince Albert to use as a curling-rink. Nowadays, the gallery contains an interesting collection of furniture, busts by Nollekens of William Pitt and of the 1st Earl, and an early organ of 1813. There is also a unique collection of papier mâché vases, lacquered by the secret *Vernis Martin* process, invented by the French coach-maker Martin in the reign of Louis XV. The Indian painting of a four-horned ram of the strange breed of Jacob's sheep is in the restaurant: a herd of these can be seen in the grounds at Scone, and they are now becoming popular elsewhere. The Slip Gallery, which displays many family photographs, leads to the bedroom prepared for Queen Victoria and Prince Albert. The small room before the exit is the Duke of Lennox's room, with a bed said to have belonged to Mary, Queen of Scots, the covering worked by her and her four ladies.

The old village of Scone, now no more than a graveyard and a cross, lay between the gateway and the palace. When the 3rd Earl came to build his new mansion, the inhabitants were re-housed in New Scone, over a mile to the E, now a suburb of Perth. The Pinetum in the grounds contains unusual conifers, including giant red-woods and some splendid Douglas firs, named after David Douglas, the botanist and traveller who was born on the Scone estate in 1798, and discovered these magnificent trees on the Oregon coast of North-West America.

Sheriffmuir   Perthshire   Tayside   1 C4

To the E of Dunblane, on the Ochil Hills, lies Sheriffmuir, a high expanse of moorland with views to Allan Water to the N and over the Forth to the s. It can be easily visited by a detour from the A9. Though the battle that took place hereabouts on 13 November 1715 marked the turning-point of the Jacobite rising of that year, Sheriffmuir goes down in the ballad as a thoroughly indecisive battle:

There's some say that we wan,
And some say that they wan,
And some say that nane wan at a', man;
But ae thing I'm sure, that at Sheriffmuir,
A battle there was which I saw, man,
And we ran and they ran,
And they ran and we ran, and they ran awa', man.

The Fifteen was a fairly well planned but thoroughly mismanaged rebellion. After the Earl of Mar had raised the standard of the Old Pretender at Braemar (q.v.), he moved to Perth to wait for the clans to come in. He planned to beat his opponent, the Earl of Argyll, to the Forth, but Argyll pre-empted this move by capturing Dunblane on 12 November. Mar's men camped, some inside the great Roman fort of Ardoch, and moved the following morning to the eastern end of Sheriffmuir, more or less astride the straight road leading to Dunblane from the Sheriffmuir Inn. Argyll's forces, smaller in number but superior in cavalry, faced the Jacobites from a position somewhat s of this road. Argyll's right wing found Mar's left wing at a disadvantage, and his cavalry, under General Cathcart, charged, slaughtering the Macraes almost to a man. Meanwhile, Argyll's own left wing had been routed by the Macleans on Mar's right, and its leader, General Whitman, had fled back towards Stirling. Both centres remained on the defensive until the hesitant Mar decided to retreat, destroying Auchterarder, Crieff and Muthil, whose inhabitants became embittered against the Jacobites. Despite Mar's tactical advantage over Argyll, the rising soon collapsed, not only because of the simultaneous defeat of the southern body of Jacobites at Preston in Lancashire but also on account of the lack of charisma of the Old Pretender, who landed at Peterhead in December 1715, to re-embark for France a mere six weeks later. The battlefield is today marked by the prominent Macrae monument, erected by the Clan Macrae Society in 1915 to show where the 'Kintail and Lochalsh companies formed part of the left wing of the Highland Army and fell almost to a man'. Near it is the Gathering Stone (where Argyll had his observation post), a small boulder now protected with iron hoops to deter souvenir hunters.

Slains *see* **Buchan Coast**

Lower Speyside Moray Grampian 7 B3-C1
The better-known parts of Speyside lie in the Highland Region, but on the 20 miles (32 km.) downstream from Ballindalloch, where the Avon (q.v.) joins the Spey, to where it runs into the Moray Firth at Speymouth, there are many beautiful reaches, beloved of the salmon fisherman, as well as a number of places of interest. The triangle Dufftown-Knockando-Rothes, to the N of the prominent peak of Ben Rinnes, is the heart of the whisky country (*see* Introduction: Whisky). The district centres on the pleasant town of Aberlour, with its wide main street. Marked on the maps as Charlestown of Aberlour, it was founded by a local landlord, Charles Grant. Craigellachie marks the northern end of the territory of Clan Grant which runs from here to the other Craigellachie, the crag behind Aviemore. The Grant motto is 'Stand Fast, Craigellachie'. It was also the text of a telegram sent by George Stephen (later Lord Mountstephen), a native of Dufftown, to Donald Smith (later Lord Strathcona), a native of Forres, at a moment of financial crisis during the construction of the Canadian Pacific Railway. When Donald Smith drove in the last spike of the famous railway on 6 November 1885 in the Eagle Pass in the Selkirk range of British Columbia, he named the spot Craigellachie. The most attractive feature of the Moray Craigellachie is the old bridge (now outflanked by a structure of 1975, more convenient for whisky lorries). This was built in 1815 by Simpson of Shrewsbury to a design by Thomas Telford, and withstood the Morayshire floods of 1829. Its lattice-work cast-metal arch of 150 ft span is light and airy, and the battlemented turrets which stand on the abutments against the rugged rock com-

bine utility with ornament. It is well worth stopping to walk over the old bridge and peer into the black depths of the Spey.

Across the new bridge, the A95 road follows the w bank to the distillery town of Rothes, and on to Elgin. Below Rothes, the valley opens out into a broad strath and the Spey becomes an actively braiding river, shifting its bed with successive spates. Over on the E bank, an unusual formation of pinnacles of red earth stands out: it can be inspected more closely from the Forestry Commission picnic area at Ordiquish, reached by a narrow lane from Fochabers. At Fochabers (q.v.), the Spey is crossed by a fine new bridge. The E bank road ends at the golf and beach resort of Speymouth. The two w bank roads converge on Garmouth, a trim village half a mile from the Moray Firth. On the beach here, Charles II was carried ashore from a Dutch warship and, as noted on a plaque on the wall of Brae House, he was 'obliged to sign the Solemn League and Covenant on 3 June 1650' as a preliminary to the abortive attempt to reclaim his father's throne that ended in the disaster of Worcester a year later. The name of the neat village of Kingston-on-Spey does not mark the royal disembarkation, but derives from the fact that, in 1786, two English timber merchants and a shipwright from Kingston-on-Hull set up a shipbuilding business here, and named the place after their native town. The Hull men made use of the fine timber rafted down the Spey from Rothiemurchus Forest to build and launch ships on the pebble beach. Some of the Kingston ships became famous as clippers on the Cape Horn route and as whaling-ships in the Arctic. The business lasted until iron and steam replaced wood and sail in the late 19th century, and the Clyde shipyards took over.

Across on the E side of the estuary at Tugnet is a pleasant two-storey house, built as an ice-house in 1800 to preserve the salmon which were then so plentiful that a catch of over 1,000 fish in a day was not unusual. Close by is the packing station for the present Crown Estates salmon netting: one should not miss seeing (in season) these huge fish collected in nets in the estuary and thrown sprawling on the floor. The Speyside footpath way is planned to run from here to Grantown-on-Spey, largely following the disused railway line. The Spey, falling at the rate of 12 ft a mile, creates problems at its mouth, where the pebble barrier is frequently changing and has, on occasions, to be breached. The beach and the marshland behind are ideal feeding grounds for sea-birds and waders, and a paradise for bird-watchers.

Stirling Central 1 B5 (*pop.* 29,776)
A 350 ft (100 m.) high volcanic rocky outcrop, dominating the point at which the River Forth ceases to be tidal, would attract the eye of any strategist, Roman, Pictish, Anglo-Norman or medieval Scots; and when that river provides a gateway to fertile Strathmore and the North-East as well as to the Highlands, there can be little doubt

that critical battles – Stirling Bridge, Bannockburn and others – will be fought for possession of the rock and its castle. From the M9, which crosses the Forth W of Stirling close by the Roman ford, there is a dramatic view of the castle and palace rising like some medieval fantasy from the isolated rock. In the background, Abbey Craig with the Wallace Monument stands out against the sharp outline of the Ochil Hills. Stirling is at the heart of Scotland's history. Both Alexander I and William the Lion died in the castle in the 12th century. It surrendered to the English under Edward I in 1296, but was re-taken by Wallace (and Andrew de Moray) after their victory at the battle of Stirling Bridge the following year. Sir William Oliphant gallantly held the castle for the Scots against Edward's second invasion in 1304 and only surrendered when the new-fangled English catapults began their bombardment. The famous bargain struck between Edward Bruce, brother of Robert I, and the English Governor, Sir Philip Moubray, led to its surrender after the Scottish victory at Bannockburn (q.v.). Bruce dismantled those fortifications, but the Stuart kings made Stirling their favourite residence until James VI went off to London, to be James I of England. On the way up to the Castle Rock, there is much of interest to be seen in the Old Town, as it straggles up out of the welter of 19th-century buildings. King Street, which leads uphill from the busy thoroughfare of Port Street, soon divides at a curious building, described in 1814 as 'genteel', with a curved front, a square clock-tower and an octagonal spire, to which a porch has been added to support a statue of Wallace, incongruously clad as a Roman. Higher up, with Spittal (continued by St John) Street to the left, and Baker and Broad Streets to the right, the medieval street pattern is preserved, and there has been much careful restoration of medieval buildings. St John Street, the former fleshers' or butchers' market, has some pleasantly restored 17th-century houses. Between St John and Broad Streets is the Tolbooth designed in 1701 by Sir William Bruce, the architect who built his own Renaissance house at Kinross (q.v.). Prisoners were confined here until the more commodious, if less pleasing, 19th-century jail added its jarring note to the Stirling skyline. Broad Street, dominated at the top by the facade of Mar's Wark (see below), was the original general market. Only the unicorn, crowning the pillar restored in the 19th century, remains of the old Mercat Cross: the cannon at its feet are 'carronades' (from the Carron factory near Falkirk) used at Waterloo.

The fine Gothic building closing the upper end of St John Street is the Church of the Holy Rude (rood being an old English word for cross). The nave, with its five bays and massive round pillars, dates from the early 15th century, as does the fine oak-beamed roof. The choir, with its high-pitched roof, was built nearly a century later. Mary, Queen of Scots, was crowned here (or, perhaps in the castle) in 1543 as an infant, and so was her son James VI in 1567. Then only a year old, he can hardly

have appreciated the sermon preached by John Knox. The square, battlemented tower at the W end was used by General Monk to bombard the castle in 1651. Like so many large Scottish churches (and, in this case, after a violent squabble between two factions), the Holy Rude was divided between two parishes in 1656 by a solid wall. When Gillespie Graham restored the West Church in 1818, the fine roof was concealed. Since the restoration and reunification in 1935, the generous proportions and the open-timbered roof of Stirling's parish kirk can be admired as a whole. The stained glass is modern, including one window by Burne-Jones, and an impressive study in blue, the 'Benedicite', in the S transept by Douglas Strachan.

Opposite the S entrance to the Holy Rude is the charming Cowane's Hospital – now the Guildhall – with its attractively leaded ogee-shaped bell-tower, built in 1639-45 from the bequest of a wealthy merchant, Cowane (whose statue looks somewhat smugly down from a niche

Cowane's Hospital, or former Guildhall, Stirling

Stirling Castle

in the tower), to support 'twelve decayed Gild breíthers'.

On Castle Wynd leading up to the castle stand the former residences of two great noblemen: Mar and Argyll. Mar's Wark, at the head of Broad Street, was the fine palace built for that Earl of Mar who was Regent to James VI for a brief period (1570-2). It was probably never finished and is now no more than a ruined, but magnificent, facade, floridly Renaissance in style, but also provided with stout walls and gunloops for defence. The royal arms are over the gateway; there are also other heraldic bearings and some curious rhyming inscriptions, boldly carved but difficult to interpret. They could indicate Mar's uneasy conscience at having used the stones from Cambuskenneth Abbey for his 'lodging'. It was used by the Mar family until the disgrace of the Earl who instigated the Fifteen. The present Earl of Mar and Kellie was reinstated as Keeper of Stirling Castle in 1923. The place fell into disuse and was used as a 'wark' or workhouse for vagrants in the 19th century.

'Argyll's Ludging', another noble town residence, was built in 1632 by Sir William Alexander, who inspired the scheme for the development of Nova Scotia by the sale of baronetcies (*see* Menstrie). After he died insolvent in 1640, the Duke of Argyll bought the house and enlarged it. The Alexander arms ('W.E.S' for William, Earl of Stirling) appear over the doorway, but the Argyll boar's head crest is to be seen elsewhere. The house was a military hospital in the Napoleonic Wars and is now put to good use as a youth hostel. The Portcullis Hotel opposite was the Stirling Grammar School of 1788. Castle Wynd curves upward into the vast Esplanade, which commands a fine panorama, and is now used as a car park for visitors to the castle. On the E side is the attractive white-harled Landmark, the well-conceived visitor centre designed to bring alive the history of Stirling. In addition to photographs of Edwardian and Victorian Stirling, a multi-screen

presentation depicts the history of the castle from Edward I to General Monk; and the bustle and activity of Stirling as a medieval market and port over the past 700 years. On the Esplanade is a statue of Bruce sheathing his sword, not as impressive as the figure on horseback at Bannockburn (q.v.). To the w of the Esplanade, down some steps in a little valley between the Castle and the Church of the Holy Rude, is the former jousting ground, now a public garden and a cemetery, dominated by a large pyramid — the Covenanters' monument.

Despite — or perhaps because of — its splendidly strong position Stirling Castle (AM) is no grim fortress, but contains the finest examples of Renaissance architecture in Scotland. Though the scene of some of the most gruesome episodes of the Stuart dynasty, such as the execution of Albany and his family in 1424, the murder and defenestration of the Earl of Douglas by James II in 1452 and numerous conflicts over the custody of successive infant sovereigns, Stirling Castle was, on the whole, a happy place for the Stuarts. Some were born, baptised and brought up here. They all hunted, jousted and feasted here, encouraging music and the arts, to say nothing of an early and unsuccessful attempt by John Damian to 'fly' from the battlements. For James III, who built the Great Hall, Stirling was the 'most pleasantest dwelling'. James IV began work on the magnificent palace. James V, who completed it, adding the unusual and grotesque figures, was the monarch who felt most at home in Stirling, not only as King, but also when he slipped out in disguise through the old Ballengeich entrance to the NE, to test the opinions of his subjects and to engage in romantic adventures. He became known as the Gudeman of Ballengeich and was the subject of Sir Walter Scott's 'Fitzjames' in his *Lady of the Lake*.

From the Esplanade, the entrance to the castle is first through the Counterguard and then over two dry ditches; the Overport Battery is to the right and Queen Anne's Battery (now a small garden) to the left. The outer wall of this little garden gives the best view of the King's Knot, the raised outline of a one-time formal garden, now grassed over, 350 ft (100 m.) below. Next comes the imposing Portcullis gateway, flanked by two (originally four) massive squat round towers. This curtain wall was the 'Foir Face' of James III and once spanned the whole width of the castle rock.

After passing through the Portcullis, with its narrow pedestrian passageways, one is in the castle proper. Across the lower square lies the Great Hall; the palace is to the left; and down to the right there is a small house, the 'Cunzie Hoose' — possibly once the Royal Mint — standing over a long vaulted passage. This leads down to the Nether Bailey on the northern slope of the rock, and the Ballengeich entrance used by James V for his incognito excursions. The Great Hall, built by James III's unpopular architect Thomas Cochrane, was left a shell after its conversion to a barracks in the Napoleonic Wars. It is now being well but slowly restored. The palace, joined corner to corner to the Great Hall by a short (19th-century) gallery at first-floor level, is the crowning glory of Stirling. James V, whose initials are over the windows, used French masons under the direction of his Master of Works, the notorious 'bloody butcher', Sir James Hamilton, who later perished on the scaffold to which he had sent many others. There is no mistaking the influence of the classic Renaissance style of the French chateaux on the Loire — the wide, grilled windows, the rich ornamentation and, above all, the fantastic array of mythological and other figures, a change in fashion from the earlier statues of saints and kings. These grotesque sculptures are worth studying in detail: some are reminiscent of the Flemish devils of Breughel or Bosch, some represent the kings's guard (a man with a claymore, a cross-bowman winding up his bow), there are women in flowing drapery and naked boys supporting scrolls. The bearded gentleman on the left end of the facade on the Upper Square is said to be James V in his Ballengeich disguise. The open court within the Palace is known as the lion's den, where the Stuarts kept a living example of the lion of the royal coat of arms. The rooms on the N side were the king's, to the south the queen's: the ornamental fireplaces continue the theme of the grotesque statues without. The king's presence chamber once had a remarkable ceiling with some 45-50 large portrait roundels carved in oak: these were removed in the 18th century, after one had fallen and injured a soldier. The roundels were later recovered, and most are now on display in the two main palace chambers. The Chapel Royal is the long, low building with six pairs of round-headed windows on the N side of the Upper Square. Now rather austerely restored and in use as the ceremonial chapel of the Argyll and Sutherland Highlanders, it was built by James VI in 1594 to impress the English with the ceremonial baptism of his son Prince Henry, elder brother of Charles I. There are portraits of James VI and of the Jacobite Earl of Mar who led the Fifteen. At the west end of the Chapel a vaulted passage leads to the Douglas Garden. It was hereabouts that in 1452 James II threw the body of the murdered Douglas over the walls. The Douglas Room above was not, however, built until later. The Argyll and Sutherland Highlanders maintain their extensive regimental museum, with memories of Lucknow, Balaclava and the Death Railway of World War II, in the building at the top of the Upper Square.

With the Union of the Crowns in 1603 and James VI's preoccupation with his English realms, the glory departed from Stirling Castle, save for a two-day visit by Charles I in 1633, and an even briefer call by Charles II in 1650. No longer a real stronghold, the old castle was to suffer two further sieges: one when General Monk bombarded it for three days in 1651 before forcing the garrison to surrender; the other, unsuccessful, by the Highland forces of Prince Charles Edward, when they were retreating northwards in January 1746; Cumberland arrived in time to relieve the English garrison. So ends the story of Stirling as capital, as royal palace, and as fortress. It suffered from neglect during the following 180 years or so of service as a barracks until the present restoration was put in hand. Back o' Hill road leads up from the King's Knot round the precipitous W and N sides of the castle, past the beheading stone on Gowan's Hill, where executions of Regents like Albany, Morton and others were carried out. The road continues down over the golf-course to the Old Bridge of Stirling, a fine but narrow stone bridge (now for foot-traffic only), which, for 400 years, was the only bridge across the Forth and in the days of the cattle trysts this meant heavy congestion. The bridge at which Wallace defeated the English in 1297 was a wooden one, a short distance upstream, and exists no more.

Crossing the Forth by the 19th-century bridge and up Causewayhead Road, one is confronted by the Wallace Tower, on top of Abbey Craig — the abbey in question being Cambuskenneth. This monument to the strong sense of Scottish patriotism was erected between 1861 and 1868 in the high period of Victorian architectural pomposity. A bronze Wallace is above the door to the tower hall, which contains busts of Scotland's famous sons, from Robert the Bruce to Burns, Scott and Carlyle. The climb up the 246 steps to the terrace below the fantastically decorated hollow spire is well worth while for the sake of the magnificent view, not only of castle and town, but of the Forth winding down through the carselands under the steep Ochil Hills and in the opposite direction to prominent Ben Vorlich and Ben Lomond.

The Causewayhead road, now the A9, leads to Bridge of Allan, once the 'Queen of Scottish Spas', a 19th-century resort for taking the waters and still a prosperous outlier of Stirling town. The spa was discovered by the

The Palace and garden, Stirling Castle

Abercromby laird of Airthrey, the estate which lies on the low saddle between Abbey Craig and the wooded Witches' Crag, a western outpost of the Ochil Hills. Airthrey is now the site of the University of Stirling, which came into being in the late 1960s, though it had been promised since the days of James VI. The university buildings, of which the earliest is the long, low 'Pathfoot' building on three separate levels, and the halls of residence are most attractively grouped round an artificial lake in grounds which were first landscaped in the 19th century by a pupil of 'Capability' Brown. They are now carefully laid out with wide lawns, trees and ornamental shrubs, including rhododendrons and plants collected by the Scottish collector George Forrest from Tibet and China. The MacRobert Centre forms a splendid cultural focus for drama, music and the visual arts. To the east rises the sharp little peak of Dumyat (*pron.* Dum-my-at), its precipitous crags giving it a more spectacular aspect than its mere 1,373 ft (418 m.) would seem to warrant. Present-day students have a most attractive campus on which to study.

Stonehaven Kincardine and Deeside Grampian 5 H3
Stonehaven was well-named, for it was not until 1826 that the big rock obstructing the harbour was removed by Robert Stevenson, the lighthouse builder. Its sheltered bay lies deep down, where the Highland Boundary Fault comes to the North Sea, between the Old Red Sandstone of Downie Point (with its prominent war memorial) to the s, and Garron Point where the Grampians end, to the N. Two streams, Cowie Water and the Carron, run into the little bay, hemming in the town between them. 'Old Steenie', the old town under the steep slope of Downie Point, a cluster of quaint old houses round the little port, is largely a 17th-century creation of George Keith, 5th Earl Marischal, but the ravages of Montrose, General Monk and Cumberland have left their mark. The principal building of note is the crowstep-gabled Tolbooth (1710) — now a museum — where in 1748 three Episcopal priests were imprisoned. Devoted members of their flock brought their babies, concealed in fishing creels, to be christened through the barred windows of the prison — a sad scene, recorded in a well-known painting by S. W. Brownlow in 1865.

The 'New Town' to the north of the Carron Water was built in the 18th century by Robert Barclay of Ury, who planned it round the wide, rather Flemish-looking square. A plaque here commemorates Robert Thomson, the inventor of the pneumatic tyre in 1845: a run for veteran vehicles still keeps his memory green. The House of Ury, abandoned and roofless, lies a mile or so up the Cowie Water, behind a conspicuous long wall. The Barclays of Ury, a great Quaker family, were a remarkable lot. Colonel David Ury (1610-86) served with Gustavus Adolphus of Sweden at Lützen in 1632, joined the Covenanters in 1647, rebuilt the House of Ury in 1648, and became an active Quaker in 1666:

Wallace Memorial

Up the streets of Aberdeen, by the Kirk and College
   Green,
Rode the Laird of Ury,
Close behind him, close beside, foul of mouth and
   evil-eyed,
Pressed the mob in fury,
Call ye coward him who stood, ankle deep in Lützen's
   blood,
With the brave Gustavus?

runs the evocative ballad of John Whittier, on the subject of the bitter persecution of the Quakers in Aberdeen. Robert Barclay (1648-90), the 'Apologist', educated at the Scots College in Rome, abandoned the Roman Catholic faith for the Society of Friends (Quakers), was a friend of William Penn, became Governor of New Jersey, and encouraged the emigration there of persecuted Quakers and Covenanters, including prisoners from Dunnottar Castle. There was another Robert, who brought back a Jamaican fortune in 1760, founded the new town of Stonehaven in 1795, introduced the new agricultural methods of his friend 'Turnip' Townsend and, in the course of 37 years, removed 100,000 tons of stones, filling and dyking to make the Mearns into an agricultural county. Then there was the famous 'Pedestrian', Captain Robert Barclay-Allardice (d. 1854). He established the first herd of shorthorn cattle in Scotland, started the 'Defiance' stage-coach, doing the 129-mile Edinburgh to Aberdeen run in 12 hours and, in 1809, walked 1,000 miles in 1,000 consecutive hours at Newmarket, dressed in a tight-fitting suit, cravat and top hat.

Of the ancient burgh of Cowie there is now no trace,

save the ruined Kirk of St Mary of the Storms (up on the cliffs by the golf-course), parts dating from 1276. To the SW, tucked away in the woods on a side-road, is the little parish church of Dunnottar, dating from 1582, but rebuilt since, and including a Marischal Aisle restored in 1913. The Covenanters' Stone records the names of nine of the prisoners who perished in 1685 at Dunnottar Castle (q.v.). It was this stone that Robert Paterson was cleaning when Sir Walter Scott found him here in 1793, and thus derived the inspiration for *Old Mortality,* his novel about the Covenanters.

The Slug Road leads NW past Durris Hill with its television mast, over into Deeside at Banchory. About 3 miles out of Stonehaven it passes below a flat-topped hill, the site of the Roman camp of Raedykes, where the Roman route from the Tay along Strathmore turned north to cross the Dee at Normandykes. The area around Raedykes was once thought to be the site of the battle of Mons Graupius, but this has now been established as at the foot of Bennachie (q.v.).

Strathbogie Gordon Grampian 7 D4-D3
The little Water of Bogie which flows from the gentle pass between the Buck of Cabrach and the Correen Hills to join the Deveron at Huntly (q.v.) has a historic and strategic importance quite out of proportion to its size. The fertile Rhynie basin is dotted with standing stones and some Pictish symbol stones. The Iron Age inhabitants selected the superb hill-top site of Tap o' Noth (1,850 ft/564 m.) for the highest hill-fort in Scotland. This is a fine example of a vitrified fort — that is to say, one in which the timber-laced masonry has been fused together by the intense heat as a result of the supporting framework of logs being kindled by accident or by enemy action. The rampart encircling the summit enclosed an area of about 330 ft by 100 ft. Tap o' Noth, a steep but short climb from the Rhynie-Cabrach road (A941), gives magnificent views down over Dufftown to lower Speyside, and out to sea beyond Buchan, as well as eastward to the neighbouring massif of Bennachie (q.v.), where the Mither Tap is crowned by a smilar hill-fort.

Later inhabitants did not aim quite so high for the defence of what became the principal route from Donside at Kildrummy into Moray by way of Huntly. Lulach the Simple, the son of Lady Macbeth by her first husband, was run to earth here and killed by Malcolm Canmore in 1058, a few months after he had slain Macbeth at Lumphanan. The Comyns held Strathbogie until Robert the Bruce broke their power, and the wardenship of the North-East passed to the Gordons of Huntly. At Craig of Auchendoir, just off the A97 near Lumsden, are two roofless churches. The 19th-century one at the road junction is less interesting than the one of the 17th century (with aumbry) hidden away up the wooded glen. The Gordons' 16th-century Castle of Craig overlooks the ravine. Its steep battlemented wall, with a formidable array of gunloops, is in sharp contrast to the cheerful

courtyard, bright with coloured coats-of-arms. (The castle is privately owned, and only open on special request).

On the E side of the Rhynie basin is the interesting castle of DRUMMINOR, restored and harled in pink, and occasionally open to the public. It was the principal seat of the Forbes chiefs from the 13th century until they moved to the 19th-century Castle Forbes near Alford. Drumminor, when built in 1440, was considerably larger than the present building, with a tall tower and a courtyard. The main hall projects on the level from the round entrance tower, in the style of a 'palace' rather than a vertical tower-house. The round tower supports on corbels a square-gabled guard-house. The lower hall bears the delightful inscription 'A Happy Room 144? I.R.' (presumably for James II) over the fireplace. The hall above cannot have been so happy for the fifteen Gordons who were murdered in it a century or so later. The story runs that the Forbes laird gave the signal for the massacre by inadvertently stroking his beard — the pre-arranged signal for suspected treachery. In 1571, the Gordons, who were in a continual state of feud with the Forbes, took their revenge by defeating them at nearby Tillyangus, and Drumminor fell into disrepair. It was acquired and lovingly restored by the late Miss Margaret Forbes-Sempill in the 1960s. North of the pleasant planned village of Rhynie, the Bogie squeezes between the Noth Hills and the hills behind Leith Hall (q.v.). A couple of dead-end roads lead up to the extensive forest of Clashindarroch, where one can walk in solitude for hours. The Forestry Commission have afforested up to, but not over, the watershed into the Cabrach basin of the Upper Deveron.

Strathbogie was the centre of Gordon power, where successively as Earls of Huntly, Marquises of Aboyne and Dukes of Gordon they earned their nickname of Cock o' the North. These titled Gordons descended through the female line from Elizabeth Gordon who, in the 15th century, married Sir Alexander Seton of Fyvie, and their descendants took the name of Gordon. Important for Strathbogie was the fact that the male line of Gordons, whose legitimacy was disputed, continued with Elizabeth's cousins Tam o' Riven (Ruthven in Strathbogie) and Jock o'Scurdargue, the farm under Tap o' Noth. They were the progenitors of many of those Gordons who, as Catholics after the Reformation, were subject to restrictions and sought their fortunes abroad in Austria, Prussia, Russia and elsewhere.

Tarland *see* **Cromar**

River Tay Stirling and Perthshire   Central and Tayside 1B1-2G2
The Tay's claim to be the longest river in Scotland is only valid if the 30 miles of the Firth of Tay, a branch of the sea, from Perth to beyond Dundee, are taken into account. Otherwise, it is slightly shorter than the Spey — just

under 100 miles (160 km.) from mountain source to tidal reach. But both are lovely rivers in their different ways, and both are world-famous among anglers for the excellence and size of their salmon. The Tay's headwaters rise far to the west, on the borders of Argyll, taking various names as it flows through the land of Breadalbane (q.v.), and does not become known as the Tay until it emerges from the west end of Loch Tay, at Kenmore. Broad Strathtay then continues past Aberfeldy (q.v.), where the river is spanned by General Wade's fine bridge of 1733, to Ballinluig, where it is joined by the joint Garry and Tummel. At Dunkeld (q.v.), it breaks through the rocky ridge marking the SE edge of the Highland Boundary Fault, and emerges to wind gracefully through the fair countryside of lowland Perthshire. The river trends eastward, away from the A9, leaving on the N bank the great Roman legion camp at Inchtuthil. At its next great bend south-westwards, the Tay is joined by the thick, muddy Isla from the Angus hills. Nearby and alongside the A93 between Perth and Blairgowrie is the remarkable Meikleour Hedge, 580 yards long, of towering beech trees which have reached the height of 90 ft. At the junction of the Isla and the Tay, too, on the w bank of the great bend, are the ruined walls of the Castle of Kinclaven — once a royal stronghold, taken by Wallace from the English in 1297, attacked in the second War of Independence in 1330.

The Tay breaks through a dyke of basalt rock at Campsie Linn, running down over a shallow fall and rapids below Stobhall, the intimate group of buildings, chapel, dwelling house and dower house, which has been the home of the Earls of Perth since the 14th century. This break-through by the Tay has been the wealth (and sometimes the misfortune) of Perth. The strong flow of water made Campsie Linn the site of the cotton mill at Stanley (1785), founded by the Arkwright family; lower down, it favoured the development of the textile-weaving, bleaching and dye-ing works for which Perth (q.v.) is famous. As Camden's *Britannica* noted in 1593

Great Tay, through Perth, through town, through
country flies,
Perth the whole Kingdom with her wealth supplies.

The sporadic misfortune was the consequent liability to floods, for the city had no lasting bridge over the Tay until Smeaton's of 1772. The classic view of Perth seen by travellers from the south was called by Pennant 'the glory of Scotland'. The Romans excitedly cried 'Ecce Tiber, ecce Campus Martium', but Sir Walter Scott proudly rebuked them centuries later with his verse

Behold the Tiber! The vain Roman cried,
Viewing the ample Tay from Baigle's side,
But where's the Scot that would the vaunt repay,
And hail the puny Tiber as the Tay?

The new nine-span Friarton motorway bridge opened in 1978 strides across the broadening Tay from the top of Moncrieffe Hill to the foot of Kinnoull Hill, leading away through the Carse of Gowrie to Dundee. The long hog's

back of Moncrieffe Hill divides the Tay from the Earn; on its N-facing slope is the fine 16th-century castle of Elcho (AM), guarding a medieval crossing-place of the Tay. Wallace's chronicler, Blind Harry, records that his hero went to ground hereabouts in 1297, but there is no trace of an early castle. The present four-storeyed castle facing the Tay is a square keep, adjoining a long hall block with three other dissimilar towers, placed rather haphazardly on the N side. Elcho has been the property of the Wemyss family from its construction about 1550 until it became an AM in 1930. There is a fine ceremonial staircase leading up to the hall. A corridor linking the ground-floor rooms and five spiral staircases leading to the upper apartments, each with its private garderobe, provided a degree of privacy and amenity unusual for the age. The majestic Tay now becomes an arm of the sea, with tidal reaches and sandbanks, flowing for 30 miles (48 km.) past the flat-lands of the Carse of Gowrie to Dundee and its mile-long rail and road bridges.

Tolquhon Castle Gordon Grampian 8 G4 (AM)
Tolquhon, pleasantly situated at the foot of a dead-end lane leading off the B999, a couple of miles N of Pitmedden, is a late-16th-century conversion of a square mansion — albeit a fortified one — by a laird of culture and taste. Originally belonging to the Prestons of Craigmillar Castle near Edinburgh, Tolquhon passed to a member of the Forbes family by marriage. Six lairds seem to have endured the rigours of life in the Auld (or Preston) Tower, but William Forbes, the 7th laird, a remarkable and enlightened gentleman, determined to enlarge his residence, employing to good purpose the architect Thomas Leiper, who also helped build Castle Fraser. The panel to the right of the gatehouse records that 'Al this Warke — Excep the Auld Tour — was begun be William Forbes 15 Aprile 1584 and endit be him October 1589'. The 10th laird, Alexander, saved the life of Charles II at Worcester in 1651, when the King's horse was shot beneath him. Sir Alexander Forbes, as he then became, was involved in financial losses over the disastrous Scottish colony on the Darien Isthmus in Central America, and Tolquhon was bought by the Earl of Aberdeen. Occupied until mid 19th century, it was allowed to decay until 1929 when the ruins were placed in the care of AM.

The massive Auld Tower, to the left of the entrance gateway, is balanced by a 16th-century round tower on the sw corner. The gatehouse, which leads into a spacious courtyard, is flanked by two guard-rooms within two small drum towers, which 'give a martial air but in fact serve no warlike purpose' (Cruden) and is decorated with fanciful gunloops and some amusing carvings. Access from the courtyard to the large dining-hall and the laird's room on the first floor is by a fine arch in the sw corner of the courtyard, and a broad flight of stairs. On the same level are two galleries, now roofless. The long one on the west side, probably the laird's library, continues over the gatehouse. In the square tower on the SE corner, a hatch leads down to the 'pit' — a grim reminder of the old baronial rights of 'pit and gallows' — where prisoners were kept. The bottom of the pit backs on the bake-house oven below. The ground floor also contains the kitchen, with large moulded fireplace; cellars, with hooks for hanging prisoners, or meat; and brew-house. A special feature of Tolquhon is the pleasant walk, with an arrangement of avenues of yews and hollies, stretching along the whole W front of the castle, which is recessed to provide 12 'bee-holes', or niches for beehives.

Tomintoul   Moray   Grampian   7 B5

Set in a wide-ranging bowl of heather-clad hills, Tomintoul (*pron.* Tomin-towl) lies along the crest of a gentle ridge between the clear-running River Avon, abundant with salmon, and the little Conglass stream which flows beside the A939 down from the Lecht Pass (2,090 ft/637 m.). Tomintoul claims, at 1,160 ft (354 m.), to be the highest village in the Highlands (this is accurate, though the highest in Britain are the lead-mining villages of Leadhills and Wanlockhead at 1,300 ft (396 m.) in the Lowlands). An attractive green square, planted with limes, sycamore and whitebeam, marks the centre of this versatile resort which offers facilities for fishing, shooting and stalking, as well as hill-walking and, with the development in 1978 of the Lecht ski-tows, skiing in winter. The village can also offer a complete range of Highland malt whiskies: the secret of many of these is locked in the clear waters of these Banffshire hills.

Each of the approach roads to Tomintoul is a delight in itself, whether up Avonside from Ballindalloch (*see* Avon), or from Corgarff (q.v.) on Donside over the Lecht, or from Dufftown across the Fae Mussach peat-moss, with the tors of the high ridge of Ben Avon dominating the southern horizon. But best of all is the A939 from Grantown-on-Spey, giving magnificent views of the whole breadth of the Cairngorm massif, before dipping down to the Bridge of Brown, which straddles the border between the Highland and Grampian Regions. Just SE of the bridge, the stream runs in a deep-cut gorge (the Linn of Brown), a few yards from the road but almost totally concealed. In this high inland area the winters are often hard: the occasional heavy snowstorm alternates with periods of clear, frosty weather, giving brilliant blue skies of almost Alpine intensity. In these winter days, Tomintoul is a remote community, close-knit and well-balanced, where members of Protestant and Catholic faiths live in harmony.

The long main street, central square and grid-iron layout mark Tomintoul as one of the planned villages founded by the improving lairds of the 18th century. About 1776, the fourth Duke of Gordon put out a prospectus advertising the allocation of 'feus' (plots) for a new community in the parish of Kirkmichael in Strathavon. There was to be a 'Lint Miln, a Spinning School' and the use of the nearby 'sleat quarry' (the

attractive stone slates from Cnoc Fergan roof most of the older houses), as well as the establishment of a 'right Publick House for the accommodation of Travilers'. Alas, the ducal plan did not immediately succeed. In the Statistical Account of 1795 for Banffshire, the Revd John Grant observes that, of the 37 families then in 'Tamantoul, all of them sell whisky and all of them drink it. When disengaged from this business, the women spin yarn, kiss their inamoratos or dance to the discordant sounds of an old fiddle'. In 1860, Queen Victoria passed through Tomintoul on her journey from Grantown-on-Spey up past Inchrory to return to Balmoral, pausing for lunch at The Queen's View near Delnabo. She noted in her diary that Tomintoul was 'the most tumbledown poor-looking place I ever saw — a long street with three inns and miserable dirty-looking houses and people and a sad look of wretchedness about it'. She would scarcely recognize it in the flourishing community of today.

For centuries before the foundation of Tomintoul, folk of the Gordon Lordship of Strathavon had worshipped at the church of Kirkmichael, now a trim 19th-century building still in use, situated on a green 'haugh' beside the Avon, 3½ miles down-stream from the village. The gravestones tell of Avonside families returning from far corners of the world to their final rest here. Tradition has it that members of the congregation rested their leisters — or salmon-spears — on the wall, having improved their attendance at church with 'eager rivalry in piscation'. Worshippers from the W bank of the Avon used stilts to cross the clear but deep water. When the community began to develop in the 19th century, more convenient Presbyterian and Catholic churches were built in Tomintoul village. Before 1776, there were only three houses of significance in the area of the village: first, St Bridget's (near the old ford across the Avon) which, in 1746, Cumberland's troops burnt over the head of Glenbucket (q.v.), that most devoted of Jacobites; next, Croughly, which produced a remarkable series of six Generals Gordon; and last, Delnabo, under the hill where the Water of Ailnack emerges from its steep-sided ravine to join the Avon. Somewhere on the side of the Ailnack gorge is a cave which was a hiding-place for a notorious outlaw of the 16th century, James (Grant) of the Hill, known in Gaelic as *Sheumas an Tuim*.

From Delnabo, a signposted walk leads a mile or so up Glen Avon, turning down on the opposite bank (there is a pedestrian right-of-way continuing up to Inchrory and past Loch Builg to the Gairn and Deeside, the route followed by Queen Victoria in 1860). The signposted walk returns past the Queen's View at the entrance to Glen Avon, described in *Highland Leaves*; but a more wide-reaching view of Ben Avon can be obtained from a point near the N exit from Tomintoul, a short distance up the old military road, marked to Campdalmore. A cairn stands here in memory of Victor Gaffney (1910-74), the historian of Strathavon.

Looking up Glen Avon from Tomintoul.

This military road is part of a remarkable route, planned by Major Caulfeild, General Wade's successor, to connect Blairgowrie with Fort George on the Inverness Firth, by way of the high passes of the Cairnwell (2,199 ft/670 m.) and the Lecht (2,090 ft/637 m.), the route now followed by the A93 and A939. Beside the well at the N foot of the Lecht ('hollow') pass, a roughly-carved tablet records that 'Lord Chas. Hay and five companies of the 33rd Regiment built the road from here to the Spey in 1754'. Near by is a pleasant picnic spot, facing up a little glen to the ruined building of the former Lecht iron mine, of which the surface workings are still to be seen on the hillside. In the 18th century, ore was carried on pony-back to be smelted near Nethy Bridge on the Spey — one of the projects of the York Buildings Company — and again in the 19th century when the mine was re-opened for a time to exploit manganese ore. One hopes that the peace of these remote Ladder Hills will remain undisturbed.

The Lecht road rises steeply from the Well to the pass, with the ski-tows. The swooping descent to Corgarff (q.v.) on Donside gives glorious views into the heart of the Eastern Cairngorms (q.v.). Both sides of the Lecht have a reputation for being blocked by drifting snow, but rarely for more than a day or two.

Towie-Barclay Castle Banff and Buchan
Grampian F3
Four miles from Turriff on the A947 to Aberdeen, the little River Ythan turns sharply from NE to SE. In the bend

of the river stands Towie-Barclay Castle, abandoned and decaying for over 200 years until happily restored in the late 1960s by the present American owner who, in 1973, earned awards from the Saltire Society and the European Architectural Heritage Year (interested visitors are welcomed by appointment). Towie-Barclay presents a rather squat appearance, as the two upper storeys were removed in 1792. They have now been replaced by a kind of penthouse. Built on a typical L-plan, the castle is harled a deep rose-red (from the local red sandstone), which will lighten with time. The master mason who built the castle for Patrick Barclay in the 16th century was probably one Conn. He had connexions with German masons, and the interior of the castle has a South German or Swiss look. The lower hall is a long, barrel-vaulted room. The principal glory is the magnificent Great Hall above, with its ribbed, double groin-vault in red sandstone, the two bosses bearing the royal arms of Stuart and the Barclay arms, indicating a Regality Court as well as a Baronial Court. The irregular red sandstone quoins (cornerstones) are left uncovered, revealing numerous mason-marks, as well as 'laird's lugs' and shot-holes. A special feature is the oratory high in the s wall, accessible by a stair in the wall; this could be curtained off if visitors hostile to the Catholic faith of the Barclays were to call. On the N wall is a magnificent fireplace. Stewart Cruden describes the hall as 'one of the noblest and most imaginative of all tower-house interiors'.

The Barclays came up to Buchan in 1136 with Malcolm Canmore, from Berkeley in Gloucestershire. The present castle became an ancestral home of the Towie branch, but was abandoned after 1753. Meanwhile, a junior branch of the Barclays of Towie had settled in Riga on the Russian shores of the Baltic. From this family came Michael Andreas Barclay (or Bogdanovitch) (1761–1818) who rose to fame as Russian Minister of War in 1810, commanded the Russian armies against Napoleon in 1812, drawing the enemy on into a land of scorched earth. He was created Prince Barclay de Tolly by the Tsar and accompanied him to London in 1814, but was not concerned to prevent the decline of the castle of his ancestors. A biography entitled *The Commander* by Michael Jesselson was published in 1980.

Turriff Banff and Buchan Grampian 8 F2
(*pop.* 2,858)
This red sandstone town on a low ridge just E of the junction of the little Idoch Water with the River Deveron is the epitome of Aberdeenshire and a thriving market-centre for the farmers of inland Buchan and the Banffshire hinterland. The burgh dates back to Malcolm Canmore and the Comyn Earls of Buchan, before their liquidation by Bruce in 1308. The Hays of Erroll, one of whose castles is nearby Delgatie (q.v.), were the ruling family in these parts in the 16th and 17th centuries, and there are memorials to Hays, as well as to Barclays of

Towie and others, in the roofless 11th-century church of St Congan. The Mercat Cross dates from 1577 at least. Turriff made a brief incursion into national history as the scene of the first engagement in the Civil War when, on 14 February 1639, the Earl of Huntly and his Gordons attacked the town, defended by Montrose (then an adherent of the Covenant), in an operation known as the Raid of Turriff, and were dispersed. Exactly three months later on 14 May, the positions were reversed when the Gordons routed the Covenanters in the Trot of Turriff. Thereafter, Turriff was spared the excitements of history and enjoyed increasing agricultural prosperity until (of all things) Lloyd George's National Health Insurance Act of 1911. The compulsory payment of stamps for his employees struck farmer Paterson of Lendrum as obnoxious. He dug in his heels and refused to pay: the authorities sent the sheriff to impound a cow in default of payment. The famous white 'Turra' Coo' was to be auctioned in Turriff, but no bids were made and the officers were pelted with eggs. After various adventures, including a trip by train to Aberdeen, the unfortunate 'Turra' Coo' was privately bought back and returned with full honours to Lendrum. Nothing could illustrate better the stubborn nature of the dour Buchan and Banffshire folk, splendid farmers that they are.

The castles of Craigston, Delgatie and Towie Barclay are all within 5 miles of Turriff, all on the fertile vein of Old Red Sandstone that runs down to the sea at Aberdour and Pennan.

River Ythan   Banff and Gordon Districts   Grampian   8 E3-H4

The little River Ythan (*pron.* eye-than), possibly from a Celtic word meaning the 'talking' river, marks the north boundary of the old thanage of Formartine ('Martin's land') lying between Don and Ythan. This historically interesting stream, though scenically unsensational, rises near the bleak hamlet of the Wells of Ythan, close to the traces of the Roman marching camp at Glenmailen, almost the furthest point known to have been reached by the legions.

The Ythan first flows NE down the fertile Howe of Auchterless, turning sharply SE at the castle of Towie-Barclay (q.v.), past the splendid castle of Fyvie (q.v.), once the 'capital' of Formartine, and then winds into a steep-sided defile. Set on a green shelf on the N bank, and reached by a rough track from the B9005 Fyvie to Methlick road, is the ivy-clad ruined castle of GIGHT (*pron.* Gicht), not to be confused with Bog o' Gight at Fochabers, on the edge of the wide gorge. The branch of the Gordon family associated with Gight since 1480 were a wild and tragic lot: killed in battle, murdered, executed, drowned or in debt. The heavy musket with which the 5th laird, William Gordon (d. 1605), terrorised the country for 30 years is to be seen in the National Museum of Antiquities in Edinburgh. The last laird was the unfortunate Catherine

Gordon, who married the profligate John Byron, father of the poet George Gordon Byron (1788-1824), who would have inherited Gight had it not been sold in 1787 to the Earl of Aberdeen to settle his father's debts. The ballad has it:

O, whaur are ye gaun, bonnie Miss Gordon, O, whaur are ye gaun sae bonnie and braw?
Ye're gaun wi' Johnny Byron, to squander the lands o' Gight awa'.

Byron's early years were spent in lodgings in Aberdeen, before he succeeded to the title in 1798 on the death of his wicked great-uncle, who had stripped his estate at Newstead Abbey in Nottinghamshire, knowing it would go to 'that brat in Aberdeen'. Gight is probably the first of the four castles built by the same master mason, Conn (the others being Towie-Barclay, Delgatie and Craig), with the characteristic ribbed groin-vault, of which only a small section in the entrance remains at Gight.

The S, or Formartine, side of the Ythan is full of delights described separately: the mansion of Haddo, the tower-house of Tolquhon, and the great garden of Pitmedden. Nearby stands the castle of Udny (not open to the public, but visible from the road), a strong, rectangular tower with ornamental battlements, completed in the 17th century, now well restored and shorn of its Victorian extensions. On the N, or Buchan, side there are two interesting tower-houses, both well restored. One is the House of Schivas, originally built in 1560 by Thomas Leiper, the master mason of Castle Fraser, for the Gray laird of the day, 'Balmoralised' in the 19th century, but skilfully restored after a fire in 1900. The other is Arnage, again built by Thomas Leiper as a Z-plan tower-house, and now well restored; it was for a time the country house of Provost Ross of Aberdeen, whose town house is in the centre of the city. Arnage was held by him and his descendants from 1702 to 1927. Nearby the little town of Ellon (*pop.* 2,000), once the 'capital' of Buchan, stands on the north bank of the Ythan, where it ceases to be tidal. Ellon Castle, to the east of the town, is a ruined tower standing above the terraced gardens created by its early-18th-century owner. It was acquired in 1752 by the 3rd Earl of Aberdeen to accommodate his brown-eyed mistress from Sussex (*see* Haddo), but could not be kept up by her son, Alexander Gordon.

The Ythan's stream broadens as it enters the tidal estuary, forcing its way by Newburgh through the sandbanks of Foveran and Forvie. Pearls have been found in the mussels here, and there was once a minor industry. The estuary is of very considerable interest to natural historians, providing just the right ecological combination for innumerable migrant wildfowl: eider duck, tern and shelduck can breed in safety; golden plover and pink-footed geese from Iceland use it as a staging-post; and there is ample food for wading birds —, sandpipers, redshanks — and for swans. It has been developed as a natural history research station by Aberdeen University.

Further Reading

Geology and Natural History

Ben Lawers and its Alpine Flowers (NTS 1972)

Jones, J. W. *The Salmon* (1959)

Millman, R. N. *The Making of the Scottish Landscape* (1975)

Nethersole-Thompson, D. and Watson, A. and others *The Cairngorms, their natural history and scenery* (1974)

Whittow, J. B. *Geology and Scenery in Scotland* (1977)

History

Brown, H. (ed.) *Early Travellers in Scotland* (1891, repr. 1978)

Crawford, O. G. S. *Topography of Roman Scotland, north of the Antonine Wall* (1949)

Dickinson, W. Croft, Duncan, Rev. A. A. M. *Scotland from earliest times to 1603* (1977)

Donaldson, G. and Morpeth, R. *A Dictionary of Scottish History* (1977)

Feachem, R. *Guide to Prehistoric Scotland* (1977)

Glover, J. *The Story of Scotland* (1977)

Hastings, M. *The King's Champion* (Montrose) (1977)

Henderson, I. *The Picts* (1967)

Mackie, E. W. *Scotland, an Archaeological Guide* (1975)

Mackie, J. D. *A History of Scotland* (1975)

Simpson, W. D. *The Ancient Stones of Scotland* (1965)

Smout, T. C. *A History of the Scottish People* 1560–1830 (1969)

Wedgwood, C. V. *Montrose* (1952)

Travel and Topography

Allan, J. R. *The North-East Lowlands of Scotland* (1974)

Finlay, I. *The Central Highlands* (1976)

Forestry Commission *Forests of North-East Scotland* (1976)

Fraser, D. *Discovering East Scotland* (1973)

Graham, C. *Portrait of Aberdeen and Deeside* (1972)

Graham, C. *Portrait of the Moray Firth* (1978)

Graham-Campbell, D. *Portrait of Perth, Angus and Fife* (1979)

Haldane, A. R. B. *New Ways through the Glens* (1962)

Haldane, A. R. B. *The Drove Roads of Scotland* (1968)

Johnston, J. B. *Place Names of Scotland* (3rd edn. 1934, repr. 1970)

Keith, A. *A Thousand Years of Aberdeen* (1972)

McLaren, M. *Shell Guide to Scotland* (1965, revised by regions 1977)

Nicolaisen, W. F. H. *Scottish Place Names* (1976)

Omand, D. *The Moray Book* (1976)

Simpson, W. D. *The Highlands of Scotland* (1976)

Smith, R. *Grampian Ways, Journey over the Mounth* (1980)

FURTHER READING

Taylor, W. *The Military Roads in Scotland* (1976)

Tranter, N. *The Queen's Scotland: The North-East* (1974); *The Eastern Counties* (1972); *The Heartland* (1971)

Watson, A. *The Cairngorms, Mounth and Lochnagar* (1975)

Wyness, F. *City by the Grey North Sea* (Aberdeen)(1965)

Architecture

Cruden, S. *The Scottish Castle* (1960)

Dunbar, J. G. *The Historic Architecture of Scotland* (1966)

Fenwick, H. *Scotland's Castles* (1976)

Fenwick, H. *Scotland's Abbeys and Cathedrals* (1978)

Tranter, N. *The Fortified House in Scotland*; Vol. 2, *Central Scotland* (1977); Vol. 4, *Aberdeenshire, Angus and Kincardineshire* (1977); Vol. 5, *North and West Scotland and Misc.* (Banff & Moray) (1970)

West, T. W. *A History of Architecture in Scotland* (1967)

Literature, Culture

Alison, J. (ed.) *Poetry of North-East Scotland* (1976)

Anson, P. F. *Fishing Boats and Fisher Folk on the East Coast of Scotland* (1974)

Anson, P. F. *A Monastery in Moray, the story of Pluscarden Priory* 1230-1948 (1959)

Barclay-Harvey, Sir M. *The Great North of Scotland Railway* (1940)

Cameron, D. K. *The Ballad and the Plough, A Portrait of Life in the old Scottish Farmtouns* (1979)

Daiches, D. *Scotch Whisky* (1976)

Dorward, D. *Scotland's Place-Names* (1979)

Dorward, D. *Scottish Surnames* (1978)

Duff, D. (ed.) *Victoria in the Highlands, the personal journal of Her Majesty, Queen Victoria* (1968)

Dunlop, J. *The Clan Gordon* (1972)

Grimble, I. *Scottish Clans and Tartans* (1977)

Lockhart, R. Bruce *Scotch, the Whisky of Scotland in Fact and Story* (1951)

Stewart of Ardvorlich, J. *The Grahams* (1973)

Stewart of Ardvorlich, J. *The Stewarts* (1973)

Vallance, H. A. *The Highland Railway* (1972)

Photograph Credits

Index

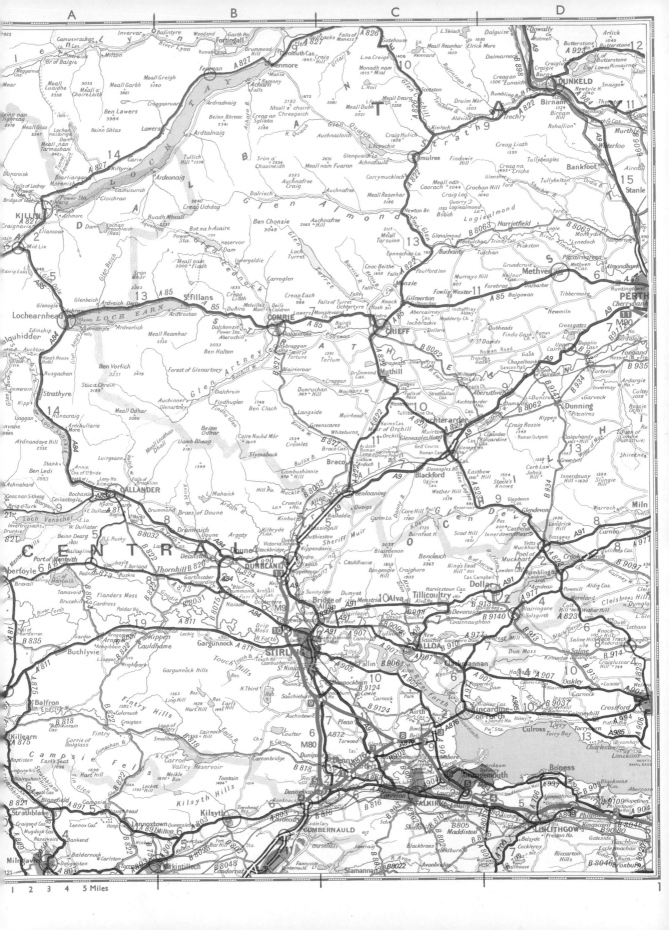

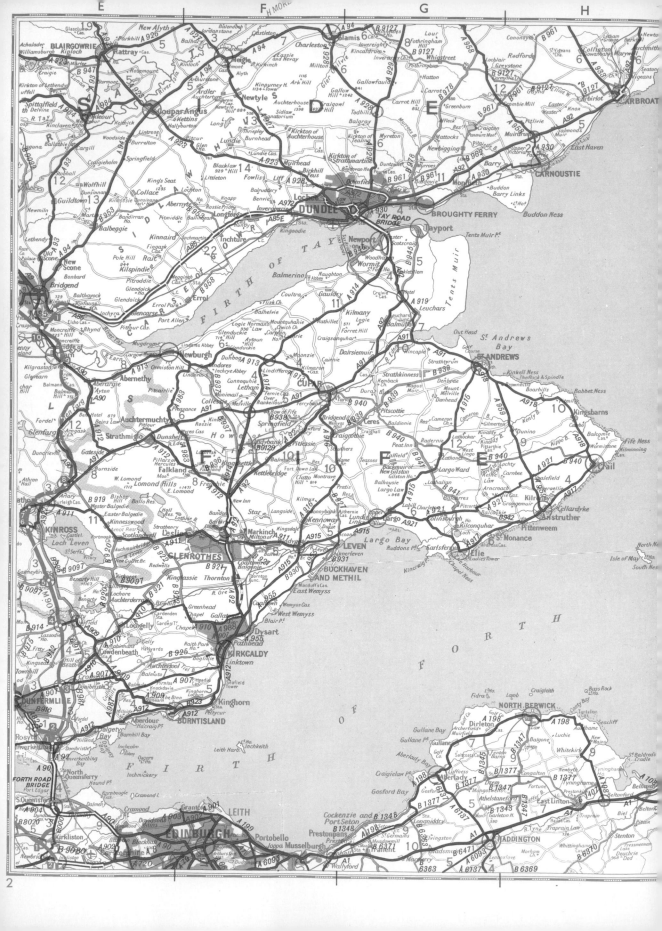

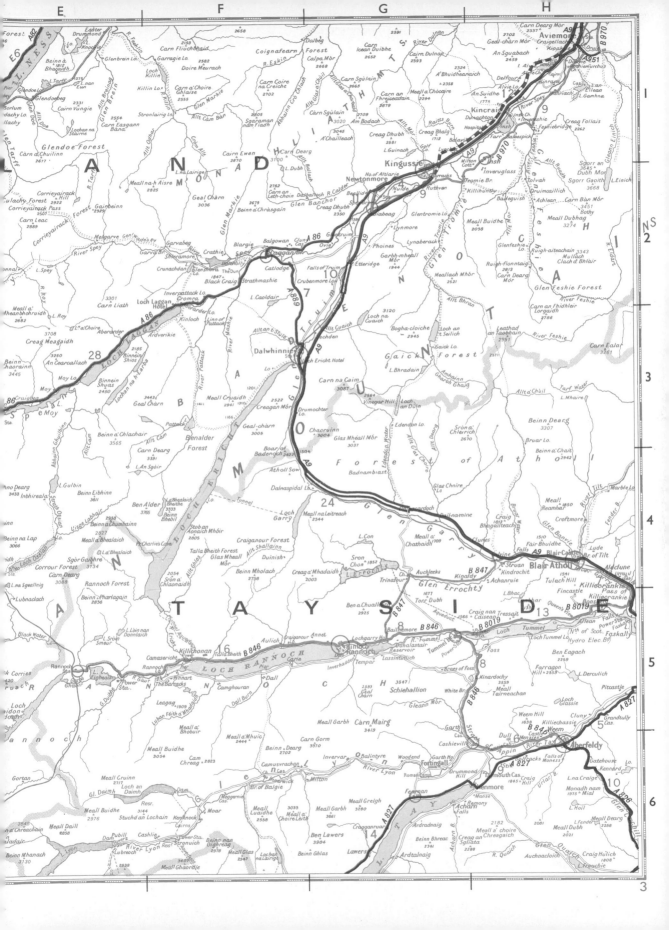

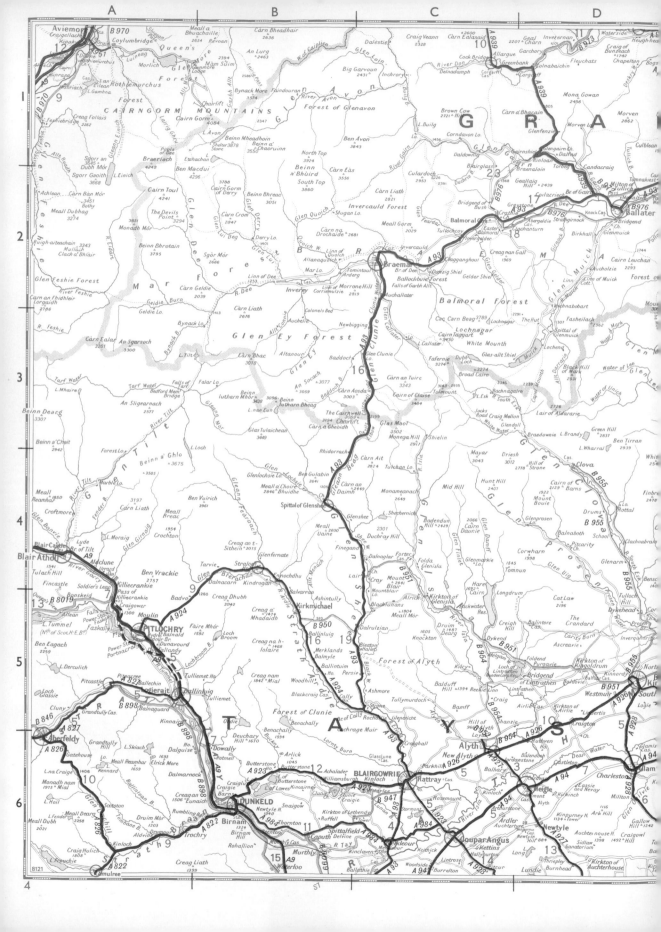

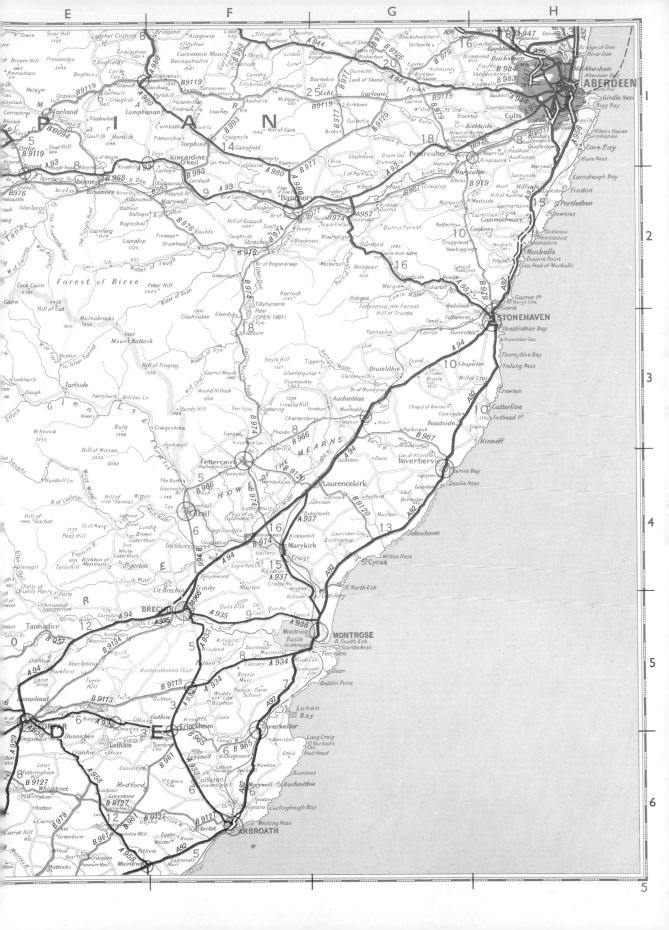

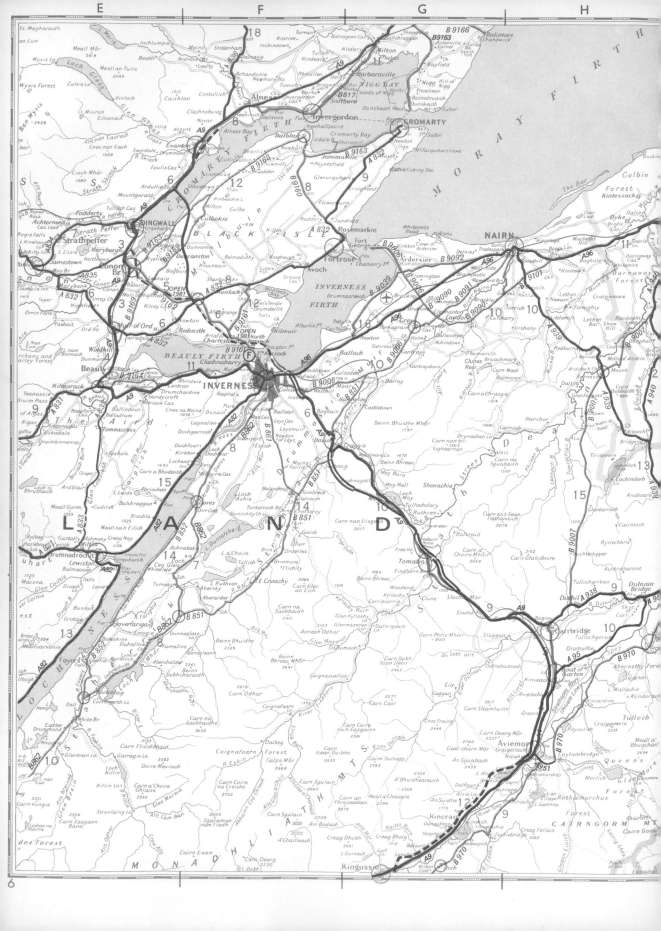

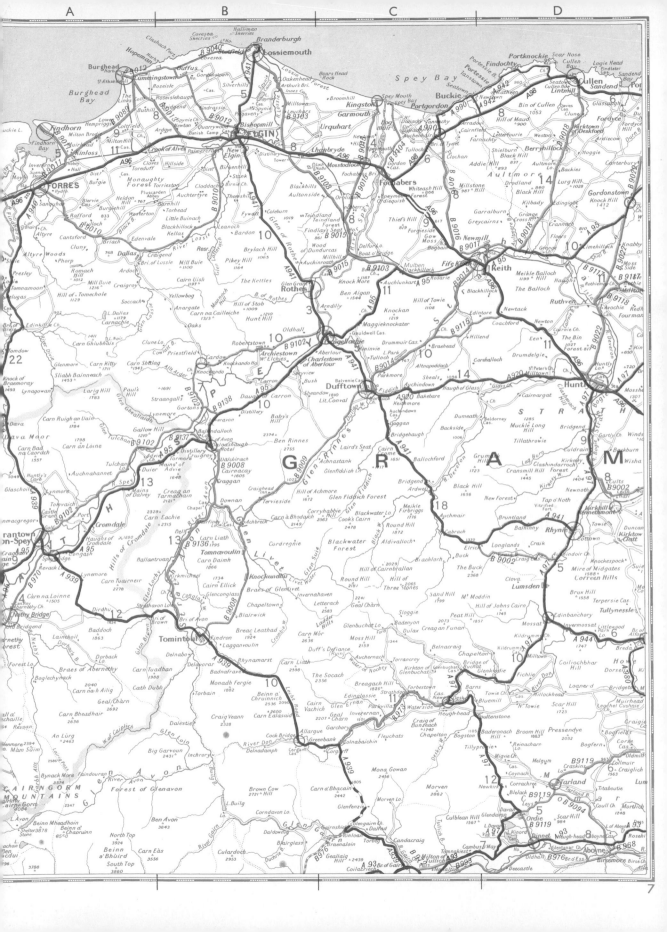

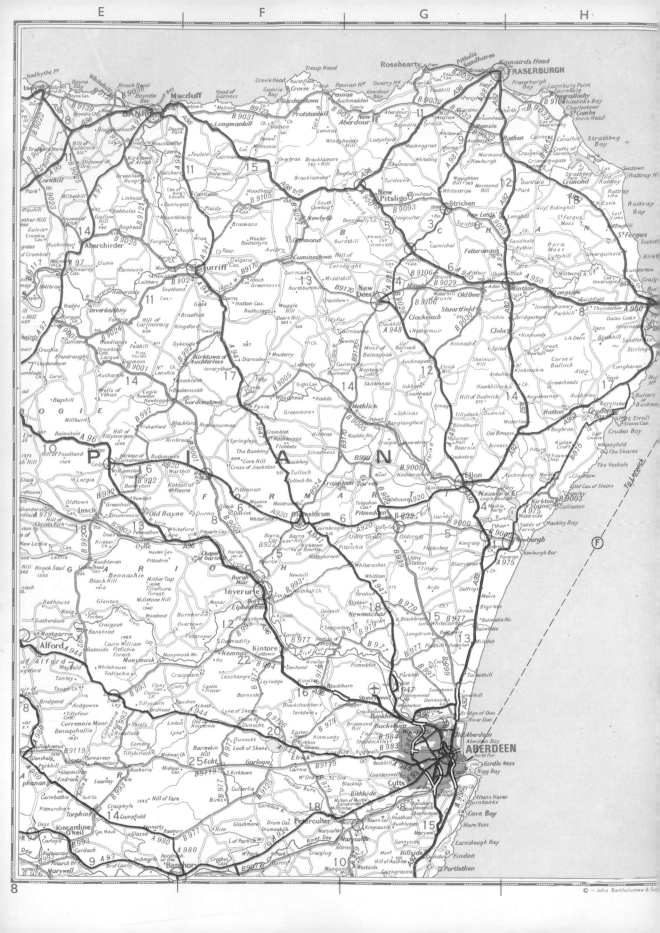